Insurable Interest and the Law

CW01091620

This book assesses the role of the doctrine of insurable interest within modern insurance law by examining its rationales and suggesting how shortcomings could be fixed.

Over the centuries, English law on insurable interest – a combination of statutes and case law – has become complex and unclear. Other jurisdictions have relaxed, or even abolished, the requirement for an insurable interest. Yet, the UK insurance industry has overwhelmingly supported the retention of the doctrine of insurable interest. This book explores whether the traditional justifications for the doctrine – the policy against wagering, the prevention of moral hazard and the doctrine's relationship with the indemnity principle – still stand up to scrutiny and argues that, far from being obsolete, they have acquired new significance in the global financial markets and following the liberalisation of gambling. It is also argued that the doctrine of insurable interest is an integral part of a system of insurance contract law rules and market practice. Rather than rejecting the doctrine, the book recommends a recalibration of insurable interest to afford better pre-contractual transparency to a proposer as to the suitability of the policy to his or her interest in the subject-matter to be insured.

Providing a powerful defence for the retention of insurable interest, this book will appeal to both academics and practitioners working in the field of insurance law.

Franziska Arnold-Dwyer, Lecturer in Insurance Law and Deputy Director of the Insurance, Shipping & Aviation Law Institute at the Centre for Commercial Law Studies, Queen Mary University of London.

Insurable Interest and the Law

Franziska Arnold-Dwyer

Routledge
Taylor & Francis Group

LONDON AND NEW YORK

First published 2020
by Routledge
2 Park Square, Milton Park, Abingdon, Oxon OX14 4RN

and by Routledge
52 Vanderbilt Avenue, New York, NY 10017

Routledge is an imprint of the Taylor & Francis Group, an informa business

British Library Cataloguing-in-Publication Data
A catalogue record for this book is available from the British Library

Library of Congress Cataloging-in-Publication Data
Names: Arnold-Dwyer, Franziska, author.
Title: Insurable interest and the law / Franziska Arnold-Dwyer.
Description: Abingdon, Oxon ; New York, NY : Routledge, 2020. |
Based on author's thesis (doctoral - Queen Mary University London, 2018) issued under title: Insurable interest in property insurance : a defence. | Includes bibliographical references and index.
Identifiers: LCCN 2020003594 (print) | LCCN 2020003595 (ebook) |
ISBN 9780367076672 (hardback) | ISBN 9780429021961 (ebook)
Subjects: LCSH: Insurance law—England.
Classification: LCC KD1859 . A76 2020 (print) |
LCC KD1859 (ebook) | DDC 346.42/086—dc23
LC record available at https://lccn.loc.gov/2020003594
LC ebook record available at https://lccn.loc.gov/2020003595

ISBN: 978-0-367-07667-2 (hbk)
ISBN: 978-0-367-49953-2 (pbk)
ISBN: 978-0-429-02196-1 (ebk)

Typeset in Galliard
by codeMantra

Contents

Abbreviations and definitions

ABI The Association of British Insurers.

AICA Australian Insurance Contracts Act 1984.

Alternative Policy In relation to the Unsuitable Policy Scenario, a contract of insurance under which the policyholder would have had an insurable interest and, accordingly, an enforceable claim. See Chapter 12.

ALRC Australian Law Reform Commission.

cash conversion argument The argument that an insured with an insurable interest may have reason to destroy the insured property to convert an asset into ready cash. See Chapter 7.

CDS Credit default swap/s.

CIDRA Consumer Insurance (Disclosure and Representations) Act 2012.

CRS *Cooperative Retail Services Ltd v Taylor Young Partnership Ltd* 2000] EWCA Civ 207; aff'd [2002] UKHL 17, [2003] 1 CLC 75.

Deepak *Deepak Fertilisers & Petrochemicals Corp Ltd v ICI Chemicals & Polymers Ltd* [1999] 1 Lloyd's Rep 387.

DISP FCA Handbook 'Dispute Resolution: Complaints'.

duty to decline A proposed statutory duty on the insurer to decline to enter into a contract of insurance if, at the time of entering into the contract, the insurer knows or ought to know that the contract would be void for lack of insurable interest. See Chapter 12.

economic interest A policyholder's interest in the insured subject-matter that is not based on legal or equitable rights in relation to the subject-matter but on pecuniary loss arising upon the loss or damage of the insured subject-matter. See Chapter 4.

factual expectation test The factual expectation test as applied to property insurance requires that for an insurable interest to exist, the insured must have a factual expectation, or reasonable prospect, of economic benefit from the preservation of the insured subject-matter, or of an economic loss on its being damaged or destroyed, which would arise in the ordinary course of things. See Chapters 4 and 5.

FCA Financial Conduct Authority.

Feasey *Feasey v Sun Life Assurance Co of Canada* [2003] EWCA Civ 885.

Financial Crisis The global financial crisis of 2008/9.

FSA Financial Services Authority (predecessor to the FCA and PRA).

FSMA 2000 Financial Services and Markets Act 2000, as amended by the Financial Services Act 2012.

FSMA regulatory framework The financial services regulatory regime as established under the FSMA 2000 and secondary legislation made pursuant to it.

GA 1845 Gaming Act 1845.

GA 2005 Gambling Act 2005.

Gard Marine *Gard Marine & Energy Ltd v China National Chartering Co Ltd* [2017] UKSC 35 [2017].

IA 2015 Insurance Act 2015.

ICA 2007 German Insurance Contract Act of 2007 (Versicherungsvertragsgesetz).

ICOBS FCA Handbook 'Insurance: Conduct of Business Sourcebook'.

IDD Directive 2016/97/EU of the European Parliament and of the Council of 20 January 2016 on insurance distribution (recast).

IIB The Draft Insurable Interest Bill published by the LC in June 2018.

IIB Notes LC, *Updated draft Insurable Interest bill for review – Accompanying Notes* (June 2018).

insurance distributor An insurer or insurance intermediary pursuing insurance distribution activities as defined in article 2(1)(8) of the IDD.

ILAG Investment and Life Assurance Group.

ILW Industry loss warranty/ies.

Internal-Contagion-Restriction Insurers are prohibited from carrying on any commercial business other than insurance business and activities directly arising from that business (PRA Rulebook for Solvency II Firms, Conditions Governing Business, 9.1; for non-Solvency II Firms, Insurance Company – Internal Contagion Risk, 2.1). See Chapter 6.

Invalid Policy In relation to the Unsuitable Policy Scenario, a contract of insurance entered into by the policyholder and the insurer which is void for lack of insurable interest. See Chapter 12.

IPID An insurance product information document to be provided to the policyholder before the contract of insurance is concluded. See Chapter 12.

Kosmopoulos *Kosmopoulos v Constitution Insurance Co.* [1987] 1 SCR 2.

LAA 1774 Life Assurance Act 1774.

LC Denotes both the Law Commission and the Scottish Law Commission in the text of this thesis, unless specifically stated otherwise.

LCCP Gambling Licence Conditions and Codes of Practice. See Chapter 6.

LC respondents Insurers, insurance industry associations, brokers and broker's associations, law firms with an interest in insurance law, lawyers' organizations, policyholder groups, insurance academics and individuals responding to the LC's consultation on the reform of doctrine of insurable interest.

legal interest test The legal interest test as applied to property insurance requires that for an insurable interest to exist, the insured must have a legal (or equitable) right in relation to the insured property. The legal interest test is derived from Lord Eldon's definition of 'insurable interest' in *Lucena* (at 321) and has been included as an example in the non-exhaustive definition of insurable interest in s.5(2) of the MIA 1906. See Chapter 4.

Leyland *Leyland Shipping Co v Norwich Union Fire Insurance Society* [1918] AC 350 (HL).

LMA Lloyd's Market Association.

Lorcom *Lorcom Thirteen v Zurich Insurance Company South Africa Ltd* [2013] ZAWCHC 64.

Loss of Chance In relation to the Unsuitable Policy Scenario, the policyholder's loss of opportunity to enter (or cause a controlled person to enter) into an Alternative Policy. See Chapter 12.

Lucena *Lucena v Craufurd* (1806) 2 Bos & Pul (NR) 269 (HL).

Macaura *Macaura v Northern Assurance Company* [1925] AC 619 (HL).

material adverse effect test Colman QC in *Stone Vickers*: 'whether the [sub-contractor] … might be materially adversely affected by loss of or damage to the … works'. See Chapter 4.

MIA 1746 Marine Insurance Act 1746.

MIA 1788 Marine Insurance Act 1788.

MIA 1906 Marine Insurance Act 1906.

MIGamblingA 1909 Marine Insurance (Gambling Policies) Act 1909.

moral certainty test The moral certainty test as applied to property insurance requires that for an insurable interest to exist, there must be a moral certainty that the insured would benefit from the continued existence of the insured property and be prejudiced by its destruction. The moral certainty test is derived from Lawrence J's definition of 'insurable interest' in *Lucena* (at 302). See Chapter 4.

multiple exposure risk Multiple insurance cover exposure on the same risk position. See Chapter 6.

National Oilwell *National Oilwell (UK) Ltd v Davy Offshore Ltd* [1993] 2 Lloyd's Rep 582 (Comm).

Nextia *Nextia Properties Limited v RBS* [2013] EWHC 3167 (QB).

NTNI activities Non-traditional and non-insurance activities. See Chapter 6.

NYCIL New York Consolidated Insurance Laws.

NYID New York State Insurance Department.

opportunity argument The argument that an insured with an insurable interest has intimate access to the insured property and is in a position to destroy it without detection. See Chapter 7.

Part 4A Permission The regulatory permission granted under FSMA 2000, Pt 4A to carry on a specified regulated activity.

PERG FCA Handbook 'Perimeter Guidance Manual'.

pervasive interest An insurable interest based on the notion (expounded in *Petrofina (UK) Ltd v Magnaload Ltd* [1984] Q.B. 127 and subsequent cases) that all insured contractors and sub-contractors working together on a construction project have an insurable interest in the whole property insured under the project insurances. See Chapter 4.

Petrofina *Petrofina (UK) Ltd v Magnaload Ltd* [1984] QB 127 (Comm Ct).

Potts Opinion Opinion prepared for the International Swaps and Derivatives Association by Robin Potts QC, Erskine Chambers, dated 24 June 1997, on the differentiation of CDS from contracts of insurance. See Chapter 6.

PRA Prudential Regulation Authority.

PRIN FCA Handbook 'Principles for Business'.

profit argument The argument that an insured with an insurable interest may seek to profit by deliberately destroying the insured property in situations in which insured property has been overvalued. See Chapter 7.

project policy A single composite property policy providing cover for the project works and assets under which the project employer, the main contractor and sub-contractors are insured. See Chapter 4.

Protection Buyer Party to a CDS who buys credit protection from the Protection Seller in respect of a Reference Entity in return for a fee. See Chapter 6.

Protection Seller Party to a CDS who sells credit protection to the Protection Buyer in respect of a Reference Entity in return for a fee. See Chapter 6.

RAO Financial Services and Markets Act 2000 (Regulated Activities) Order 2001.

Reference Entity A third party whose credit risk is the subject-matter under a CDS. See Chapter 6.

regulatory product information requirement A regulatory obligation on insurers to produce IPID information, and on insurance distributors to give the prospective policyholder information on the insurable interest requirement as applicable to the contract. See Chapter 12.

reinstatement Basis of settlement terms providing for the reinstatement or repair of insured buildings or personal property that have been damaged, or the replacement of lost items. See Chapter 10.

Rights of Actions Regulations Financial Services and Markets Act 2000 (Rights of Action) Regulations 2001, SI 2001/2256 (amended by SI 2013/472).

Risk Control Terms Property policy terms such as exclusions, conditions precedent, warranties, notice provisions or termination events relating to the use of the insured property and changes in circumstances relating to the property, aimed at protecting the insurer from an increase in risk after the inception of the policy. See Chapter 10.

RSA Royal & Sun Alliance.

s.20(3) action An action at the suit of a person who suffers loss as a result of a Part 4A permission contravention under FSMA 2000, s 20(3). See Chapter 12.

s.138D(2) action An action at the suit of a person who suffers loss as a result of a FCA rule contravention under FSMA 2000, s.138D(2). See Chapter 12.

SC A sub-contractor responsible for the insured loss. See Chapter 4.

SCRs Solvency Capital Requirements under the Solvency II regime. See Chapter 6.

Solvency II Directive Directive 2009/138/EC of the European Parliament and of the Council of 25 November 2009 on the taking-up and pursuit of the business of Insurance and Reinsurance (Solvency II) (recast).

Solvency II regime Solvency II Directive as implemented by the Solvency 2 Regulations 2015 (SI2015/575) and the PRA Rulebook for Solvency II firms and the FCA Handbook.

STOLI Stranger-originated life insurance: an investment scheme facilitated or instigated by a third party investor pursuant to which a person, in whose life the investor has no insurable interest, takes out life insurance, with the premium payments being funded by the investor, and with the intention that the policy be assigned to the investor shortly after the policy has been issued.

Stone Vickers *Stone Vickers Ltd v Appledore Ferguson Shipbuilders Ltd* [1991] 2 Lloyd's Rep. 288 (Comm); decision reversed on appeal [1992] 2 Lloyd's Rep. 578 (CA).

The Moonacre *Sharp v Sphere Drake Insurance* [1992] 2 Lloyd's Rep 501 (Comm).

Three Strategies The courts have developed three strategies 'to lean in favour of an insurable interest' and let a defence of insurable interest fail: (1) 'finding' an insurable interest on the facts of the case, (2) construing the policy so as to 'embrace' any interest that the insured might have and (3) stretching the concept of insurable interest to extend to any interest that the insured might have. See Chapter 3.

Traditional Justifications The traditional justifications for the doctrine of insurable interest are that an insurable interest requirement differentiates contracts of insurance from wagers, prevents or reduces moral hazard and supports the indemnity principle. See Chapters 6–8.

Uninsured Loss In relation to the Unsuitable Policy Scenario, a genuine loss suffered by the policyholder in relation to which he had thought to have insurance protection but for which he is not in fact covered as that loss does not relate to an interest protected by the policy in question. See Chapter 12.

Unsuitable Policy Scenario See Chapter 12.

Western Trading *Western Trading Limited v Great Lakes Reinsurance* (UK) Plc [2015] EWHC 103 (QB); reversed in part on a different issue [2016] EWCA Civ 1003.

Wilson *Wilson v Jones* (1866–67) L.R. 2 Ex. 139 (ExchCham).

Cases

Cases from England and Wales and House of Lords/ Supreme Court decisions

Anderson v Commercial Union Assurance Corp (1885) 55 LJQB 146

Andrews v Herne (1662) 1 Lev 33

Arab Bank plc v John D Wood Commercial Limited [2000] 1 WLR 857

Arnold v Britton [2015] UKSC 36

Assievedo v Cambridge (1711) 88 ER 634

Bankers Insurance Co Ltd v South [2003] EWHC 380 (QB)

Basma Al Sulaiman v Credit Suisse Securities (Europe) Limited, Plurimi Capital LLP [2013] EWHC 400 (Comm)

Bell v Lever Bros Ltd [1932] AC 161

Belmont Park Investments Pty Ltd v BNY Corporate Trustee Services Ltd [2011] UKSC 38

Black King Shipping Corp v Massie (The Litsion Pride) [1985] 1 Lloyd's Rep 437

British Eagle International Air Lines Ltd v Compagnie Nationale Air France [1975] 1 WLR 758

Brotherton v Aseguradora Colseguros SA (No.2) [2003] EWCA Civ 705

Carlill v Carbolic Smoke Ball Company [1892] 2 QB 484

Caparo Industries Plc v Dickman [1990] 2 AC 605

Castellain v Preston (1883) 11 QBD 380

Carter v Boehm (1766) 3 Burr 1905

Cattle v Stockton Waterworks Co (1875) LR 10 QB 453

Cepheus Shipping Corp v Guardian Royal Exchange Assurance Plc (The Capricorn) [1995] 1 Lloyd's Rep 622 (QB) 641

CGU International Insurance Plc v AstraZeneca Insurance Co Ltd [2005] EWHC 2755 (Comm)

Chapman v Pole (1870) 22 LT 306

City Index v Leslie [1992] QB 98

City Index Limited (t/a FinSpreads) v Romeo Balducci [2011] EWHC 2562 (Ch)

Colonia Versicherung AG v Amoco Oil Co [1997] 1 Lloyd's Rep 261

USA

Legislation

UK primary legislation

Civil Partnership Act 2004, s.253
Consumer Insurance (Disclosure and Representation) Act 2012, ss
    2, 4, 5, Sch 1
Consumer Rights Act 2015, s 9
Corporation Tax Act 2009, Pts 3 and 7
Equality Act 2000
Finance Act 1994, ss 48–74, Sch 6A, 7 and 7A
Financial Services Act 2012
Financial Services and Markets Act 2000, ss 1B, 1C, 1D, 2B, 2C,
    3B, 19, 20, 22, 59, 138D, 229, 398, 404B, 412, Pt 4A, Pt XV
Fires Prevention (Metropolis) Act 1774, s 83
Forfeiture Act 1982, s 1
Friendly Societies Act 1992, s.99
Gambling Act 2005, ss 3, 10, 33, 334, 335, 356, Sch 17
Gaming Act 1845, ss 1, 3, 9, 10, 18, 334, 335, 356, Sch 17
Insolvency Act 1986, s 107
Insurance Act 2015, ss 3–12, 13A, 14–18, Sch 1
Insurance Companies Amendment Act 1973, s.50
Insurance on Ships Act 1785
Law Reform (Frustrated Contracts) Act 1943, s 2
Life Assurance Act 1774, ss 1, 2, 3
Marine Insurance Act 1746, Preamble; ss 1, 2, 4
Marine Insurance Act 1788, s 1
Marine Insurance Act 1906, ss 1, 3–6, 14, 16, 17–20, 27, 55,
    60–63, 67, 78, 79, 82, 84
Marine Insurance (Gambling Policies) Act 1909, s 1
Sale of Goods Act 1979, s 14
Shipping Act 1795, s 21
Unfair Contract Terms Act 1977

UK secondary legislation

Financial Services and Markets Act 2000 (Regulated Activities)
    Order 2001, SI 2001/544, arts 3, 10, Sch 1
Financial Services and Markets Act 2000 (Rights of Action)
    Regulations 2001, SI 2001/2256 (amended by SI 2013/472)
Gaming Machine (Miscellaneous Amendments and Revocation)
    Regulations 2018, SI 2018/1402
Insurers (Reorganisation and Winding Up) Regulations 2004, SI 2004/353
Solvency II Regulations 2015, SI 2015/575
Unfair Terms in Consumer Contracts Regulations 1999, SI 1999/2083

Regulatory and taxation materials

PRA Rulebook for SII Firms: Conditions Governing Business;
    Investments; Minimum Capital Requirements; Reporting;
    Solvency Capital Requirement – General Provisions; Solvency
    Capital Requirement – Internal Models; Solvency Capital
    Requirement – Standard Formula
FCA Handbook: Principles for Business; Insurance: Conduct of
    Business Sourcebook; Dispute Resolution; Compensation; The
    Enforcement Guide; The Perimeter Manual
HMRC, 'VAT Notice 701/29: betting, gaming and lotteries'
HMRC, 'VAT Notice 701/36: insurance'
HMRC, 'Notice IPT1: Insurance Premium Tax'

EU legislation

Directive 2009/138/EC of the European Parliament and of the
    Council of 25 November 2009 on the taking-up and pursuit of
    the business of Insurance and Reinsurance (recast)
Directive 2014/65/EU of the European Parliament and of the
    Council of 15 May 2014 on markets in financial instruments and
    amending Directive 2002/92/EC and Directive 2011/61/EU
    Text with EEA relevance (applicable from 3 January 2018)
Directive 2016/97/EU of the European Parliament and of the
    Council of 20 January 2016 on insurance distribution (recast)
Regulation (EU) No 236/2012 of the European Parliament and
    of the Council of 14 March 2012 on short selling and certain
    aspects of credit default swaps
Regulation (EU) No 648/2012 of the European Parliament and
    of the Council of 4 July 2012 on OTC derivatives, central
    counterparties and trade repositories
Regulation (EU) No 1215/2012 of the European Parliament and
    of the Council of 12 December 2012 on jurisdiction and the

recognition and enforcement of judgments in civil
and commercial matters (recast)

Regulation (EU) No 1215/2012 of the European Parliament
and of the Council of 12 December 2012 on jurisdiction
and the recognition and enforcement of judgments in civil and
commercial matters (recast)

Regulation (EU) No 575/2013 Of the European Parliament and
of the Council of 26 June 2013 on prudential requirements
for credit institutions and investment firms and amending
Regulation (EU) No 648/2012

Regulation (EU) No 596/2014 of the European Parliament and of
the Council of 16 April 2014 on market abuse and repealing
Directive 2003/6/EC of the European Parliament and of
the Council and Commission Directives 2003/124/EC,
2003/125/EC and 2004/72/EC

Regulation (EU) 2016/679 of the European Parliament and of the
Council of 27 April 2016 on the protection of natural persons
with regard to the processing of personal data and on the free
movement of such data, and repealing Directive 95/46/EC

Regulation (EU) 2017/2402 of the European Parliament and of the
Council of 12 December 2017 laying down a general framework
for securitisation and creating a specific framework for simple,
transparent and standardised securitisation, and amending
Directives 2009/65/EC, 2009/138/EC and 2011/61/EU and
Regulations (EC) No 1060/2009 and (EU) No 648/2012

Legislation from other jurisdictions

Australia

Insurance Contracts Act 1984, ss.16, 17, 49, 50
Marine Insurance Act 1909, ss.10, 11

Canada

Alberta Insurance Act 2000, s.514, ss.646–648
British Columbia Insurance Act, s.47
Civil Code of Quebec, s.2418, s.3150
Manitoba Insurance Act, s.155
Marine Insurance Act 1993, s.8

China (PR)

Insurance Law 2009, art.12, 31, 33, 48

Germany

Bürgerliches Gesetzbuch, §138
Gesetz über den Versicherungsvertrag vom 23. November 2007, §§
    43–49, 80, 95, 150

USA

Dodd-Frank Act, Title VII
McCarran-Ferguson Act (15 U.S.C.) §1012
New York State Insurance Act, §3205, §3401, §6901, §7813, §7815
Securities and Exchange Act of 1934, s15G

1 Introduction

The UK insurance industry has a long history in the international insurance and reinsurance markets. Today, the UK insurance and long-term savings provider industry is the largest in Europe, and fourth largest in the world,[1] but faces new challenges from technical innovations, consumer protection demands, the sharing economy, alternative risk transfers and financings in the capital markets and Brexit. Since 2006 the Law Commission of England and Wales and the Scottish Law Commission (together, the 'LC') have been engaged in a joint project to transform English and Scottish insurance contract law into a modern insurance law fit for the 21st century. Thus, the Consumer Insurance (Disclosure and Representations) Act 2012 ('CIDRA') significantly rebalanced the approach to the pre-contractual provision of information by consumer insureds to their insurers. The Insurance Act 2015 ('IA 2015') reformed, inter alia, the pre-contractual duty of disclosure of non-consumer insureds and, for consumer and non-consumer insureds alike, the law on breach of insurance warranties and conditions and fraudulent claims.

The final outstanding piece of the LC's insurance contract law reform project is the doctrine of insurable interest. The doctrine of insurable interest is concerned with the insured's relationship with the subject-matter of insurance. The LC have identified a number of issues with the current law on insurable interest, including its complexity and uncertainty. Some commentators argue that the doctrine of insurable interest is an anachronism which is no longer needed. In contrast, the insurance industry has overwhelmingly supported the retention of the doctrine of insurable interest. The LC have put forward proposals for a 'Draft Insurable Interest Bill'[2] (the 'IIB'), which widens and clarifies the ambit of the doctrine of insurable interest in relation to life and life-related insurance. At the time of writing, it is uncertain whether, when and to what extent the IIB will be introduced in, and passed into law by, Parliament. The IIB leaves the law relating to other types of insurance, including property and liability insurance,

---

1 Association of British Insurers ('ABI'), 'UK Insurance & Long-Term Savings – The State of the Market 2019' (February 2019), 2.
2 LC, *Insurable Interest Bill* (June 2018).

largely untouched. In the United States, the doctrine of insurable interest has attracted judicial and legislative attention in relation to stranger-originated life insurance ('STOLI'). STOLIs are investment schemes facilitated or instigated by a third party investor pursuant to which a person, in whose life the investor has no insurable interest, takes out life insurance, with the premium payments being funded by the investor and with the intention that the policy be assigned to the investor shortly after the policy has been issued.

This book examines the English law on insurable interest and contributes to the debate whether the doctrine remains relevant to modern English insurance law and market practice and whether and how the doctrine of insurable interest should be reformed. Thus far, the debate has been focussed on the doctrine's failings in delivering on what it promises to do: namely to differentiate contracts of insurance from wagers, to prevent or reduce moral hazard and to support the indemnity principle (together, the 'Traditional Justifications'). Rather than rejecting the doctrine of insurable interest for its flaws, it is examined what the doctrine still has to offer and how its shortcomings might be fixed. It is argued that the doctrine of insurable interest is part of a system of insurance contract law rules and market practice. The Traditional Justifications are still relevant and command new significance. Moreover, the doctrine can be rationalized on two novel grounds: its existence (1) is integral to the operation of other doctrines and principles of insurance law and, in relation to property insurance, the operation and performance of standard terms contracts, and (2) is a defining characteristic of property indemnity insurance contracts. However, the doctrine of insurable interest would operate more fairly and effectively if it were to be supported by (1) a statutory duty on an insurer to decline to enter into a contract of insurance which it knows would be void for lack of insurable interest, and (2) a regulatory obligation on insurers to provide information to the insured on the insurable interest requirement specific to the type of policy in question before the contract is entered into.

This book is structured as follows: Chapter 2 looks into the history, and Chapter 3 identifies the legal bases for the requirement for an insurable interest and discusses the courts' approach to dealing with insurable interest issues. Chapter 4 discusses the meaning of insurable interest, namely what kind of relationship between the insured and the insured property is needed to satisfy the insurable interest requirement. Chapter 5 takes stock of the existing debate on the law on insurable interest – the criticisms raised and how it might be reformed – including the LC's IIB proposals and academic contributions, and provides an overview of the approaches taken by a number of foreign jurisdictions. Chapters 6–8 reassess whether the Traditional Justifications are still relevant to modern insurance law and market practice. Chapter 9 explores the interconnectedness of the doctrine with other doctrines and principles of insurance law. Chapter 10 considers the extent to which the notion of an insurable interest is embedded in property insurance policy wordings. Chapter 11 examines whether, in addition to being a validity requirement, the requirement for an insurable interest is a definitional characteristic of contracts of indemnity insurance. Chapter 12 evaluates the doctrine of insurable interest's remedial and enforcement mechanisms and puts forward suggestions for making the operation of the doctrine fairer and more effective. Chapter 13 concludes with some observations on reforming the doctrine of insurable interest.

2   The historical development of the insurable interest requirement

Formative period

Insurable interest under the lex mercatoria and common law

English insurance law emerged from the lex mercatoria, a body of transnational customary law which had gradually developed as a result of dealings between merchants.[1] By the beginning of the 17th century, the use of insurance had become so established that the preamble to the Policies of Assurance Act 1601 stated that it had been 'time out of mind a usage' among English and foreign merchants to procure insurance on ships and goods. Inherent in the concept of a contract of insurance under the lex mercatoria was that the contract was subject to the indemnity principle and that the insured should run part of the risk, or share into the adventure, itself.[2] In early insurance practice, the insured 'running the risk', whilst not using the terminology of insurable interest, translated into a requirement that the insured had a proprietary interest in the subject-matter of the insurance, most commonly ships or goods in transit, so that in the event of (physical) loss or damage, the insured would suffer an actual loss. Thus ownership and interest tended to coincide. At the close of the 17th century it appears to have been settled law in England that a lack of insurable interest rendered a contract of insurance void:

> Take it that the law is settled, that if a man has no interest, and insures, the insurance is void, although it be expressed in the policy interested or not interested, and the reason the law goes upon, is the encouragement of trade, and not that persons unconcerned in trade, nor interested in the ship, should profit by it.[3]

---

1 HN Bennett, '*Mapping the Doctrine of Utmost Good Faith in Insurance Contract Law*' [1999] LMCLQ 165, 186.
2 John Weskett, *A Compleat Digest of the Theory, Laws, and Practice of Insurance* (London 1781) 226–227, 587.
3 *Goddart v Garrett* (1692) 23 ER 774.

In *Lynch v Dalzell*[4] the House of Lords affirmed a decision by Lord Chancellor King that the party claiming for a loss under a contract of insurance must have an interest in the insured subject-matter at the time of the loss. In *Sadlers' Company v Badcock*,[5] the court said that it is necessary for the insured to have an interest at the time of entering into the contract and at the time of the loss. Lord Hardwicke noted the rationales for an insurable interest: the prevention of fraud and the wilful destruction of insured property. Moreover, without any interest the insured could not suffer any loss. These rationales solidified into the Traditional Justifications are discussed in Chapters 6–8.

Wager and wager policies

In contrast, wagering contracts were enforceable at common law[6] unless they contravened a specific public policy or were injurious to a third party or were prohibited by statute. In the 18th century, gambling was a popular pastime and was not regarded as morally objectionable. Wager insurance or wager policies constituted a grey area between the dichotomy of wagering contracts on the one hand and contracts of insurance on the other. Across Europe a practice had developed to write insurance policies on an 'interest or no interest' or 'without further proof of interest' or 'valued free from average' or 'without the benefit of salvage' basis. The perceived commercial benefits of these clauses – in a world of limited communication – were that a merchant could take out insurance in circumstances when it was unclear whether cargo had been lost or sold, a specified value could be assigned to the cargo and, upon a claim being made, the insured did not have to produce evidence of interest.[7] However, such policies were soon used in circumstances where the insured had no interest at all in the insured subject-matter of the policy; they were acquired for purely speculative or even fraudulent purposes. Park reported that since the Revolution of 1688 'interest or no interest, or without further proof of interest policies' had been "increasing at an alarming degree and by such rapid strides as to threaten to speedy annihilation of that lucrative and most beneficial branch of trade [insurance]".[8] By the end of the 17th century, a number of seafaring countries and port cities had enacted insurance laws or ordinances which prohibited insurances not founded upon an interest of the insured.[9] In England there was no legislative

---

4 (1729) 4 Bro PC 431.

5 (1743) 2 Atk 554, at 556 (Lord Hardwicke LC).

6 *Andrews v Herne* (1662) 1 Lev 33; *Da Costa v Jones* (1778) 2 Cowp 729, 734.

7 Samuel Marshall, *A Treatise on the Law of Insurance: In Four Books*, vol 1 (Butterworth 1802) 99; see also *Thellusson v Fletcher* (1789) 1 Doug 315.

8 J Park, *A System of the Law of Marine Insurance* (6th edn, Butterworth 1809) 348.

9 Park (n 8, at 346) lists France, Middlebourg (Middelburg), Konyngsburg (Königsberg), Genoa, Rotterdam and Stockholm as having passed positive laws prohibiting policies without interest by the end of the 17th century. Marshall (n 7, at 99) lists France, Amsterdam, Rotterdam, Conningsberg (Königsberg), Genoa and Stockholm as having such laws but notes that Portugal and some parts of Italy "still tolerate" policies without insurable interest.

intervention until 1746, and the 18th-century courts did not offer a consistent doctrinal treatment of wager policies. The earliest reported case on an 'interest or no interest' policy is *Assievedo v Cambridge*,[10] where the court held that such policies entitled the insured to recovery even if he held no interest. In *Depaba v Ludlow*,[11] the court held that "such insurance was good" but clarified that the effect of the words 'interest or no interest' was that the insured did not have to prove his interest (which is different to no interest being required). In *Sadlers' Company v Badcock*,[12] the Lord Chancellor, Lord Hardwicke, acknowledged the existence of 'interest or no interest' policies but commented, "The common law leant strongly against these policies for some time, but being found beneficial to merchants, they winked at it".

Early legislation

The Marine Insurance Act 1746

By the early 1740s, there had been a number of notorious insurance fraud cases in connection with wager policies,[13] and there was a growing body of opinion that this was prejudicial to trade and that statutory regulation was required.[14] This was, however, not a universally held opinion as the parliamentary debates on a predecessor bill to the Marine Insurance Act 1746 ('MIA 1946') show.[15] The MIA 1746 came into force on 1 August 1746.[16] By s. 1, all insurance contracts made on British ships and their cargoes were declared "null and void" if written "interest or no interest or, without further proof of interest other than the policy or, by way of gaming or wagering or, without benefit of salvage to the insurer...". The Preamble to the MIA 1746 explains the reasons for constraining wagering policies:

> Whereas, it hath been found by experience, that the making of assurances, interest or no interest, or without further proof of interest than the policy, hath been productive of many pernicious practices, whereby a *great number of ships, with their cargoes, have either been fraudulently lost and destroyed*, or taken by the enemy in time of war; and such assurances have *encouraged the exportation of wool, and the carrying on of many other prohibited and clandestine trades*, which by means of such assurances have been concealed,

---

10 (1711) 88 ER 634.

11 (1721) 92 ER 1112.

12 n 5.

13 Park (n 8) 228–237; Weskett (n 2) 226–227; see also *The Gentleman's Magazine, and Historical Chronicle*, vol XII (London 1742) 8.

14 M Postlethwayt, *The Universal Dictionary of Trade and Commerce*, vol 1 (London 1751)142.

15 *The Gentleman's Magazine* (n 13) 3–12. A bill to restrict marine insurance on enemy ships and to prohibit wager polices was introduced to Parliament in 1741 but eventually failed.

16 The Act is also referred to as the Marine Insurance Act 1745 in some of the literature because it was passed in 1745.

and the parties concerned secured from loss, as well to the *diminution of the publick revenue*, as to the great detriment of fair traders: and *by introducing a mischievous kind of gaming or wagering*, under the pretence of assuring the risque on shipping, and fair trade, the institution and laudable design of making assurances, hath been perverted; and that which was intended for the encouragement of trade, and navigation, has in many instances been hurtful of, and destructive to the same....

(Emphasis added)

The MIA 1746 did not prohibit wagering contracts – they remained lawful for the time being – but one could no longer wager on British ships and their cargo under the guise of an insurance contract. Nor did the MIA 1746 create the requirement for an insurable interest in English law. Rather the MIA 1746 reversed the 'winking'[17] and established that the common law requirement for an insurable interest could not be evaded by express agreement that no (proof of) interest would be required or by entering into a wager policy.

Section 1 of the MIA 1746 only applied to British ships and their cargo, so that it remained open to insurers to write wager policies in respect of foreign ships and cargo. Why? One reason, as explained in *Thellusson v Fletcher*,[18] was that it would have been difficult to bring witnesses from abroad to prove interest. Moreover, it was thought that permitting wager policies on foreign vessels would encourage fraud and aggression against enemy ships as it would make such ships, if insured against capture by British subjects, attractive targets for 'friendly' British privateers.[19] Similarly, the express exclusion of British privateer ships (i.e. those fitted out by a British subject for the purpose of capturing enemy prize during war) in s.2 of the MIA 1746 was intended to encourage acts of warfare against enemy ships.[20] Section 3 contains a specific exception permitting wager policies in respect of cargo from Spanish and Portuguese dominions. The reason for this exception was said to be to encourage the smuggling by British subjects of such goods in contravention of the Spanish and Portuguese embargo on trading between their respective dominions and foreigners. On account of the embargo, it would not have been possible for British traders to obtain bills of lading or other evidence of their cargo, and accordingly they had no choice but to leave their insurance arrangements vague on interest.[21] These exceptions to s.1 were consistent with the intended purpose of the MIA 1746 to reduce insurance fraud and wilful destruction by declaring wager policies null and void.

17 See text to n 12 above.
18 n 7.
19 AB Leonard, '*Underwriting Marine Warfare: Insurance and Conflict in the Eighteenth Century*' (2013) 15 Int JMH 173, 183.
20 Ibid., 184.
21 Marshall (n 7) 104, citing the French advocate and Counsellor of the Marseille Admiralty B.-M. Emerigon, *Traité des assurances et des contrats a la grosse*, vol 1 (Marseille 1783) 212.

Whilst wagering under the guise of marine insurance had been curtailed by the MIA 1746, other classes of insurance still provided opportunities for gambling and fraud. Significantly, Parliament saw it necessary to reinforce the MIA 1746 with the Insurances on Ships Act 1785, making it illegal to issue policies on ships or goods without the name of all the persons interested therein (or their agents) being inserted in the policy. However, the 1785 Act itself and its subsequent interpretation created "such mischiefs and inconveniences"[22] that it was repealed and replaced by the Marine Insurance Act 1788 ('MIA 1788'), which also applied to ships and goods but only required the insertion into the policy of the names of any one person interested in it. The MIA 1788 remains in force in so far as it applies to non-marine insurance. The MIA 1746 remained in force until it was superseded by the Marine Insurance Act 1906 ('MIA 1906').

The Life Assurance Act 1774

There was some small-scale life and funeral expenses insurance written by mutuals, such as the Amicable Society, in the first decade of the 18th century, and from the 1720s the Royal Exchange Assurance Corporation and the London Assurance Corporation wrote a small volume of life insurance.[23] The Society for Equitable Assurances on Lives and Survivorship (the Equitable Society) started writing life insurances in 1762, and, interestingly, its Deed of Settlement contains the following rule:

> No person can make assurance upon the life of another, unless he makes it appear to the Court of Directors of the Society, that he hath an interest in the life of such other person, at least equal to the sum which he proposes to assure.[24]

Rather than insuring one's own life or that of one's spouse, at that time it was much more common practice to insure the lives of well-known or notorious personages as a way of betting on their surviving a reported illness or their conviction for a capital offence.[25] *Wittingham v Thornborough*[26] is an early authority for the proposition that a life insurance where the insured has no interest in the insured life is an 'ill use', but there appears to have been no crystallized common law rule that required an insurable interest in life insurance.[27] In the case of *Earl*

22 Park (n 8) 18–20.
23 Geoffrey Clark, *Betting on Lives: The Culture of Life Insurance in England, 1695–1775* (Manchester University Press 1999) 103–104.
24 ER Mores, *A Short Account of the Society for Equitable Assurances on Lives and Survivorship; Established by Deed* (London 1762) 21 (rule VI).
25 T Mortimer, '*Every Man His Own Broker*' (London, WJ & J Richardson 1801) quoted in J Lowry and P Rawlings, *Insurance Law: Cases and Materials* (Hart Publishing 2004) 315 [701].
26 (1690) Prec. Ch. 20.
27 R Merkin, '*Gambling by Insurance – A Study of the Life Assurance Act 1774*' (1980) 9 Anglo-Am L R 331, 331–333.

of March v Pigot[28] two young heirs, Codrington and Pigot, had betted as to whose father would live longer. This bet was documented in an insurance policy. Unknown to the parties (Codrington had assigned to the Earl of March), Pigot's father had already died at the time of the bet. Codrington's counsel argued that the contract was void for want of consideration, but the court, upon evidence of the trial jury that the intention of parties was to bet on the chances of survivorship, enforced the contract.

The Life Assurance Act 1774 ('LAA 1774'), which is still in force today, was enacted to counteract a 'mischievous kind of gaming' resulting from the insurance of lives in which the insured has no interest. The LAA 1774 appears to have been uncontroversial: any amendments to the Bill debated in Parliament were agreed upon on the same day and Royal Assent was received within two months of the Bill being introduced.[29] Section 1 of the LAA 1774 prohibits any insurance on lives and "on any other event or events whatsoever" without interest or by way of gaming or wagering. Section 2 requires the insertion into the policy of the names of all persons interested in it (s.2). Section 3 limits the insured's recovery to an amount not exceeding his interest.

Professor Merkin identified three factors that did influence, or may have influenced, the passing of the LAA 1774:

1   the social waste of gambling;
2   the belief that the knowledge that one's life had been insured could hasten one's death; and
3   the temptation to take the life of the person insured.[30]

In addition to curtailing gambling on lives, it is suggested that the LAA 1774 was intended to bring life insurance and insurance on "other events" in line with (1) the common law which had already established the requirement for an insurable interest in insured property, and (2) the MIA 1746 which rendered wager policies on British ships and cargo null and void. Thus, s.1 of the LAA 1774 contains a prohibition on policies without interest and mirrors the MIA 1746 by rendering wager policies 'null and void'. The scope of the LAA 1774 dovetails with the MIA 1746: it applies to insurance on lives and "other events", and under s.4 expressly excludes those types of insurances (on 'ships, goods and merchandise') which had already been regulated separately in the MIA 1746. Although the phrase "other events" was given a restrictive meaning towards the end of the 20th century,[31] on a literal interpretation, it would be apt to describe loss or damage to property. On that interpretation of the LAA 1774, the

---

28 (1771) 5 Burr 1802.
29 *Journal of the House of Commons, From November the 26th, 1772, in the Thirteenth Year of the Reign of King George the Third, to September 15th, 1774, in the Fourteenth Year of the Reign of King George the Third*, vol. 34 (26 November 1772 to 15 September 1774) 614, 682 and 776.
30 Merkin (n 27).
31 See Chapter 3.

common law, the MIA 1746 and the LAA 1774 together could be said to have required an insurable interest across all types of insurance known at the time. Moreover, to align the regulation of marine and life (non-marine) insurance further, the Insurance on Ships Act 1785 and the MIA 1788 followed suit with introducing a requirement equivalent to s.2 of the LAA 1774, namely for the names of interested parties to be inserted in the policy.

Consolidation

The Gaming Act 1845

The early 19th century saw the publication of a number of anti-gambling pamphlets drawing attention to the detrimental effects of gambling on the individual and society. The emerging middle class, which had gained a stronger voice in Parliament following the Reform Act 1831, saw gambling as a vice "counter the demands of thrift, industry, and the rational pursuit of leisure".[32] Gambling was thought to be particularly prevalent in the lower classes (where gambling was said to promote idleness and crime), and the aristocracy (where gambling was associated with scandals and the ruin of young men).[33] The judiciary felt that adjudicating wagers was undignified and a wasteful use of resources.[34] In 1845, Parliament passed the Gaming Act 1845 ('GA 1845') which provided in s.18:

> ... all Contracts or Agreements, whether by Parole or in Writing, by way of gaming or wagering, shall be null and void; and that no Suit shall be brought or maintained in any Court of Law or Equity for recovering any Sum of Money or valuable Thing alleged to be won upon any Wager ...

The GA 1845 repealed a number of obsolete anti-wagering statutes but left the MIA 1746 and the LAA 1774 untouched. It is important to note that s.18 of the GA 1845 was directed at *all* wager and gaming contracts (subject to specific exceptions). The GA 1845 did not define wagering contracts and the classic definition is that of Hawkins J in *Carlill v Carbolic Smoke Ball Company*:

> [A] wagering contract is one by which two persons, professing to hold opposite views touching the issue of a future uncertain event, mutually agree that, dependent upon the determination of that event, one shall win from the other, and that other shall pay or hand over to him, a sum of money or

---

32 David Miers, *Regulating Commercial Gambling: Past, Present and Future* (OUP 2004) 54–55.

33 Ibid., Ch 2.

34 The Parliamentary Select Committee set up to look into the effectiveness of the then existing gaming laws noted: "... there seems to be [no] sufficient reason why the valuable time of the Courts of Law should be consumed by adjudicating disputes that may arise in consequence from such Wagers ... [they are] little suited to the dignity of a Court of Law" (*Report from the Select Committee Report on Gaming Together with the Minutes of Evidence*, dated 20 May 1844, vi).

other stake; *neither of the contracting parties having any other interest* in that contract than the sum or stake he will so win or lose ...[35]

(Emphasis added)

Accordingly, in the context of contracts of insurance, any contract where the insured had no genuine interest in the subject-matter beyond the agreement itself was at risk of being void and unenforceable under s.18 of the GA 1845, but s.18 itself did not require insurance contracts to be supported by an insurable interest. The real significance of s.18 in relation to the doctrine of insurable interest was that wagers on the loss or destruction of property (outside the application of the MIA 1746 and the LAA 1774) were no longer an enforceable alternative to contracts of insurance. An insurable interest in the subject-matter could differentiate a (valid) contract of insurance from a (void) wager.

The Marine Insurance Act 1906

The MIA 1906 is a codifying statute based on 200 years' worth of case law, drafted by Sir Mackenzie Chalmers, which sets out the law as it applied to marine insurance in 1906. The doctrine of insurable interest occupies a prominent place within its structure. Section 4(1) declares wagering contracts void. Section 4(2) deems contracts of marine insurance where the insured has no (expectation of acquiring an) interest, and policies made "interest or no interest", or "without further proof of interest than the policy itself", or "without benefit of salvage to the insurer", or subject to any other like term, to be wagering contracts. Section 5 provides a non-exhaustive definition of an insurable interest in marine insurance, followed by specific examples of insurable interest in ss.7–14 of the MIA 1906, which will be discussed in detail in Chapter 4. According to s.6(1) of the MIA 1906 the insured must have an insurable interest at the time of the loss but need not have one at the time of entering into the contract, subject to the proviso that a contract made by the insured with no expectation of acquiring an interest is void pursuant to s.4(2)(a). The MIA 1906 did not replicate the exceptions to the prohibition on wager policies for foreign ships and privateers contained in the MIA 1746. The MIA 1906 was supplemented by the Marine Insurance (Gambling Policies) Act 1909 ('MIGamblingA 1909') pursuant to which effecting a contract of marine insurance without having any bona fide interest is a criminal offence.[36]

The MIA 1906 and the MIGamblingA 1909 did not settle all aspects of the doctrine of insurable interest: neither Act applies to non-marine insurance contracts, and s.5 of the MIA 1906 does not set clear boundaries to the meaning of insurable interest. Moreover, as the MIA 1906 was designed to represent the

---

35 [1892] 2 Q.B. 484, 490–491.
36 MIGamblingA 1909, s.1. According to the LC there are no known prosecutions that have been brought under s.1 of the MIGamblingA 1909 (LC, *Insurance Contract Law: Post Contract Duties and Other Issues* (Law Com CP No 201, December 2011) para 12.52).

marine insurance law as it stood in 1906, it has been described as a retrospective measure,[37] which arguably has not kept pace with all subsequent developments and changes.[38]

The Gambling Act 2005 ('GA 2005')

The GA 2005 has repealed the GA 1845 generally,[39] and s.18 of the GA 1845 specifically.[40] Pursuant to s.335(1) of the GA 2005, gambling contracts are generally enforceable, save that under s.335(2) any rule of law that does not relate specifically to gambling and that renders the contract unenforceable remains operative. This raises the question whether a contract of insurance made without interest is now enforceable as a gambling contract. In Issues Paper 4, the LC suggested that the GA 2005 had abolished the requirement for an insurable interest in non-marine non-life insurance.[41] The prevailing academic opinion is that the GA 2005 is not intended to have, and has not, that effect for a number of reasons, which are summarized below.[42]

First, insurance contracts may not be caught by the definition of 'gambling' in s.3 of the GA 2005. The most pertinent category of gambling is 'betting', which in s.9 is defined as, inter alia, "the likelihood of anything occurring or not occurring". Insurance is more aptly described as the possibility, not the likelihood, of an event occurring. Moreover, s.10 of the GA 2005 excludes from the definition of 'bet' any regulated activity within the meaning of s.22 of the FSMA 2000 since they are separately regulated under the FSMA 2000 regulatory regime. Pursuant to art.10 of the Financial Services and Markets Act 2000 (Regulated Activities) Order 2001 ('RAO'), "effecting and carrying out contracts of insurance" is a regulated activity. In *Feasey v Sun Life Assurance Co of Canada* ('*Feasey*') the Court of Appeal rejected the proposition that gambling is the antithesis of insurable interest,[43] so that a contract of insurance unsupported by an insurable interest would not necessarily be a contract related to gambling caught by s.335(1) of the GA 2005.

Secondly, it is almost inconceivable that it was the intent of Parliament to remove the doctrine of insurable interest with the GA 2005: the GA 2015 (which contains a list of specific repeals)[44] does not mention insurance, the scope of

---

37 Robert Merkin, '*Australia, Still a Nation of Chalmers?*' (2011) 30 UQLJ 189, 195.
38 See Chapter 5.
39 GA 2005, s.356 and Sch.17.
40 GA 2005, s.334(1)(c).
41 LC, '*Issues Paper 4 – Insurable Interest*' (January 2008) paras 5.23 and 5.30. This suggestion was later retracted in LC, '*Post Contract*' (n 36) paras 11.31–11.35.
42 Jonathan Gilman, Mark Templeman and others, *Arnould's Law of Marine Insurance and General Average* (19th edn, Sweet & Maxwell 2018) paras 11-10–11-13; John Birds, Ben Lynch and Simon Paul, *MacGillivray on Insurance Law* (14th edn, Sweet & Maxwell 2018) para 1–39; Robert Merkin, *Colinvaux's Law of Insurance* (12th edn, Sweet & Maxwell 2019) paras 4-0012–4-018.
43 [2003] EWCA Civ 885, [58] and [150–151].
44 The GA 2005 contains a list of specific repeals: s.356 and Sch 17.

s.335 is restricted to gambling and Hansard does not record any discussion of insurance of insurable interest when the Gambling Bill passed through Parliament. Even if the GA 2005 represents a more liberal attitude to regulated gambling, there are policy and regulatory reasons to suppose that Parliament would not wish to permit insurers to gamble under the guise of insurance.[45]

Thirdly, for specific types of insurance there are further arguments that s.335(1) of the GA 2005 does not apply. In respect of *marine insurance* it has been argued that s.335(1) only relates to the enforcement of a contract, not its illegality. Thus, s.335(1) does not capture the MIGamblingA 1909, which makes the effecting of a contract of marine insurance without interest illegal. Moreover, the saving provision in s.335(2) of the GA 2005 arguably applies in relation to marine insurance: whilst s.4 of the MIA 1906 is phrased by reference to "gaming and wagering", it is clear from the preamble of the MIA 1746 (which the MIA 1906 repealed and replaced) that the prohibition on certain wager policies was not just to curtail gambling but to prevent gambling under the guise of insurance and also to prevent other unlawful practices, such as fraud, tax evasion and unlawful trading. A similar point could be made in relation to the types of *contracts of insurance to which the LAA 1774 applies* as it does not simply render a policy in which the insured has no insurable interest void but also prohibits such policies.

Fourthly, from *Sadlers' Company v Badcock*[46] it appears that the (common law) rationale for an insurable interest was not (exclusively) concerned with gambling – after all, pre-GA 1845, wagering contracts were generally enforceable at common law – but the prevention of fraud and the wilful destruction of insured property. Accordingly, it is arguable that the common law rule, being a rule of law which does not specifically relate to gambling, remains operative pursuant to s.335(2) of the GA 2005. If it is accepted, as has been argued above, that s.18 of the GA 1845 did not create an insurable interest requirement, then it should follow that the repeal of s.18 of the GA 1845 by s.334(1)(c) of the GA 2005 should leave the common law on insurable interest unaffected. This proposition is supported by the post GA 2005 decision in *Western Trading Limited v Great Lakes Reinsurance (UK) Plc*[47] ('*Western Trading*') where the court accepted that the insured was required to have an insurable interest in the insured subject-matter (a building) in order to insure it. In sum, the weight of evidence is against an (inadvertent) abolition of the doctrine of insurable interest by the GA 2005.

The historical background to the meaning of insurable interest, recent case law developments and the reform proposals put forward by the LC are examined in the following three chapters.

---

45 See Chapter 6.
46 n 5, 556.
47 [2015] EWHC 103 (QB); reversed in part on a different issue [2016] EWCA Civ 1003.

3 The legal bases for insurable interest

The requirement for an insurable interest was developed in a number of early cases developing the common law and took hold in successive statutes which were enacted in relation to specific, but not all, types of insurance. The resulting legal landscape is a "bewildering mix"[1] of common law and statute law in which the legal basis for insurable interest differs depending on the type of insurance. This Chapter identifies the legal bases for an insurable interest requirement in different types of insurance. The significance of the underlying legal basis is that it is determinative of the timing of the requirement and the consequences that flow from a lack of insurable interest, how insurable interest can be utilized as a defence and whether the requirement can be waived.

Legal bases

The classification by type of insurance for the purposes of insurable interest depends on the underlying subject-matter of insurance and/or on the perils insured against. This classification is neither identical to the classes of insurance listed in Schedule 1 to the RAO nor does it correspond to any conventional categorization of property interests and in personam actions. Moreover, in *Feasey*[2] the Court of Appeal said there is "no hard and fast rule" that, because the nature of an insurable interest relates to one type of insurance, insurable interest could not also be covered by other types of insurance.

Marine property

The legal basis for insurable interest in contracts of marine insurance is MIA 1906, s.4(1), which provides that "every contract of marine insurance by way of gaming or wagering is void". Section 4(2) provides that such contracts are deemed to be by way of gaming or wagering if the insured does not have

---

1 LC, '*Insurance Contract Law: Post Contract Duties and Other Issues*' (Law Com CP No 201, December 2011) para 10.2.
2 [2003] EWCA Civ 885.

(an expectation of acquiring) an insurable interest or where the policy is made "interest or no interest" or "without further proof of interest than the policy itself", or "without benefit of salvage to the insurer", or subject to any other like term. Contracts of marine insurance to which the MIA 1906 applies are contracts of indemnity insurance that cover marine adventures, including ships and goods exposed to maritime perils.

Non-marine goods

Tangible personal property that is not exposed to maritime perils ('non-marine goods') is not captured by the insurable interest provisions of the MIA 1906 and is excluded from the application of the LAA 1774 by s.4.

Some commentators take the view that s.18 of the GA 1845 – which provided that all contracts or agreements by way of gaming or wagering should be null and void – had been the sole basis for an insurable interest requirement for non-marine goods and that, following its repeal by the GA 2005, policies covering non-marine goods are no longer rendered invalid or unenforceable on the grounds of lack of an insurable interest.[3] It is suggested that the requirement for an insurable interest in non-marine goods was never solely governed by s.18 of the GA 1845: first, the case of *Lynch v Dalzell*[4] is a pre-GA 1845 House of Lords authority for the proposition that at common law the party claiming for a loss under a fire insurance policy must have an interest in the insured house and contents at the time of the loss. Moreover, the common law requirement for an insurable interest preceded the first insurable interest statute – the MIA 1746.[5] A textual analysis of the MIA 1746 indicates that the Act assumes that the common law requirement for an insurable interest already existed and would continue to apply: s.1 declares 'null and void' wager policies etc. There are no provisions for the scenario where there is no insurable interest which one might expect if an insurable interest was a newly created requirement of the Act (and which is indeed the language used by the LAA 1774, s.1 in relation to life insurance). In *Lucena v Craufurd* ('*Lucena*'), Lord Eldon doubted the view that no insurable interest was required pre-MIA 1746:

> Lord Kenyon in Craufurd v Hunter considered [the MIA 1746] as a statutory declaration that insurance might have been effected before the Statute without interest. It is with great deference that I entertain doubts on the subject.[6]

3 LC, '*Issues Paper 4 – Insurable Interest*' (January 2008) paras 5.22–5.23; Robert Merkin, *Colinvaux's Law of Insurance* (12th edn, Sweet & Maxwell 2019) para 4-018.

4 (1729) 4 Bro PC 431 (HL). In *Williams v Baltic Insurance Association of London* [1924] 2 K.B. 282, at 288 Roche J stated that "there is nothing in the common law of England which prohibits insurance, even if no interest exists", but he did not consider any of the earlier authorities.

5 See Chapter 2.

6 (1806) 2 Bos & Pul (NR) 269 (HL) 321–322.

The MIA 1746 made it clear that the common law requirement for an insurable interest in contracts of insurance could not be evaded by express agreement that no (proof of) interest would be required or by entering into a wager policy.

Secondly, in *Macaura v Northern Assurance Company* ('*Macaura*') the House of Lords considered the requirement for an insurable interest by reference to the case authorities, and not as a requirement under the GA 1845.[7] Lord Sumner said that the insurers were entitled to deny liability as no insurable interest could be demonstrated at the time of loss on the terms of the policy itself.[8] Similarly, the editors of MacGillivray argue that in indemnity insurance where "the insurer has undertaken to indemnify the assured against loss caused by or arising from particular risks, an interest is required by reason of the nature of the contract itself".[9]

Thirdly, the proposition that sufficient insurable interest is demonstrated if it can be shown that a policy is not a wager contract was rejected in *Feasey*.[10] The question whether a contract of insurance is a wagering contract for the purposes of the GA 1845, s.18 is distinct from the enquiry into whether there is an insurable interest. As noted in Chapter 2, the significance of s.18 of the GA 1845 to insurance contracts was that wagers ceased to be an enforceable alternative. To demonstrate an insurable interest in the subject-matter would have been a means of differentiating insurance contracts from wagers, and thus eliminating any risk of the contract being (re)characterized as the latter.[11] In that sense, the GA 1845 would have had the indirect effect of reinforcing the doctrine of insurable interest, but it did not create a legal requirement for insurable interest.

It has also been suggested that s.1 of the MIA 1788, which is still in force in so far as it applies to non-marine risks, may have been a legal basis for insurable interest in non-marine goods.[12] It renders unlawful insurance policies "upon any … goods, merchandises, effects or property whatsoever" that do not contain the name of at least one person "interested in such assurance". Given the marine context of the 1788 Act, it has been doubted whether non-marine goods were intended to be covered.[13] Yet 18th-century Parliamentary draftsmen could distinguish between marine and non-marine goods: for example the MIA 1746, s.1 specifically refers to "goods, merchandise, or effects, laden … on board of any ship". On the other hand, the 1788 Act was not primarily intended to regulate insurable interest as such; its main purpose was to stop the practice of using

---

7 [1925] AC 619 (HL) 627–628 (Lord Buckmaster) and 630–631 (Lord Sumner).

8 Ibid., 631–632.

9 John Birds, Ben Lynch and Simon Paul, *MacGillivray on Insurance Law* (14th edn, Sweet & Maxwell 2018) paras 1–14. See also Chapter 11.

10 *Feasey* (n 2) [58–59] and [150–151].

11 Wagers have been defined by reference to the absence of an interest other than the sum at stake under the contract – see *Carlill v Carbolic Smoke Ball Company* [1892] 2 QB 484 (QB) 490–491 and Chapter 6.

12 Malcolm Clarke, *The Law of Insurance Contracts* (Service Issue 37, Informa 2016) fn 22 to para 3-2.

13 John Birds, Ben Lynch and Simon Paul (n 9) fn 134 to para 1-042.

blank policies following complaints from insurers about the moral hazard in not knowing the counterparty to a contract of insurance.[14] Moreover, on its wording s.1 of the MIA 1788 does not require an insurable interest of every insured – it is sufficient that the name of one person interested is inserted in the policy. For these reasons, it is suggested that the MIA 1788 on its own is a relatively weak basis for an insurable interest requirement in non-marine goods and that the better view is that the requirement is rooted in the common law.

Buildings and land

Lynch v Dalzell[15] and *Sadlers' Company v Badcock*[16] are authorities for the proposition that at common law the insured was required to have an insurable interest in the insured land or buildings.

At one time it was thought that land and buildings were also subject to the LAA 1774. Section 1 of the LAA 1774 prohibits and renders null and void any insurance on lives and "on any other event or events whatsoever" without interest or by way of gaming or wagering. In *Re King*, Lord Denning MR noted obiter that "other events" in s.2 of the LAA 1774 (which requires the name of the interested person to be inserted in the policy) could refer to damage to or the destruction of land and buildings.[17] In contrast, in *Mark Rowlands Ltd v Berni Inns Ltd* the Court of Appeal held that the LAA 1774 did not apply to any kind of indemnity insurance, but only to insurances which provide for the payment of a specified sum upon the happening of an insured event, for three reasons[18]: first, a literal interpretation of the reference to "other events" in s.2 would "create havoc in much of our modern insurance". Secondly, the LAA 1774, being aimed at gambling, was not intended to deal with indemnity insurance. Thirdly, the court interpreted the decision in *Dalby v The India and London Life Assurance Company*[19] as drawing a distinction between insurances covered by the LAA 1774 (i.e. contingency insurance), and indemnity insurance to which the LAA 1774 does not apply.[20] Faced with this conflict of authority in *Siu Yin Kwan v Eastern Insurance Co Ltd*[21] the Privy Council preferred the decision in *Mark Rowlands*. Lord Lloyd of Berwick gave two reasons: first, the reference to "other events" in s.2 of the LAA 1774 is "not apt to describe" employers' liability (the subject-matter of the insurance in *Siu Yin Kwan*) and, secondly,

---

14 Samuel Marshall, *A Treatise on the Law of Insurance: In Four Books*, vol 1 (Butterworth 1802) 212.
15 n 4.
16 (1743) 2 Atk 554 (Ch) 556 (HL).
17 *Re King*, also known as *Robinson v Gray* [1963] Ch 459 (CA) 485.
18 [1986] 1 QB 211 (CA) 227 [E-G] (Kerr LJ).
19 (1854) 15 CB 365 (ExchCham).
20 Contrary to the Court of Appeal's analysis, *Dalby* does not in fact support the proposition that indemnity insurance is not covered by the LAA 1774. The court in *Dalby* held that life insurance is not a contract of indemnity and that for life insurance the LAA 1774 only required an interest to exist at the time the contract is made (n 19, 390–392).
21 [1994] 2 AC 199 (PC).

indemnity insurance cannot be described as "a mischievous kind of gaming" and was therefore not within the "legislative intent" of the LAA 1774.[22] *Siu Yin Kwan* is not binding on the English courts, although as the board who heard the appeal was constituted by Law Lords, who also sat in the House of Lords at that time, the decision is highly authoritative.

Most commentators now accept that, on the balance of the authorities, the LAA 1774 does not apply to land and buildings. Nevertheless, it is suggested that *Siu Yin Kwan* has not conclusively ruled out that s.1 of the LLA 1774 is a statutory basis for requiring an insurable interest in respect of policies insuring land or buildings: first, the Privy Council only considered the interpretation of s.2 of the LAA 1774 but not s.1. It is the latter provision that prohibits insurances on lives and on any other events without interest. Secondly, the Privy Council reasoned that the words 'event or events' are not apt to describe an employers' liability. Yet, the phrase would be apt to describe damage to or the destruction of land or buildings,[23] an interpretation which is in fact supported by its literal meaning. In addition, land and buildings are not caught by the exceptions (namely insurance "on ships, goods and merchandise") in s.4 of the 1774 Act, and, prima facie, the 1774 Act should therefore be read as applying to all other kinds of insurance except those expressly excluded. Thirdly, although the Privy Council notes that indemnity insurance cannot be described as "mischievous kind of gaming", it is conceivable that a wager policy unsupported by insurable interest could be effected on land or buildings in the same way that wagers were made on ships under the guise of marine insurance policies. A wager contract under the guise of insurance was precisely the "mischievous kind of gaming" that the LAA 1774 (as well as the MIA 1746) sought to curtail.[24] Although the weight of authority is against the application of the LAA 1774 to land and buildings, many commentators still note the argument on this point, and the IIB (cl.6(1)(a)) repeals s.1 of the LAA 1774 only "to the extent that it applies in relation to contracts of life-related insurance", leaving open the possibility that it may have wider application.

To the extent contracts of insurance on land or buildings were effected by way of gaming or wagering, s.18 of the GA 1845, prior to its repeal by the GA 2005, would have rendered such a contract null and void. As has been argued in relation to non-marine goods, the GA 1845 indirectly supports the doctrine of insurable interest but does not constitute the legal basis for the doctrine in relation to land and buildings or indeed any kind of insurance. The recent decision in *Western Trading*[25] supports the proposition that in relation to contracts

22 Ibid., 211.
23 John Birds, *Birds' Modern Insurance Law* (10th edn, Sweet & Maxwell 2016) para 3.9.1.
24 MIA 1746, Preamble; LAA 1774, Preamble.
25 [2015] EWHC 103 (QB); reversed in part on a different issue [2016] EWCA Civ 1003.

of insurance for land and buildings, there is an insurable interest requirement at common law independent of the provisions of the GA 1845.

Profit and future income

The insurability of profits on goods or business assets merits special consideration as there is a conceptual difficulty with seeking to indemnify anticipated future loss or loss of an expected asset, as opposed to an actual loss. To what extent an insurable interest can exist in anticipated profits and future income by anchoring the interest in the underlying asset will be considered in Chapter 4. If profits on goods are regarded as additional value on goods or are subsumed into the value of goods by way of a valued policy, the legal bases for an insurable interest must be the same as for marine goods and non-marine goods respectively, as set out above. Similarly, in business interruption insurance, the legal basis for an insurable interest in the future income and increased running costs as a result of business premises or equipment being destroyed or damaged must be the same as for the business premises and business assets in question.[26] It is consistent with that analysis that, in the UK, business interruption insurance is almost always offered as a business insurance package with property insurance so that the loss of profits is linked to physical damage to business assets in which the business has an insurable interest by virtue of its proprietary rights in, or contractual rights in relation to, such property.

Life

The legal requirement that an insured must have an insurable interest in the life insured derives from the LAA 1774. Section 1 prohibits any insurance made by A on the life of B, where the person or persons "for whose use, benefit, or on whose account such policy" is made has no interest, or where the policy is made by way of gaming or wagering. In addition, s.2 makes such policies unlawful unless the name of the person/s interested or whose benefit the policy is made is inserted.[27] Under s.3, the 'interested' person cannot recover more than the value of his interest. These provisions also serve as the legal basis for an insurable interest requirement in life-related insurance, such as insurance where the insured event is an accident resulting in personal, injury, ill-health or incapacity or indeed survival.[28]

---

26 Richard P. Lewis, Nicholas M. Insua, *Business Income Insurance Disputes* (2nd edn, Wolters Kluwer 2012) para 2.04[A][1].

27 Section 2 was amended by s.50 of the Insurance Companies Amendment Act 1973 so that policies for the benefit of unnamed persons falling within a specified class or description are not invalidated provided the policy states that class or description with sufficient particularity.

28 By way of short-hand, the term 'life insurance' will be used as short-hand to cover both life and life-related insurance, unless expressly stated otherwise.

Liability

The subject-matter of liability insurance is commonly described as the liability itself.[29] On this view, an insurable interest exists in liability insurance if the insured is exposed to the type of liability the policy covers by reason of owing a legal duty or obligation to a third party. Following the decision in *Siu Yin Kwan*,[30] it is highly unlikely that an English Court would now regard the provisions of the LAA 1774 as the basis for an insurable interest requirement in liability insurance. Professor Merkin suggests that, following the repeal of s.18 of the GA 1845 by the GA 2005, this type of policy is not rendered invalid in the absence of an insurable interest, subject to that the insured must still prove his loss in order to recover under the principle of indemnity.[31] However, if the insured is not exposed to the liability covered by the policy, there is no possibility of the insurer being liable to indemnify and such a contract of insurance would therefore be unenforceable for lack of consideration. In the Australian decision *Rados v General Construction Co Ltd & Zurich Australian Insurance Ltd*, the court held that an employee had no insurable interest under an employer's liability policy since he was not exposed to workers' compensation claims.[32] The legal basis for insurable interest in relation to marine liability insurance is s.4 of the MIA 1906.

In contrast, Clarke notes that the subject-matter of liability insurance is not the liability itself but "the patrimony ... of the insured ... which is vulnerable to the effect of liability, *viz*, awards of damages".[33] On his analysis, an insurable interest must inevitably exist because everyone owns some assets – and accordingly, the nature of the asset/s would be determinative of the legal basis for an insurable interest.

Debtor's property and debtor's life

An unsecured creditor has no insurable interest in his debtor's property.[34] In contrast, a secured creditor may have an insurable interest in the debtor's property by reason of a security interest[35] in a specific piece of property of the debtor or over his assets generally. The legal basis for insurable interest in each case depends on the type of the underlying property in which the security interest is held.

---

29 *Feasey* (n 2) [95] (Waller LJ); *CGU International Insurance Plc v AstraZeneca Insurance Co Ltd* [2005] EWHC 2755 (Comm). See also John Birds (n 23) para 3.9; Adolfo Paolini and Deepak Nambisan, *Directors' and Officers' Liability Insurance* (Informa 2008) para 2.18.

30 (n 21).

31 Robert Merkin (n 3) para 4-018.

32 VSC BC9606907.

33 Malcolm Clarke, *Law of Liability Insurance* (Informa 2013) para 1.2.2. Clarke's 'asset' view of insurable interest in liability insurance is shared by a number of continental commentators.

34 *Macaura* (n 7), 626.

35 Such as a mortgage (*Samuel & Co v Dumas* [1924] AC 431 (HL)); MIA 1906, s 14(1)), a lien (*Godin v London Assurance Company* (1758) 1 Burrow 489 (KB)), or a pledge (*Hibbert v Carter* (1787) 1 TR 745 (KB)).

In contrast, a creditor has an insurable interest in the life of the debtor[36] regardless of whether or not the creditor has security over the debtor's property.[37] The requirement for insurable interest in lives derives from s.1 of the LAA 1774.

Debt

Creditors, such as banks and sellers of goods, can insure against the non-payment of a debt or default by an obligor under a credit (or non-payment) policy. The insurer provides an indemnity if the obligor, such as a borrower or buyer of goods, fails to (re)pay a debt. The subject-matter of the insurance is the debt. The insured's interest is a legally enforceable contractual right to (re)payment arising under the loan agreement between the insured (as the lender) and the borrower/obligor. There does not appear to be any direct authority on the legal basis for the requirement, if any, of an insurable interest in debt, or more generally in intangible property. In *Belmont Park Investments Pty Ltd v BNY Corporate Trustee Services Ltd*,[38] Lord Mance accepted indirectly that an insurable interest is required in credit insurance when he rejected the comparison of credit default swaps ('CDS') with credit insurance for want of insurable interest in the former. Arguably, the common law requirement for insurable interest in non-marine property insurance is extendable to intangible property. If the subject-matter of the policy is a debt, the insured will only be able to recover if it has a legally enforceable right to (re) payment under that debt. Conversely, if there is no legally enforceable right to (re)payment, because the right has been lost, transferred or compromised or (re) payment is on a voluntary basis, the creditor does not have an insurable interest in the debt. This is not just a question about whether the insured has suffered a loss governed by the principle of indemnity, but it is also a matter of construction of the contract as to whether or not the policy embraces the insured's repayment rights in the insured debt in the event that the obligor fails to repay.[39]

Reinsurance

In *Wasa International Insurance Co Ltd v Lexington Insurance Co*[40] the House of Lords were unanimously of the view that the nature of a reinsurance contract is not liability insurance but a further insurance of the underlying risk. Lord Mance said:

> … a reinsurance such as the present is an independent contract, under which the subject-matter reinsured is the original subject-matter. The insurable interest which entitles the insurer to reinsure in respect of that subject-matter is the insurer's exposure under the original insurance.[41]

36 *Godsall* v *Boldero* (1807) 9 East 72; *Von Lindenau* v *Desborough* (1828) 3 Car & P 353.
37 *Macaura* (n 7) 626.
38 [2011] UKSC 38 [135].
39 *Feasey* (n 2) [97]; and see Chapter 8.
40 [2009] UKHL 40.
41 Ibid., 33.

If the House of Lord's 'underlying risk as subject-matter of reinsurance' analysis is taken to its logical conclusion, the legal basis for an insurable interest in reinsurance will depend on that subject-matter of the underlying insurance contract – that is, s.4 of the MIA 1906 for marine reinsurance, the common law for non-marine property, s.1 of the LAA 1774 for life reinsurance, etc.

Timing and consequences of lack of insurable interest

The point in time when the insured must have an insurable interest in the insured subject-matter and the consequences of failing to have an insurable interest at that time depend on the legal basis for an insurable interest in the type of insurance in question.

Marine insurance

Timing: Section 6(1) of the MIA 1906 provides that the insured must have an insurable interest at the time of the loss. The insured need not have an insurable interest at the time of entering into the contract, subject to the proviso that a contract made by the insured with no expectation of acquiring an interest is deemed to be a wagering contract.[42]

Invalidity: Section 4(1) of the MIA 1906 provides that "every contract of marine insurance by way of gaming or wagering is void". Such contracts are deemed to be by way of gaming or wagering if the insured does not have (an expectation of acquiring) an insurable interest at the time of the loss or where the policy is made "interest or no interest" or "without further proof of interest than the policy itself", or "without benefit of salvage to the insurer", or subject to any other like term.[43] Thus, indirectly, an insurable interest (or the expectation of acquiring one) is transformed into a validity requirement of a contract of marine insurance since a marine insurance contract without an insurable interest is deemed to be by way of gaming or wagering.

Return of premium: In situations where the policy is *not effected by way of gaming or wagering*, s.84(3)(c) of the MIA 1906 provides that the premium is returnable if the insured has no insurable interest throughout the currency of the risk. The insured would be entitled to retain the premium if not yet paid.[44] Conversely, if at any point during the term of the marine insurance contract the insured had the prerequisite insurable interest, the risk would 'attach' at that point and the premium would be considered 'earned' and payable (and not be returnable) once the risk has attached.[45]

However, where the policy *is effected by way of gaming or wagering* within the meaning of s.4 of the MIA 1906, s.84(3)(c) does not apply, and accordingly

---

42 MIA 1906, s.4(2)(a).
43 Ibid., s.4(2) and 6(1).
44 Ibid., s.82(b).
45 *Heath Lambert Ltd v Sociedad de Corretaje de Seguros* [2004] EWCA Civ 792.

there would be no statutory entitlement for the return of premium for failure of consideration.[46] Nevertheless, in *In Re London County Commercial Reinsurance Office, Limited*,[47] it was held that premium would be returnable in respect of a marine policy which was deemed to be by way of gaming and wagering under the MIA 1906, s.4(2) as the insured had an insurable interest in the insured subject-matter as a matter of fact. The position is further complicated if the contract of marine insurance is, in addition to being void, also regarded as illegal under s.1(1) of the MIGamblingA 1909. Until recently, under the principle *in pari delicto potior est conditio possidentis*, the illegality of the contract would have barred the insured from claiming a return of a premium already paid,[48] and, vice versa, the insurer would not have been entitled to the payment of any premium not yet paid under the illegal contract. However, following the Supreme Court's decision in *Patel v Mirza*,[49] a claimant is not necessarily debarred from an unjust enrichment claim in relation to recovering monies paid to another party under an illegal contract.

Illegality and criminal liability: Marine policies that fall within s.1(1)(a) or (b) of the MIGamblingA 1909 are illegal. Effecting a contract of marine insurance (a) "without ... any bona fide interest ..., or a bona fide expectation of acquiring such an interest" or (b) "interest or no interest", or "without further proof of interest than the policy itself" constitutes a criminal offence.[50]

Life insurance

Timing: Reversing the earlier decision in *Godsall v Boldero*,[51] the court in *Dalby v The India and London Life Assurance Company* held that the LAA 1774 only required an interest to exist for the purposes of life insurance at the time the contract is made.[52] Parke B said that a contract of life insurance was not a contract of indemnity but a contract to pay a certain sum of money upon the death of a person for premium fixed upon the value of the interest at the time the contract is made (i.e. a contingency contract). It would be contrary to the terms of such a contract, justice and commercial practice if the value of the interest at

46 See MIA 1906 ss.84(1) and 84(3)(c).
47 [1922] 2 Ch. 67 (Ch) 85.
48 Jonathan Gilman, Mark Templeman and others, *Arnould's Law of Marine Insurance and General Average* (19th edn, Sweet & Maxwell 2018) paras 6–45. See also *Hughes v Liverpool Victoria Friendly Society* [1916] 2 KB 482 (CA), 492 (Phillimore LJ).
49 [2016] UKSC 42. The Supreme Court said that in deciding whether monies would be recoverable, regard must be had to "(a) ... the underlying purpose of the prohibition which has been transgressed, (b) ... conversely any other relevant public policies which may be rendered ineffective or less effective by denial of the claim, and (c) ... the possibility of overkill unless the law is applied with a due sense of proportionality. We are, after all, in the area of public policy" (at [101] (Toulon SCJ).
50 MIGamblingA 1909, s.1(1)(a) and (b).
51 n 36.
52 n 19.

the time of death could vary the sum payable by the insurer. Parke B was also guided by life insurance market practice which solely relied on the existence of an insurable interest at the outset. Since *Godsall*, life and life-related insurance has been treated as contingency insurance: namely cover that pays out a pre-determined sum upon a specified contingent event. Although s.3 of the LA 1774 limits the insured's recovery to an amount not exceeding his interest, there is no requirement that the insured must prove interest at the date of loss. The time of valuing the insured's interest is the date when the contract is made.[53] An expectation to acquire an interest after the date of the contract does not satisfy the LAA 1774.

Invalidity: Section 1 of the LAA 1774 provides that any contract of insurance made contrary to the prohibition on insurance on life without an insurable interest of the insured in the life insured is 'null and void'.

Illegality: Contracts made in contravention of s.1 of the LAA 1774 are not on the wording of s.1 'illegal', and s.1 does not impose any criminal penalty. Section 2 renders unlawful any policy not containing the name of any person interested. Based on these two provisions, the Court of Appeal in *Harse v Pearl Life Assurance Co* adopted the 'hypothesis' – which was the accepted position of both parties to the litigation – that life insurance contracts unsupported by an insurable interest are illegal, as well as void.[54] Since then this hypothesis appears to have hardened into a proposition of law for which *Harse* is frequently cited as authority.[55]

Return of premium: If it is accepted that contracts of life insurance made in contravention of ss.1–2 of the LAA 1774 are illegal, the illegality of the contract would prevent the insured from claiming a return of a premium already paid,[56] and, vice versa, the insurer would not be entitled to the payment of any premium not yet paid under the illegal contract, under the above-mentioned principle of *in pari delicto potior est conditio possidentis*. However, following the Supreme Court's decision in *Patel v Mirza*,[57] a claimant is not necessarily debarred from an unjust enrichment claim in relation to recovering monies paid to another party under an illegal contract. Even before *Patel v Mirza*, there were a number of exceptions to the general rule that premiums are non-returnable if the contract of insurance is illegal.[58] The most relevant exception in the context of lack of insurable interest is that it may be open to an insured ignorant of the

---

53 *Feasey* (n 2) [73] (Waller LJ)
54 [1904] 1 KB 558, 562 (Collins MR). In the earlier case of *Evans v Bignold* (1868–1869) L.R. 4 Q.B. 622, the court held that a contravention of s.2 of the LAA 1774 rendered a contract of life insurance illegal. *Evans* was not cited in *Harse*.
55 John Birds (n 23) paras 3.6–3.7; John Lowry, Philip Rawlings and Robert Merkin, *Insurance Law: Doctrines and Principles* (3rd edn, Hart Publishing 2011) 183; LC, *'Post Contract'* (n 1) para 11.40.
56 *Harse v Pearl Life Assurance Co* (n 52), 562 (Collins MR).
57 n 49.
58 John Birds, Ben Lynch and Simon Paul (n 9) paras 8-010–8-026.

facts,[59] or perhaps even the law,[60] which rendered the contract illegal, to claim a return of premium. In addition, it is said to be the practice of the Financial Ombudsman not to allow insurers to retain the premium in respect of consumer contracts of insurance that are void or illegal for lack of insurable interest.[61]

Non-marine goods, buildings and land and liability insurance

Timing: It is unclear at what point(s) in time the insured's insurable interest in non-marine goods, buildings and land must exist. In *Lynch v Dalzell*[62] it was held that the insured must have an interest in the insured subject-matter at the time of the loss. In *Sadlers' Company v Badcock*[63] Lord Hardwicke said that the insured must have an interest at the time of insuring, and at the time of the loss. If the LAA 1774 applied to land and buildings, pursuant to s.1, the insured would be required to have an interest at the time the contract is effected. The principle of indemnity, which precludes the insured from recovering more than the value of the actual loss sustained, presupposes an interest at the time of the loss.[64] The insurer is entitled to require proof of insurable interest at the time of loss.[65]

Invalidity/unenforceability: Whilst the GA 1845, s.18 was in force, any contract by way of gaming or wagering was null and void and contracts of insurance unsupported by an insurable interest were at risk of being re-classified as wagers.[66]

It is unclear whether at common law a lack of insurable interest throughout the duration of the contract renders void the whole contract or simply renders any claim thereunder unenforceable. In *Goddart v Garrett*[67] the court stated: "Take it that the law is settled, that if a man has no interest, and insures, the insurance is void". In contrast, in *Lynch v Dalzell*[68] the court appears to have been of the view that an absence of an interest would simply render a claim unenforceable. In *Macaura* Lord Sumner indicated that it is not necessary for the insurer to dispute the validity of the whole contract,[69] whereas Lord Buckmaster

---

59 *Cousins v Nantes and Another* (1811) 3 Taunton 513 (ExchCham) 524.
60 Ignorance of the law relating to insurable interest was not a basis for entitling the insured to a return of premium in *Harse v Pearl Life Assurance Co* (n 54) 563 (Collins MR). However, the LC have suggested that following case of *Kleinwort Benson v Lincoln City Council* [1999] 2 AC 349 (HL) that ignorance of the law may entitle a party to an illegal contract to claim restitution for sums paid under a mistake of law – see LC 'Issues Paper 4' (n 3) para 3.56.
61 LC *Issues Paper 4* (n 3) para 4.20.
62 n 4.
63 n 16, 556.
64 See Chapters 6 and 8.
65 *Macaura* (n 7).
66 See Chapter 2.
67 (1692) 23 ER 774 (Ch).
68 n 4.
69 n 7, 631–632.

expressed himself more ambiguously in terms of a policyholder lacking an insurable interest not being 'entitled' or 'at liberty' to insure, perhaps suggesting that the whole contract would be invalid.[70] The 'invalidity' analysis would be in line with s.4(1) of the MIA 1906 and is the position that LC have taken to be the current law.[71] The 'unenforceability' analysis is rooted in contractual interpretation: if the insured has no insurable interest in the insured subject-matter, and no prospect of acquiring one, at any point during the term of the contract, he cannot suffer an indemnifiable loss that gives rise to a claim covered by the policy in question. Ergo, any claim made by an insured without insurable interest at the time of the loss would be unenforceable.

In addition, MIA 1788, s.1, in so far as it applies to non-marine risks, renders null and void any policy which does not contain the name of any person interested in the insured (non-marine) goods. Arguably, such details could not be included in the policy if the policyholder does not have an insurable interest (although in a policy insuring several insureds, the 'interest' details of one of them would suffice). If the LAA 1774 applied to contracts insuring land and buildings, any such contract of insurance without an interest would be rendered null and void and may also be regarded as illegal.[72]

If the insured had an insurable interest at inception or at any point during the term of the contract, but not at the time of loss, the contract would not be void but the insured may not have a valid claim on account of being unable to prove his loss.[73]

Return of premium: The general rule is that the premium is returnable (or if not yet paid, not payable) if the risk has not been run.[74] If the insured has no insurable interest in the insured subject-matter, and no prospect of acquiring one at any point during the term of the contract, the risk cannot attach since no interest of the insured will be exposed to an insured peril and, accordingly, the insurer would not be running the risk of being liable to indemnify the insured in the event of a loss.[75] If the contract of insurance is void for lack of insurable interest, it could also be argued that premium is returnable on the basis that it was paid for a consideration that has failed.

Policies to which the LAA 1774 applies and made in contravention of its provisions may also be illegal. Under the above-mentioned principle of *in pari delicto potior est conditio possidentis*, the illegality of the contract would have prevented the insured from claiming a return of a premium already paid, and, vice versa, the insurer would not be entitled to the payment of any premium not yet paid under the illegal contract. However, as noted above, following the Supreme Court's decision in *Patel v Mirza*,[76] a claimant is not necessarily debarred from

70 Ibid., 625–627.
71 LC, *Issues Paper 4* (n 3) para 4.19.
72 LAA 1774, ss.1–2 and see above.
73 See Chapter 8.
74 *Tyrie v Fletcher* (1777) 2 Cowper 666 (KB) 668.
75 *In Re London County Commercial Reinsurance Office, Limited* (n 47) 85 (PO Lawrence J).
76 n 49.

an unjust enrichment claim in relation to recovering monies paid to another party under an illegal contract. The US courts are divided on whether premium is returnable if the contract is illegal for lack of insurable interest.[77]

Defence of lack of insurable interest

The insured does not have to prove his interest to make an insurance claim, but the insurer is entitled to raise the insured's lack of insurable interest as a defence to liability.[78] Insurers rarely use this defence because the courts have made it clear repeatedly that they do not look favourably upon it being raised.[79] The courts' attitude to the defence is summarized in the often quoted passage from Brett MR in *Stock v Inglis*:

> In my opinion it is the duty of a Court always to lean in favour of an insurable interest, if possible, for it seems to me that after underwriters have received the premium, the objection that there was no insurable interest is often, as nearly as possible, a technical objection, and one which has no real merit, certainly not as between the assured and the insurer.[80]

A 'technical objection' is a defence raised by the insurer in response to an otherwise meritorious claim when the insurer was, or should have been, aware that the insured had no insurable interest at the time of the contract. Thus, in *Feasey* the (re)insurers' defence of lack of insurable interest was criticized for its unattractiveness and "moral bankruptcy"[81] given that the insurer had devised the structure of the insurance in question and had been content to collect the premium.

The courts' strategies to 'lean in favour of an insurable interest'

The courts have developed three strategies 'to lean in favour of an insurable interest' and let a defence of insurable interest fail by:

1 'finding' an insurable interest on the facts of the case;
2 construing the policy so as to 'embrace' any interest that the insured might have; and
3 stretching the concept of insurable interest to extend to any interest that the insured might have (together, the 'Three Strategies').

---

77 *Penn Mutual Life Ins Co v GreatBanc Trust Co* 887 F.Supp.2d 822 (2011) (no); *Principle Life Ins Co v Lawrence Rucker* 77 F.Supp.2d 674 (2011) (yes).
78 *Macaura* (n 7) 631–632 (Lord Sumner).
79 *Stock v Inglis* (1884) 12 QBD 564 (CA) 571 (Brett MR). Also see *Cepheus Shipping Corp v Guardian Royal Exchange Assurance Plc (The Capricorn)* [1995] 1 Lloyd's Rep 622 (QB) 641; *Feasey* (n 2) [6] (Waller LJ), [144] (Ward LJ); *Western Trading* (n 25) [59–60].
80 (1884) 12 QBD 564 (CA) 571.
81 n 2 [6] and [144].

The Three Strategies are exemplified in two modern cases: *Western Trading*[82] and *Feasey*.[83] In *Western Trading*, Western Trading took out in its name a property insurance policy in respect of a building which was owned by Mr Singh, who was the majority shareholder of Western Trading. Mr Singh had set up Western Trading for managing his property portfolio. The insurer alleged that Western Trading was merely a conduit for rental income for tax and accounting purposes and, accordingly, had no insurable interest in the insured building and had not suffered any loss when the building was destroyed by fire.[84] Judge Mackie QC preferred Western Trading's evidence that Western Trading was Mr Singh's rent-paying tenant who managed the insured building and was responsible for the upkeep and maintenance of the building and, in return, had the right to sub-let the insured building and to receive and enjoy the rent payable by its sub-tenants. On its facts, *Western Trading* is not a revolutionary decision given that there is long-standing authority that a proprietary interest in property constitutes an insurable interest[85] and that a tenant has an insurable interest in the property he rents.[86] But the decision also demonstrates that the enquiry as to whether or not the insured has an insurable interest can be extremely fact-sensitive and that the courts will strive to find an insurable interest on facts that suit the existing categories of insurable interest.

The Court of Appeal's decision in *Feasey*[87] illustrates the courts' strategies to construe a policy so as to embrace any insurable interest that the insured might have and to expand the meaning of insurable interest. The case is more fully considered in Chapter 4. By a 2:1 majority, the Court of Appeal held that Steamship had an insurable interest in the lives and well-being of 'original persons' (employees) as defined by the policy and, properly construed, the policy embraced that insurable interest. To arrive at this result, first, the Court of Appeal had to construe a personal accident policy as personal injury/death liability cover for the losses which Steamship would suffer (i.e. legal liability) by reference to the bodily injury or death of original persons. Secondly, the court had to extend the categories of what constitutes a valid insurable interest under the LAA 1774 to include an insured's *potential* pecuniary liability in respect of bodily injury or death of a group of persons. This constitutes an extension as, following *Dalby v The India and London Life Assurance Company*,[88] the LAA 1774 requires an insurable interest to exist for the purposes of life insurance at the time the contract is made.

The Three Strategies are affirmative of the existence of the doctrine of insurable interest, but, as will be argued further in Chapters 4 and 12, they undermine the doctrine of insurable interest and can make the legal outcome unpredictable.

---

82 n 25.
83 n 2.
84 Ibid., [57].
85 *Lucena* (n 6).
86 *Castellain v Preston* (1883) 11 QBD 380 (CA); *Mark Rowlands v Berni Inns Ltd* (n 18).
87 n 2.
88 n 19.

Another strategy should be mentioned for completeness: where the policy-holder lacks an insurable interest in the insured goods, it has been held that he had insured on behalf of, or as agent for, others with an insurable interest.[89] For this strategy to succeed, it must be shown that the agent had express or implied authority to enter into the insurance contract to bind another party, that that party had an insurable interest and that the agent intended to insure that party's interest.[90] Moreover, s.2 of the LAA 1774 should render this strategy ineffective in relation to contracts of insurance to which the Act applies. There are no recent cases where the agency strategy has been deployed to satisfy the insurable interest requirement, but effecting insurance as an agent for an unnamed or undisclosed principal is frequently argued to deny subrogation rights in a co-insurance context.[91]

Although available, the lack of insurable interest is almost never raised by the insured. There is usually no practical or tactical advantage to do so. In a claims scenario, the invalidity or unenforceability of the contract of insurance for lack of insurable interest would defeat the policyholder's claim and the premium may not be returnable. One notable exception is *Glengate-KG Properties Ltd v Norwich Union Fire Insurance Society Ltd*,[92] where the insurer pleaded the existence of an insurable interest, and the insured argued that he had none, in architectural drawings belonging to a third party in relation to a material damage proviso which effectively barred a claim in respect of material damage to other people's property. *Glengate-KG* shows that the courts are prepared to arbitrage between construing 'interest' broadly for the purposes of insurance coverage and narrowly for the purposes of an exception to cover, in order to prevent an insurer from raising the defence on technical grounds.

The defence of lack of insurable interest and good faith

Would the courts be entitled to deny the defence of lack of insurable interest on the grounds of bad faith where the insurer knew at the time of contracting that the insured had no insurable interest? As a matter of black letter law, such a 'defence' to the defence of lack of insurable interest would be problematic: first, the decision in *Macaura*[93] remains authority for the proposition that the lack of insurable interest in the insured subject-matter is a valid defence to a claim in respect of the insured subject-matter. Secondly, as regards insurance contracts to which the LAA 1774 or the MIGamblingA 1909 apply, such contracts would not merely be void but also be tainted by illegality. Thirdly, to the extent the

---

89 *Prudential Staff Union v Hall* [1947] KB 685 (KB).
90 *National Oilwell (UK) Ltd v Davy Offshore Ltd* [1993] 2 Lloyd's Rep 582 (Comm Ct), 596 (Colman J).
91 Most recently in *Haberdashers' Aske's Federation Trust Ltd v Lakehouse Contracts Ltd* [2018] EWHC 558 (TCC), and see the 'pervasive interest' cases in Chapter 4.
92 [1996] CLC 676 (CA).
93 n 7.

lack of insurable interest renders a contract of insurance void, any subsequent unconscionable conduct by the insurer in raising the defence must be immaterial. Fourthly, it is at best unclear whether a breach of good faith by the insurer affords the policyholder any remedy for breach under s.14(1) of the IA 2015. The LC have said that the duty of utmost good faith has become a mere "interpretative principle"[94] that supports separate remedies regimes for breaches of more specific duties in the IA 2015, although the editors of 'The Law of Reinsurance' suggest that s.14(1) opens the possibility for remedies other than avoidance.[95]

Assuming a 'bad faith' counter-defence is not available, it is suggested that the Three Strategies achieve a similar practical outcome of letting the defence of lack of insurable interest fail (albeit through the route of 'finding' an insurable interest). Reference is made to Chapter 12, where it will be argued that as a matter of good faith, the insurer should be under a pre-contractual duty to decline to enter into a contract of insurance which he knows would be void for lack of insurable interest.

Waiver and assignment

This section gives a brief overview (1) of the debate of whether the requirement for an insurable interest can be waived by the parties, and (2) to what extent the requirement can be circumvented by subsequent assignment of the policy itself, or rights thereunder. It highlights that the applicable legal basis for an insurable interest may also have a bearing on whether the parties can 'contract out' from the requirement.

Marine insurance

The MIA, s.4(2)(b) does not leave any scope for the requirement of an insurable interest to be waived,[96] as marine insurance contracts made 'interest or no interest' are automatically rendered void. In addition, where a marine insurance contract effected without insurable interest is tainted by illegality under the MIGamblingA 1909 s 1(1), the court must take notice of the illegality even if the parties agree to treat the policy as enforceable.[97]

An assignment of a marine insurance policy (whether under s.50 of the MIA 1906 or pursuant to s.136(1) of the Law of Property Act 1925) to a third party without an insurable interest in the subject-matter does not assist the parties in circumventing the requirement for an insurable interest: the assignment is not valid unless (inter alia) the assignor has an insurable interest in the subject-matter

---

94 LC, *Insurance Contract Law: Business Disclosure; Warranties; Insurers' Remedies for Fraudulent Claims; and Late Payment* (Law Com No 353, July 2014) paras 30.22–23.

95 PT O'Neill and JW Woloniecki, *The Law of Reinsurance* (5th edn, Sweet & Maxwell 2019) paras 6–125.

96 See also Robert Merkin (n 3) para 4-016.

97 *Gedge* v *Royal Exchange Assurance Corp* [1900] 2 QB 214 (Comm) 219.

and that interest is assigned to the assignee.[98] In contrast, an insured can assign a particular right under the contract – such as the right to make claims and claims proceeds – to a third party who does not need to have an insurable interest of its own. This is because the assignor remains the insured under the contract, and it is its insurable interest that is relevant, whereas the assignee is a mere loss payee.

Life insurance

In relation to life insurance and any other type of insurance that falls within the scope of the LAA 1774, the requirement for insurable interest cannot be waived because the Act prohibits, and renders illegal, contracts of insurance where the insured has no interest in the insured subject-matter. The parties cannot 'contract out' from the requirement in contravention of the Act. The same position is adopted in the IIB. However, as an insurable interest is only required to exist at the time the contract is made, no insurable interest issue would arise in life insurance if the insured has no longer any such interest at the time of the loss.

Subject to the terms of the policy, the insured can assign a policy to a third party without an insurable interest after the contract is entered into. However, where the contract is effected with the real intention to benefit a third party with no interest in the insured life, then LLA 1774, ss.1–2 cannot be evaded by a subsequent assignment of the policy or benefits thereunder or a bequest.[99] In *Wainwright v Bland*,[100] the insured, Miss Abercromby, took out several life insurance policies in her own name on the instructions of Wainright, who had no interest in Miss Abercromby's life but who funded the premium and to whom the policies were assigned just before her death. Lord Abinger CB instructed the jury as follows:

> [T]he question in this case is, who was the party really and truly effecting the insurance. Was it the policy of Miss Abercromby? Or was it substantially the policy of Wainwright …, he using her name for purposes of his own? … [I]f…you come to the conclusion that the policy was in reality effected by Wainwright; that he merely used her name, himself finding the money, and meaning (by way of assignment, or by bequest, or in some other way) to have the benefit of it himself; then I am of the opinion such a transaction would be a fraudulent evasion of the [1774 Act]….

The factors a court may take into account in deciding whether the policy was effected for the benefit of the insured or a third party include whether the

---

98 MIA 1906, ss.50–51; *Raiffeisen Zentralbank Österreich AG v Five Star Trading LLC* [2001] EWCA Civ 68, [64] (Mance LJ).

99 *Wainwright v Bland* 26 (1835) 1 M & Rob 481; *Shilling v The Accidental Death Insurance Company* 175 E.R. 651; *Fitzsimmons v City of Glasgow Friendly Society* [1933] I.A.C.Rep. 24; *M'Farlane v Royal London Friendly Society* (1886) 2 T.L.R. 755.

100 n 99, 486–487.

premium was paid by the insured or the third party,[101] whether the insurance and the assignment were effected (near) simultaneously and whether the insurance was effected for a bona fide purpose not captured by the mischief of the LAA 1774.[102] The limitation on the assignment of policies to parties without interest is consistent with the view that the requirement for an insurable interest cannot be waived: the statutory requirement cannot be evaded by the (deceptive) agreement of the parties to the contract and/or third parties.

In the United States, assignments of life policies to persons without an insurable interest came into sharp focus in relation to STOLI schemes. The US courts tend to recognize the insured's general right to assign a life policy regardless of whether the assignee has an insurable interest in the life insured, subject to that such an assignment is void as against public policy if the policy was taken out in bad faith with the intention to circumvent the insurable interest requirement with the assignment.[103] Most US courts have held that the lack of a bona fide interest at the inception of the STOLI policy renders the transaction void and the majority of States have now enacted legislation that ban or restrict STOLI schemes.[104] In contrast, viatical settlements pursuant to which the insured – typically an elderly or terminally ill person – 'sells' his or her policy for a cash price in excess of its surrender value to a third party who did not initiate the purchase of the policy are not void for lack of insurable interest.

Non-marine property insurance

In relation to non-marine property insurance that falls within the scope of the LAA 1774, the parties cannot 'contract out' from the statutory requirement for an insurable interest in contravention of the law. In relation to other non-marine insurance contracts, the position is less clear and academic opinion is divided.[105] In *Anctil v Manufacturers' Life Insurance Company*, the Privy Council held that for public policy reasons, the parties cannot waive the requirement for an insurable interest.[106] In contrast, in *Thomas v National Farmers' Union Mutual Insurance Society*[107] the court decided that on the terms of the policy, the insurer was still required to pay a claim for hay and straw even though at the time of the loss, the hay and straw had been divested to the landlord and the insured tenant had no longer an insurable interest therein. In *Prudential Staff Union v Hall*[108] the court did not address the permissibility of waiver, relying instead on

---

101 See n 99.
102 *M'Farlane v Royal London Friendly Society* (n 99), 756 (Pollock CB).
103 *Warnock v Davies* 104 U.S. 775 (1881); *Grigsby v Russell* 222 U.S. 149 (1911).
104 See Chapter 5.
105 Pro waiver: John Birds (n 23) para 3.11. Contra: Malcolm Clarke (n 12) paras 3-6E and 4-1D; J Lowry and P Rawlings, 'Rethinking Insurable Interest' in Sarah Worthington (ed.), *Commercial Law and Commercial Practice* (Oxford: Hart Publishing. 2003) 335, 361–363.
106 [1899] AC 604 (PC).
107 [1961] 1 WLR 386 (QB).
108 n 89.

a contractual loss payee, trust and agency analysis. The US authorities too are divided on this issue.[109]

It is suggested that the better view is that the parties should not be permitted to waive the requirement of an insurable interest even in relation to those types of insurance where the requirement is not derived from statute but from common law. If it is accepted that contract of insurance unsupported by an insurable interest is void, the contract does not exist at all and cannot be resurrected by the parties agreeing to do so. In *Feasey* the Court of Appeal said that it is desirable for there to be some alignment in the treatment of insurable interest in different classes of insurance.[110] If it is accepted that the requirement of insurable interest cannot be waived in life and marine insurance, there is an argument that non-life non-marine insurance should be treated in the same way. As will be discussed in the following Chapters, there are policy reasons for requiring an insurable interest in insurance contracts, and it will also be argued that an insurable interest is an integral part and hallmark of contracts of indemnity insurance.

Similarly, the requirement for an insurable interest cannot be circumvented by an assignment of the policy (as opposed to rights under the policy). Upon an assignment of the policy, the assignee replaces the assignor as the insured and it will be the assignee's insurable interest in the insured subject-matter that determines whether the contract is valid and enforceable. If there is no contemporaneous assignment of the subject-matter and the policy, the policy lapses since either (1) assignee of the policy has not acquired any insurable interest in the subject-matter and can suffer no loss[111] or (2) the assignee of the property has not become an insured under the policy (whereas the assignor has ceased to have an insurable interest in the property).[112]

Within the framework of the general law and regulation, the parties are free to conclude other forms of contracts that do not require an insurable interest, or to agree loss of payee provisions or an assignment of claims and claims proceeds where it is intended that claims are paid to third parties. The courts have been able to stay clear of considering 'waiver' by resorting to the Three Strategies, in particular stretching the meaning of insurable interest to embrace any interest that the insured might have. The meaning of insurable interest will be considered in the next chapter.

109 *Couch on Insurance 3D* (Thomson Reuters 2011) §41:7 and §41:8.
110 n 2 [90–96], [114], [174].
111 *Lloyd v Fleming* (1871–1872) L.R. 7 Q.B. 299, 302 (Blackburn J).
112 *Rayner v Preston* (1881) 18 Ch. D. 1, 7 (Cotton LJ).

4 The meaning of insurable interest

The MIA 1746 and the LAA 1774 did not define the term 'interest', and it was left to the courts to explain the meaning of insurable interest. In *Feasey*, Waller LJ acknowledged that 'insurable interest' "... has been a concept which has proved difficult of precise definition"[1] and commentators too are reluctant to commit.[2] Yet the meaning of insurable interest is central to the scope of the doctrine of insurable interest: a narrow definition risks that certain interests cannot be validly insured, whilst too wide a definition could render the requirement for an insurable interest meaningless and incapable of serving the policy reasons behind the doctrine. Traditionally, the courts focussed on legal relationships in defining insurable interest in all classes of insurance, but this Chapter looks at property insurance and life insurance separately as the courts have developed different approaches in each group.

Property insurance

The classic definition of insurable interest

The test(s) in Lucena v Craufurd: The seminal case on what constitutes an insurable interest in property insurance is *Lucena*.[3] The House of Lords considered the interest of the Commissioners of Admiralty in Dutch ships and their cargo of which the Commissioners had taken possession under protective powers conferred onto them by statute[4] but to which they had no rights. The court concluded that the Commissioners had no insurable interest. Giving the leading speech, Lord Eldon formulated what has become the classic definition of insurable interest synonymous with the 'legal interest test':

---

1 [2003] EWCA Civ 885, [64].
2 John Birds, Ben Lynch and Simon Paul, *MacGillivray on Insurance Law* (14th edn, Sweet & Maxwell 2018) paras 1-051 and 1-118; Robert Merkin, *Colinvaux's Law of Insurance* (12th edn, Sweet & Maxwell 2019) Ch 4, Sec 5.
3 (1806) 2 Bos & Pul (NR) 269 (HL).
4 Shipping Act 1795, s.21.

[Insurable interest is] a right in the property, or a right derivable out of some contract about the property, which in either case may be lost upon some contingency affecting the possession or enjoyment of the property.[5]

Lord Eldon's definition underscores that the purpose of insurance is the protection of legal interests, but it does not require absolute ownership rights in the insured property: a legally enforceable right to the possession of, or contractual rights in relation to, the insured property suffices.

In the same case, Lawrence J, giving an advisory opinion to the House of Lords, put forward an alternative test that has become known as the 'moral certainty test':

A man is interested in a thing to whom advantage may arise or prejudice happen from the circumstances which may attend it ... and where a man is so circumstanced with respect to matters exposed to certain risks or dangers, as to have a moral certainty of advantage or benefit, but for those risks or dangers he may be said to be interested in the safety of the thing. To be interested in the preservation of a thing is to be so circumstanced with respect to it as to have the benefit from its existence, prejudice from its destruction.[6]

Lawrence J's moral certainty test assesses insurable interest by reference to the probability – pitched at a level of 'moral certainty' – of the insured being prejudiced by the loss of the insured property. The 'prejudice' to the insured is not confined to proprietary rights as long as the insured can show that a benefit from the continuing safety of the insured property would have arisen but for the peril.[7]

Lord Eldon rejected the moral certainty test: first, he found it impossible to differentiate between a 'moral certainty' and an expectation, and, in his opinion, a mere expectation, even if founded "upon the highest probability", would not be insurable.[8] Secondly, he argued that the moral certainty test could lead to a proliferation of insurance by a wide range of persons in the same property: "If moral certainty be a ground of insurable interest, there are hundreds, perhaps thousands, who would be entitled to insure ... and of course get something by it".[9] Thirdly, Lord Eldon said that courts could decide only on enforceable rights, not unascertained speculations.[10] This is a causational and quantum concern – namely how the insured would prove, and quantify, a loss of property

5 n 3, 321.
6 Ibid., 302.
7 Ibid., 301–302.
8 Ibid., 321 and 323. Lord Eldon also said that, to the extent *Le Cras v Hughes* (1782) 3 Dougl 79 was decided on the basis of an expectation, he could not "give [his] assent to such a doctrine".
9 Ibid., 324.
10 Ibid., 325.

in relation to which he does not have any rights. All three reasons will be recurring themes in this and the following Chapters.

Despite the different tests put forward, it has been noted that Lawrence J's advice read as a whole is consistent with Lord Eldon's opinion.[11] They have in common the notion of a relationship between the insured and the insured subject-matter. Lawrence J qualified his moral certainty test by also requiring the insured to have "some relation to, or concern in the subject-matter",[12] and his conclusion that the Commissioners had no insurable interest rested on the absence of their "authority and duty" (i.e. legal responsibility) until after the ships' arrival in England.[13] A relationship between the insured and the insured property based on legal responsibility is not dissimilar to having "a right derivable out of some contract about the property". Both phrases are apt to cover an entitlement or power to deal with the property and neither requires an in rem right. There is a further overlap in that both judges identify as problematic the causational link between the insured peril and the loss and the valuation of the loss, where there is no legal interest.[14] Both judges reached the same conclusion that the Commissioners had no insurable interest.

Yet, Lawrence J's moral certainty test and Lord Eldon's legal interest test are frequently presented as rival tests for insurable interest in case law[15] and commentary,[16] with the former being ascribed a wider scope than the latter. This appears to be the result of a reductionist interpretations of both tests. In particular, Lawrence J's moral certainty test is often cited as an isolated passage without the context of his full advice[17] that, as has been shown above, qualifies the moral certainty test. In other instances, his test has been paraphrased so as to reduce it to a mere advantage/prejudice test. For example, in *Wilson v Jones*, Blackburn J summarized as follows:

> I know no better definition of an interest in an event than that indicated by Lawrence, J., in Barclay v. Cousins, and more fully stated by him in Lucena v. Craufurd, that if the event happens the party will gain an advantage, if it is frustrated he will suffer a loss.[18]

---

11 John Birds, Ben Lynch and Simon Paul (n 2) para 1-118, cited with approval in *Comlex Ltd (in Liquidation) v Allianz Insurance Plc* [2016] CSOH 87, [2016] Lloyd's Rep IR 631 [33] (Lord Doherty).
12 n 3, 302.
13 Ibid., 306.
14 Ibid., 301–303 (Lawrence J) and 324–326 (Lord Eldon).
15 See e.g. *Feasey* (n 1) [68–70] (Waller LJ).
16 Robert Merkin (n 2) paras 4-018–4-019; John Lowry and Philip Rawlings, *Insurance Law: Cases and Materials* (Hart Publishing 2004) notes to [613]. See also LC, '*Insurance Contract Law: Post Contract Duties and Other Issues*' (Law Com CP No 201, December 2011) paras 11.46–11.51.
17 See e.g. *Sharp v Sphere Drake Insurance (The Moonacre)* [1992] 2 Lloyd's Rep 501 (Comm Ct) 512; *Glengate-KG Properties Ltd v Norwich Union Fire Insurance Society Ltd* [1996] CLC 676 (CA) 691; *O'Kane v Jones* [2003] EWHC 3470 (Comm), [2004] 1 Lloyd's Rep. 389 [145].
18 (1866–1867) L.R. 2 Ex. 139 (ExchCham) 150–151.

Similarly, Lawrence J's moral certainty test has been equated with the 'factual expectation', 'factual expectancy' or 'economic interest' tests used for determining insurable interest on an economic interest basis,[19] whilst ignoring the 'relational' element in Lawrence J's advice. A 'factual expectation' sets a lower certainty threshold than a 'moral certainty', and 'mere expectation' of loss was ruled out as insufficient for an insurable interest not just by Lord Eldon but also by Lawrence J on the grounds that economic loss could arise from "a variety of probable contingencies" and not just the insured peril.[20]

Conversely, Lord Eldon's legal interest test has been reduced to requiring a proprietary right in the property insured,[21] which ignores that his test does not insist on in rem rights but also considers contractual rights in relation to the property as sufficient interest.[22] As explained below, the MIA 1906, s.5(2) does not treat the two tests as alternatives but requires them to be applied cumulatively. Similarly, in *Moran Galloway & Co v Uzielli*, Walton J thought it unremarkable to synthesize both tests into one definition.[23] It is suggested that a polarized and antithetical presentation of the two tests is not justified.

The definition in the MIA 1906: The MIA 1906, s.5(1) provides that "every person has an insurable interest who is interested in a marine adventure", which is further defined in s.5(2):

> In particular a person is interested in a marine adventure where he stands in any legal or equitable relation to the adventure or to any insurable property at risk therein ['first limb'], in consequence of which he may benefit by the safety or due arrival of insurable property, or may be prejudiced by its loss, or by damage thereto, or by the detention thereof, or may incur liability in respect thereof ['second limb'].

The first limb of this definition is similar to, but not the same as, Lord Eldon's legal interest test as s.5(2) employs the term 'relation' instead of 'right'. The 'relation' has to be 'legal or equitable', and, according to the draftsman of the MIA 1906, Makenzie Chalmers, "cognizable by law".[24] A mere economic relationship, or a moral obligation, which is not legally enforceable, cannot be the basis of a legal or equitable relationship with the property. The first limb is not restricted to proprietary rights and is apt to cover contractual rights in respect of property. The wording of the second limb derives from Lawrence J's advice in *Lucena*. The two limbs are not alternatives but integrated tests. This is apparent from (1) the connective drafting: the second limb is "in consequence" of

---

19 See Chapter 5.
20 *Lucena* (n 3), 321 and 323 (Lord Eldon), 301 (Lawrence J).
21 See e.g. *Feasey* (n 1) [81] (Waller LJ); *The Moonacre* (n 17); and M. Clarke, 'An Introduction to Insurance Contract Law' in J Burling and K Lazarus (eds), *Research Handbook on International Insurance Law and Regulation* (Edward Elgar, Cheltenham 2011) 17.
22 n 3, 321.
23 [1905] 2 KB 555 (KB) 561–562.
24 Makenzie Chalmers, *The Marine Insurance Act 1906* (1st edn, William Clowes & Sons 1907) 12.

the first limb and (2) the commentary to s.5(2) of the MIA: Chalmers did not merely rely on the moral certainty test but cited another passage in Lawrence J's advice that emphasizes the 'relation' between the insured and the subject-matter of insurance:

> [I]nterest ... [implies] ... the having some *relation* to, or concern in the subject of the insurance, which *relation* or concern by the happening of the perils insured against may be so affected as to produce a damage, detriment, or prejudice to the person insuring.[25]

(Emphasis added)

The introductory language, "In particular ...", in s.5(2) suggests that the definition is non-exhaustive. Arguably, the MIA 1906, s.5(1) should therefore be elastic enough to accommodate interests that fall outside s.5(2). However, such a construction would be inconsistent with the pre-existing marine insurance law,[26] contrary to Chalmers' commentary on s.5 and the specific examples of insurable interest that follow in ss.7–14 of the MIA 1906, which are all instances of interest based on "legal or equitable relations". The better view is that the first limb is a minimum requirement, which reflects the legal interest test.

Endorsement of the legal interest test: The legal interest test was applied by the House of Lords in a non-marine context in *Macaura*.[27] Mr Macaura, the sole shareholder and unsecured creditor in a company, 'insured' the company's main asset, a timber estate, against fire under several policies effected in his own name. When the timber was subsequently destroyed by fire, the insurers declined Mr Macaura's claim. It was held that the insurers were not liable to pay the claim as Mr Macaura had no insurable interest in the timber. Borrowing from the language in the MIA 1906, Lord Sumner said that in order to show an insurable interest, the insured must stand in "legal or equitable relation" to the property.[28] As an unsecured creditor, Mr Macaura had a right to the repayment of the debt, but "the debt was not exposed to fire".[29] The decreased probability of repayment of the debt as a result of the fire did not give rise to legal or equitable rights in relation to the timber.[30]

Moreover, Mr Macaura had no interest qua shareholder for three reasons: First, echoing the concerns expressed in *Lucena*, Lord Buckmaster anticipated valuation problems in determining the extent to which the loss of a company's asset would be reflected in the diminution of the share value upon the

---

25 n 3, 302, cited in Chalmers (n 24) 12.
26 *Moran Galloway & Co v Uzielli* (n 23). The MIA 1906 sought to codify the existing marine insurance law as it stood at the time (see Preamble).
27 [1925] AC 619 (HL).
28 Ibid., 630.
29 Ibid., (Lord Sumner).
30 Ibid., 626 (Lord Buckmaster) citing *Moran Galloway & Co v Uzielli* (n 23).

dissolution of the company.[31] Secondly, following Lord Eldon in *Lucena*,[32] he said that a moral certainty of loss was insufficient to establish a causal connection between the loss of a company's asset and the diminution in the share value an insurable interest with any (legal) certainty.[33] Thirdly, on a proper construction of the policy, Macaura's interest was not covered: he had suffered loss as a result of the decrease in share value, but not as a result of the destruction of the timber by fire.[34] In contrast, a majority shareholder's insurable interest in the company's property has been recognized in the United States on the basis that the destruction of a major corporate asset would materially affect the amount of dividends and the share price.[35]

Since *Macaura*, there has been no House of Lords or Supreme Court decision on the meaning of insurable interest, although the Supreme Court in *Petrodel Resources Ltd v Prest*[36] cited *Macaura* with approval on the point that a shareholder has no insurable interest in company assets. Accordingly, to the extent the legal interest test and the moral certainty test as originally conceived in *Lucena* are different, the weight of legal authority favours the legal interest test with its roots in two House of Lords decisions and its embodiment in s.5(2) of the MIA 1906 as the most authoritative and binding test for determining insurable interest in property insurance.[37] Nevertheless, as will be discussed below, some lower courts have sought to expand the definition of insurable interest by rejecting a reductionist version of the legal interest test as too narrow in order to justify reliance on a (wider and unqualified) version of the moral certainty test.

Expanding the meaning of insurable interest

There are a number of cases that are regarded as expanding upon (the reductionist version of) the legal interest definition of insurable interest, although some of them can be explained on the basis of the legal interest test as originally conceived in *Lucena*.

Profits and business interruption: The conceptual difficulty with insuring profits is that the indemnity sought is for anticipated future loss or loss of an expected asset, as opposed to an existing legal right to receipts. To bring the notion of 'profits' within the realm of the legal interest test, the courts have derived an insurable interest in profits from an insurable interest in the underlying

---

31 Ibid., 627. Note also the reflective loss principle in tort law: see Chapter 8.
32 n 3, 325.
33 *Macaura* (n 27) 627.
34 Ibid., 630 (Lord Sumner).
35 *Travelers Indemn. Co. v Israel* 354 F.2d 488 (2d Cir. 1965).
36 [2013] UKSC 34, [8] (Sumption JSC).
37 This conclusion was reached by Ward LJ in *Feasey* (n 1) [181] (see below) and the Scottish Court of Session (Outer House) in *Comlex Ltd (in Liquidation) v Allianz Insurance Plc* (n 11) [35–37] (Lord Doherty).

asset or adventure generating the profit.[38] For example, in *Stockdale v Dunlop*, Parke B explained:

> I admit that profits may be insured, but that is on the ground that they form an additional part of the value of the goods, in which the party has already an interest. Thus, the owner of goods on board a vessel may insure the profits to arise from them … In these cases there is either an absolute or a special property in possession. There the profits are insured as an additional value upon the goods, in which the insurer has a present interest.[39]

The profits can be absorbed into the value of the goods themselves by agreeing their value for the purposes of the policy. Similarly, in business interruption insurance, the insurable interest in future income is derived from the insurable interest in the business premises and assets that generate that income.[40] In the UK, business interruption insurance is almost always offered as a package together with property insurance so that the loss of profits is linked to physical damage to business assets.

In *Wilson v Jones*[41] ('*Wilson*'), the court held that a shareholder in the Atlantic Telegraph Company had an insurable interest in profits (i.e. the increase in share value) to be derived from the success of 'the adventure' to lay a telephone cable in the Atlantic Ocean. The subject-matter of the insurance was 'the adventure'. Willes J considered two alternative formulations as to what the shareholder's interest in 'the adventure' was: (1) "the profit to be made by successfully laying down the cable on that occasion" or (2) the success of the adventure to lay down the cable "generally".[42]

It seems that Willes J and Blackburn J (with whom the other judges agreed) favoured (1): had the adventure been successful, the profit would have derived from the increased share value realizable upon the sale of the shares.[43] Arguably, the insurable interest of the shareholder was anchored in his title to the shares and the profits would have been an additional part of the (agreed) value of his shares upon the cable being successfully laid. This analysis can be criticized on three grounds: first, in their reasoning the judges did not refer consistently and clearly to the insurable interest subsisting in the shareholder's shares. Being confined by the policy language describing the insured subject-matter by reference to "the adventures … attending the conveyance and successful laying of the cable",

---

38 *Eyre v Glover* (1812) 16 East 218 (KB); *Stockdale v Dunlop* (1840) 6 Meeson Welsby 224 (Exch) 232–233 (Parke B); *M'Swiney v Royal Exchange Assurance Company* (1849) 14 QB 634 (QB); *Wilson v Jones* (1866–1867) L.R. 2 Ex. 139 (ExchCham); *Arab Bank plc v John D Wood Commercial Limited* [2000] 1 WLR 857 (CA) [97] (Mance LJ).

39 n 39, 232–233.

40 Richard P. Lewis, Nicholas M. Insua, *Business Income Insurance Disputes* (2nd edn, Wolters Kluwer 2012) para 2.04[A][1]. Also see *Glengate-KG Properties Ltd v Norwich Union Fire Insurance Society Ltd* (n 17).

41 n 18.

42 Ibid., 144 and 150.

43 Ibid., 146 (Willes J) and 152 (Blackburn J).

Willes J was careful to formulate the interest in broader terms by reference to the success of "the adventure".[44] The notion of 'adventure' is much harder to reconcile with the legal interest test as the relationship between the adventure and the shareholder is limited to the shareholder's rights deriving from his shares.

Secondly, the concept of an insurable interest in profits is problematic to the extent that there is a mere expectation to realize a gain on the sale of goods or shares. A mere expectation is insufficient to found an insurable interest.[45] In *Wilson* the shareholder would have been able to prove that he would have made a profit as the return on the shares – if the adventure should be successful – had been contractually agreed at the outset, but it is telling that Blackburn J cites with approval Lawrence J's moral certainty test, rather than relying on the legal interest test.[46]

Thirdly, the decision in *Wilson* is heavily reliant on a construction of the policy that is consistent with the presence of an insurable interest, which is one of the Three Strategies used by the courts "to lean in favour of an insurable interest".[47] If the insured subject-matter had been the cable (rather than the adventure), the shareholder would not have had an insurable interest. In *Macaura* Lord Buckmaster distinguished *Macaura* from *Wilson* on the basis that the insured subject-matter in *Macaura* was the timber owned by the company. Thus, the different outcomes in *Wilson* and *Macaura* are pivoted on the construction of the respective policies.

The courts' approach to insurable interest in future profits as an add-on to an underlying asset cannot be easily reconciled with Lord Eldon's legal interest test, and the editors of MacGillivray argue that it would be better to analyse the subject-matter of an insurance on profits as a vested or contingent right of sale[48] which, as a species of intangible property, would constitute an insurable interest under the legal interest test.

Bailment, enjoyment and management of property: Consistent with the legal interest test, bailees being in possession of, and responsible for, the property of their customers, as well as having a lien on the property to the extent of any reward or charge for their services, have an insurable interest when they insure the property entrusted to them.[49] Despite their limited interest, for reasons of commercial convenience, bailees may insure the full value of the property but must account for any recoveries in excess of their interest to the true owner of the property.[50]

In *Sharp v Sphere Drake Insurance*[51] ('*The Moonacre*') one of the issues was whether Mr Sharp had an insurable interest in a yacht insured in his name but owned and registered in the name of a company, Roarer. The court held that

---

44 Ibid., 147–148.
45 *Lucena* (n 3), 321 and 323 (Lord Eldon).
46 n 18, 145.
47 See Chapter 3.
48 John Birds, Ben Lynch and Simon Paul (n 2) para 1-122.
49 *Waters v The Monarch Fire and Life Assurance Company* (1856) 5 Ellis and Blackburn 870, 880–881 (Campbell CJ).
50 *Hepburn v A Tomlinson (Hauliers) Ltd* [1966] AC 451 (HL); *Ramco (UK) Ltd v International Insurance Co of Hannover Ltd* [2004] EWCA Civ 675.
51 n 17.

Sharp had an insurable interest in the yacht as a result of two powers of attorney issued by Roarer, giving Sharp rights of use, control, management and disposal of the yacht.[52] In addition, as a result of the wide terms of the powers of attorney, Mr Sharp had also become a bailee of the yacht, giving rise to an insurable interest based on the bailment relationship.[53] Arguably, the decision in *The Moonacre* is consistent with the MIA 1906 definition of insurable interest and Lord Eldon's legal interest test. The powers of attorney gave Mr Sharp extensive rights over the yacht. Although not "right(s) derivable out of some contract about the property" strictu sensu, Mr Sharp's rights derived from these instruments relating to the use of the yacht.

And yet, the decision in *The Moonacre* has been regarded as extending the meaning of insurable interest beyond the legal interest test.[54] One explanation for this may be that the court cited Lawrence J's moral certainty test (and not Lord Eldon's legal interest test) in support of its conclusion that an insurable interest may subsist without a proprietary right in the insured subject-matter,[55] although that conclusion would have been equally consistent with Lord Eldon's legal interest test. Possibly as a result of how the case was pleaded by the insurer's counsel,[56] the judge adopted the kind of 'reductionist' interpretation of *Lucena* discussed earlier.

Moreover, the judge's (obiter) "provisional view" that Sharp also may have had an insurable interest on the basis that he owed a duty of care to Roarer[57] represents an extension of the legal interest test. Lord Eldon's test only refers to 'rights', but not 'liability', in relation to the insured property. It is suggested that there is no departure from the legal interest test as long as the insured has obligation as well as existing rights in respect of the insured property – as was indeed the case in *The Moonacre*. Examples of a non-owner with rights and obligations in respect of the property are lessees,[58] bailees[59] and licensees[60] who enjoy a right to possession (or other contractual rights), and are subject to liability, in respect of the property.

In *O'Kane v Jones*, the insured's insurable interest in a vessel was founded upon management and control rights over a vessel, combined with the insured's exposure to liability in the event of the loss of the vessel, derived from a management agreement (which was said to represent the legal relationship with the vessel).[61] The court's obiter comments in *O'Kane* go beyond *The Moonacre* since the insured did not have a right to possession of the vessel. By comparison, in

52 Ibid., 512 (Colman, QC sitting as Deputy Judge).
53 Ibid., 513.
54 *Feasey* (n 1) [90] (Waller LJ).
55 *The Moonacre* (n 17).
56 Ibid., 509: insurer's counsel pleaded that Sharp did not have an insurable interest because he was neither the owner nor the bailee of the property.
57 Ibid., 513.
58 *Castellain v Preston* (1883) 11 QBD 380 (CA).
59 See 49 and 50.
60 *Comlex Ltd (in Liquidation) v Allianz Insurance Plc* [2016] (n 11).
61 n 17 [154].

the US case *Judge v Travelers Ins. Co* a mother's management duties in relation to her son's property did not give her an insurable interest.[62] The notion that an insurable interest may subsist (solely) because the insured may become liable by reason of the loss or damage of the insured property was also recognized in the pervasive interest cases considered next.

Expanding insurable interest to pervasive interests

The question whether potential liability for damage to property can create an insurable interest in that property has been considered by the courts in a number of construction cases. In construction projects involving a main contractor and multiple sub-contractors, insurance cover for the project works and assets is frequently arranged for all (sub-)contracting parties in a single composite property policy (the 'project policy'). If the project works are defective, or are damaged, as result of a sub-contractor's negligence, the owner/employer and/or main contractor of the project may claim under the project policy and the insurers may seek to pursue a subrogation claim against the sub-contractor responsible for the loss or damage (the 'SC'). In *Petrofina (UK) Ltd v Magnaload Ltd* ('*Petrofina*'),[63] *Stone Vickers Ltd v Appledore Ferguson Shipbuilders Ltd* ('*Stone Vickers*')[64] and *National Oilwell (UK) Ltd v Davy Offshore Ltd* ('*National Oilwell*'),[65] it was considered whether the SC would have a defence to the insurers' subrogation claim on the basis that the SC was a co-insured with an insurable interest in the whole project works under the project policy in question.

In *Petrofina* the SC had neither proprietary nor contractual rights in respect of the insured property. Its interest was limited to potential liability if, in the event of its negligence, the insured property was damaged or destroyed. Nevertheless, Lloyd J held, by analogy to a bailee who can insure the full value of the goods held by him, and in reliance on the decision of the Canadian Supreme Court in *Commonwealth Construction Co. Ltd. v. Imperial Oil Ltd*,[66] that all insured contractors and sub-contractors had an insurable interest in the *whole insured property* based on their potential liability (to be referred to as a "pervasive interest").[67] The court relied on the SC's pervasive interest in the project works to deny the insurers' subrogation claim. Lloyd J gave two reasons for a (sub-)contractor's pervasive interest: first, taking out a single project policy for all contractors and sub-contractors as co-insureds is a matter of commercial convenience; and secondly, it was the means to defeat an insurer's subrogation rights against a co-insured, which, in turn, is necessary to avoid circuity of action.[68]

---

62 *Judge v Travelers Ins. Co.*, 262 A.D.2d 983, N.Y.S.2d 288 (1999) and see Chapter 5.
63 [1984] QB 127 (Comm Ct).
64 [1991] 2 Lloyd's Rep. 288 (Comm Ct); decision reversed on appeal [1992] 2 Lloyd's Rep. 578 (CA).
65 [1993] 2 Lloyd's Rep 582 (Comm Ct).
66 (1977) 69 D.L.R. (3d) 558.
67 n 63, 137–140.
68 Ibid., 136, 139–140.

As noted in subsequent decisions,[69] the circuity argument is logically impossible: given that the project policy indemnified against property damage rather than liability, the insurers discharged their obligations when they settled the freeholder/manager's claim; the sub-contractor could not have asked insurers to pay out a second time. As discussed below, there are other solutions that allocate risk and liability between contractors, sub-contractors and insurers that do not entail straining the concept of insurable interest.

The decision has also been criticized for the analogy with bailment.[70] A bailee's insurable interest is based on his possession of, and responsibility for, the insured goods, as well as having a lien on the property to the extent of any reward or charge for the bailment. Lloyd J acknowledged that the SC did not have any right of possession in relation to the project works and assets.[71] In addition, there is a line of cases that has held that where a bailee insures "goods in trust for which they are responsible" such insurance is of the bailee's legal liability, not of the bailed goods.[72] The same words, "… for which they are responsible", appeared in the project policy in *Petrofina*. In *Ramco (UK) Ltd v International Insurance Co of Hannover Ltd* the Court of Appeal doubted the decision in *Petrofina* that the SC could have a pervasive interest in the whole contract works as the policy language expressly limited the property insured.[73]

In *Stone Vickers* the relevant SC was a supplier of a component constructed on its own premises and who was not contracted to work on the project site. Yet, Colman QC (sitting as a Deputy Judge) held that the SC had an insurable interest in the whole project works. He put forward two tests to determine whether a SC has a pervasive interest in the whole contract works: (1) "whether the [SC] … might be materially adversely affected by loss of or damage to the … works" (the "material adverse effect test"), and (2) "whether such a [SC] would have had sufficient interest to have taken out a policy in his own name on the whole of the vessel or contract works …".[74] Whilst expressing his approval[75] of the 'commercial convenience' rationale relied upon in *Petrofina*, Colman QC reasoned that the insurers could not seek to subrogate against the SC qua co-insured with a pervasive interest on the basis of an implied term "that an insurer will not … use

69 *National Oilwell* (n 65) 613 (Colman J); *Cooperative Retail Services Ltd* v. *Taylor Young Partnership Ltd* [2000] EWCA Civ 207, [72] (Brooke LJ) and aff'd [2002] UKHL 17, [65] (Lord Hope).
70 John Birds, Ben Lynch and Simon Paul (n 2) para 1-162; Jonathan Gilman, Mark Templeman and others, *Arnould's Law of Marine Insurance and General Average* (19th edn, Sweet & Maxwell 2018) paras 11–37.
71 n 63, 135.
72 See *North British & Mercantile Insurance Co v Moffat* (1871) LR7 CP 25 (Ct of Com Pl).; *Engel v Lancashire & General Assurance Co* (1925) 21 Lloyd's Rep 327 (KB); *Ramco (UK) Ltd v International Insurance Co of Hannover Ltd* (n 50).
73 n 72. See also John Birds, *Birds' Modern Insurance Law* (10th edn, Sweet & Maxwell 2016) para 4.2.2.
74 n 64, 300–301.
75 Ibid., 300.

rights of subrogation in order to recoup from a co-assured the indemnity which he has paid to the assured".[76]

The material adverse effect test is even wider than an insurable interest based on potential liability for causing loss or damage to the insured property. The addition of the second test seems odd: it is not obvious that a supplier of a part would have been able to obtain separate insurance on the project itself. It is more likely that such a supplier would have been offered liability insurance instead precisely because he would be regarded as lacking an insurable interest in the project.

The Court of Appeal reversed Colman QC's decision on the grounds that, on the construction of the project policy, the parties did not intend to include the SC as a co-insured under the project policy.[77] It was therefore not necessary for the Court of Appeal to comment on the pervasive interest point, but the decision indicates that 'commercial convenience' cannot override the actual agreement of the parties to the project policy, which made it clear that the SC in question was not intended to have cover under the project policy. Similarly, in In *Hopewell Project Management Ltd v Ewbank Preece Ltd* the court held that, on the true construction of the project policy, a firm of engineers providing advisory services, but not carrying out physical construction works, were not co-insureds defined as "contractor or sub-contractors".[78]

In *National Oilwell* Colman J (as he had by then become) held that, as a matter of commercial convenience, a supplier of equipment had a pervasive interest in the project property, even though he had taken no part in the construction at the project site and had no legal rights in relation to the project property. By reference to his decision in *Stone Vickers*, he held that the insurer could not bring a subrogated claim against the supplier on the basis that to do so would be in breach of an implied term in the project policy.[79] Abandoning the *Stone Vickers* material adverse effect test, Coleman J said that an insurable interest in property could arise "from the assured's proximate physical relationship to the property…".[80] Moreover, he noted that (1) the availability of liability insurance to protect against liability for property damage, and vice versa, (2) the unavailability of a separate project insurance policy with the SC as the sole insured in the insurance market did not preclude an insurable interest in that project property for the purposes of the project policy in question.[81]

Petrofina, *Stone Vickers* and *National Oilwell* blur the line between property and liability insurance. The distinction between property insurance and liability insurance should be maintained, and can be easily maintained by clear drafting, since they are recognized as distinct types of insurance in s.3(2)(a) and (c) of the

---

76 Ibid., 300–302.
77 [1992] 2 Lloyd's Rep. 578, 585.
78 [1998] 1 Lloyd's Rep 448 (QB) 455.
79 n 65, 611, 613–614.
80 Ibid., 611.
81 Ibid.

MIA 1906 and in Schedule 1 Part 1 of RAO. In *Wasa International Insurance Co Ltd v Lexington Insurance Co*[82] the House of Lords noted that there are reinsurance and regulatory implications flowing from characterizing a particular insurance to fall into one class or another. The distinction is also embedded in the insurance market: most general insurers organize their business by different lines of insurance which distinguish between different types of property (casualty) insurance and different types of liability insurance. The terms and structure of property policies are distinct from liability policies. Even in all risks policies that combine different types of cover, property and liability cover tend to be presented in separate sections of the policy document.

The temporal scope of the concept of 'pervasive interest' was reined in by the Court of Appeal in *Deepak Fertilisers & Petrochemicals Corp Ltd v ICI Chemicals & Polymers Ltd*[83] ('*Deepak*'). The Court of Appeal held that the relevant SC had had an insurable interest "in the plant under construction and on which they were working" since they would have lost "the opportunity to do the work and to be remunerated" if the plant had been damaged or destroyed.[84] However, the SC ceased to have an insurable interest in the plant after completion of its construction – thereafter the SC's potential liability for causing loss of or damage to the contract works should have been covered with liability insurance.[85] The court did not comment on whether the pre-completion insurable interest in the plant would have been 'pervasive' or more limited.

The Court of Appeal's approach in *Deepak* reinstated, at least to some extent, a dividing line between property insurance and liability insurance.[86] On the other hand, an interest based on earning opportunities cannot necessarily be justified on the grounds of the commercial convenience of pooling insurance arrangements (which was the rationale put forward for a pervasive interest in *Petrofina*): the earning opportunities of different parties and deriving from different contractual relationships may not have sufficiently in common to make 'pooling' commercially convenient and their pooling would not address how liability claims by one (sub-)contractor against another should be dealt with.

Pervasive interest – v – legal interest test – v – moral certainty test

Legal interest test: The notion of a 'pervasive interest' is inconsistent with the legal interest test for insurable interest to the extent that a (sub-)contractor does not have any legal or equitable rights in the project works.[87] Lord Eldon's legal

---

82 [2009] UKHL 40, [33] (Lord Mance) and [114–115] (Lord Collins).
83 [1999] 1 Lloyd's Rep 387.
84 Ibid., 399 (Stuart-Smith LJ).
85 Ibid.
86 Note that the Court of Appeal in *Feasey* (n 1) [94–95] (Waller LJ) doubted *Deepak* on that point, and the majority held that insurable interest in liability could be covered by a policy insuring property or life if it could be construed to embrace such an insurable interest – see below.
87 *Feasey* (n 1) [90–94] (Waller LJ). See also John Birds, Ben Lynch and Simon Paul (n 2) para 1-162.

interest test only refers to 'rights', but not 'liability', in relation to the insured property. Moreover, the type of contract that the SCs entered into in *Petrofina*, *Stone Vickers* and *National Oilwell* would not constitute a 'contract about property' under the legal interest test. In a building project, the subject-matter of a contract between the main contractor and the SC is the provision of goods or services in respect of the project – not the insured project or works itself. The SC's rights are against the main contractor, primarily for remuneration in respect of the goods supplied or services rendered. This would not usually create a contractual link between the sub-contractor and the insured works as a whole. Any tortious duty in relation to the project works is most likely owed to the owner of the project works and does not create a separate legal relationship with the project works itself. The risk of loss vis-à-vis the SC is a mere expectation: damage to the insured project works by itself does not cause a loss to the SC. The SC would only suffer a loss (i.e. liability for damages) if the project works are damaged as a result of his negligence and if his liability is established. In *Lucena* and in *Macaura* the House of Lords held that expectation of loss is insufficient for an insurable interest in property.

As regards an interest based on the opportunity to earn income as noted in *Deepak*, there are parallels to an insurable interest in the profits on goods. However, an insurable interest in profits on goods must be anchored in an insurable interest in the underlying asset which generates the profit or can be absorbed into the value of the goods themselves by agreeing their value for the purposes of the policy.[88] This nexus does not exist between the SC and the project works.

Moral certainty test: There is some overlap between the notion of a pervasive interest and an insurable interest as defined by the moral certainty test: the insured could be prejudiced by the exposure to liability and the loss of opportunity to earn income resulting from the destruction of the insured property. However, the benefit from its existence, and the prejudice from the destruction of the property, is not necessarily a 'moral certainty': the SC can be exposed to liability, and his opportunity to earn remuneration can be prejudiced, for reasons unrelated to the safety of the project property/works. Conversely, the destruction of the project property/works may not give rise to a liability of the SC if the SC has not been in breach of any duty relating to the safekeeping of the project property/works, and the SC's rights to payment may not be conditional upon the safety of the project property/works. American decisions also distinguish between interests based on (1) legal liability and (2) factual expectation of loss.[89] Moreover, a loss of income as a result of loss of, or damage to, the insured property is arguably mere consequential loss that is not proximately caused by the applicable insured peril.[90] Thus, the link between the SC's prejudice/advantage

---

88 *Stockdale v Dunlop* (n 38) 232–233 and see above.
89 *Beatty v USAA Cas. Ins. Co.*, 330 Ark. 354, 954 S.W.2d 250 (1997).
90 Peter MacDonald Eggers, 'The Marine Insurance Act 1906: Judicial Attitudes and Innovation – Time for Reform?' in D Rhidian Thomas (ed.), *Marine Insurance: The Law in Transition* (Informa 2006) para 10.22. Also see Chapter 9.

and the safety of the project property is far from 'morally certain' – they can exist independently from each other. This is why Lawrence J considered that with a non-proprietary interest, it could be difficult to prove a causational link between the peril insured against and the loss suffered by the insured.[91] Moreover, Lawrence J qualified his moral certainty test requiring 'some relation to, or concern in the subject-matter',[92] which a pervasive interest based merely on an exposure to liability in relation to the project works would not provide. It is therefore suggested that the notion of a pervasive interest is also inconsistent with the moral certainty test. Notably, none of the pervasive interest decisions discuss, rely on or even cite the moral certainty test.

Has the notion of pervasive interest become obsolete?

The 'pervasive interest' cases are now of mostly academic interest in the insurable interest debate: first, as a matter of market practice, construction of all risk policy wordings now frequently include a 'subrogation waiver', which is a contractual term by which the insurer promises not to pursue subrogation rights against any co-insured. With an express waiver of subrogation rights, there is no need for an SC to rely on a pervasive interest in order to defeat an insurer's subrogation rights against him.

Secondly, there has been a shift in the judicial approach to subrogated claims brought in the name of one co-insured against another co-insured. From the Court of Appeal's decision in *Cooperative Retail Services Ltd v Taylor Young Partnership Ltd*[93] ('*CRS*'), which was affirmed by the House of Lords,[94] and approved by the Supreme Court in *Gard Marine & Energy Ltd v China National Chartering Co Ltd*[95] ('*Gard Marine*'), it appears that the circuity of action rationale (*Petrofina*) and the implied term theory (*Stone Vickers* and *National Oilwell*) are no longer favoured. Instead, the question whether or not insurers can exercise subrogation rights is to be answered by reference to the intention of the (projects) parties as ascertained from the construction of the underlying contract.[96] There may be an implied term to the effect that co-insureds cannot sue one another in respect of damage in respect of which they are co-insured under the same policy.[97] On the true construction of the underlying contract it may also be apparent that the intention of the co-insureds was to create an insurance fund which would be the only avenue for making good the relevant loss or damage, and that, accordingly, insurers would not be able to pursue any

91 *Lucena* (n 3), 301 and 303.
92 Ibid., 302 and see above.
93 n 69.
94 Ibid.
95 [2017] UKSC 35.
96 *CRS* (n 69) [72–73] (Brooke LJ); approved obiter dicta by the House of Lords (n 83) [64–65] (Lord Hope); *Gard Marine* (n 95) [114] (Mance JSC).
97 Ibid., [65] (Lord Hope).

subrogated actions.[98] Significantly, neither the House of Lords in *CRS* nor the Supreme Court in *Gard Marine* referred to the concept of a 'pervasive interest'.

Thirdly, the courts no longer insist on an absolute subrogation immunity between co-insureds. In *Tyco Fire & Integrated Solutions (UK) Ltd v Rolls-Royce Motor Cars Ltd*[99] Rix LJ observed that in situations where the underlying construction contract preserves a liability of the co-insured party in respect of which there is co-insurance cover, there can be no implied term to exclude the insurer's subrogation rights. Similarly, in *Gard Marine*, the Supreme Court stressed that whether the insurance arrangements between the project parties had the effect of exempting one of the co-insured's from liability (thereby extinguishing the insurer's subrogation rights) was a matter of construction of the underlying contract.[100]

As immunity from subrogation is no longer a foregone conclusion and can be rationalized without recourse to the concept of a pervasive interest, the 'pervasive interest' extension to the meaning of insurable interest in property insurance is arguably redundant. Nevertheless, it was heavily relied upon in *Feasey* (discussed below) in support of a broad and expanded definition of insurable interest.

Life insurance

As noted in Chapter 3, life insurance is contingency insurance. In life insurance there are three broad categories of insurable interest: (1) where the insured must have a pecuniary interest in the life insured, (2) where an insurable interest in the life insured is presumed on the basis of specified familial relationships and (3) where an insurable interest is deemed to exist for the purposes of specific statutory provisions. Categories (2) and (3) represent exceptions to Category (1).

Pecuniary interests

Although the LAA 1774 does not provide a definition of insurable interest, it appears from s.3 that an insurable interest exists if the insured has a pecuniary interest in the life insured since the amount payable is limited to the "value of the interest of the insured in such life". This has been interpreted as meaning that the interest must be capable of being valued in money at the time of the contract,[101] but it does neither require "any detailed examination of the values of insurable interests" nor "any assessment whether the value was arrived at without negligence or reasonably".[102]

Moreover, a pecuniary insurable interest in a particular life depends upon a pecuniary loss flowing from a legal obligation, or from the loss of some legal or

---

98 n 137 [115] (Mance JSC), [139], [141]–[142] (Toulson JSC).
99 [2008] EWCA Civ 286, [2008] 1 CLC 625 [77].
100 n 95 [139] (Toulson JSC).
101 *Halford v Kymer* 109 ER 619 (KB) 620–621 (Bayley J), *Feasey* (n 1) [97] (Waller LJ).
102 *Feasey* [2002] EWHC 868 (Comm), [2003] 2 CLC. 936 [187] (Langley J).

equitable right, that will or might be suffered on the death of the life insured provided that the fixed sum that is payable upon that death does not exceed the maximum which might have flowed from the loss estimated at the time of the contract.[103] A voluntary undertaking cannot be the basis for an insurable interest in a life. The technical meaning of 'pecuniary interest' in life insurance introduces two issues: (1) which pecuniary interests the law recognizes, and (2) to what extent s.3 of the LAA 1774 limits recoveries in relation to expected or diminishing interests. As for the dividing line between life insurance and liability insurance, in *Feasey* the Court of Appeal held that the LAA 1774 applied to insurances covering the insured's liability to a third party upon the accidental injury or death of an insured life.

Business relationships: A creditor has an insurable interest in the life of its debtor on account of the debt, an employer has an insurable interest in the life of its employee[104] (and vice versa)[105] on account of the service to be rendered by the employee in return for payment, and a partner has an insurable interest in the lives of the other partners in a partnership,[106] always provided that the insured would suffer a pecuniary loss recognized by law upon the other person's death. Conversely, an employee has no insurable interest in his or her employer's life on account of a non-enforceable promise by the employer to forbear a debt.[107]

A strict application of s.3 of the LAA 1774 – as put forward in two Scottish decisions[108] – would preclude an employer from insuring the life of an employee beyond the value of the employee's service during the notice period as this is the only legally recognized right to the employee's service that the employer has. Yet, 'key person insurance' frequently covers amounts that are multiples of a key employee's annual salary on the basis that the pay-out would cover the costs for recruiting and training a replacement, and possibly any resulting loss of profits until the replacement employee is settled in. It has been noted that the law is out of step with modern expectation and practice.[109]

In contrast, s.3 of the LAA 1774 does not prevent a creditor from recovering an amount that is equivalent to the debt owed (plus interest outstanding) by the debtor at the time of the contract, even if at the time of the death of the debtor the debt has been discharged or partially repaid or has become unenforceable. This anomaly arises since the insurable interest is fixed at the time of the insurance contract. This can give rise to opportunities for speculation: for example, an insured may keep the life insurance contract in place even though the liability

103 *Feasey* (n 1) [82] citing with approval Nicholas Legh-Jones, John Birds J and David Owen, *MacGillivray on Insurance Law* (10th edn, Sweet & Maxwell 2003) paras 1-074–1-075.
104 *Simcock v Scottish Imperial Insurance Co* (1902) SLT 286 (CSOH).
105 *Hebdon v West* (1863) 3 B&S 579 (QB).
106 *Griffith v Fleming* [1909] 1 KB 805 (CA) 815 (dicta per Vaughan Williams LJ).
107 *Hebdon v West* (n 105).
108 See *Simcock v Scottish Imperial Insurance Co* (n 104) and *Turnbull v Scottish Provident Institution* (1896) 34 SLR 146 (CSOH).
109 LC, '*Issues Paper 10 – Insurable Interest: Updated Proposals*' (March 2015) paras 1.4 and 3.14; John Birds, Ben Lynch and Simon Paul (n 2) paras 1-072 and 1-116; John Birds (n 73) para 3.4.2.

in respect of the life insured has been discharged speculating that an imminent death would result in a sum payable larger than the premium payments.

Family relationships: A pecuniary interest in the life insured is also required in familial relationships where the presumption of an insurable interest (see below) does not apply. Therefore, a parent does not have an insurable interest in the life of a child,[110] or vice versa,[111] merely based on natural affection or familial dependence. A pecuniary interest in the life insured may arise if there is a legal obligation to provide maintenance, make financial contributions or pay funeral expenses. In contrast, on the older authorities an insured has no insurable interest in the life of a family member who has been supporting him financially where there was no legal obligation to do so.[112] The requirement for a financial link between the insured and the life insured based on some legal right or obligation has been criticized for (1) inhibiting the sale of socially beneficial insurance, and (2) being contrary to modern market practice that is responding to the demand for life-insurance products (such as travel insurance) allowing parents to insure their children and providinglife insurance for co-habitants.[113]

Presumed interests

There are several categories of life insurance where an insurable interest is presumed, need not be proved and is not limited by s.3 of the LAA 1774:

1   on the insured's own life;[114]
2   on the life of a spouse;[115]
3   on the life of a civil partner;[116] and
4   possibly on the life of a financé(e).[117]

The reason for the existence of these categories is that they are said to fall outside the mischief of the LAA 1774 – to counteract a 'mischievous kind of gaming'[118] – since, according to Kennedy LJ: "A man does not gamble on his own life to gain a Pyrrhic victory by his own death" and "that the same principle must be applied to the insurance by the husband of the wife's life"[119] and by the wife of the husband's life.[120] This rationale has been doubted and will be discussed further in Chapters 6 and 7.

---

110 *Halford v Kymer* (n 100).
111 *Harse v Pearl Life Assurance Co* [1904] 1 KB 558.
112 *Griffith v Fleming* (n 106), 820 (Vaughan Williams LJ); *Halford v Kymer* (n 110).
113 LC, *Issues Paper 10* (n 109) paras 1.4 and 3.14; John Birds, Ben Lynch and Simon Paul (n 2) para 1-116; John Birds (n 72) para 3.4.1.
114 *Wainwright v Bland* (1835) 150 ER 334 (Exch).
115 *Griffith v Fleming* (n 106) (presumed insurable interest in life of wife); *Reed v Royal Exchange Assurance* 170 ER 198 (Assizes) (presumed insurable interest in life of husband).
116 Civil Partnership Act 2004, s.253.
117 See John Birds (n 73) para 3.4, n 32.
118 See Chapter 2.
119 *Griffith v Fleming* (n 106), 821 (Vaughan Williams LJ).
120 *Reed v Royal Exchange Assurance* (n 115).

Statutory extensions

No pecuniary interest is required under certain statutory exceptions, including in endowment policies pursuant to s.1 of the Industrial Assurance and Friendly Societies Act 1929, and, within certain parameters, life insurance taken out by a parent on his or her child's life pursuant to s.99 of the Friendly Societies Act 1992.

In addition, subject to the terms of the policy, the insured can assign policy to a third party without an insurable interest in the life insured after the contract is entered into (see Chapter 3). In the United States, assignment has been used as a mechanism to write STOLI as a speculative investment of third parties with no insurable interest but legislation has now put a stop to this in the majority of States. Reference has already been made to the reality that the insurance market is already under pressure to write life insurance policies which cover interests beyond traditional pecuniary interests. An expanded definition of insurable interest in life insurance was also put forward in *Feasey* (see below) and has been the centrepiece of the LC's reform proposals (see Chapter 5).

A new approach to insurable interest: *Feasey*

In *Feasey* a P&I Club (Steamship) insured the liabilities of its members for personal injury and illness of their crews on board of their ships (Original Persons). For accounting purposes, Steamship did not reinsure its exposure through conventional reinsurance but instead took out insurance in the form of a master lineslip policy in which Sun Life Assurance Co of Canada and Phoenix Home Life Mutual Insurance Co promised to pay to Steamship fixed benefits on the occurrence of personal injury or illness of an Original Person, which would then be returnable to the insurers where the relevant P&I Club member's liability to that Original Person could not be established. The insurers declined liability for claims, inter alia, on the grounds that Steamship had no insurable interest in the lives of Original Persons. The Court of Appeal decided that a contingent liability arising upon death/personal injury/illness can constitute an insurable interest in life insurance for the purposes of s.1 of the LAA 1774 and also took the opportunity to review the general principles applicable to determining insurable interest across all classes of insurance.

The principles

Waller LJ restated the principles for determining an insurable interest, as distilled from the authorities, as follows:

> (1) It is from the terms of the policy that the subject of the insurance must be ascertained; (2) It is from all the surrounding circumstances that the nature of an insured's insurable interest must discovered; (3) There is no hard and fast rule that because the nature of an insurable interest relates to a liability to compensate for loss, that insurable interest could only be

covered by a liability policy rather than a policy insuring property or life or indeed properties or lives; (4) The question whether a policy embraces the insurable interest intended to be recovered is a question of construction ... (5) It is not a requirement of property insurance that the insured must have a 'legal or equitable' interest in the property as those terms might normally be understood. It is sufficient for a sub-contractor to have a contract that relates to the property and a potential liability for damage to the property to have an insurable interest in the property. It is sufficient under section 5 of the Marine Insurance Act for a person interested in a marine adventure to stand in a 'legal or equitable relation to the adventure.' That is intended to be a broad concept (6) In a policy on life or lives the court should be search-ing for the same broad concept. It may be that on an insurance of a specific identified life, it will be difficult to establish a 'legal or equitable' relation without a pecuniary liability recognised by law arising on the death of that particular person. There is however no authority which deals with a policy on many lives and over a substantial period and where it can be seen that a pecuniary liability will arise by reference to those lives and the intention is to cover that legal liability. (7) The interest in policies falling within section 1 of the 1774 Act must exist at the time of entry into the policy, and be capable of pecuniary evaluation at that time.[121]

Construction

Principles (1) to (4) suggest that Waller LJ regards determining an insurable in-terest to be primarily a question of construction, employing a three-step process:

1   ascertaining the subject-matter of the policy from the terms of the policy;
2   ascertaining the insured's interest in the subject-matter; and
3   considering whether his interest is 'embraced' by the policy as a matter of policy construction.

There is a degree of overlap, if not circularity, in making both the subject-matter of the insurance contract and whether the interest is embraced by that subject-matter matters of construction as the interest(s) that a policy embraces will depend upon the scope of the subject-matter. The court's construction of the insured subject-matter is likely to be coloured by any interest that the in-sured has given to the courts' approach "to lean in favour of an insurable in-terest".[122] Thus, in *Feasey*, the insured was exposed to the risk of liability to indemnify its members against their liability for injury and illness of Original Persons, yet the subject-matter of the policy was the well-being of those persons.

---

121 n 1 [97].
122 See Chapter 3.

Despite the apparent mismatch, both Waller LJ[123] and Dyson LJ[124] said that an insurable interest relating to liability need not necessarily be insured under a liability policy and, accordingly, the insured in *Feasey* had an insurable interest in the well-being of Original Persons under the terms of the policy. Dyson LJ indicated that the distinction between insurable interest in liability and property insurance should be overlooked in accordance with the courts' approach "to lean in favour of an insurable interest".[125] Reference is made to the discussion above on the classification of insurance.

In relation to life insurance, the Court of Appeal also had regard to statutory construction: noting that s.50 of the Insurance Companies Act 1973 had amended s.2 of the LAA 1774 so that the latter would not invalidate group life insurance for the benefit of unnamed persons from time to time falling within a specified class or description stated in the policy, Waller LJ said that Parliament must be taken not to have intended that s.1 of the LAA 1774 would render void an insurance on lives of persons unidentified as at the date of the policy but falling within the class or description stated in the policy.[126]

When an interest is an 'insurable interest'

In Waller LJ's judgment, the question whether an interest that is covered under the terms of the policy is also recognized at law as being an 'insurable interest' is relegated to being a secondary enquiry.[127] Principles (5) and (6) suggest that not every interest qualifies as a valid insurable interest but, rather than defining insurable interest with a test "which will apply in all situations", and "slavishly following" existing definitions, Waller LJ indicated that the meaning of insurable interest would vary between four different groups of cases, depending on the type of insurance, the context and the terms of the policy.[128]

In respect of marine insurance, Waller LJ considered himself bound by the wording of s.5(2) of the MIA 1906, requiring the insured to stand in "legal or equitable relation to the adventure" but noting that this should be seen as "a broad concept".[129]

In relation to non-marine property insurance, Waller LJ rejected any requirement that the insured "must have a 'legal or equitable' interest in the property as those terms might normally be understood".[130] The qualification "as those terms might be normally understood" is perhaps a tacit acknowledgement that Lord Eldon's legal interest test is frequently reduced to requiring in rem rights which overlooks that he also considered contractual rights in relation to

123 n 1 [95], [97], [101].
124 Ibid., [114], [120], [123].
125 Ibid., [122].
126 Ibid., [61–63].
127 Ibid., [97].
128 Ibid., [71], [81–90].
129 Ibid., [97].
130 Ibid., – see Principle (5).

property to be sufficient interest.[131] Waller LJ stated that it "is sufficient for a sub-contractor to have a contract that relates to the property and a potential liability for damage to the property…".[132] This suggests that a SC's exposure to a potential liability for damage to the insured property on its own is not sufficient – he also needs "to have a contract that relates to the property" in order to have an insurable interest (i.e. 'bare' tortious liability is insufficient). However, elsewhere Waller LJ seemingly rejects the proposition that legal liability by itself can never be enough to create an insurable interest in the property.[133] It has been argued above that the types of contract entered into *Petrofina*, *Stone Vickers* and *National Oilwell*[134] would not constitute a 'contract relating to property' but, citing these decisions with apparent approval,[135] it seems that Waller LJ would be prepared to give a broader meaning to the contractual relations between the insured and the insured property than Lord Eldon intended. Nevertheless, basing a SC's insurable interest on potential liability for causing loss or damage to the insured property seems narrower than the material adverse effect test and the proximate physical relationship test in *Stone Vickers* and *National Oilwell* respectively. It is also to be contrasted with the approach in *Deepak*,[136] where the court anchored a SC's insurable interest in the project in his opportunity to work on, and to earn remuneration from working on, the project. For the reasons set out above, it is suggested that Principle (5), in so far as it relates to sub-contractors, is also inconsistent with Lawrence J's moral certainty test.

As for life insurance, Waller LJ draws a distinction between (1) life insurance on the life of a specific identified person, where a pecuniary interest linked to a legal or equitable obligation as at the date of the policy is required, and (2) group life insurance, where a contingent liability upon the death of a member of the group may be sufficient to constitute an insurable interest.[137] Thus, he extends the meaning of insurable interest in relation to group life insurance to interests based on a contingent pecuniary loss consequent upon death/personal injury/illness. Given that the older authorities are clear that a mere chance or expectation of loss is insufficient for a pecuniary interest,[138] Waller LJ's wider meaning hinges upon differentiating a contingent liability from a mere chance or expectation. He seeks to do so by reference to the pervasive interest cases in property insurance.[139] Arguably this analogy is (1) over-extended, given that in Principle 5 Waller LJ was not prepared to state clearly that a SC's exposure to potential liability for damage to the insured property on its own – without any contractual

---

131 *Lucena* (n 3) 321 and see above.
132 *Feasey* (n 1) [97].
133 Ibid., [95].
134 n 63–65.
135 *Feasey* (n 1) [94].
136 n 83.
137 n 1 [97] Principle 6.
138 *Hebdon v West* (n 105); *Griffith v Fleming* (n 106); *Simcock v Scottish Imperial Insurance Co* (n 104).
139 n 1 [90–96].

link to the insured property – is sufficient,[140] and (2) now anachronistic if it is accepted that the notion of a pervasive interest is redundant.[141] Reference is also made to Ward LJ's dissenting judgment (see below).

In contrast, Dyson LJ seeks to establish an insurable interest on the facts of *Feasey* by noting that the insured would have had an insurable interest if the policy had been framed as a liability insurance, and concluding:

> It is a non-sequitur to reason that because (a) [the reinsured] would have an insurable interest in the liability of its members to those persons, therefore (b) it cannot have an insurable interest in those persons themselves.[142]

Dyson LJ refers to the courts' strategy "to lean in favour of an insurable interest",[143] in support of his conclusion and to *Dalby v The India and London Life Assurance Company*[144] as authority for the proposition that no legal or equitable right in the life insured is required. In *Dalby* the policy in question was euphemistically described as "cross or counter assurance" but was in essence a reinsurance policy at a time when reinsurance was unlawful[145] and poorly understood in legal terms. In any event, the (re)insurer in *Dalby* was under an existing liability, not a contingent one, to pay in the event of the death of the Duke of Cambridge. Parke B's reported decision does not address whether the underlying insured – a Mr Wright – had an insurable interest in the life of the Duke of Cambridge. Moreover, this question did not arise on the facts of *Dalby* as Mr Wright had terminated the policies before the Duke of Cambridge died.

In the (post-*Feasey*) case of *Wasa International Insurance Co Ltd v Lexington Insurance Co*, the House of Lords clarified that "[t]he insurable interest which entitles the [reinsured] to reinsure in respect of [the original] subject matter is the [reinsured's] exposure under the underlying insurance".[146] According to this analysis, a reinsurer's arguments on the facts of *Dalby* (or *Feasey* (had it been a conventional reinsurance case) might be that the reinsurer cannot be liable to indemnify the reinsured where the reinsured has no exposure under the underlying insurance on account that the original insured had no insurable interest in the life insured.

Ward LJ's dissenting judgment

Ward LJ dissented from the majority's decision reasoning that the insured's liability to indemnify a member was only triggered upon the personal injury or

---

140 Ibid., [97] and see above.
141 See above.
142 n 1 [114].
143 See Chapter 3.
144 (1854) 15 CB 365 (ExchCham).
145 MIA 1746, s.4.
146 n 82, at [33] (Mance LJ).

illness of an Original Person but only if and when a member's liability for such injury/illness was established later, so that the actual injury/illness of an Original Person itself gave rise only to an expectation of loss.[147] On the basis of case law[148] and academic authorities,[149] he found that an expectation of loss was insufficient to support an insurable interest in the lives of the Original Persons insured.[150] With some regret, Ward LJ said that Lord Eldon's opinion in *Lucena* and the House of Lord's decision in *Macaura* were binding authority for the proposition that an expectation of loss was insufficient to found an insurable interest.[151] Permission to appeal was granted to the insurers but the parties settled before the case reached the House of Lords.

Reception and analysis

The decision in *Feasey* was received with great interest as it "affords a rare insight into contemporary judicial thinking on the requirement"[152] of insurable interest. Given the general paucity of judicial pronouncements on insurable interest, some commentators now tentatively take the *Feasey* proposition that, in certain contractual situations, an insurable interest in property can be founded upon potential liability for damage to that property if the relevant liability is embraced by the subject-matter of the policy, to represent the current law.[153] By reference to *Feasey*, the LC make more radical claims that in relation to property "[t]he courts have inched towards a 'factual expectation' test, which now appears to represent the current law",[154] and in group life insurance an insurable interest may be founded upon a potential liability in respect of the lives covered, combined with an intention to cover that liability.[155] Thomas argues that *Feasey* is affirmative of a line of cases that show that courts take a 'pragmatic commercial approach' to insurable interest, which is distinct from the legal interest test and the factual expectation test, seeking to uphold the validity of the insurance contract.[156]

147 n 1 [166].
148 Ibid., [167–169] citing *Hebdon v West* (n 105), *Griffiths v Fleming* (n 106).
149 n 1 [170–171] citing Nicholas Legh-Jones, John Birds and David Owen, *MacGillivray on Insurance Law* (n 103) para 1-49 and Malcolm Clarke, *The Law of Insurance Contracts* (4th edn) para 3-6.
150 n 1 [172].
151 Ibid., [181].
152 John Lowry, Philip Rawlings and Robert Merkin, *Insurance Law: Doctrines and Principles* (3rd edn, Hart Publishing 2011) 187.
153 See e.g. Jonathan Gilman, Mark Templeman and others (n 70) paras 11-38; Robert Merkin (n 2) para 4-020; and more cautiously, John Birds, Ben Lynch and Simon Paul (n 2) paras 1-163, 1-070 and 1-119 and John Birds (n 73) para 4.2.2.
154 LC, *Insurance Contract Law: Post Contract* (n 16) paras 11.51 and 11.66.
155 Ibid. para 11.92.
156 D Rhidian Thomas, 'Insurable Interest – Accelerating the Liberal Spirit' in D Rhidian Thomas (ed.), *Marine Insurance: The Law in Transition* (Informa 2006) paras 2.72–2.75.

In considering whether *Feasey* has extended the meaning of insurable interest in property insurance, the following observations could be made: first, *Feasey* concerned a life insurance policy and accordingly the Court of Appeal's review of the principles applying to insurable interest in a non-life context ought to be regarded as obiter dicta. Secondly, as Ward LJ pointed out, there is binding House of Lords authority which requires a legal or equitable relation between the insured and the insured property in order for a valid insurable interest to exist.[157] That authority is in conflict with the wider analysis of Waller and Dyson LJJ of what constitutes an insurable interest. Thirdly, although Waller LJ sought to reconcile his reasoning with the Court of Appeal's decision in *Deepak*, there is a conflict between the decisions to the extent that the court in *Deepak* declined to recognize potential liability in respect of loss or damage to the insured property as giving rise to an insurable interest in property. In *Tyco Fire & Integrated Solutions (U.K.) Ltd v Rolls-Royce Motor Cars Ltd.*[158] the Court of Appeal cited *Deepak* as authority for the proposition that, following completion, a sub-contractor has no insurable interest in the works and must insure his liability in respect of loss of or damage to the works under a liability insurance. The Court of Appeal in *Tyco* did not refer to *Feasey*. *Feasey* has only been cited in two subsequent cases, *Western Trading*[159] and *Comlex Ltd (in Liquidation) v Allianz Insurance Plc*,[160] neither of which broke any novel ground on the meaning of insurable interest. Fourthly, *Feasey* expands the concept of insurable interest on the basis of the preceding pervasive interest cases which are no longer favoured by the courts in subrogation cases and are arguably obsolete.[161]

In relation to insurable interest in life insurance, the Court of Appeal in *Feasey* made it clear that its decision is specific to the (unusual) policy wording in the case.[162] Waller LJ also sought to limit the extended meaning of insurable interest to life insurance "on many lives and over a substantial period".[163] The editors of *MacGillivray* note that *Feasey* has "not dispensed with the insurable interest rule that a mere expectancy or hope of future of future pecuniary benefit from the prolongation of the life insured ... is insufficient",[164] whilst Birds hails *Feasey* as setting out a new approach to the meaning of insurable interest in specific factual circumstances whilst not clearly challenging the traditionally understanding of life insurance in "straightforward" cases.[165]

It is suggested that the majority's decision in *Feasey* produced a pragmatic and commercial result on the facts of the case. It therefore has its place amongst

---

157   n 1 [177] and see above.
158   n 99 [63] (Rix LJ).
159   [2015] EWHC 103 (QB), [53]; reversed in part on a different issue [2016] EWCA Civ 1003.
160   n 11. Lord Doherty did in fact prefer Ward LJ's dissenting judgment ([35–37]).
161   See above.
162   n 1 [98–101] (Waller LJ).
163   Ibid., [97].
164   John Birds, Ben Lynch and Simon Paul (n 2) para 1-070.
165   John Birds (n 73) para 3.5.

the line of cases where 'commercial convenience' has been a relevant factor in determining the existence of an insurable interest, as well as being an example of the courts' approach "to lean in favour of an insurable interest". However, the decision has introduced further complexity and unpredictability to an already complicated area of law: first, given the emphasis placed on considering insurable interest as a matter of construction of the policy in question, even slight variations in policy wordings and the factual matrices can produce different outcomes. In construing the terms of a contract of insurance, the courts are bound by established rules of construction, but in consumer insurance contracts, there may be a greater emphasis on a *contra proferentem* construction of coverage than in a commercial context where the insured has the bargaining power and capability to choose and negotiate a policy that clearly defines the insured subject-matter in a manner that is consistent with the legal interest test. Secondly, Waller LJ's rejection of a single test or definition of insurable interest in favour of different tests applicable in different categories means that the validity of an insurable interest may now need to be considered by reference to the group into which the case falls, as well as the type of insurance in question. Moreover, the situation is further complicated by the possibility that liability-based interests can support (1) liability and (2) property or life insurance. Thirdly, it is by no means clear in what circumstances an insurable interest in property can arise solely on the basis of potential liability in respect of loss or damage to that property. Within the same judgment, Waller LJ is inconsistent as to whether potential liability must be paired with "a contract that relates to the [insured] property".[166] In addition, there is conflicting authority in *Deepak* to the effect that, following completion, a sub-contractor has no longer an insurable interest in the works, regardless of whether or not he is exposed to liability for loss or damage to the works. Fourthly, in relation to life insurance, it is also unclear whether potential liability upon the death of the life insured is sufficient, or whether it needs to be coupled with an "intention to cover that liability", and whether that kind of limited pecuniary interest can only be sufficient in life insurance "on many lives and over a substantial period".

The House of Lords decision in *Lucena* and *Macaura* and s.5(2) of the MIA 1906 continue to be binding authority for the legal interest test for insurable interest in property insurance. However, there has been a tendency in the lower courts to look for a wider meaning of insurable interest on the grounds of commercial convenience and in order to give effect to the bargain struck between the insurer and the insured. As a result, there now seem to be two broad categories of interests in relation to property insurance: (1) a core set of 'strong' interests based on a legal or equitable relationship with the property which would always qualify as an 'insurable interest', and (2) a penumbra of 'weaker' interests based on potential liability, or earning potential, in relation to the insured property which have not been consistently recognized as an 'insurable interest' by the courts.

166 See above.

Similarly, pushing the constraints of the LAA 1774 to its limits, the meaning of insurable interest in life insurance has been extended beyond the traditional categories to include a new category of *Feasey*-style insurable interests based on contingent liability upon the death of the lives insured.

The uncertainty about the precise meaning of 'insurable interest' in relation to any specific policy in any given set of circumstances has added the complexity to an already complex area of law. *Feasey* has pushed the boundaries of insurable interest by shifting the focus of enquiry to a construction of the policy that is consonant with covering the interest that an insured has. The LC has put forward statutory reform proposals to deal with some of the issues that have been highlighted, and they will be examined in Chapter 5.

5 Insurable interest – Quo Vadis?

Having taken stock of the current law on insurable interest in the previous Chapters, this cChapter reviews the LC's reform proposals and the academic debate on the role of insurable interest in modern insurance law, and it surveys the insurable interest approaches taken in selected foreign jurisdictions. From this discussion, a number of reform themes will be extrapolated, which will then serve as yardsticks for the discussion of the rationales for insurable interest in the following Chapters.

The LC's proposals

The LC's review of the doctrine of insurable interest as part of their insurance contract law reform project has a history of U-turns.[1] The latest instalment is the IIB published in June 2018, which contains the LC's evolved proposals for reforming the law on insurable interest in life-related insurance, whilst abandoning its previous proposals on non-life insurance. It had been envisaged that the IIB would be introduced as a third Insurance Bill in Parliament under the expedited procedure for uncontroversial Law Commission bills,[2] but it is now uncertain when and to what extent the IIB will be brought forward given the priority of Brexit-related legislation in the Parliamentary timetable.

The case for reform of the doctrine

From the outset, the LC advocated the retention of the doctrine of insurable interest in contingency (including life) insurance on the grounds that "[t]aking out an insurance policy on someone's life could be used as a threat" and feels "uncomfortable".[3] In contrast, the LC initially took the 'tentative' view that the requirement for an insurable interest in relation to indemnity insurance should

---

1 See further: Franziska Arnold-Dwyer, 'Insurance Law Reform by Degrees: Late Payment and Insurable Interest' (2017) 80 MLR 489, 500–501.
2 LC, 'Issues Paper 10 – Insurable Interest: Updated Proposals' (March 2015) para 1.5.
3 LC, 'Issues Paper 4 – Insurable Interest' (January 2008) para 7.40.

be abolished,[4] but respondents to the LC's initial proposals – mainly form the insurance industry – "argued strongly in favour of retaining the requirement for insurable interest, for both life and indemnity insurance".[5] The LC distilled four main reasons for the retention of the doctrine of insurable interest from the feedback received:

1   It is a "hallmark of insurance" which distinguishes between contracts of insurance and other contracts of speculation.
2   It promotes market discipline and guards against moral hazard.
3   It protects insurers from invalid claims.
4   Its abolition would be disruptive without significant benefits.[6]

These reasons will be evaluated as part of the discussion of the Traditional Justifications and other rationales in Chapters 6–10. The LC also identified several problems with the law relating to insurable interest:

1   the complexity of the law;
2   the uncertainty surrounding the definition of insurable interest in relation to property insurance;
3   the restrictiveness of the law in relation to life insurance; and
4   the applicability of different rules for different types of insurance.[7]

Complexity of law: "The law is a bewildering mix of common law and statute, including various eighteenth century statutes" and "there is uncertainty over the effect of the GA 2005, which may or may not affect insurance contracts".[8] The convoluted legal landscape relating to the legal bases for, timing of and the consequences for the lack of insurable interest has been described in Chapter 3.

Ambit of definition: According to the LC, the definition of insurable interest in property insurance is unclear as it has been "continuously expanding" in case law.[9] Chapter 4 illustrated that the lower courts have sought to widen the definition of insurable interest, which has resulted in definitional inconsistencies and has created a conflict with the earlier House of Lords authorities in *Lucena*[10] and *Macaura*.[11] Moreover, *Feasey*'s[12] rejection of a single test or definition of insurable interest in favour of a contractual construction approach and different tests applicable in different categories of cases that cut across the existing classification

---

4   Ibid. para 7.50.
5   LC, '*Insurance Contract Law: Post Contract Duties and Other Issues*' (Law Com CP No 201, December 2011) para 12.2.
6   LC, '*Issues Paper 10*' (n 2) para 2.3; LC, *Post Contract* (n 5) paras 12.6–12.25.
7   Ibid. paras 1.8 and 3.3.
8   Ibid. para 1.8.
9   Ibid., and LC, '*Post Contract*' (n 4) para 10.2.
10   (1806) 2 Bos & Pul (NR) 269 (HL).
11   [1925] AC 619 (HL).
12   [2003] EWCA Civ 885, [94] and [97].

of insurance into life, property, marine and liability has contributed to the uncertainty as to the precise scope of the doctrine of insurable interest.

Restrictiveness of the law in life insurance: The narrow application of the category of presumed interest, and the combined effect of the LAA 1774, s.3 and the narrow definition of pecuniary interest were discussed in Chapter 4. In 2014, the LC were approached by the Investment and Life Assurance Group ('ILAG') on behalf of life insurers raising the issue that the law on insurable interest in life insurance is too restrictive, "hindering the development of socially useful products".[13] The LC notes that some insurers "are willing to write policies which may not strictly fall within [the LAA 1774]", including cover on the lives of children, co-habitants and 'key persons' for substantial amounts, which means that those insurers who comply with the law strictly are at competitive disadvantage.[14] The LC consider it "unsatisfactory" that the black letter law may be ignored as a matter of practice.[15]

Different rules for different types of insurance: The doctrine of insurable interest differs depending on the type of insurance.[16] The type of insurance determines the applicable legal basis for insurable interest, has an impact on the timing when an insurable interest must exist, determines the legal consequences if no insurable interest exists and may be relevant to the availability of waiver.[17] For the purposes of determining the relevant insurable interest rules, insurance contracts are generally classified according to the underlying subject-matter (marine, property, liability, etc.), but *Feasey* has added an additional gloss stating that there is "no hard and fast rule" that because the nature of an insurable interest relates to one type of insurance that insurable interest could not also be covered by other types of insurance.[18] *Feasey* and the 'pervasive interest' cases[19] are examples of how the dividing line between different types of insurance may become blurred.

The IIB

The LC's latest proposals are encapsulated in the IIB. The IIB's main substantive provisions in cl.2–4 apply only to contracts of life-related insurance defined as contracts of insurance "under which the insured event is the death, injury, ill-health or incapacity of an individual, or the life of an individual continuing".[20] The aim of the LC's proposals is to modernize the law by creating a more "permissive regime" conducive to the "development and sale of economically and socially useful products in the UK", which "would therefore fuel additional

---

13 LC, *'Updated Draft Insurable Interest Bill for Review – Accompanying Notes'* (June 2018) (the 'IIB Notes') para 1.11.
14 Ibid., Chapter 3.
15 LC, *'Post Contract'* (n 5) paras 10.4–10.5, 13.2; LC, *'Issues Paper 10'* (n 2) para 1.5.
16 LC, *'Issues Paper 10'* (n 2) para 1.8.
17 See Chapter 3.
18 n 12 [97].
19 See Chapter 4.
20 IIB, cl. 1

economic activity among UK insurers while making it possible for people and businesses to protect their legitimate interests".[21]

At the time of writing, the IIB remains a draft bill that has not been introduced into Parliament.

Statutory basis and timing: Clause 2(1) of the IIB establishes the requirement for an insurable interest at the time of the contract as a validity requirement for life-related contracts of insurance on a statutory basis. However, where a life-related contract of insurance defines the lives insured by reference to a category or description, it is sufficient for the insured to have an insurable interest in the life of a person who subsequently falls within that category or meet that description at that point in time.[22]

Consequences of lack of insurable interest: (1) A contract of life-related insurance under which the insured has no insurable interest at the time of the contract is void.[23] Considering that an insurable interest would be a statutory validity requirement, the parties should not be able to agree to waive the requirement. (2) The IIB does not prohibit assignment and an assignee of a life-related contract who has no insurable interest in the life insured at the time of the insured event should therefore not be precluded from claiming under the contract on the grounds of lack of interest. (3) Retention of premium: under cl.3(1) of the IIB an insurer need not return any of the premium paid if the insured deliberately or recklessly made an untrue statement as to the insurable interest concerned in entering a contract of insurance which is void for lack of insurable interest. There is an exception in cl.3(2) for consumer insurance that applies if "it would be unfair to the insured to retain the premiums". In all other cases (i.e. those not captured by cl.3), it is a matter for the general law as to whether or not premium paid under an invalid contract is returnable.[24] (4) The combined effect of cl.2(1) and 6 is that contracts of life-related insurance would no longer be rendered illegal for lack of insurable interest.

Defining insurable interest: Clause 2(2) sets out a broad economic interest test for determining whether the insured has an insurable interest in the life insured. Instead of requiring a pecuniary interest recognized by law, the insured has an insurable interest "if there is a reasonable prospect" of suffering "economic loss" on the occurrence of the insured event.

Clause 2(3) proceeds to give a non-exhaustive list[25] of specific examples of "other circumstances" in which the insured would have an automatic insurable interest where the life insured:

> a   i is the insured,
>   ii is the spouse or civil partner of the insured or lives with the insured as a spouse or civil partner,
>   iii is, or is treated as, the child or grandchild of the insured;

---

21 LC, '*IIB Notes*' para 3.1.
22 IIB, cl 2(5).
23 IIB, cl 2(1).
24 LC, '*IIB Notes*' para 2.21.
25 IIB, cl.2(3) "Other circumstances … include"; also see LC, '*IIB Notes*' para 2.26.

b the individual who is the subject of the contract is a member of a pension or other group scheme which is administered by the insured (whether as a trustee or otherwise);

c … the individual who is the subject of the contract [and for whose benefit the contract is made], or a nominee of that individual.

The examples in cl.2(3)(a) are a restatement of the presumed interest category, save that it has been extended to cohabitants, children, grandchildren and those treated as children or grandchildren. Example (b) provides that the person who administers a pension or other group scheme has an automatic insurable interest in the lives of the members of the scheme – regardless of financial loss – thus clarifying the post-*Feasey* law on the test for insurable interest in group life insurance. Example (c) gives an automatic insurable interest to an insured who takes out a life-related insurance which is for the benefit of the life insured or their nominee, the insured. This is aimed at employers who would have "an unlimited interest in the lives of its employees when entering into a group scheme the purpose of which is to provide benefits for its employees or their families"[26] but does not cover key person insurance where the insurance would be for the employer's own benefit. The effect of cl.2(4) of the IIB is that, where insurance is taken out by a trustee, the trustee has an insurable interest in the relevant life if the settlor of the trust would have such an interest. This provision was added to cater for life investment-linked products where the investor (the settlor) puts money in trust and the trustee then purchases a life assurance bond.

Effect on existing legislation: The provisions of the IIB replace any other rule of law relating to the requirement for an insurable interest for the purposes of a contract of life-related insurance.[27] This is aimed at the common law rules relating to insurable interest in life-related insurance but does not affect the law on insurable interest in non-life-related insurance. Pursuant to cl.6(1)(b) and 6(2), the LAA 1774 ss.2 and 3, the MIGamblingA 1909 and the MIA 1788 are repealed in relation to all contracts of insurance. The repeal of s.3 of the LAA 1174 would mean that there will no longer be a cap as to the amounts payable under life-related insurance, and non-life-related contracts of insurance to which the LAA 1774 applies. In contrast, the provisions relating to insurable interest in the MIA 1906 are expressly preserved by cl.5 of the IIB. Clause 6(1)(a) preserves implicitly the LAA 1774, s.1 in so far as it relates to contracts of non-life-related insurance covering "other events". Thus, the LC keep alive the debate on whether the LAA 1774 applies to land and buildings.

No reform of insurable interest in non-life-related insurance: Clauses 2–4 of the IIB are limited to 'contracts of life-related insurance'. The LC decided not to pursue proposals relating to the definition of insurable interest and the statutory basis of insurable interest in non-life-related contracts of insurance "at a time when parliamentary time is scarce", since they were (1) "clarificatory only"

---

26 LC, '*IIB Notes*' para 2.57.
27 IIB, cl 4.

and therefore unnecessary, and (2) there was "no call [for reform] from stake-holders".[28] Contracts of non-life-related insurance would be a residual category capturing all contracts that do not fall into the definition of contract of life-related insurance.

The first justification gainsays the LC's earlier analysis that there are problems with the law on insurable interest affecting all classes of insurance, in particular that the law on insurable interest is complex and unclear. It is suggested that the second justification for abandoning the insurable interest reforms in non-life-related insurance goes to the heart of the matter: insurers have no appetite for change in an area that is unproblematic in practice, which has produced little litigation and where the courts have recourse to the Three Strategies. The ABI noted: "Insurers are currently able to write policies that are required by customers ... There is no significant customer problem or market opportunity creating an imperative for legislative change".[29] Similarly, Kees van der Klugt (Director of Legal & Compliance at the Lloyd's Market Association ('LMA')) noted that the current definition of insurable interest has not created any problems in the Lloyd's Market; he was not aware of any risks not being written or rejected because the definition of insurable interest is too narrow.[30] A LexisNexis search shows that, over the last 25 years, there were only 11 reported cases in the English courts in which an insurable interest was a contested issue in the case. The fact-pattern of six of those cases fully supported, or would have supported, a decision on the existence or absence of an insurable interest consistent with the legal interest test.[31] Out of the remaining five cases, two are 'pervasive interest' cases, a category of cases which, arguably, has become obsolete;[32] two did not require a decision on insurable interest,[33] and the remaining case is *Feasey*.[34] A review of the reported Financial Ombudsman decisions between 2012 and 2017 showed that there were only 35 complaints with an insurable interest element, and in 32 of those complaints

---

28 LC, '*IIB Notes*', para 1.12.

29 Cited in: LC, '*Post Contract Duties*' (n 5) para 12.26.

30 Interview with Kees van der Klugt, Director of Legal & Compliance at the Lloyd's Market Association (London 29 September 2015).

31 *Wunsche Handelsgesellschaft International mbH v Tai Ping Insurance Co Ltd* [1998] 2 Lloyd's Rep 8 (CA); *King v Brandywine Reinsurance Co (UK) Ltd* [2004] EWHC 1033 (Comm); *Ramco (UK) Ltd & Ors v International Insurance Co of Hannover Ltd* [2004] EWCA Civ 675; *Linelevel Limited v Powszechny Zaklad Ubezpieczen S.A.* [2005] EWHC 421 (Comm); *Western Trading Limited v Great Lakes Reinsurance (UK) Plc* [2015] EWHC 103 (QB), reversed in part on a different issue [2016] EWCA Civ 1003; *Fresca-Judd v Golovina* [2016] EWHC 497 (QB).

32 *National Oilwell* [1993] 2 Lloyd's Rep 582 (Comm); *Glengate-KG Properties Ltd v Norwich Union Fire Insurance Society Ltd* [1996] CLC 676 (CA); and see Chapter 4.

33 *Hopewell Project Management Ltd v Ewbank Preece Ltd* [1998] 1 Lloyd's Rep 448 (QB); *O'Kane v Jones* [2003] EWHC 2158 (Comm).

34 n 12.

the Financial Ombudsman rejected or confirmed the existence of an insurable interest in accordance with the legal interest test.[35]

Would the IIB address the issues identified?

This section is concerned with the question whether the IIB, if implemented, would address the issues identified by the LC; it is not a wider normative evaluation of the more fundamental question of whether the doctrine of insurable interest should be retained (which is discussed in the following Chapters).

Complexity of law and different rules for different types of insurance: As the substantive provisions of the IIB only apply, and s.1 of the LAA 1774 is only repealed, in relation to life-related contracts of insurance, the IBB would create four different insurable interest regimes: (1) contracts of insurance to which the IIB applies, (2) contracts of insurance to which the LAA 1774 continues to apply, (3) contracts of marine insurance to which the MIA 1906 applies and (4) contracts of insurance where the insurable interest requirement is rooted in common law. Thus, the problem that the doctrine of insurable interest differs depending on the type of insurance has not been addressed. Although the MIA 1788 and the MIGamblingA 1909 would be repealed, there would still be a complex mix of statutes and common law.

Definition of insurable interest: The IIB redefines the categories of insurable interest for life-related insurance but does not define insurable interest for property/indemnity insurance. Therefore, the definitional inconsistencies for insurable interest in relation to property insurance remain unresolved. Despite the lack of interest from the insurance industry, excluding insurable interest in non-life-related insurance from the reforms is a missed opportunity to clarify its ambit. As argued in Chapters 6 and 11, the requirement for an insurable interest is a definitional characteristic of contracts of indemnity insurance and creates a doctrinal dividing line between contracts of insurance and other kinds of contracts. Some contracts, such as parametric polices and industry loss warranties ('ILW'), can be structured as insurance or as a derivative contract, and the requirement for an insurable interest and proof of at least a nominal loss ensure that a parametric policy or ILW are characterized as the former, and not the latter.[36] The definition of insurable interest must be clear and flexible enough so that parametric policies and ILW written as insurance are recognized as insurance contracts for legal, regulatory and tax purposes but, at the same time, the definition of insurable interest must also be meaningful enough to serve its purpose of differentiating contracts of insurance from derivatives. If the definition is too wide, that distinction will become blurred.

---

35 These numbers should be considered in the light of 42,346 complaints made relating to insurance (excluding PPI) and 180,507 PPI complaints made in the year from 1 April 2018 to 31 March 2019 (source: Financial Ombudsman Service Annual Review 2018/19, '*Data in more depth 2018/2019*', 5.

36 LC, '*Insurable Interest and Parametric Policies*' (April 2016) paras 1.22–1.26.

A clearer definition of insurable interest would have also been useful for the development of Smart Contract insurance products. Smart Contracts are self-executing transactions, written in computer code and performed in an automated way and without human control.[37] Therefore, the definition of insurable interest needs to be translatable into code. This will be more difficult to achieve if the definition is unclear and/or open-ended. The terms of the Smart Contract and the state of facts relating to the performance of the contract are programmed into a decentralized blockchain that cannot be overridden by the parties, and some argue, not even the courts in so far as they would be interpreting the intention of the parties.[38] Accordingly, the scope for using the Three Strategies would be eliminated or greatly reduced.

The law needs to be flexible enough to embrace new market developments, but the doctrine of insurable interest should not be demonized as an obstacle to innovation. The requirement for an insurable interest, whether defined widely or restrictively, does not necessarily prevent the development of new risk transfer/finance products; rather, it is relevant to whether or not the product in question is to be structured as property insurance, contingency insurance or a non-insurance contract. Consequently, the width of the definition of insurable interest may have an impact on whether new selling opportunities arise in the (property) insurance sphere or other financial markets, but it is suggested that (property) insurance market share should not be the sole consideration in determining it.

Restrictiveness of the law/creating a more permissive regime: The economic interest test for insurable interest in cl.2(2) and the recast and new categories of automatic insurable interest in cl.2(3) and (4) of the IIB would expand the scope of insurable interest in relation to life-related insurance. The economic interest test for insurable interest is not limited to pecuniary interests based on legal rights or obligations, and it should therefore be possible to insure a life on which the insured is economically dependent, or where the insured would incur an economic loss upon the death, based on a voluntary undertaking. The new economic interest test for insurable interest should cover cases such as son's insurable interest in mother's burial costs (*Harse v Pearl Life Assurance Co*[39]), or a debtor's insurable interest in life of the creditor who has made a gratuitous promise not to enforce the debt (*Hebdon v West*[40]). The categories where an insurable interest is presumed, or automatic, have been expanded to cohabitants, children, grandchildren and those treated as children or grandchildren, trustees of group schemes and employers who set up group life insurance schemes for the benefit of their employees and their families. Clause 2(3) should allow insurers to write family travel- and personal accident policies that are taken out by parents for their children. It also modernizes the law on insurable interest, putting cohabitants

---

37 See further: Max Raskin, '*The Law and Legality of Smart Contracts*' (2017) 1 Geo L Tech Rev 305, 309–11.

38 Ibid.

39 [1904] 1 KB 558.

40 (1863) 3 B&S 579 (QB).

on the same footing as spouses, as well as elevating non-pecuniary interests in connection with group pensions schemes into automatic interest (thus, codifying the *Feasey*[41] majority view on insurable interest in group life insurance).

However, parents and grandparents are not included in the list of automatic interests, so that an insured wishing to insure the life of a (grand)parent would need to show an insurable interest under the economic interest test in cl.2(2). The LC thought that there were "strong moral hazard arguments" against giving an automatic insurable interest in the lives of (elderly) (grand)parents in light of the assisted dying debate and concerns that care cost insurance proceeds could be misapplied.[42] The moral hazard argument will be considered further in Chapter 7.

The repeal of the LLA 1774, s.3 (which limits the amount of any recovery to the value of the interest) means that there would be no longer a statutory restriction on the value of life-related policies. Thus, employers could purchase 'key person' insurance that would not be limited to the value of that person's service during the notice period. The LC consider that limiting the value of the policy by statute can lead to practical and valuation difficulties without a clear rationale for doing so.[43] Setting a value of the policy is therefore left to the agreement of the parties, depending on the risk appetite of the insurer and the willingness of the insured to pay a higher premium for a higher valuation. However, the LC have not ruled out that this might be a matter for further regulatory guidance.[44] Moreover, by analogy to the law on valued policies in marine insurance,[45] excessive or fraudulent valuations on the life insured may not be conclusive and may not satisfy the insurable interest test in cl.2(2).

The IIB does not impose any restrictions on the transfer or assignment of life-related insurance contracts to third parties (as some US and Canadian statutes do).[46] It is unlikely, but open to interpretation, that cl.4 of the IIB has the effect of abolishing the common law rule of free assignability to a third party with or without insurable interest, subject to the evasion exception in *Wainwright v Bland*.[47]

Academic debate

The academic debate on the questions whether and to what extent the doctrine of insurable interest should be reformed has centred on whether there ought to be an insurable interest requirement, and how insurable interest ought to be defined. The following literature review identifies trends for reform and distils

---

41 n 12.
42 LC, '*IIB Notes*' para 2.40.
43 Ibid. para 2.74.
44 LC, '*Issues Paper 10*' (n 2) para 3.25.
45 *Lewis v Rucker* (1761) 2 Burr 1167.
46 See below.
47 (1835) 150 ER 334 (Exch).

strands of reasoning. To avoid going over the same grounds repetitively, the proposals and arguments will be evaluated as part of the examination of the justifications and rationales for the doctrine of insurable interest in Chapters 6–10.

Examining the Traditional Justification

Hartnett and Thornton's 1948 article on insurable interest in property[48] is frequently taken as the starting point of the modern debate on, and the socio-legal analysis of the Traditional Justifications for, the doctrine of insurable interest. Hartnett and Thompson's premise is that, given the social and economic importance of insurance, the legal requirement for an insurable interest which allows insurers to "escape from contractual liability" must be re-evaluated for "utility and correspondence to social and economic practices and expectations".[49] They argue that at the heart of the concept of insurable interest lies a public policy against wagering: the presence of an insurable interest differentiates a socially useful insurance contract from an economically unproductive wager. This distinction can be maintained with an insurable interest based on a factual expectation of damage since that would be probative that the insured contemplated a genuine risk transfer.[50] The indemnity principle, they argue, is simply another manifestation of the policy against wagering but does not represent an independent justification for the doctrine of insurable interest.[51] They also reject that the doctrine of insurable interest is justified on the basis that the existence of an insurable interest reduces the temptation to destroy insured property.[52] Their central point is that insurance protection should not be denied at law on the grounds of a narrowly defined concept of insurable interest if the insured has an insurable relationship with the insured property that is based on a factual expectation of damage if that property is lost or destroyed, since to do so would impinge upon the parties' freedom to contract and would prevent risk transfers to insurers which is "a valuable function in society ...."[53] They concede that an open-ended factual expectation test may give rise to uncertainty but consider that it will produce fairer outcomes than "calcified legal rules".[54]

Hartnett and Thornton's article has been influential on subsequent judicial thinking,[55] and their arguments relating to the justifications for the doctrine of insurable interest continue to be discussed.[56] Their suggestion that the concept

---

48 B Hartnett and JV Thornton, '*Insurable Interest in Property – A Socio-Economic Reevaluation of a Legal Concept*' (1949) Ins LJ 420.

49 Ibid., 421.

50 Ibid., 431–435.

51 Ibid., 434.

52 Ibid., 433–434.

53 Ibid., 434–436, 464.

54 Ibid., 464.

55 *Constitution Ins Co v Kosmopoulos* [1987] 1 SCR 2 (Canadian Supreme Court).

56 Malcolm Clarke, *The Law of Insurance Contracts* (Service Issue 37, Informa 2016) para 4-2; Robert Merkin, *Colinvaux's Law of Insurance* (12th edn, Sweet & Maxwell 2019) paras 4-001–4-002.

of insurable interest "must be constantly re-evaluated" to ensure that it corresponds to "social and economic practices" lives on in the LC's aim in relation to life-related insurance to bring the law on insurable interest in line with modern market practice and customer demands.[57] Hartnett and Thornton do not advocate legislative reform of the doctrine of insurable interest but suggest judicial oversight to ensure that insurance contracts do not fail for lack of insurable interest where the insured has an economic interest in the insured property. There are obvious parallels to be drawn to the Three Strategies employed by the English courts, although, as has been argued above, the English courts are bound, at least in theory, by existing House of Lords authorities[58] and s.5(2) of the MIA 1906.

Abolition

Some commentators have suggested that the doctrine of insurable interest should be abandoned completely. Clarke argues that preventing gambling under the guise of insurance is no longer a sound reason for the requirement of an insurable interest in contracts of insurance since gambling is now widespread and has been legalized by the GA 2005. He also questions whether insurable interest stops insureds from destroying the insured subject-matter in order to make a (fraudulent) claim. He concludes that "the legal requirement of insurable interest in property is arguably an irrelevance and an anachronism".[59] Similarly, Davey argues that "the insurable interest rule does not prevent murder."[60] Merkin suggests that an insurable interest is already no longer a requirement in non-marine non-life insurance[61] but, to eliminate any legal uncertainty whether and when an insurable interest is required and what qualifies as an insurable interest, he recommends that the requirement for an insurable interest be abolished. He cites the 'Australian experience' in support of making similar changes in English law.[62]

Lowry and Rawlings question whether the requirement for an insurable interest serves any useful purpose in the context of modern commercial practice.[63] They argue that the Traditional Justifications are no longer relevant: gaming has become a legitimate activity and, in their opinion, in so far as regulation is required,

---

57 LC, '*IIB Notes*' paras 1.3, 3.1–3.3.
58 *Lucena* (n 10); *Macaura* (n 11).
59 M Clarke, 'An Introduction to Insurance Contract Law' in J Burling and K Lazarus (eds), *Research Handbook on International Insurance Law and Regulation* (Edward Elgar, Cheltenham 2011), 18.
60 J Davey, '*Dial M for Moral Hazard? Incentives to Murder and the Life Assurance Act 1774*' (2014) 25 ILJ 120, 133; and see Chapter 7.
61 Robert Merkin (n 56) para 4-019.
62 Robert Merkin, '*Reforming Insurance Law: Is There a Case for Reverse Transportation? A Report for the English and Scottish Law Commissions on the Australian Experience of Insurance Law Reform*' (undated) paras 8.6–8.10.
63 J Lowry and P Rawlings, 'Rethinking insurable interest' in Sarah Worthington (ed), *Commercial Law and Commercial Practice* (Oxford, Hart Publishing 2003) 335.

such regulation should be a matter of public law, not contract law. Further, they doubt that an insurable interest is an effective deterrent against moral hazard. They conclude that "[o]nce those policy arguments are removed, the justifications for the requirement disappear" and that "the principle of indemnity ... is in itself sufficient to render the requirement redundant".[64] Birds suggest that in life insurance the insurable interest requirement could be replaced with a requirement to obtain the consent from the person whose life is to be insured.[65]

Davey offers a different perspective on why the doctrine of insurable interest in its current form should be abolished: he argues that there is now an inconsistency of regulatory standards between wagers and insurance since straightforward wagers are enforceable under the GA 2005, whereas insurance contracts deemed to be wagers for lack of insurable interest are void.[66]

Retention and expansion

There are some voices that favour an incremental development of the common law to modernize the doctrine of insurable interest. *Feasey*[67] is an example of how the courts seek to adjust the doctrine of insurable interest despite the constraints of the LAA 1774. Commenting extra-judicially, Sir Jonathan Mance (later Lord Mance PSC) considers that the common law, and the definition in s.5(2) of the MIA 1906, offers sufficient flexibility so that "courts need not be too rigid in ascertaining an insurable interest ....".[68] First, the court need not adopt a literal construction of the policy in order to uphold an insurable interest. Secondly, he argues that s.5(2) frames an insurable interest in terms of "any legal or equitable relation to the adventure or to any insurable property at risk therein" and is sufficiently open-textured to accommodate interests beyond proprietary and contractual rights in the property at risk. Whilst noting that insurers' general commercial interests operate as restraint "to raise too many points on insurable interest" and that the practical implications of the current law on insurable interest are "less obviously prejudicial", he does not offer any affirmative reasons why the doctrine of insurable interest should be retained.

Birds considers that, given the insurance market's preference for retaining the doctrine, for clarity a "broad statutory definition would be the best solution".[69] Similarly, Thomas suggests that one option would be to retain the existing framework of the law on insurable interest but to widen the definition of insurable interest "so that it reflects the full breadth of the legal approach adopted by

64 Ibid., 361–363.
65 John Birds, *Birds' Modern Insurance Law* (10th edn, Sweet & Maxwell 2016) para 3.8.
66 James Davey, '*The Reform of Gambling and the Future of Insurance Law*' (2004) 24 LS 507, 513–514.
67 n 12.
68 Jonathan Mance, '*Commentary on rethinking insurable interest*' in Sarah Worthington (n 63) 365, 365–367.
69 Ibid.

the contemporary courts", and to make this shift more transparent by amending s.5 of the MIA 1906. In his opinion, such a "liberalisation" of the concept of insurable interest would reflect "the contemporary demands for insurance and the varied and sophisticated insurance packages provided for by the contemporary markets".[70] Douds considers that the criticisms of the doctrine are overstated in relation to marine insurance and that, despite its deficiencies, it provides a workable framework for an ex ante enquiry as to who can insure.[71]

There is academic opinion in favour of expanding the doctrine of insurable interest. Posner and Weyl advocate the adoption of a more sophisticated insurable interest rule across all financial instruments for regulatory purposes in order to assess ex ante whether they are socially valuable or costly and argue that all socially costly financial instruments should be banned.[72] The test for 'insurable interest' they employ – whether the pay-out to the beneficiary is linked to a financial loss – is necessarily an open-textured one as it is supposed to apply to various financial instruments. Risk retention regimes that draw on the concept of 'interest' have recently been introduced in relation to securitizations.[73] Similarly, the anti-STOLI legislation in several US States[74] – which prohibits any arrangement, at or prior to the time of the contract, to initiate or facilitate the issuance of a life insurance policy for the intended benefit of a person who, at the time of policy origination, has no insurable interest – is seen by some commentators as a reaffirmation of the doctrine of insurable interest and its role in curtailing wagers on human lives.[75]

Remedies

As Davey notes, in the debate on whether an insurable interest is required and constituted, the consequences of failing to have an insurable interest are often overlooked.[76] He has criticized that the remedial regime for lack of insurable interest is rendered ineffective since its enforcement depends upon the insurer raising the matter as a defence and describes the ensuing invalidity of the contract of insurance lacking an insurable interest as "anti-competitive and archaic". Davey argues that the proper role of the doctrine of insurable interest should be as an "interpretative principle" that defines the extent of the cover, so that in the

---

70 D Rhidian Thomas (ed), *Marine Insurance: The Law in Transition* (Informa 2006) paras 2.93–2.94, 2.97.

71 Graham Douds, '*Insurable Interest in English Marine Insurance Law: Do We Still Need It*' (2012) 25 USF Mar LJ 323, 338–340.

72 EA Posner and EG Weyl, '*An FDA for Financial Innovation: Applying the Insurable Interest Doctrine to the 21st Century Financial Markets*' (2013) 107 Nw U L Rev 1307, 1344, 1357.

73 See Chapter 6.

74 See below.

75 PN Swisher, '*Wagering on the Lives of Strangers: the Insurable Interest Requirement in the Life Insurance Secondary Market*' (2015) 50 Tort Trial Ins Prac LJ 703.

76 James Davey, '*Insurable Interest – A Rule in Search of a Rationale*', presentation at a BILA seminar at Lloyd's on 18 September 2015. The slides are available from BILA.

absence of an insurable interest, any loss would be irrecoverable.[77] Lowry and Rawlings too have pointed out that the doctrine of insurable interest, if used as a technical defence by insurers, is enforced "at the whim of insurers" and that its validity/enforceability function can be fulfilled by the indemnity principle.[78]

From this overview it is apparent that there is a wide spectrum of academic opinion ranging from the abolition of the doctrine of insurable interest to expanding the concept to apply to other types of financial instruments. The majority of commentators has focussed on the extent to which the Traditional Justifications (reflected in the LC's reasons) for insurable interest still serve as rationales for the doctrine today. There is a noticeable sparseness of contributions in relation to the doctrine's place within the framework of insurance contract law and the role that insurable interest plays as a definitional element of insurance contracts.

Foreign law approaches

The following overview of the law on insurable interest in Australia, the USA, Canada, Germany, South Africa and China is not a comprehensive comparative law study but is intended as an illustration that different jurisdictions have adopted different solutions. Australian law, US American law, Canadian law and South African law share a common law history with English law. German insurance law and English insurance law have common roots in the lex mercatoria, and China has been looking West to modernize its insurance law.

Australia

Until 1984 Australian insurance contract law, including the law on insurable interest, was largely the same as English insurance contract law.[79] In 1982, the Australian Law Reform Commission ('ALRC') produced a report on insurance contract law which proposed wide-ranging reforms, including the abolition of the requirement of insurable interest in relation to non-life non-marine insurance.[80] The ALRC dismissed the requirement for an insurable interest as "the result of a combination of imprecise drafting and historical accident rather than coherent implementation of clear legislative policy" and noted that the public policy against wagering and the policy against unnecessary creation of a risk of destruction of the subject-matter of the insurance would be "adequately protected by the indemnity principle, since potential recovery is limited to actual loss".[81] Accordingly, the Insurance Contracts Act 1984 (the 'AICA'), s.16 provides that a contract of general (i.e. non-life non-marine) insurance is not inval-

---

77 Ibid.
78 J Lowry and P Rawlings (n 63) 361–363.
79 Robert Merkin (n 62) para 2.1.
80 The Australian Law Reform Commission, *Report No.20 – Insurance Contracts* (1984) para 117.
81 Ibid.

idated by a lack of insurable interest. Moreover, in general insurance the lack of "an interest at law or in equity in the [insured] property" at the time of the loss is no bar to recovery as long as the insured has suffered "a pecuniary or economic loss by reason that the subject-matter of the contract has been damaged or destroyed".[82] The AICA was later amended to abolish the requirement for an insurable interest in life insurance.[83] The requirement for an insurable interest in marine insurance remains in force.[84]

Merkin notes that he "has been informed that the insurable interest sections have not given rise to any difficulties in Australia ...".[85] A number of observations may be made in response: First, under the AICA, s.17 the insured is implicitly required to have an insurable interest at the time of the loss in order to have a valid claim and to measure the loss – he must suffer a pecuniary or economic loss as a result of the damage or destruction of the insured property. Proof of loss would necessarily involve proof of the insured's 'interest'.[86] Secondly, the AICA contains provisions that suggest that the concept of insurable interest remains a live issue. For example, pursuant to s.49, the insured is required, under certain circumstances, to disgorge any sums recovered that exceed his interest. Under s.50 of the AICA, the purchaser of an insured building is automatically deemed to be an insured under the existing policy of the vendor to cover the time from when the risk in the insured property passes until completion. The rationale of this provision is to construct a relationship between the insured subject-matter and an insured. Thirdly, although insurable interest is no longer a legal requirement, it has remained an underwriting requirement in Australia.[87] Fourthly, a search on LexisNexis Australia revealed that insurable interest issues still arise in claims litigation.[88] There are several cases since 1984 in which insurable interest has been pleaded by the claimant under a policy in support of its case, or in defence to subrogation claims, rather than as a defence to liability by the insurer.[89] For example, in *GBRH Holdings Pty Ltd v Helicopter Services Cairns Pty Ltd*, the hirer of a helicopter, GBRH, sought a share of the insurance proceeds for the loss of the helicopter that had been paid to the owner. On appeal,

---

82 AICA, s.17.

83 AICA, s.18.

84 See ss.10 and 11 of the Australian Marine Insurance Act 1909.

85 Robert Merkin (n 62) para 8.7.

86 K Sutton, *Insurance Law in Australia* (3rd edn, LBC Information Service 1999) para 6.29. Note that the book is now in its fourth edition as Enright and Merkin, *Sutton on Insurance Law* (4th edn, Thomson Reuter 2014).

87 LC, '*Issues Paper 4*' (n 3) n 26 to para 7.33, citing an email from Peter Mann, partner, Clayton Utz.

88 A search on CaseBase LexisNexis Australia for 'insurable interest' carried out on 22 May 2019 returned 17 post-1984 results (including three life insurance cases).

89 *GBRH Holdings Pty Ltd v Helicopter Services Cairns Pty Ltd* [2012] QCA 198; *Competitive Business Solutions Pty Ltd v Kim* (2002) 1 DCLR (NSW) 194; *Woodside Petroleum Development Pty Ltd v H & R – E & W Pty Ltd* (1997) 18 WAR 539; *Co-operative Bulk Handling Ltd v Jennings Industries Ltd* (1996) 17 WAR 257.

GBRH argued that the first instance judge had failed to consider the AICA, s.17. The Queensland Court of Appeal held that GBRH did have an insurable interest, but on the terms of the hire agreement, the insurance proceeds were payable to the owner.[90] The LC cite "anecdotal evidence" provided by the LMA that insurable interest was still the subject of litigation and that the abolition of the requirement had led to an increase in fraudulent claims with a higher level of out of court settlements (due to the difficulty in proving fraud) in non-marine business.[91] Fifthly, Halsbury's Laws of Australia states that an insured is required to have an insurable interest by the nature of an indemnity insurance contract and under a number of statutes directed against gaming and wagering.[92] Commentaries still refer to insurable interest as a feature of insurance contracts that distinguishes them from wagers.[93]

The United States/New York

One of the earliest reported American decision on insurable interest is *Pritchet v Insurance Co. of North America*,[94] where the court adopted the doctrine from the English MIA 1746 as a matter of American common law and commercial usage, whilst also referring to its role as a definitional characteristic of contracts of indemnity insurance. Similarly, an insurable interest requirement for life insurance policies was derived from the LAA 1774.[95] In the 19th century, the American courts developed the insurable interest doctrine to distinguish insurance contracts from wagers.[96] In the 20th century the predominant justifications for the requirement of an insurable interest became its roles as deterrent to moral hazard and protection against societal waste,[97] but the anti-wagering justification has recently resurfaced in the STOLI context (discussed below).

Pursuant to the McCarran-Ferguson Act (15 U.S.C. §1012), insurance law is the subject of State law. According to a survey carried out by the US insurance law firm Tressler LLP in 2009, the doctrine of insurable interest applies in property insurance in all 50 States.[98] The majority of States have adopted a form of the factual expectation test (also known as 'factual expectancy' test in the United States), but some States continue to define insurable interest on the basis of proprietary or contractual rights.[99] The most common statutory definition of

---

90 [2012] QCA 198, [32].
91 LC, '*Post Contract*' (n 5), fn 4 to para 12.16.
92 *Halsbury's Laws of Australia: Insurance* (LexisNexis Loose-leaf, 6 May 2013) para 235-20.
93 K Sutton (n 86) para 1.7.
94 3 Yeates 458, 464 (Pa. 1803).
95 *Connecticut Mutual Life Insurance Co. v. Schaefer* 94 U.S. 457 (1876), 460.
96 *Warnock v Davis* 104 U.S.775 (1881) (US Supreme Court).
97 *Couch on Insurance 3D* (Thomson Reuters 2011) §41:1 n 7.
98 Tressler LLP, '*50 State Survey: Insurable Interest Doctrine*' (July 2009) (hard copy available from author).
99 California, Colorado, Georgia, Missouri, Nebraska, North Dakota and Vermont – see Tressler LLP (n 98).

insurable interest used is "[actual,] lawful and substantial" interest in the safety or preservation of the property,[100] but this provision has not been interpreted consistently across those States that use it.[101] Almost all American jurisdictions, by statute or pursuant to case law, require that an insurable interest exist for life insurance, and the majority of States do so by statutory provisions that list the persons and entities that have an insurable interest in the life of another person.[102]

Property insurance: It is a statutory requirement under the New York Consolidated Insurance Laws ('NYCIL'), §3401 that the insured has an insurable interest. The definition of insurable interest ("any lawful and substantial economic interest in the safety or preservation of the property") does not require the insured to have legal or equitable title in the property,[103] but, in order to show that his interest is 'substantial', the insured must demonstrate an interest of pecuniary value.[104]

NYCIL §3401 does not operate in a socio-legal vacuum. First, §3401 (or similar provisions in other States) has been interpreted by the courts. The interest in the property must have some pecuniary value and, if the insured cannot prove that value, he will not be able to establish an interest.[105] A broad economic interest in the continued existence of the property which does not result in a direct pecuniary loss from its destruction or loss by the peril insured against is not sufficient to constitute an insurable interest.[106] Thus, in *Arthur Andersen LLP V. Federal Insurance Company* the accounting firm did not have an insurable interest in the World Trade Center. Their loss in revenue caused by the economic downturn was consequential, not direct, loss from the destruction of the building. Similarly, a mother's management duties in relation to her son's property did not give her an insurable interest, absent any current relationship with the property that directly affected her economically.[107] An unsecured creditor does not have an insurable interest in the debtor's property.[108] There must be a current relationship to the property directly affecting the insured's economic

---

100 See Tressler LLP (n 98).
101 For example, in Georgia the notion of 'lawful interest' has been interpreted as requiring a proprietary or contractual right in property, although that interest may be slight or contingent, legal or equitable – see *Conex Freight Sys., Inc. v Georgia Ins. Insolvency Pool*, 561 S.E. 2d.221, 225 (Georgia Court of Appeal 2002).
102 RH Jerry II and DR Richmond, *Understanding Insurance Law* (5th edn, LexisNexis 2012) 282.
103 *Taylor v. Allstate Ins. Co.*, 214 AD2d 610, 611; *Scarola v. Insurance Co. of North Amer.*, 31 NY2d 411; *Cross v. The National Fire Ins. Co.*, 132 NY 133, 137.
104 *Italian Designer Import Outlet, Inc. v New York Cent. Mut. Fire Ins. Co.*, 891 N.Y.S. 2d 260 (N.Y. Sup. Ct. 2009.
105 *Arthur Andersen LLP V. Federal Insurance Company* 3 A.3d 1279 (N.J. Super. Ct. App. Div. 2010). This was a New Jersey case but New York has an identical statutory insurable interest requirement to N.J. Stat. Ann. §17:37A-8 (West 2009).
106 *Arthur Andersen* (n 105).
107 *Judge v Travelers Ins. Co.*, 262 A.D.2d 983, N.Y.S.2d 288 (1999).
108 *Grevemeyer v Southern Mut. Fire Ins. Co.* 15 F.707 (C.C.Or. 1883).

well-being which will not be satisfied if there is mere expectancy to benefit from the property in the future, or the insured only uses or benefits form the property occasionally.[109]

Some commentators argue that in most 'economic interest' situations a contractual relationship in relation to the property either exists or could have been constructed.[110] Arguably, an economic interest under §3401 is not, as it might appear at first glance, significantly wider than an interest that qualifies under the legal interest test (and which also allows for interests based on contractual rights in relation to the property).

Secondly, the doctrine of proximate cause may act as barrier to recovery if the insured has a bare economic interest in the property as it may be difficult to prove that the loss suffered by the insured was proximately caused by an insured peril. New York courts have interpreted the proximate cause doctrine with a focus on the "direct" and "obvious" cause of the loss, so that "a causation inquiry does not trace events back to their 'metaphysical beginnings'".[111] Damage or loss of property in which the insured has a mere economic interest in property may not cause the insured direct pecuniary loss – that is, the loss will be too remote to be covered by the policy.[112]

Thirdly, it is common practice in the US insurance market that the policyholder of a property insurance policy is required to make representations and that property policies contain conditions precedent to recovery, as to the policyholder's ownership or title of the property insured.[113] As a result, an insured with no proprietary title in the property insured may be prevented from recovery as a matter of misrepresentation and/or under the terms of such policy. More significantly, if a proposer declares his interest in the property to be insured at the pre-contractual stage, the insurer has the opportunity to decline the risk, or to offer insurance on modified terms, or offer a type of policy that is suitable to the proposer's interest. It is also noteworthy that there are a number of additional standard representations and warranties which a proposer with a mere economic interest may not be able to give, either because he is unlikely to have the relevant information or because he has no control over the insured property: for example, detailed description of property and current and future use of property, prior loss history in relation to property and information on hazards associated with business activities carried on the property.[114]

109 RH Jerry II and DR Richmond (n 102) 271–273.
110 Ibid., 273.
111 *Album Realty Corp. v American Home Assurance Company* 80 N.Y.2d 1008, 607 N.E.2d 804, 592 N.Y.S.2d 657 (1992).
112 *Arthur Andersen* (n 105).
113 EM Holmes (ed), *Appleman on Insurance* (St. Paul, Minn. West Pub. Co. 1996–2014) §41.05[1] [a] and §197.01[A].
114 Ibid., §41.04[1] [a].

Life insurance: The NYCIL §3205(b)(2) prohibits the procurement of insurance upon the life of another person (A) unless the benefits under the contract are payable to A or to a person who has an insurable interest in A's life at the time of the contract. In life insurance, 'insurable interest' is defined as (1) an interest in the insured's own life, (2) in the case of a close relationship by blood or law with A, a substantial interest engendered by love and affection and (3) in all other cases, a lawful and substantial economic interest in the continued life and health of A.[115] NYCIL §3205 lists other specific kinds of persons or entities that may have a presumed insurable interest in A or are excepted from the requirement. NYCIL §3205(c) requires the prior consent of A to any insurance upon its life even if the insured has an insurable interest in A except where A is the spouse of the insured or where A is minor who is financially dependent upon the insured.

It is generally recognized that an insurable interest based solely on love and affection arises in insurance upon a spouse's life and a parent's insurance on his/her minor child's life.[116] The closer the familial relationship, the more likely it is that an insurable interest exists since it is presumed that a strong familial bond engenders love and affection that will preclude the moral hazard that the doctrine seeks to curtail.[117] Conversely, if the familial relationship is remote, the courts will look for an economic interest to substantiate a weak familial interest.[118]

In the 'substantial economic interest' category, an insurable interest is generally found in certain business relationships, such as (business) partners, key employees and debtors. As regards key employee insurance, an employer has an insurable interest only if the employee "is crucial to the operation of the employer's business".[119] The insured must be able to quantify the alleged economic interest, and the value of the insurance must be proportionate to that interest.[120] As illustrated in *Rubenstein v Mutual Life Insurance Co. of New York*, an employer has no insurable interest in a "non-crucial" employee: when Rubenstein took out life insurance for $240,000 on his employee Connor, Connor had just started working for Rubenstein, he had no relevant experience for the job, and Rubenstein's business had just been set up.[121] The court also found that Rubenstein did not have an insurable interest as creditor of Connor, as "the value of the life insurance [was] grossly disproportionate to the amount actually owed" ($2,000). The existence of an insurable interest owing to an economic interest in the insured's survival is a question of fact where the parties dispute the basis

---

115 NYCIL §3205(a) and (b).
116 RH Jerry II and DR Richmond (n 102) 277.
117 Ibid., 277. See also Chapter 7.
118 *Holmes v Nationwide Mut. Ins. Co.* 244 N.Y.S.2d 148 (Sup. Ct. 1963).
119 *Wagner v G. Gaudig & Blum Corp.* 228 N.Y.S. 139, 144 (App. Div. 1928).
120 *Rubenstein v Mutual Life Insurance Co. of New York* 584 F. Supp. 272 (E.D.La. 1984).
121 Ibid.

for the pecuniary interest.[122] Where the parties simply contest sufficiency of the economic interest, the question becomes one of law for the court.[123]

In *Kramer v Phoenix Life Ins. Co.*,[124] the court was asked to consider a STOLI investment scheme, under which the insured, Kramer, procured life insurance (totalling $56,200,000) on his own life with the pre-conceived intent to assign the policy immediately to an investor without an insurable interest in Kramer's life and where the premium was funded by the investment scheme. The New York Court of Appeals held by a majority that this STOLI scheme did not contravene NYCIL §3205(b)(1) and (2). NYCIL §3205(b)(1) expressly permits an insured to effect insurance on his own person for the benefit of another person and to assign the contract immediately. The requirement that he must do so "on his initiative" does not prohibit a non-coercive arrangement with an investor.[125] Whilst acknowledging that the STOLI scheme was tantamount to a wager on Kramer's life, Ciparick J said that "[i]t is not our role ... to engraft an intent or good faith requirement" onto §3205(b)(1), which permits immediate assignment.[126] In contrast, many other US courts have held that STOLI schemes entail contracts of life insurance that are void for lack of a bona fide insurable interest at their inception and are wagering contracts contrary to public policy.[127] Postdating the events in *Kramer*, the New York legislature intervened passing legislation to ban STOLI transactions where at the inception of the life insurance contract, the investor has no insurable interest in the insured (NYCIL §7815) and to prohibit life settlement contracts within a two-year period commencing with the date of the policy (NYCIL §7813(j)(1)). Forty-two US States have similar anti-STOLI statutes.[128] STOLI schemes will be considered further in relation to the anti-wagering and moral hazard justifications.

Further, a life insurer has a duty to use reasonable care not to issue a life insurance policy in favour of a beneficiary who has no interest in the continuation of the insured life, so that where the beneficiary murders the insured life, a cause of action may lie against the insurance company for wrongful death.[129] This principle has not been extended into other classes of insurance, although the

---

122 *Country Life Ins. Co. v. Marks* 592 F.3d 896, 899 (8th Cir. 2010) (applying Missouri law).
123 *Renchie v John Hancock Mut. Life Ins. Co.* 174 S.W.2d 87, 91 (Tex. App. 1943).
124 15 N.Y.3d 539 (2010) (Court of Appeals of New York).
125 Ibid., [3–7].
126 Ibid., [7].
127 See e.g. *First Penn-Pacific Life Ins. Co. v Evans* 2007 WL 1810707 (D. Md. 2007); *Lincoln Nat'l Life Ins. Co. v Calhoun* 596 F. Supp. 2d 662 (D.N.J. 2009); *Sun Life Assurance Co. of Canada v. Moran*, 2009 WL 2450443 (D. Ariz. 2009); *Am. Gen. Life Ins. Co. v Goldstein* 741 F. Supp. 2d 604 (D. Del. 2010); *Sun Life Assurance Co. of Canada v Berck* 770 F. Supp. 2d 728 (D. Del. 2011); *Sciaretta v Lincoln Nat'l Life Ins. Co.* 899 F. Supp. 2d 1318 (S.D. Fla. 2012); *PHL Variable Ins. Co. v Charter Oak Trust* 2012 WL 2044416 (Conn. Sup. Ct. 2012); *PHL Variable Ins. Co. v P. Bowie 2008 Irrevocable Trust* 718 F.3d 1 (1st Cir. 2013).
128 Life Insurance Settlement Association, *Life Settlement Regulation* (September 2018).
129 *Liberty Nat. Life Ins. Co. v Weldon* 267 Ala. 171,100 So.2d 696.

Wisconsin Insurance Statute §631.07 prohibits insurers from knowingly issuing a policy to a person without an insurable interest in the subject of the insurance.

In the past, it has been suggested that American and English insurance law developed differently in the last century since the United States has not traditionally been a welfare state and, accordingly, insurance assumed a vital role in private welfare arrangements. As a result, insurance has been regarded as having a 'public interest' dimension in the United States, and courts, legislators and insurance regulators alike have treated the insured favourably.[130] This may be one of the underlying reason why most States have adopted a wider definition of insurable interest to protect the insureds. Given that the austerity measures implemented following the global financial crisis of 2008/9 (the 'Financial Crisis') have significantly cut back on the welfare state in the UK, private (insurance) arrangements may become more significant. Thus, the LC considered it to be a relevant factor in reforming insurable interest in life insurance that wider categories of persons should be regarded to have an insurable interest in life insurance.[131]

Canada

The insurance law of the Canadian common law provinces (all provinces other than Quebec) has its origins in English insurance law. Substantive insurance law, other than marine insurance law, falls within the remit of the provinces. Most provinces have enacted insurance statutes that require that the insured has an insurable interest in the insured subject-matter for the contract of insurance to be valid. Insurable interest in property insurance is also relevant to determining the jurisdiction in which the contract was made and the applicable law.[132]

Until 1987 the common law provinces followed the legal interest test for determining insurable interest in non-marine property insurance. In *Kosmopoulos v Constitution Insurance Co.*[133] ('*Kosmopoulos*') the Canadian Supreme Court adopted a factual expectation test holding that a sole shareholder of the company was so placed in respect of the company's assets as to have the benefit from their existence and prejudice from their destruction.[134] The Canadian Supreme Court reviewed the Traditional Justifications and concluded that they did not mandate adherence to the legal interest test. Wilson J, giving the leading judgment, said that the legal interest test was an "imperfect tool" for policing wagering because the insurer alone can raise the lack of insurable interest as a defence.[135] Quoting

---

130 R Hasson, '*The Special Nature of the Insurance Contract: A Comparison of the American and English Law of Insurance*' (1984) 47 MLR 505, 521.
131 LC, '*Post Contract*' (n 5) para 10.5.
132 See e.g. Ontario Insurance Act, s.123; Alberta Insurance Act, s.514; and the Civil Code of Quebec, s.3150.
133 n 55.
134 Ibid., [43].
135 Ibid., [33–34].

Hartnett and Thornton,[136] she concluded that the policy against wagering is satisfied with an interest meeting the factual expectation test.[137] She further rejected the idea that an insurable interest under the legal interest test furthers the indemnity principle since a narrow notion can prevent the insured from recovering for a loss he has suffered.[138] Finally, she rejected the proposition that a narrow conception of insurable interest minimizes the insured's incentive to destroy the insured subject-matter. She argues that "an insured with legal or equitable title in the subject-matter of insurance has intimate access to it and is in a position to destroy it without detection".[139] The court's reasoning on this point will be considered further in Chapter 7.

Only a few years after the Supreme Court of Canada widened the meaning of insurable interest for non-marine property, the Canadian Parliament re-affirmed the legal interest test ("legal or equitable relation") for marine insurance in s.8(2) of the Canadian Marine Insurance Act 1993, which applies in all provinces and territories.

A contract of life insurance which is not supported by an insurable interest at the time of the contract is void.[140] The provincial and territorial legislatures have created lists of relationships that give rise to an insurable interest, such as an insurable interest in the insured's own life, the insured's spouse and (grand) children, any person on whom the insured is dependent for support or education, employees and any person in whose life the insured has a pecuniary interest.[141] An insurable interest is not required in group insurance and where the person whose life is to be insured has given his or her prior written consent. The consent exemption overrides the public policy against wagering on lives and extends the categories of relationship ad infinitum (provided an insurer agrees to provide cover). However, the relatively flexible categories of insurable interest and the insurable interest exemptions have been counter-balanced with a right of the person (A) whose life has been insured by another person (B) to apply to the court to order the termination of the life insurance contract (or a the reduction of cover) on the grounds that B no longer has an insurable interest in A's life[142] and/or that A reasonably believes that his life or health is endangered by the insurance contract.[143] Whilst the availability of such a court order may protect A, it would also have the effect of unilaterally varying or terminating the contractual rights and obligations between B and the insurer.

---

136 B Hartnett and J V Thornton (n 48).
137 n 55 [34].
138 Ibid., [35].
139 Ibid., [37].
140 See e.g. Ontario Insurance Act, s.178(1); Alberta Insurance Act, s.646; and the Civil Code of Quebec, s.2418.
141 See e.g. Ontario Insurance Act, s.179; Alberta Insurance Act, s.647; and the Civil Code of Quebec, s.2418.
142 Manitoba Insurance Act, s.155(4).
143 Ontario Insurance Act, s.179.1; Alberta Insurance Act, s.648.1; British Columbia Insurance Act, s.47; Manitoba Insurance Act, s.155.1.

The assignment of life insurance policies to a third party in exchange for payment is prohibited by legislation in most provinces (but not in Saskatchewan, Quebec, Nova Scotia and New Brunswick). Thus, US-style STOLI schemes would be illegal in most provinces, although a third party without an insurable interest in A's life could, of course, take out insurance on A's life with A's consent and thus be exempt from the insurable interest requirement. The Canadian consent exemption has the advantage of transparency and allows the insurer to consider as part of its underwriting decision whether to grant cover and, if so, on what terms.

Germany

German law follows the civil law tradition of legal codes. Yet, English and German insurance law have common roots in the lex mercatoria of the Late Middle Ages and the Renaissance. Through the Hanseatic League, English merchants had close ties to German maritime cities, and the maritime trade in the North Sea and Baltic Sea was governed initially by a transnational lex mercartoria.[144] From the 17th century onwards, the lex mercatoria was supplemented by local ordinances, including ordinances from the German cities of Königsberg (1730) and Hamburg (1731), relating to insurance (including insurable interest) which were of "considerable Authority; [were] paid great Regard to, and frequently *quoted*, as such, by the Judges themselves, in our Courts of Justice ..." in England.[145] German non-marine property insurance was developed from English fire insurance policy templates.[146] The MIA 1906 is a British version of the Continental codification approach.

The concept of an insurable interest has been part of German law for a long time, and German scholars have identified a number of purposes that are served by the concept of insurable interest[147]: First, it differentiates insurance contracts from other types of contracts of speculation. Secondly, it is said that an insurable interest helps to minimize the risk of (fraudulent) over-insurance since the nature of the interest will inform its value. Thirdly, the concept of an insurable interest identifies the nature of the relationship between the insured and the insured subject-matter and allows different people to insure different types of interest in the same subject-matter. The German Insurance Contract Act of 2007

---

144 In the English courts, the law merchant was considered to be part of the law of nations and judicial notice was taken of it. See *Meggadow v Holt* (1691) 12 Mod 15 and *Lethulier's case* Mich. 4 W.& M. 2 Salk. 443.

145 John Weskett, *A Compleat Digest of the Theory, Laws, and Practice of Insurance* (London 1781), Preliminary Discourse p. lxix., 381.

146 Peter Koch, '*100 Jahre Versicherungsvertragsgesetz*' Versicherungswirtschaft Nr.11 (June 2008) 54.

147 Victor Ehrenberg, *Versicherungsrecht* (Verlag von Duncker & Humblot, 1893) vol. 1, 293; Heinrich Honsell (ed), *Berliner Kommentar zum Versicherungsvertragsgesetz* (Springer Verlag 1999) vol. III, 814 [44]; Bruck-Möller, *Kommentar zum Versicherungsvertragsrecht - Vol.3 – Feuerversicherung* (8th edn, De Gruyter Recht, Berlin 2002) para C20-22.

(the 'ICA 2007'), §80 requires the insured to have an insurable interest at the time of the contract and throughout its currency in indemnity insurance. An indemnity insurance contract is rendered void for lack of insurable interest, if the insured entered the contract with the intention to profit unlawfully – that is to say that the insured intended, at the time of the conclusion of the contract, to claim in circumstances where he had not suffered an insured loss.[148] In contrast, in the absence of such an intention of the insured, the contract ceases to be enforceable: the insured is no longer liable for the premium since the insurer cannot be liable to pay any claims in respect of an insured subject-matter in which the insured has no insurable interest,[149] although the insurer may be entitled to charge reasonable costs. The prevailing academic opinion is that such costs are limited to administrative costs incurred in relation to issuing a policy and cannot be claimed by the insurer if the insurer knew that the insured was lacking an insurable interest at the time of the conclusion of the contract.[150] There is also academic opinion to the effect that if both parties purport to enter into a contract of insurance knowing that the insured lacks on insurable interest in the insured subject-matter, the contract is void as being contrary to public policy pursuant to §138 (*Sittenwidriges Rechtsgeschäft*) of the German Civil Code.

The ICA 2007, §80 does not contain a definition of 'insurable interest' (*versichertes Interesse*). The term has been defined generally in respect of all types of insurance by the Bundesgerichtshof (the highest court in civil matters) as "a pecuniary disadvantage which the parties, at the time of the contract, consider may be suffered by the insured and for which he would be indemnified by the insurer".[151] In relation to property insurance (*Sachversicherung*), an insurable interest means the relationship between the insured and the insured subject-matter, as a result of which the insured would suffer a pecuniary disadvantage if the insured subject-matter were lost, damaged or destroyed.[152] The relationship between the insured and the insured subject-matter must be of a legal nature, in the sense that the insured must have an enforceable legal right either in relation to the property itself or in relation to profits or income deriving from that property.[153] In addition, the insurance contract may limit or define the insurable interest that is covered.

Thus, in relation to property insurance, the meaning attributed to the concept of 'insurable interest' under German law is similar to the 'legal interest test' used in English law. Nevertheless, the parallels must not be overstated, in particular as the ICA 2007 contains other provisions that mitigate the narrow meaning of

---

148 Bruck-Möller *Grosskommentar zum Versicherungsvertragsrecht – Vol.3* (9th edn, De Gruyter Recht, Berlin 2010) paras 86–87.
149 This is the interpretation given to §80 by the Bundesgerichtshof in Decision BGH 24.5.1962 VersR 1962, 659, 660.
150 Bruck-Möller (n 148) paras 59 and 67.
151 BGH 20.1.1988 NJW-RR 1988, 727.
152 Bruck-Möller (n 148) para 18; Bruck-Möller (n 147) para C.20.
153 Heinrich Honsell (n 147) para 56, citing further academic authorities.

insurable interest: German law recognizes the valid conclusion of an insurance contract for the benefit of a third party (*Versicherung für fremde Rechnung*). Thus, a policyholder may enter into a contract of insurance under which a third party becomes the insured, whether or not that third party is named in the policy, and regardless of whether or not the third party knows of, or has consented to, the conclusion of the contract (although the standard case would be that the third party is a named insured in the policy and that the third party has been informed).[154] In those circumstances, it is the insurable interest of the third party insured that is relevant.[155] Whilst the third party insured is entitled to the claims proceeds in the event of an insured loss, the policyholder can retain control over the exercise and enforcement of the contractual rights of the third party insured vis-à-vis the insurer.[156] The policyholder remains liable for the premium. The idea behind this legal construct is that a person with an economic interest in the preservation of a specific item of property but no legal interest (whether proprietary or contractual) therein – such as Mr Macaura and Mr Kosmopoulos – can obtain insurance cover for the benefit of the owner of that property (i.e. the company's assets) and, at the same time, ensure that all contractual obligations are fulfilled and that contractual rights are exercised in a way that benefits him.

German law does not require an insurable interest in life insurance. The ICA 2007, §150(1) expressly permits life insurance on one's own life (*Eigenversicherung*) or on another person's (A's) life (Fremdversicherung). According to §150(2), where the insured event is A's death and exceeds 'reasonable funeral costs' (which may be set by regulation), the insured (B) must obtain A's prior written consent for the contract to be valid. The consent requirement is intended to reduce the risk that B procures A's death as A can withhold his or her consent if he or she considers that the proposed life insurance would endanger his or her life.[157] The consent requirement does not preclude wagering on another person's life. However, some commentators have noted that where B would not suffer any economic detriment if the insured event occurs, the contract in question should be characterized as an unenforceable wager,[158] rather than life insurance. Therefore, in borderline cases the insured would need to prove that the policy was intended to protect an identifiable interest.

South Africa

The doctrine of insurable interest was absorbed into Cape Colony law through the adoption of English insurance law and developed into a validity requirement

---

154 ICA 2007 §§43–49.
155 Bruck-Möller (n 148) para 46.
156 ICA 2007 §§44–45.
157 BGH 27.6.2018 JurionRS 2018, 24573 [24].
158 Bruck (ed), *Kommentar zum Versicherungsvertragsrecht – Vol. 5/2 – Lebensversicherung* (8th edn, De Gruyter Recht, Berlin 2013) paras B.99–B.101; and see §762(2) of the German Civil Code (BGB).

for contracts of insurance.[159] English law ceased to be applicable in 1977 and there is no South African statute which requires an insurable interest.[160] Traditionally, an insurable interest in property insurance had to be based on a legal interest in relation to the insured property but, striving to find an insurable interest where the lack of it is alleged as an insurer's defence, the South African courts have moved towards an economic interest-based test:

> ...in our law of indemnity insurance an insurable interest is an economic interest which relates to the risk which a person runs in respect of a thing which, if damaged or destroyed, will cause him to suffer economic loss ...[161]

Moreover, some courts have started to question whether an insurable interest is indeed a validity requirement for insurance contracts under South African law.[162] In the High Court decision in *Lorcom Thirteen v Zurich Insurance Company South Africa Ltd* ('*Lorcom*', concerning a shareholder insuring a company asset) the attack on the doctrine is three-pronged: first, on a juridical level, the court concluded that there was no justification for importing the English law concept of insurable interest and found that the applicable modern Roman-Dutch law was merely concerned with distinguishing enforceable insurance contracts from unenforceable wagers.[163] Secondly, on a theoretical level, the court considered that insurable interest is no "self-standing requirement" but merely an aspect in determining whether the contract is a wager.[164] Thirdly, it is a matter of contractual interpretation what losses are covered by the contract of insurance and to what extent the insured must prove its loss. On the construction of some insurance contracts, the insured may not be limited to its patrimonial (pecuniary) loss.

The decision in *Lorcom* is not a binding on other courts and has not escaped criticisms.[165] Some commentators have suggested that legislative intervention is needed to clarify and modernise the South African law on insurable interest. In relation to life insurance, there is very little case law and the main textbooks generally refer to the English law insurable interest rules.[166] Although insuring human life was not permitted under Roman-Dutch law, it seems to have become accepted that an insured has an insurable interest in its own life, in the life of its

---

159 FMB Reinecke, PM Nienaber and JP van Niekerk, *South African Insurance Law* (Juta 2013) 25–26; *Lynco Plant Hire & Sales BK v Univem Versekeringsmakelaars* BK 2002 5 SA 8 (T) [21].
160 *Lorcom Thirteen v Zurich Insurance Company South Africa Ltd* [2013] ZAWCHC 64 [23].
161 *Refrigerated Trucking (Pty) Ltd v Zive NO* 1996 2 SA 361, 372.
162 *Steyn v AA Onderlinge Assuransie Assosiasie Bpk* 1985 4 SA (T); *Lorcom Thirteen v Zurich Insurance Company South Africa Ltd* (n 160).
163 *Lorcom* (n 160) [23] [26–28] [31].
164 Ibid.
165 Estian Botes and Henk Kloppers, '*Insurable Interest as a Requirement for Insurance Contracts: A Comparative Analysis*' (2018) 26 AJ Int CL 130, 141 and 153–154.
166 Office of the Ombudsman for Long Term Insurance (MFB Reinecke – Assistant Ombudsman), '*Insurable Interest in the Context of Long-Term Insurance*' (undated).

spouse and the life of its child.[167] However, a number of open questions have been highlighted, including what other relationships can be the basis for an insurable interest, to what extent an insurable interest in another person's life can be purely pecuniary and the timing of the interest.[168]

People's Republic of China

Article12 of the Insurance Law 2009 requires the insured to have an insurable interest. In property insurance, the insurable interest must subsist at the time of the loss and must be based on a legally recognized right in respect of the subject-matter. The courts have interpreted the meaning of 'legally recognised right' relatively narrowly in terms of ownership rights, management or operation rights in the insured property.[169] Some commentators advocate that the meaning of insurable interest should evolve to a factual expectation test.[170] Lack of an insurable interest at the time of the loss means that the insured does not have an enforceable claim, although the contract continues to exist.[171]

Pursuant to art.12 and 31 of the Insurance Law, in life insurance, the insurable interest must subsist at the time of entering into the contract and can be based on the following categories: (1) own life, (2) spouses (but not civil partners), parents, children, (3) other family relationships where there is also a relationship of foster, support or maintenance and (4) employees. In addition, an insured can be deemed to have an insurable interest in another person's life if that person consents.[172] The value of insurance on the life of a minor child is limited by law.[173] The background to China's comparatively generous categories of insurable interest in life insurance is its 'one child' family planning policy, which has distorted the balance between generations and necessitates inter-generational financial planning and support with annuity and endowment policies.[174] A life insurance policy in which the insured is lacking an insurable interest at the time of the contract is void.[175]

The different approaches to insurable interest in different jurisdictions provide interesting perspectives and showcase different models for the legal rules relating to insurable interest. However, it is also apparent that individual rules and legal definitions of other legal systems cannot be read in isolation: to understand their true application and effect, they must be considered within the legal framework and socio-cultural context in which they operate in their home jurisdiction.

---

167 *Lorcom* (n 160) [31].
168 Office of the Ombudsman for Long Term Insurance (n 166).
169 Zhen Jing, *Chinese Insurance Contracts* (Routledge 2017), Section 7.3.
170 HY Yeo, Y Jiao and J Chen, '*Insurable Interest Rule for Property Insurance in the People's Republic of China*' (2009) 8 JBL 787.
171 PRC Insurance Law 2009, art.48.
172 Ibid., art.31(2).
173 Ibid., art.33.
174 Zhen Jing (n 169), 198.
175 PRC Insurance Law 2009, art.31.

Conversely, if the insurable interest rules of another jurisdiction are considered for transplantation into English law, one must consider their interaction with other doctrines and principles of English insurance contract law, local (London) market practice and the regulatory environment – these aspects will be examined in Chapters 8–11.

Themes for reform

This Chapter has highlighted that the LC's proposals are not the only option for reform – the LC's previous proposals, the academic discussion and the insurance contract laws of other jurisdictions show that there is a wide spectrum of possible approaches to insurable interest. The LC accept that the doctrine of insurable interest remains central to the insurance industry and, accordingly, the IIB restates the doctrine of insurable interest as a statutory requirement to the validity of a contract of life-related insurance. Regrettably, the IIB does not clarify the meaning of insurable interest in non-life-related insurance.

Although many of the proposals, and those foreign law models examined, are nuanced, three basic models can be extrapolated in relation to indemnity insurance (including property insurance):

1   *Abolition of the doctrine of insurable interest*: Without the doctrine of insurable interest, the parties would enjoy flexibility as they could choose to enter into a contract of insurance in circumstances where the insured has no insurable interest in the insured subject-matter. However, this option disregards any policy reasons for the retention of the doctrine, its potential interconnectedness with other doctrines and principles of insurance law and its role as hallmark of contracts of insurance.
2   *Retention of the doctrine of insurable interest with a wide (moral certainty/ factual expectation test) definition*: Adopting a moral certainty/factual expectation test would broaden the range of insureds that can validly insure and thus allows economic risks to be transferred. It needs to be examined whether the policy reasons underlying the doctrine of insurable interest can still be satisfied if the concept of insurable interest is expanded to lesser interests that do not meet the legal interest test (i.e. economic interests). Further consideration should also be given to whether a factual expectation test definition would have an impact on the operation of other doctrines and principles of insurance law, and the definition of contracts of insurance.
3   *Retention of the doctrine of insurable interest with a narrow (legal interest test) definition*: Retaining a narrowly defined insurable interest requirement does not preclude reforms to address some of the complexity/legal uncertainty problems identified by the LC, e.g. by restating the doctrine of insurable interest as a statutory requirement for all types of insurance and by reconfirming that the legal interest test is the sole test for determining insurable interest. There are concerns that a definition that is too restrictive can hamper the development of new insurance products but there is a

boundary to be drawn where interests become too speculative to support a contract of insurance and other types of financial contracts may provide more suitable formats.

If it is accepted that the categories of insurable interest in life-related insurance are too restrictive, the core options for reform are (1) to abolish the requirement for an insurable interest, (2) to widen the categories of relationships, whether based on familial ties or economic interests, that can found an insurable interest and (3) to keep the categories of insurable interest relatively narrow but to permit life insurance outside those categories if the person whose life is insured give its consent. The socio-cultural context in which the doctrine of insurable interest operates is more prominent in life insurance as a balance needs to be struck between limiting speculation on other people's lives and allowing life insurance to make financial provisions for dependants in the event of death or ill-health. Even in those jurisdictions that do not require an insurable interest in life insurance, the law draws a distinction between contracts of insurance and wagers, and the absence of any kind of interest is indicative of the latter.

Views are also diverging as to what the legal consequences should ensue if the insured lacks an insurable interest and whether the insurers should take some responsibility for ascertaining the interest of the proposer at the outset. The methods for implementing reform are either incremental judicial development of the doctrine of insurable interests, including the applicable tests, or statutory restatement. Whilst it has been shown that some courts have taken a pro-active approach in widening the meaning of insurable interest, other members of the judiciary feel restrained by the doctrine of precedent. The LC is promoting a statutory reform of the law on insurable interest in relation to life-related insurance but is now proposing to leave the definition of insurable interest in non-life-related insurance to the courts.

Each model needs to be assessed in light of the public policies that make up the rationales for the doctrine of insurable interest. The next Chapters will look at the Traditional Justifications for insurable interest and consider to what extent they still apply today and, if so, whether or not the relevant public policies could be equally supported by a wider notion of insurable interest.

6 The anti-wagering justification

Does the anti-wagering justification represents a well-founded rationale for the requirement of an insurable interest in modern English insurance law? The anti-wagering justification has been expressed in two different ways. First, its narrow expression is that there is a public policy against wagering under the guise of insurance and that the presence of an insurable interest demonstrates that the policy is a genuine contract of insurance, rather than a wager policy.[1] Secondly, a wider formulation of the anti-wagering justification is that the doctrine of insurable interest serves as a dividing line between insurance and gambling more generally.[2]

The MIA 1746 and the LAA 1774 were examples of the narrow expression: these Acts did not prohibit wagering but were passed to counteract "a mischievous kind of gaming" under the guise of insurance. Whilst the GA 1845 was in force, the existence of an insurable interest in the insured subject-matter was a means of differentiating an enforceable contract of insurance from an unenforceable wager.[3] Both formulations of the anti-wagering justification are based on the premise that it is the concept of insurable interest that distinguishes contracts of insurance from wagers and wager insurance. This premise will be tested in the first part of this chapter. The following two sections will examine the contemporary relevance of the wider expression of the anti-wagering justification and its narrow expression, respectively. This chapter also looks at CDS as a case study of the potential issues that can arise in contracts of speculation which are characterized by the absence of an insurable interest requirement and concludes with an examination of whether the anti-wagering justification requires a narrow definition of insurable interest.

---

1 MIA 1746, Preamble; LAA 1774, Preamble; MIA 1906, s.4(1); *Lucena* (1806) 2 Bos & Pul (NR) 269 (HL) 323 (Lord Eldon).
2 LC, '*Insurance Contract Law: Post Contract Duties and Other Issues*' (Law Com CP No 201, December 2011) para 10.12; Robert Merkin, *Colinvaux's Law of Insurance* (12th edn, Sweet & Maxwell 2019) para 4-001.
3 See Chapter 2.

Wagers and insurance distinguished

Both formulations of the anti-wagering justification for the doctrine of insurable interest rely on 'insurable interest' as a characteristic that differentiates contracts of insurance from wagers. Both types of contracts are aleatory agreements, where the performance of at least one party is contingent upon the occurrence of an uncertain event, or its timing or extent, which is beyond the control of the parties.

Doctrinal distinction

The classic definition of a wagering contract is that of Hawkins J in *Carlill v Carbolic Smoke Ball Company*:

> [A] wagering contract is one by which two persons, professing to hold opposite views touching the issue of a future uncertain event, mutually agree that, dependent upon the determination of that event, one shall win from the other, and that other shall pay or hand over to him, a sum of money or other stake; *neither of the contracting parties having any other interest in that contract* than the sum or stake he will so win or lose, whether he will win or lose being dependent on the issue of the event, and therefore, remaining uncertain until the issue is known.[4]

(Emphasis added)

There is no legal definition of 'contract of insurance', but in *Prudential v Commissioners of Inland Revenue* Channell J described a number of its characteristics, including the following: "A contract which would otherwise be a mere wager may become an insurance by reason of the assured having an interest in the subject-matter...".[5]

Whereas Hawkins J relies on the absence of any interest in the contract beyond the money to be won or lost upon the occurrence of the uncertain event as one of the characteristics of a wagering contract, Channell J indicates that a contract that would otherwise be a wager may be a contract of insurance on account of the insured having an insurable interest which makes the uncertain event adverse to the interest of the insured. Thus, both judges' focus is on an 'interest' as the characteristic that differentiates one type of contract from the other. Similarly, the MIA 1906 s.4(2) deems a marine insurance contract lacking an insurable interest to be a wagering contract. Conversely, the absence of an interest being a hallmark of a wager is underscored by betting and racing rules that restrict specified persons that have a connection with the subject-matter from wagering. For example, directors, employees and contractors of Camelot cannot buy or

---

4 [1892] 2 QB 484 (QB) 490–491.
5 [1904] 2 KB 658 (Ch) 663. See also Chapter 11.

claim on National Lottery tickets,[6] and an owner, jockey or trainer of a racehorse cannot lay a bet on that horse or instruct another person to do so.[7]

The Financial Services Authority ('FSA') opined that "for regulatory purposes, it would still be possible to distinguish insurance from other products without insurable interest".[8] A number of points can be made in response:

1   The FSMA regulatory framework is distinct from the common law. The RAO does not seek to define "contracts of insurance". Instead "it makes some specific extensions and limitations to the general common law meaning of the concept".[9]

2   The FSMA regulatory framework does have regard to insurable interest as a definitional characteristic of contracts as contracts of insurance for regulatory purpose. Reference is made to Chapter 11.

3   In *Belmont Park Investments Pty Ltd v BNY Corporate Trustee Services Ltd*, the Supreme Court indicated that it regarded 'insurable interest' as a differentiating characteristic of insurance contracts. Lord Mance rejected a description of a swap agreement as 'credit insurance' in the legal sense because the entity acting as a swap counter-party to the note issuer lacked an insurable interest in the performance of the obligations by the reference entities.[10]

4   In a Legal Opinion commissioned by the International Swaps and Derivatives Association ('ISDA'), Robin Potts QC concluded that CDS should not be treated as contracts of insurance since they were structured to pay out on the occurrence of a default irrespective of whether or not the protection buyer had an insurable interest or had suffered a loss.[11] CDS and other contracts for differences might have been treated as wagers at common law,[12] but financial wagers that concern regulated investments are now regulated under the FSMA regulatory regime, and not the gambling legislation.[13]

5   Whilst the Court of Appeal in *Feasey* rejected the idea that if the contract is not a wager sufficient insurable interest is demonstrated, the court reaffirmed that a policy written on an "interest or no interest" basis is a wager policy.[14]

6   The National Lottery, '*Rules for Draw-Based Games*' (Edition 18a) cl 1.5.
7   British Horseracing Authority, '*The Rules of Racing*' (2019), J5-11.
8   LC, '*Issues Paper 4 – Insurable Interest*' (January 2008) fn 26 to para 7.4.
9   FCA Handbook, 'The Perimeter Manual' ('PERG'), PERG 6: Guidance for the Identification of Contracts of Insurance, 6.3.2. The definition of 'contracts of insurance' in art 3(1) of the RAO extends to certain fidelity bonds and other contracts of guarantee which would not be considered contracts of insurance under the common law.
10   [2011] UKSC 38 [135] (Lord Mance).
11   Opinion prepared for ISDA by Robin Potts QC, Erskine Chambers, 24 June 1997 (the 'Potts Opinion') – a copy of the opinion was unavailable and the author is quoting from LC, *Issues Paper 4* (n 8) para 7.12.
12   *City Index v Leslie* [1992] QB 98 (CA) 112 (Leggatt LJ) (contract for difference); *Westdeutsche Landesbank Girozentrale Respondent v Islington London Borough Council* [1996] AC 669 (HL) 680 (Lord Goff) (interest swap agreement); contra *Morgan Grenfell & Co Ltd v Welwyn Hatfield DC* [1995] 1 All ER 1 (QB).
13   FSMA 2000, s.412; GA 2005, s.10(1).
14   [2003] EWCA Civ 885, [58] (Waller LJ), [151] (Ward LJ).

6   In contracts of life insurance where an insurable interest is presumed based
on a close familial relationship and not an indemnity for contingent loss,
such an interest may be the sole distinguishing factor between insurance
and another contract of speculation.

Economic analysis

Many commentators have noted that the difference between contracts of insurance and wagering is that the former are socially beneficial and the latter
are economically inefficient and socially costly as insurance enables a person
to transfer risk (i.e. reduce his own risk exposure), whereas gambling increases
his risk.[15]

The insured transforms his risk of a large financial loss upon the loss of an
asset with the certainty of 'losing' a relatively small amount by way of premium
payments and gains peace of mind.[16] The insurer is able to absorb the risk more
efficiently as a result of the law of large numbers, because of risk diversification
and because an insurer can pool and invest the premium income more profitably
compared to an insured investing his premium saving if he does not buy insurance for a particular risk.[17] Thus, the transaction is mutually advantageous since
"it should mitigate their aggregate exposure to risk" and there is an overall social
gain.[18] In addition, insurance also has a wider social benefit in that it "provides
fast compensation to victims of disasters, accident, and torts", easing the burden
on tax-funded benefits and compensation schemes.[19] In contrast, under a wager
contract one party will gain at the expense of the other. The risk of winning or
losing is created by the contract itself.[20] At best, a wager is a "zero-sum game"
but wagering may even be "welfare-reducing" since both parties expose themselves to risk that they would not otherwise face[21] without gaining the "peace of
mind" effect. Wagering is also welfare-reducing since it can produce "negative
externalities" – that is costs suffered by third parties or the general public as a
whole – as a result of the transaction.[22]

---

15 B Hartnett and J V Thornton, '*Insurable Interest in Property – A Socio-Economic Reevaluation of
a Legal Concept*' (1949) Ins. L.J. 432–433; EA Posner and EG Weyl, '*An FDA for Financial Innovation: Applying the Insurable Interest Doctrine to the 21ˢᵗ Century Financial Markets*' (2013)
107 Nw U L Rev 1307, 1308, 1314–1317, 1345.

16 B Hartnett and J V Thornton (n 15) 432. Behavioural economics theory has it that most people are 'risk adverse'. In the insurance context that means that they have a preference for the
certainty of paying a (small) premium over the uncertainty of a large future financial loss. See
Ronen Avraham, '*The Economics of Insurance Law –A Primer*' (2012) 19 Conn Ins. LJ 29, 37.

17 EA Posner and EG Weyl (n 15) 1314.

18 Ibid.,1314. See also LR Cohen and ME Boardman, 'Methodology: Applying Economics to
Insurance Law – An Introduction' in J Burling and K Lazarus (eds), *Research Handbook on
International Insurance Law and Regulation* (Edward Elgar, Cheltenham 2011) 19, 22–23.

19 R Avraham (n 16) 41.

20 *Cousins* v *Nantes* (1811) 3 Taunt 513 (ExchCham) 524 (Mansfield CJ).

21 EA Posner and EG Weyl (n 15) 1314.

22 See below as to the harmful effects of gambling and the social costs in connection with CDS.

Hartnett and Thornton acknowledge that without an interest in the property to be insured, "there is no genuine risk to be hedged".[23] Posner and Weyl argue that an insurable interest requirement can distinguish between transactions where risk transfer takes place and those transactions where no risk is transferred.[24] Risk of loss can only be transferred from an insured to the insurer if the insured is exposed to that risk in the first place. An interest in the insured property establishes the exposure to the risk of loss or damage to the property which, in turn, provides the basis for the capacity or potential to suffer an insured loss. Without any interest in the property that pre-exists independently of the contract, there is no risk since the insured is not exposed to the possibility of an adverse outcome – that is, loss of or damage to the insured property. The Financial Conduct Authority ('FCA') identifies the "assumption or transfer of risk" as one of the main factors pointing towards a contract of insurance (but stops short of linking the notion of risk transfer to the concept of insurable interest).[25]

It is suggested that the existence of a risk exposure is a necessary pre-condition to the transfer of that risk under a contract of insurance. In property insurance, this risk is the insured's exposure to loss or prejudice if the insured property is lost, damaged or destroyed. An insurable interest of the insured in the insured property is the mechanism that links the insured's relationship with the insured property to his exposure to that loss. Indemnification for loss can only be triggered if the insured has something of value that can be lost or damaged.

Although contracts of life insurance are considered to be contingency contracts that do not require proof of loss when the contingent event has occurred, where such a contract is based on a pecuniary interest of the insured, there may still be a risk transfer, namely the risk of suffering a pecuniary loss or disadvantage on the death of the life insured. The bargain struck between the parties is that the insured gains peace of mind that the fixed sum that is payable upon that death will compensate for the expected pecuniary disadvantage – so there is an element of indemnity – whereas the insurer receives a premium income which it can pool and invest with other premium receipts.

The facts of *Dalby v The India and London Life Assurance Company*[26] serve as an example of how the loss of an insurable interest in the life insured after the contract has been entered into may allow for post-contract gambling: the insured might choose to continue paying the premium speculating that, as long as the aggregate premium payments do not exceed the sum payable upon the death of the life insured, he will make a profit. Similarly, STOLI investors as assignees of a life insurance contract, who do not have any interest in the life insured, do not expect pecuniary gain from its continuance or financial loss as a result of death; to the contrary: they lose from the continuance of the insured life and profit from an (early) death.

---

23 B Hartnett and JV Thornton (n 15) 433.
24 EA Posner and EG Weyl (n 15) 1314.
25 PERG 6.6.2G. See also Chapter 11.
26 (1854) 15 CB 365 (ExchCham).

Where the insured has a presumed insurable interest based on a familial relationship with the life insured, there is not necessarily an exposure to any concrete economic risk: for example, where the insured insures the life of his or her
spouse who is not making any financial contribution to the relationship, the
insured would not suffer an actual financial loss upon the spouse's death. Yet,
there would still be a loss in a more abstract sense (as reflected in the language
of condolences when we say 'I am sorry for your loss'): the loss is the death of a
cherished person who may have contributed to the relationship in non-monetary
terms. German law recognizes that life insurance provides an 'abstract indemnity' (*abstrakte Bedarfsdeckung*), where a pre-agreed amount is payable upon
death regardless of any actual economic loss, but with the intent to address an
abstract economic need.[27] Insuring one's own life, the wagering aspect is overridden by the social utility of the contract as an investment to benefit others.[28]
Own life insurance contracts are frequently structured and intended as instruments of financial planning to provide for future economic needs rather than
retrospectively covering for financial loss. Given that there may not be a concrete
indemnity element and an identifiable transfer of economic risk in life insurance,
it might be said that the requirement for an insurable interest – which establishes
the link between the insured and the insured life – is even more important as the
main distinguishing factor – approved by the LAA 1774 – between life insurance
and wagers.[29]

The existence of an insurable interest is not a fail-safe indicator but is a generally reliable doctrinal solution to differentiate between a contract of insurance and a wager. Industry feedback received by the LC clearly shows that the
insurance industry perceives an insurable interest as a "hallmark of insurance"
which provides a dividing line between contracts of insurance and other forms
of speculative contracts, and in particular gambling, and reinforces market discipline restraining insurers from entering into the latter type.[30] However, the fact
that the doctrine operates as a dividing line does not explain why the distinction
between wagers and contracts of insurance is significant. This will be explored
in the next section.

Public policy and the differentiation between insurance
and wagers

Historically, the distinction between wagers and contracts of insurance was necessary since wagers under the guise of insurance, and later on wagers generally,
were void.[31] Detractors of the doctrine of insurable interest have pointed out

---

27 Bruck (ed), *Kommentar zum Versicherungsvertragsrecht – Vol.5/2 – Lebensversicherung* (8th
   edn, De Gruyter Recht, Berlin 2013) para B.79.
28 *New England Mut Ins v Caruso* 73 N.Y.2d 74 (N.Y. 1989).
29 *Feasey* (n 14) [58] (Waller LJ).
30 The LC, '*Post Contract*' (n 2) para 10.1.
31 See Chapter 3.

that gambling has become a legalized and widespread activity and it is therefore no longer necessary to insist upon an insurable interest in insurance contracts to prevent gambling. Nevertheless, the policy objectives pursued in relation to gambling remain different to those in relation to insurance, and this difference is reflected in distinctive regulatory regimes. It is clear from the GA 2005, s.10(1) and the FSMA 2000, s.412 that Parliament intended to keep the two regulatory regimes separate. The case for differentiating contracts of insurance by way of insurable interest becomes more (not less) compelling because gambling contracts are now generally enforceable and have become widespread.

Policy on gambling

Gambling has become a "mainstream leisure activity": in 2018/19, the British commercial gambling industry generated a gross gambling yield of £14.4billion and it employed 107,940 people.[32] Although no longer regarded as morally objectionable, gambling is considered to be (potentially) harmful as it can result in addictive behaviour, mental health problems, financial hardship and bankruptcy with subsequent welfare dependency and associated crime, the consequences of which are borne by family members, creditors, tax payers and society as a whole.[33] Therefore, Parliament has put in place a regulatory regime that seeks to prevent gambling from being a source of crime, to ensure transparency and to protect vulnerable persons from the harmful consequences of gambling.[34] The GA 2005 introduced a system of governmental licensing, control and supervision of commercial operators providing any form of gambling, their personnel and premises. Moreover, licensed gambling is impersonal in the sense that it is not connected to a person's well-being or property. As noted above, betting contracts in which one party has an interest are frequently condemned by industry rules and may as a result be declared void by the Gambling Commission.[35]

The comparison between enforceable wagers and insurance contracts that are void for lack of insurable interest is flawed as the GA 2005 primarily regulates gambling operators and premises, including by criminalizing the provision of facilities for gambling without licence.[36] Moreover, the Gambling Commission has the power under the GA 2005, s.336 to declare an unfair gambling contract void.

Whilst the current gambling legislation does not prevent individuals from gambling privately or in licensed betting shops, there are restrictions on betting on another person's life imposed by the LAA 1774, ss.1–3. As noted in Chapter 3, the LAA 1774 was enacted to counteract a "mischievous kind of

---

32 Gambling Commission, '*Annual Report and Accounts 2018/2019*', 16.
33 Department for Culture, Media and Sport: Gambling Review Body, '*The Gambling Review Report*' (July 2001) Part 3. See also the Explanatory Memorandum to the Gaming Machine (Miscellaneous Amendments and Revocation) Regulations 2018, which implemented restrictions on fixed odds betting.
34 GA 2005, s.1.
35 GA 2005, s.336(2), 336(4)(b).
36 GA 2005, s.33.

gaming" in relation to human life in which neither party has an interest. The main concerns are that wagering on another person's life (1) creates a moral hazard that the party who stands to benefit from that person's death might be tempted to bring about the death of the life insured and (2) has been regarded as inherently immoral and blunting human empathy,[37] or at least instinctively "uncomfortable".[38] The US STOLI schemes show that gambling on human life is not an obsolete concern. The LC acknowledge that 'moral hazard' remains a policy concern bearing upon the breadth of the insurable interest requirement.[39] The moral hazard argument against gambling also applies in the property insurance context and will be explored further in Chapter 7.

Policy on insurance

In contrast, the purchase of insurance is not associated with addiction: over-insurance and double insurance tend to be the result of ill-informed buying choices rather than addictive behavioural patterns. The UK Government's stated policy in relation to insurance is "to drive growth across the insurance industry and strengthen the sector's contribution to the UK economy" noting:

> The insurance sector makes a vital contribution to the UK economy, employing over 300,000 people across the country, attracting global capital, serving the needs of consumers, and generating UK exports. It plays a fundamental role in assessing and managing risk – whether strengthening the resilience of local communities, sustaining regional growth, or underpinning global trade.[40]

Insurance companies conducting insurance business in the UK are subject to the FSMA regulatory framework, the primary objectives of which are consumer protection and ensuring the integrity, effective competition and the financial stability of financial services providers.[41]

Reasons against gambling by insurers

The FSMA regulatory framework imposes restrictions upon insurers engaging in gambling in line with the objectives to protect policyholders and to safeguard

---

37 G Clark, *Betting on Lives: The Culture of Life Insurance in England 1695–1775* (MUP 1999) 49–60.

38 LC, '*Issues Paper 4*' (n 8) para 7.40. In *Gilbert v Sykes* (1812) 16 East 150 (KB), Lord Ellenborough CJ described the subject-matter of the wager – Napoleon's life – as "injurious to the interest of mankind" and Blanc J said that "it is both impolitic and immoral to bet concerning the life of a Sovereign".

39 LC, '*IIB Notes*' para 2.40.

40 HM Treasury, '*The UK Insurance Growth Action Plan*' (December 2013) 5.

41 FSMA 2000, ss.1B and 2B.

the financial stability of insurers.[42] As the editors of Arnould's observe, "even if the social mores [on gambling] have changed, there is no reason why insurers should be permitted to gamble...".[43]

Policyholder protection means protection for those who are or may become policyholders,[44] as well as the fair treatment of policyholders.[45] The FCA's Insurance: Conduct of Business Sourcebook ('ICOBS') imposes a number of obligations on insurance distributors (insurers selling insurance directly, and insurance intermediaries) to ensure that customers buy policies that meet their needs. The ICOBS rules and guidance should prevent an insurer from 'marketing' and 'selling' wagers to customers who seek insurance protection.[46] There are a number of policyholder protection mechanisms that would not be available to counter-parties to wagers: first, consumer policyholders benefit from special protections under the ICOBS.[47] Secondly, consumer policyholders are entitled to avail themselves of the Financial Ombudsman Service to bring complaints against insurers.[48] Thirdly, policyholders enjoy a qualified priority over other unsecured creditors upon the insolvency of a UK insurer[49] and may be entitled to compensation under the Financial Services Compensation Scheme if an authorized insurer is unable, or likely to be unable, to meet claims against it.[50]

From the insurer's perspective, mis-selling unsuitable products to customers in breach of the ICOBS rules may lead to disciplinary action being taken by the FCA against the insurer[51] and to the payment of compensation to (private person) customers who have suffered loss as a result.[52] Conversely, insurers are not licensed and supervised under the GA 2005 regime, which contains safeguards for consumers in the gambling context.

The *financial stability of insurers* could be undermined by entering into gambling contracts since financial resources that should be held by insurers to meet their insurance liabilities could be depleted and diverted. In 1796 Park noted that the prevalence of wagering prior to the MIA 1746 had "threaten[ed] the speedy annihilation" of the insurance industry. The same point was made more recently by Langley J in *Feasey v Sun Life Assurance Corp of Canada* when he suggested that gambling by means of insurance could undermine the security of insurers.[53] Promoting the financial safety and soundness of insurers and the protection of

---

42 FSMA 2000, ss.1C, 2B and 2C.
43 Jonathan Gilman, Mark Templeman and others, *Arnould's Law of Marine Insurance and General Average* (19th edn, Sweet & Maxwell 2018) para 11–12.
44 FSMA 2000, s.2C(2).
45 FCA Handbook, 'Principles for Business' ('PRIN') PRIN 2.1.1R, Principle 6.
46 FCA Handbook, 'ICOBS' Rules and Guidance in 5.1, 5.2, 5.3 and 6.1. See also Chapter 12.
47 E.g. cancellation rights (ibid., 7.1.1R) and claims handling protections (8.1.1R and 8.1.2R).
48 FSMA 2000 s.229(3); FCA Handbook, 'Dispute Resolution' ('DISP') DISP 3.
49 Insurers (Reorganisation and Winding Up) Regulations 2004, SI 2004/353.
50 FSMA 2000, Part XV.
51 FSMA 2000, Part XIV; FCA Handbook, 'The Enforcement Guide' ('EG'') EG 7–9.
52 FSMA 2000, s.138D; see also Chapter 12.
53 [2002] EWHC 868 (Comm), [162].

existing and future policyholders are amongst the regulatory objectives of the Prudential Regulation Authority ('PRA') for insurers.[54]

As gambling contracts do not require an insurable interest, an unlimited number of unrelated parties could take out bets on the same subject-matter. Stahl (Head of Complex Claims at Allianz Group) says that, if an insurer were to do so, this would lead to "an accumulation for a single risk position, turning a standard risk into a catastrophe scenario where multiple claims would be paid out over and over again above the true value of the insured subject-matter" ('multiple exposure risk').[55] This would undermine the 'law of large numbers' principle, which is the economic foundation of insurance.[56] The multiple exposure risk was one of the reasons why Lord Eldon in *Lucena* rejected 'moral certainty' of loss as a sufficient basis for insurable interest.[57] Insurability of a risk presumes that "[i]t must be unlikely to produce loss to a very large percentage of the exposure units at the same time".[58] By insisting upon an insurable interest in insurance contracts, the number and classes of persons eligible to insure a single risk remain limited, predictable and transparent and any pay-outs are limited to each insured's loss suffered in respect of his insurable interest. Bets or wagers that are structured as insurance, in particular if multiple bets are placed in relation to the same risk, could have an (unexpected) impact on an insurer's liquidity to fund all policyholders' claims and lead to the insurer' insolvency and may even imperil the financial stability of interconnected insurers and financial institutions.

Hartnett and Thornton,[59] echoed by Wilson J,[60] pointed out that insurers can avoid multiple insurance situations by declining cover, or by limiting their liability, or by charging a larger premium. Although this seems a compelling argument on an individual policy level, the CDS case study below shows that risk multiplication can occur unintentionally due to lack of transparency and the interconnectedness of different parties. The multiple exposure risk is not just an 'underwriting issue' given that it can affect the financial stability of an insurer and could potentially even create systemic risk issues. The CDS case study also shows that the market cannot necessarily be trusted to 'self-regulate'.

The gambling industry deals with multiple bets on the same event by not just assessing the probability of the event occurring but also adjusting the odds by reference to the ratio of pay-off to stake.[61] In statistical terminology, the concept

---

54 FSMA 2000, ss.2B and 2C.

55 Interview with Andreas Stahl, Head of Complex Claims at Allianz Group (London, 14 October 2015).

56 R Avraham (n 16) 37–28.

57 n 1, 324.

58 EJ Vaughan and T Vaughan, *Fundamentals of Risk and Insurance* (10th edn, John Wiley & Sons, Inc 2008) 42–43.

59 B Hartnett and JV Thornton (n 15) 433.

60 *Kosmopoulos* [1987] 1 SCR 2, [23].

61 Lawrence V Fulton, Francis A Mendez et al, '*Confusion between Odds and Probability, a Pandemic?*' (2012) 20 J Stat Edu 1, 3.

of 'odds' used in betting denotes the ratio of the probability of an event occurring to the probability of the event not occurring.[62] Pay-offs from bets are frequently calculated taking into account the number and amount of stakes placed on either side of the bet. In contrast, the insurance industry does not generally underwrite on 'odds' but makes an assessment of the risk classifying it according to the likelihood, frequency and magnitude of a loss incurred by the insured. This assessment is based on past experience, demographical statistics and the individual characteristics of the subject-matter and the insured. Claims payment under indemnity policies are measured by reference to the insured's actual loss – they are not tied to the odds and they are not set or adjusted according to the number of insurances placed on the same risk. Pay-outs under contingency policies are pre-determined amounts and the premium payments are set at a level so that their total is likely to exceed the pay-out.

The FSMA regulatory framework seeks to ensure financial stability and to minimize the risk of insurers being unable to pay claims in a number of ways that are relevant to the wager and insurance contract distinction:

1   Insurers are prohibited from carrying on any commercial business other than insurance business and activities directly arising from that business ('Internal-Contagion-Restriction'),[63] since any losses or liabilities from a non-insurance activity could deplete or divert financial resources held to meet insurance liabilities. The Internal-Contagion-Restriction should preclude insurers from engaging in commercial gambling. AIG's pre-2008 securities lending programme, which significantly contributed to AIG's near collapse, serves as an illustration of how non-insurance activities can drain away funds: AIG Investments, AIG's institutional asset management unit, loaned securities from AIG insurance companies to institutional borrowers in return for cash collateral. Borrowers were entitled to return the securities and demand the return of their cash collateral. As it became apparent that AIG was in financial difficulties, borrowers wanted to reduce their exposure to AIG by demanding the return of their cash collateral. This en masse cash demand contributed to AIG's illiquidity and its inability to access the capital markets to raise additional capital.[64] Other examples of insurers running into catastrophic financial difficulties on account of engaging in non-insurance business are MBIA, Inc (monoline insurer writing CDS and collateral debt obligations who had to be rescued by the New York Insurance Department in 2009) and Swiss Re (writing CDS incurring a $1.1 billion loss – bailed out by a $2.6 billion emergency loan from Berkshire Hathaway in 2009).[65]

---

62 Ibid.
63 PRA Rulebook, 'SII Firms: Conditions Governing Business' 9.1.
64 W Sjostrom Jr, '*The AIG Bailout*' (2009) 66 Wash Lee L Rev 943, 961; D Schwarcz and S Schwarcz, '*Regulating Systemic Risk in Insurance*' (2014) 1 U Chi L Rev 1569, 1585–1586.
65 MC Turk, '*The Convergence of Insurance with Banking and Securities Industries, and the Limits of Regulatory Arbitrage in Finance*' (2015) 2015:3 Col Bus L Rev 968, 991–993.

2   The Solvency II regime[66] contains rules to value assets and liabilities, to calculate 'Solvency Capital Requirements' ('SCRs') and to identify eligible 'own funds' to cover the SCRs to ensure that an insurer has sufficient financial resources to pay its policyholders' claims and to create an environment of fair and stable markets.[67] The SCRs are calculated by reference to an assessment of all quantifiable risks, including underwriting risk, market risk, credit risk and operational risk.[68] The risk to which the insurer is exposed under a gambling contract – that is the gambling risk of losing the stake money – would not be captured by the underwriting risk as this solely relates to the risk arising from *insurance liabilities*.[69] Wagers may also not be adequately captured in the market risk, credit risk and operational risk categories. Gambling risk is not a type of risk that is captured in the Standard Formula for calculating an insurer's SCRs.[70] Accordingly, an insurer with a material gambling risk exposure would need to use an internal model for the calculation of its SCRs, which requires the prior approval of the PRA.[71] Alternatively, or in addition to using an approved internal model, the PRA could ask for a revision of the calculation of the SCRs,[72] or for additional capital,[73] if a specific risk is not adequately covered by the SCRs. Any material gambling-related risk that is not accounted for in the insurer's calculation of its SCRs, whether under the standard formula or an approved internal model, could distort its SCRs calculation, which could result in insufficient eligible 'own funds'.[74] Moreover, there could also be a breach of an insurer's notification obligations if a significant change to its SCR calculation is not reported to the PRA.[75]

3   The Solvency II regime also sets standards for the quality of the capital to be held by insurers as their 'own funds' to cover its SCRs. The excess of assets over liabilities, less the amount of own shares held by the insurer, represents that insurer's basic 'own funds'. Cash actually received by an insurer counts into its 'own funds' but it is unlikely that any contingent payment of wager stakes to the insurer would qualify since it would not have the capacity to absorb losses unless and until the contingency materializes.

---

66 Directive 2009/138/EC of the European Parliament and of the Council of 25 November 2009 on the taking up and pursuit of the business of Insurance and Reinsurance (recast) ('Solvency II Directive'), as implemented by the Solvency II Regulations 2015, SI 2015/575 and the PRA Rulebook for Solvency II firms and the FCA Handbook: together the 'Solvency II regime'.
67 Solvency II Directive, Recitals 15 and 16.
68 PRA Rulebook, 'SII Firms: Solvency Capital Requirement – General Provisions' 3.3.
69 PRA Rulebook, 'SII Firms: Glossary', definition of 'underwriting risk'.
70 PRA Rulebook, 'SII Firms: Solvency Capital Requirement – Standard Formula' 2.1.
71 PRA Rulebook, 'SII Firms: Solvency Capital Requirement – Internal Models' 2.1.
72 PRA Rulebook, 'SII Firms: Solvency Capital Requirement – General Provisions' 4.5.
73 Ibid., 5.
74 Ibid., 2.1.
75 PRA Rulebook, 'SII Firms: Solvency Capital Requirement – Internal Models' 6.1; 'Reporting' 5.1–5.5.

4   It may not be permissible for insurers to invest their assets in wagers as to do so may be in contravention of the requirement to invest assets "in accordance with the prudent person principle" and "in the best interest of all policyholders".[76] An insurer may invest in assets whose risks it "can properly identify, measure, monitor, manage, control and report and appropriately take into account in the assessment of its overall solvency needs …".[77] Insurers must file annual regulatory returns containing accounts and statements with details on, inter alia, their solvency, capital resources, technical provisions and investments,[78] so that any significant wagering contracts would fall to be disclosed.

Dividing line for tax treatment

The concept of insurable interest may also serve as a dividing line for tax purposes.[79] Generally speaking, insurance transactions are exempt from value added tax[80] and instead insurance premium tax is payable on premiums received under taxable insurance contracts.[81] In contrast, stake money (the money risked by each player in a bet and returned to the winning player) is outside the scope of value added tax as it is not considered to be "consideration for any supply",[82] but bookmakers and gambling operators pay gambling duties on their profits.[83] Notice IPT1 mentions "insurable interest" as a feature that characterizes contracts of insurance for the purposes of insurance premium tax,[84] and Notice 701/36 cross-refers to the identification of contracts of insurance under the FSMA regulatory regime.[85]

Dividing line for takaful insurance

The LC noted that it is important to isolate insurance from gambling for those communities that do not permit gambling.[86] Islamic (*Sharia*) law forbids gambling (*maysir*). Sharia-compliant "takaful insurance" is usually sold by specialist insurers structured as not-for-profit mutuals where takaful members contribute a certain sum of money to a common pool (investing in permissible assets) with

---

76 PRA Rulebook, 'SII Firms: Investments' 2.1.
77 Ibid., 2.1(1).
78 PRA Rulebook, 'SII Firms: Reporting'.
79 LC, '*Post Contract*' (n 2) para 10.12.
80 HMRC, 'VAT Notice 701/36: insurance' (February 2013).
81 Finance Act 1994, ss.48–74, Schedules 6A, 7 and 7A, as amended by subsequent Finance Acts.
82 HMRC, 'VAT Notice 701/29: betting, gaming and lotteries' (February 2013). Gambling profits generated by the operators of gambling facilities attract betting and gaming duties.
83 HMRC, 'Guidance on General Betting Duty, Pool Betting Duty and Remote Gaming Duty' (August 2014).
84 HMRC, 'Notice IPT1: Insurance Premium Tax' (October 2014).
85 n 80.
86 LC, '*Post Contract*' (n 2) para 10.12.

a view to share the risk of loss amongst members,[87] so as not to contravene the prohibitions of uncertainty (*gharar*), maysir and charging interest (*riba*). A member must have an insurable interest in the insured subject-matter in order to come within the precautionary measure principle (*sadd-al-dhara 'i'i*) and to stay clear of maysir. Insuring another person's property or life in which the member has no interest would contravene the Islamic law against interference with the affairs of another person without any justifiable legal basis.[88]

Policy against wagering under the guise of insurance

Sham transactions

Wagers under the guise of insurance are contracts that take the form of an insurance policy but on their (express) terms are indifferent as to whether or not the 'policyholder' has an insurable interest in the 'insured' subject-matter. Historically, the terms commonly used in wager policies were 'interest or no interest' or 'without further proof of interest' or 'without the benefit of salvage'. Under the MIA 1906, s.4(2)(b) such policies are deemed to be gaming or wagering contracts. If a wager policy is regarded as a sub-species of a wager contract, then the same reasons for distinguishing as between insurance contract and wager as discussed above apply. However, there is an additional dimension to wager policies on account of their true nature being concealed by giving the agreement between the parties the appearance of a contract of insurance. The preamble to the MIA 1746 records that this "concealment" appears to have provided opportunities for "pernicious practices", such as the procurement of fraudulent losses, evasion of trade restrictions and tax evasion as well as creating unfair competition. It is suggested that it remains unacceptable to wager under the guise of insurance. If the policyholder and the insurer collude in entering into a wager under the guise of insurance with a common intention to give to third parties and to the courts the appearance that their contract is a contract of insurance when their real intention is to create a wager, their transaction may be characterized as a 'sham'.[89] The "pernicious practice" in this scenario is that innocent third parties may be prejudiced as a result of the true character of the agreement being disguised and that the court (and the insurer's regulators) may be deceived.[90] Moreover, by entering into a sham transaction the insurer may be in breach of the FCA's PRIN, Principles 1, 5 and 11. It is a criminal offence

---

87 YA Azeez and AS Ishola, '*Insurable Interest in Takaful: A Theoretical Contrivance for Islamic Insurers*' (2015) 6(S3) IJEFI 109, 110.

88 Ibid., 111.

89 See definition of 'sham transactions' in *Snook v London and West Riding Investments Ltd* [1967] 2 QB 786 (CA) 802 (Diplock LJ).

90 *National Westminster Bank Plc v Rosemary Doreen Jones, Harold Delwyn Jones, Neuadd Goch Farm Limited* [2001] EWCA Civ 1541, [40–42] and [59].

to make misleading statements to the regulator(s) in purported compliance with any regulatory requirements under the FSMA regulatory regime.[91]

From the insured's perspective, there should be little incentive to 'disguise' a bet as an insurance contract given that betting contracts are no longer void and that bets can generally be placed at a relatively low cost, on short notice and with minimal documentation, in betting shops that are ubiquitous on every High Street. Payments on bets are frequently made instantly. In comparison, the insurance placement and claims processes can be cumbersome – in particular in relation to non-standard risks – and the premium costs can be comparatively high.

Loshin argues that the insurable interest requirement creates a perverse incentive for insurers to accept wager insurance since it can be exploited as an "embedded option" to invalidate the contract in the event of a claim, thereby escaping liability whilst retaining the premium.[92] The 'perverse incentive' argument does not undermine the anti-wager justification but it highlights that the law does not hold an insurer responsible for failing to consider whether the insured has an insurable interest at the time of the contract. This will be considered further in Chapter 12.

Modern variants of wagers under the guise of insurance are (some of) the STOLI schemes that were until recently prevalent in the United States. A STOLI scheme is a wagering device where the investor speculates that the insured life dies before the total amount of premium paid exceeds the death benefits payable. It is not the life insurance contract itself that is a disguised wager but instead the pre-conceived and immediate assignment of the life policy to a third party without an insurable interest made in bad faith and with the intention to circumvent the insurable interest requirement may cloak a wager. The insured/assignor and the investor/assignee collude to mislead the insurer, third parties and the public. As noted in Chapter 5, several US States have introduced anti-STOLI legislation to prohibit or restrict wager policy assignments.

Misrepresentation

If a policyholder misrepresents his lack of interest in the insured subject-matter at the pre-contractual stage, the insurer may have recourse to the remedies regimes under the CIDRA, s.4 and Schedule 1 (consumers), and the IA 2015, ss.3(1), 8 and Schedule 1 (non-consumers), respectively. Given the availability of those remedies, is a separate insurable interest requirement that, if breached, entitles the insurer to deny liability and/or treat the contract as void needed? Arguably, yes: first, if the insurer knew of the lack of insurable interest at the time of the contract, there would be no qualifying misrepresentation or qualifying breach of the duty of fair presentation and the CIDRA/IA 2015 remedies

---

91 FSMA 2000, s.398.
92 J Loshin, '*Insurance Law's Hapless Busybody: A Case against the Insurable Interest Requirement*' (2007) 117 Yale LJ 474, 494–497.

regimes would not be triggered.[93] Secondly, further to the CIDRA and the IA 2015's respective proportionate remedies regimes, the insurer's remedy is not necessarily a right to avoid but, in relation to qualifying misrepresentation and breaches that are not deliberate or reckless, are based on what the insurer would have done if the insured had complied with his pre-contractual duty.[94] If, on the available evidence, the applicable remedy is not avoidance, the CIDRA and the IA 2015 would effectively endorse the validity/enforceability of wager policies and create an inconsistency as between the CIDRA/IA 2015 remedies regimes and the statutory and common law requirements for an insurable interest. Thirdly, the CIDRA/IA 2015 remedies regimes are not triggered automatically but are available upon the election of the insurer who could instead elect to affirm the contract. An election to affirm would result in a sham transaction, as discussed above.

The risk of fraud and increased moral hazard in situations where the insured lacks an insurable interest in the insured subject-matter is discussed in Chapter 7. Subject to the application of an incontestability clause,[95] misrepresentation and non-disclosure defences may also be relevant to STOLI schemes, where the insurer asked questions in the life insurance application documentation intended to discover whether the proposer is intending to purchase the policy as part of a STOLI scheme (e.g. "Is the current intent to sell the policy in the future?" and "How are the premium payments financed?").[96] If the proposer answers truthfully and accurately, the insurer may be able to determine whether the policy is intended to be purchased in circumvention of the insurable interest requirement.

Unintentional wager policies

In some cases the requirement for, and absence of, an insurable interest may simply not have been a matter on the insured's mind at the outset, whereas the insurer may have (wrongly) assumed that the insured has an insurable interest. In those circumstances, there would be no intention of the parties to conceal the true nature of the contract, although the reasons for distinguishing as between insurance contract and wager as discussed above still apply. In addition to the contract being void for lack of insurable interest, it may be void on the grounds of common mistake.[97] The invalidity of the contract, if combined with

---

93 CIDRA, s.4(1); IA 2015, ss.3(5) and 8(1).
94 CIDRA, Schedule 1 paras 3–7; IA 2015, Schedule 1 paras 3–6.
95 Incontestability clauses are terms contained in life insurance policies that prevent the insurer from declining liability on the grounds of pre-contractual misrepresentation by the insured after a specified amount of time. They are mandatory by the insurance statutes of most US States.
96 RS Bloink, '*Catalysts for Clarification: Modern Twists on the Insurable Interest Requirement for Life Insurance*' (2010) 17 Conn Ins LJ 56, 90.
97 See Lord Phillips's criteria for common mistake in *Great Peace Shipping Ltd v Tsavliris Salvage (International) Ltd* [2002] EWCA Civ 1407, [76].

a return of premium, would provide the policyholder with an 'escape route' from a contract that is unlikely to be of value to him, since, without any interest in the insured subject-matter, he would not be able to establish a loss for which he could make a claim.

Contracts of insurance differentiated from CDS

The doctrine of insurable interest delineates insurance contracts not just from wagers but also from other financial contracts that are speculative in nature,[98] such as CDS. The widespread (ab)use of certain CDS structures leading into the Financial Crisis has highlighted a number of issues correlated to the inapplicability of the doctrine of insurable interest to CDS. These issues corroborate the continuing relevance of the anti-wagering and moral hazard justifications of the doctrine in relation to contracts of insurance.

What are CDS?

A CDS is a contract under which the credit risk associated with a third party (the 'Reference Entity') is transferred from one party (the 'Protection Buyer') to the other (the 'Protection Seller') in exchange for a fee. If a specified credit event (specified type(s) of credit deterioration) occurs in relation to the Reference Entity, the Protection Seller will either make a payment (a 'cash settlement') to the Protection Buyer that represents the difference between the market value and a reference price (often the face (par) value) of certain reference obligations or reference assets or the Protection Seller is required to buy from the Protection Buyer the reference obligations or reference assets at face (par) value (a 'physical settlement').[99] The Protection Seller may be required to provide 'collateral' to limit the Protection Buyer's counter-party risk. CDS can be used as a hedge on the credit risk of a third party (who is a counter-party of the Protection Buyer under a separate transaction so-called 'covered CDS') or for purely speculative purposes (where the Protection Buyer does not hold any debt obligations of the Reference Entity – so-called 'naked CDS'). Financial wagers that concern regulated investments fall to be treated under the FSMA regime (and not the gambling legislation).[100] CDS are specified investments under art.85(1) or (3) of the RAO so that any party dealing in CDS must be authorized,[101] unless any specific exemption applies.

---

98 LC, *Post Contract* (n 2) para 12.6.

99 S Firth, *Derivatives Law and Practice* (Sweet & Maxwell, Release 49 2019) paras 16.001, 16.004–16.006.

100 FSMA 2000, s.412; GA 2005, s.10(1); *Nextia Properties Limited v RBS* [2013] EWHC 3167 (QB) ('*Nextia*') [74] (Behrens J).

101 FSMA 2000, s.19.

CDS and insurance contracts distinguished

The Potts Opinion argues that CDS

> ... differ from contracts of insurance in the following critical respects:
> (1) The payment obligation is not conditional on the payee's sustaining a
> loss or having a risk of loss; (2) The contract is thus not one which seeks
> to protect an insurable interest on the part of the payee. His rights do not
> depend on the existence of any insurable interest ...[102]

Although some CDS transactions may have the same economic effect as insurance (covered CDS used to hedge against counter-party credit risk), the key
differences – the absence of a requirement for an insurable interest and a loss –
are crucial to the tradability of CDS.[103]

Since the Potts Opinion, CDS have been generally structured to include an
express term providing that there is no requirement for the Protection Buyer to
hold the reference asset or to suffer a loss in order to make a claim under the
instrument. The payment trigger events are defined to include developments
that do not cause any actual loss.[104] In the United States, the New York State
Insurance Department ('NYID') opined in 2000 that a CDS transaction did
not constitute a contract of insurance under New York insurance law on the
grounds that CDS transactions did not contractually indemnify for loss.[105]
A 2004 amendment to NYCIL §6901(j-1) provides that a CDS agreement does
not constitute insurance business unless it is an insurance contract. Although
tautologically phrased, this was meant to confirm that CDS were not contracts
of insurance.[106] After the Financial Crisis, the NYID suggested that covered
CDS should be regulated as insurance, but this proposal was superseded by the
(federal) Dodd-Frank Act, which regulates all types of CDS.[107] In the UK, CDS
are generally understood not to be insurance contracts on the basis of the reasoning in the Potts Opinion.[108]

The distinction is significant: first, investment banks, who are the main participants in the CDS market, do not usually have permission to carry on insurance

102 Potts Opinion (n 11) para 7.
103 P Walker-Bright and TP Law, '*AIG's Financial Distress: How Credit Default Swaps and the Lack
of Regulation Brought Down an Insurance Giant and Implications for the Insurance Industry*'
(2009) C Crit Issu Ins Law 1, 28–29.
104 2006 ISDA Definitions, definition of 'credit event'.
105 A Kimball-Stanley, '*Insurance and Credit Default Swaps: Should Like Things Be Treated Alike?*'
(2008) 15 Conn Ins LJ 242, 247.
106 A Kramer, A Harris and R Anschl, '*The New York State Insurance Department and Credit Default Swaps: Good Intentions, Bad Idea*' (2009) 22 JT Reg F Inst 29.
107 Ibid., 29, 31–33.
108 E.g. *Belmont Park Investments Pty Ltd v BNY Corporate Trustee Services Ltd* (n 10); *Nextia* (n
100); *Credit Suisse International v Stichting Vestia* Group [2014] EWCH 3103 (Comm), [76]
(Andrew Smith J).

business, whilst insurance companies are subject to the Internal-Contagion-Restriction, as well as being limited to regulated activities in relation to investments for which they have permissions.[109] There are now additional layers of regulations applicable to CDS at European level[110] and in the United States.[111] Secondly, the tax treatment differs: an insurance company's profits are subject to corporation tax under Part 3 of the Corporation Tax Act 2009 (and the insured must pay insurance premium tax on the premium), whereas profits and losses arising from a CDS transaction that meet specific tests are covered by a specific taxation regime under Part 7 of the Corporation Tax Act 2009 and their taxation follows their accounting treatment.[112] Thirdly, the accounting treatment of CDS is different to the accounting treatment of contracts of insurance: UK Financial Reporting Standard 25 (International Accounting Standard 31) applies to the former and International Financial Reporting Standard 4 applies to the latter. Fourthly, the classification as one or the other is also relevant as to whether other principles of insurance law, such as the duty of good faith and the doctrine of subrogation, and the provisions of the IA 2015, apply.[113] Fifthly, different regimes apply upon insolvency: in relation to CDS, the non-insolvent party has the right to set off any mutual claims and obligations under the CDS.[114] In contrast, if an insurance company becomes insolvent and is wound up, direct insurance debts (i.e. claims monies owed to an insurer's own policyholders) are to be paid in priority to all other unsecured debts, except staff remuneration and pensions contributions, under the Insurers (Reorganisation and Winding Up) Regulations.[115] According to the Bank for International Settlements the total notional amount of CDS at the end of 2018 amounted to US$8.143 billion.[116] Given the size of the CDS market that relies on the classification of CDS as non-insurance contracts, it is important to maintain a clear distinction, the importance of which has been noted by the insurance industry and other stakeholders.[117]

Restraining effect of insurable interest requirement

The distinction between CDS transactions and contracts of insurance came into sharp focus in the aftermath of the Financial Crisis. In September 2008,

---

109 FSMA 2000, s.20.
110 Regulation (EU) No 648/2012 of the European Parliament and of the Council of 4 July 2012 on OTC derivatives, central counterparties and trade repositories ('EMIR Regulation'); Regulation (EU) No 596/2014 of the European Parliament and of the Council of 16 April 2014 on market abuse; Directive 2014/65/EU (EU) of the European Parliament and of the Council of 15 May 2014 on markets in financial instruments (MiFID II).
111 Dodd-Frank Act, Title VII.
112 S Firth (n 99) para 9.004.
113 *Nextia* (n 98).
114 2002 ISDA Master Agreement, cl.6(e)(i) and 6(f).
115 See n 49.
116 Bank for International Settlements, '*OTC Derivatives Outstanding*' (4 June 2019).
117 Responses from the ABI, the City of London Law Society, ISDA and the LMA to LC, *Issues Paper 4* (n 8), cited in LC, '*Post Contract*' (n 2) paras 12.6–12.10.

AIG collapsed financially and had to be bailed out by the US Government to avoid a catastrophic knock-on effect on the wider financial markets as a result of AIG's size and interconnectedness with other financial institutions.[118] The principal cause of AIG's collapse was its liquidity problem as a result of the CDS transactions that AIG companies entered into as protection seller, and as an institutional investor in CDS.[119] The example of AIG has led some academics and policy analysts to argue that insurers that (directly, or indirectly through an affiliate) engage in non-traditional and non-insurance activities ('NTNI activities'), such as CDS, can contribute to 'systemic risk' – that is the "risk of disruption to financial services that is (i) caused by an impairment of all or parts of the financial system and (ii) has the potential to have serious negative consequences for the real economy"[120] – whilst insurers carrying on traditional (core) activities only do not generally generate systemic risk.[121] The argument that insurers that engage in NTNI activities are more vulnerable to systemic risk draws support from the fact that, during the Financial Crisis, NTNI insurers and insurers with NTNI affiliates were far more severely affected than insurers that carried on traditional activities as a result of their greater interconnectedness with other (banking) financial institutions and the capital markets.[122] Moreover, as the example of AIG shows, NTNI activities have tended to be complex and the financial products and risk involved were not always fully understood by all parties leading to modelling and valuation errors and unforeseen liquidity problems. Whilst some commentators have pointed out that the distinction between NTNI insurers and traditional insurers is unhelpful[123] and that the insurance industry as whole (including traditional insurers) can pose systemic risk,[124] the derivatives market and in particular CDS were identified as one of the main causes of the Financial Crisis.[125] Some of the criticisms that have been made in relation to CDS are directly relevant to the insurable interest debate:

---

118 For a history of the collapse and bail-out of AIG, see W Sjostrom Jr (n 64).

119 Ibid., 959–961; R McDonald and A Paulson, '*AIG- In Hindsight*' (2015) 29 J Econ Pers 81, 82.

120 Financial Stability Board, '*Guidance to Assess the Systemic Importance of Financial Institutions, Markets and Instruments: Initial Considerations*' (Report to G20 Finance Ministers and Governors, October 2009).

121 See e.g. The Geneva Association (The International Association for the Study of Insurance Economics), '*Systemic Risk in Insurance – An Analysis of Insurance and Financial Stability*' (March 2010) 3 and ch 3; S Harrington, '*The Financial Crisis, Systemic Risk, and the Future of Insurance Regulation*' (2009) 76 J Risk Ins 785, 786 and 794.

122 The Geneva Association (n 121), 12 and ch 3.

123 M Goldby and A Keller, 'Oversight of Systemically Relevant Insurance Practices in the EU: the Role of Macro-Prudential Supervision' in A Georgosouli and M Goldby (eds), *Systemic Risk and the Future of Insurance Regulation* (Informa 2016) ch 6.

124 D Schwarcz and S Schwarcz (n 64) Part II.

125 FSA, '*The Turner Review – A Regulatory Response to the Global Banking Crisis*' (March 2009), ch 1; The US Financial Crisis Inquiry Commission, '*The Financial Crisis Inquiry Report – Final Report of the National Commission on the Causes of the Financial and Economic Crisis in the United States*' (February 2011), ch 3, 50–51 and ch 8, 155.

Moral hazard: CDS have been criticized for allowing a creditor/Protection Buyer who holds CDS protection to exercise its creditor control rights in a way that triggers a credit event under the CDS motivated by the knowledge that the payment under the CDS would exceed its credit exposure to the Reference Entity (i.e. a net short position). This has been labelled as "empty creditor problem".[126] There is moral hazard since the Protection Buyer is incentivized to push the Reference Entity towards default or insolvency in order to trigger a pay-out under the CDS in circumstances where a restructuring of the Reference Entity could have protected its going concern value and perhaps ensured its continuing existence. As an empty creditor, the Protection Buyer may behave 'inefficiently' or act in 'value-destroying' ways because it does not have any exposure or has a minimal exposure to the Reference Entity that is significantly exceeded by its CDS protection.

An extreme example of the empty creditor problem is the (alleged) modus operandi of some so-called vulture funds (funds trading in distressed debt). Following Argentina's default on its sovereign debt in 2001, Argentina sought to restructure its debt by offering bondholders new debt instruments which would have entitled them to recover around 30% of their debt over the term of the bond. Whilst about 93% of bondholders agreed to a restructuring,[127] a small minority of bondholders, including Paul Singer's NML Capital Ltd. fund, opposed the restructuring and sued Argentina for payment of the full value of the bonds in the New York courts. NML Capital had bought the bonds heavily discounted for US$72 million in the secondary market in 2008 (after Argentina's default).[128] It has been reported,[129] and it is alleged in some of the filings in the US Court of Appeals (Second Circuit, New York),[130] that NML Capital or its affiliates also bought a large amount of CDS protection against another Argentine default and that, by declining the restructured bond offer and pursuing litigation to obtain payment in full, NML Capital was pursuing a strategy of triggering such a default event under the CDS contracts. Subsequently, Argentina did in fact default as a result of the New York court ruling that no payment could be made to the bondholders who had agreed to the restructuring without a concurrent payment at full face value to the bondholders not taking part in the restructuring.[131] This was determined to constitute a 'selective default' under

---

126 HTC Hu and B Black, '*Debt, Equity and Hybrid Decoupling: Governance and Empty Voting II: Importance and Extension*' (2008) 156 U Penn L Rev 625; Part V; HTC Hu and B Black, '*Debt, Equity and Hybrid Decoupling: Governance and Systemic Risk Implications*' (2008) 14 Eur F Man 663.

127 Rupert Neate, '*Argentina Appeals against US Hedge Fund Ruling*' The Guardian (27 November 2012).

128 Letter from Cleary Gottlieb Steen and Hamilton LLP (Argentina's lawyers) to the Clerk of the US States Court of Appeals for the Second Circuit (29 March 2013) fn 6.

129 C Russo, '*Singer Denial Failing to Quell Win-Win Charge: Argentina Credit*' Bloomberg (11 April 2013); F Salmon, '*Elliott vs Argentina: Enter the Crazy*' Reuters (US edition, 27 August 2013).

130 Letter from Cleary Gottlieb (n 127) fn 8.

131 The original order of the District Court (Southern District of New York) dated 7 December 2011 was affirmed by the US Court of Appeals in *NML Capital, Ltd. v. Republic of Argentina*, 699 F.3d 246 (2d Cir. 2012).

the Argentine bonds CDS and was reported to have triggered payments of US$1 billion under those CDS.[132]

Equally controversially, an empty creditor or naked CDS Protection Buyer can seek to accelerate the occurrence of a credit event by (financially) incentivizing the Reference Entity to intentionally default under the reference obligations. This has been labelled a "manufactured credit event".[133] The moral hazard in this scenario is that the Protection Buyer brings about –manufactures – the trigger for a pay-out under the CDS. Naked or empty creditor Protection Buyers can act in "value-destroying" ways because they do not have any exposure or a minimal exposure to the Reference Entity that is significantly exceeded by its CDS protection. These opportunistic strategies may also "raise various issues under securities, derivatives, conduct and antifraud laws, as well as public policy concerns".[134]

The Hovnanian Enterprise, Inc, restructuring is a recent example of a (potential) manufactured loss.[135] Hovnanian was not a company in financial distress but sought to restructure some of its debt. In 2018, Hovnanian agreed to a debt refinancing deal with hedge fund GSO on below-market terms in exchange for Hovnanian deliberately defaulting on an interest payment of just over $1m on certain notes held by its affiliate Sunrise on the following interest payment date in May 2018 (a payment which Hovnanian was easily in a position to make). GSO hoped that this manufactured default would trigger a credit event under a $600m worth of CDS (with Hovnanian as the Reference Entity), which it had started to buy from Solus in 2016. Solus sued GSO for market manipulation seeking an injunction in advance of the planned credit event, but the case was eventually settled for an undisclosed amount and GSO's undertaking not to cause Hovnanian to trigger a credit event.

Despite the reporting obligations under EMIR Regulation in the EU and the Dodd-Frank Act in the United States, Hovnanian is not an isolated incident,[136] and there has been growing concern about manufactured credit events in the CDS market, culminating in a Joint Statement by the US Commodities and Futures Trading Commission, the US Securities and Exchange Commission and the FCA in June 2019 announcing that these agencies will make collaborative efforts to address these concerns.[137] ISDA has now published a 'Narrowly Tailored Credit Events Protocol' to its 2014 Definitions, which requires that the failure to pay triggering a credit event is the result of the credit deterioration of the

---

132 A Moses, C Russo and K Porzecanski, '*Argentine Bonds Decline as Default Triggers $1 Billion of Swaps*' Bloomberg (2 August 2014).

133 See US CFTC Chairman J. Christopher Giancarlo, US SEC Chairman Jay Clayton, and (UK) FCA Chief Executive Andrew Bailey, '*Joint Statement on Opportunistic Strategies in the Credit Derivative Markets*' (24 June 2019).

134 Ibid.

135 For the background facts see the court filings for *Solus Alternative Asset Management LP v. GSO Capital Partners L.P.*, No. 18 CV 232-LTS-BCM (SDNY January 29, 2018).

136 Other reported cases of (alleged) manufactured defaults are restructuring transactions relating to Codere SA, iHeart Communications Inc and Windstream Serviced LLC.

137 See n 133.

Reference Entity.[138] The US bond market has responded by making changes to the standard definition of "Event of Default" in the indenture documentation. Greater transparency might lead towards price adjustments that make excessive CDS positions unattractive and it might flag up abuses such as those alleged against the Paul Singer funds.

The empty creditor problem and manufactured credit events are directly related to the characteristic of CDS that the Protection Buyer is not required to have an insurable interest commensurate with the CDS protection. If the protection against the credit risk were in the form of a contract of insurance – that is, credit risk insurance or non-payment insurance – the creditor's insurable interest would be limited to the amount of the principal and interest due over the lifetime of the debt instrument. The indemnity principle would prevent the recovery of any amount exceeding the repayment value of its credit exposure. The moral hazard justification for insurable interest will be analysed in more detail in Chapter 7.

Devaluation: There has been a debate on whether the practice of taking short positions on CDS on sovereign debt may have exacerbated the European sovereign debt crisis that started in 2009. Shorting a CDS is a practice that entails the purchase of a 'naked' CDS, where the Protection Buyer has no underlying exposure to the reference entities or reference assets, allowing such Protection Buyers to 'bet' on the default of the underlying reference entity or asset. It has been argued that 'shorting' can have adverse consequences on sovereign bond prices, pushing them into a downwards spiral and can thus significantly raise the costs of sovereign debt.[139] In response to the (perceived) problem, short selling of certain financial securities and naked CDS on sovereign debt was banned within the European Union under the Short Selling Regulations.[140] Similar emergency measures were adopted in the United States and Japan.[141]

Is it conceivable that multiple insurance policies taken out by policyholders without, or with insufficient, insurable interest could devalue the insured subject-matter? Multiple insurance on the same property might indicate that the property is perceived to be 'at risk' and this market perception could, hypothetically, decrease investor confidence, which could depress its market value. By analogy, the late-18th-century practice of wagering on the lives of other people (in whose lives the wagerers had no interest) was thought at the time to 'devalue' the 'insured' life by hastening the death of that person:

---

138 ISDA, '2019 NTCE Protocol' (August 2019).

139 H-W Sinn, *Casino Capitalism* (OUP 2010), ch 2 and 7; G Soros, '*One Way to Stop Bear Raids*' Wall Str J (24 March 2009). However, note that other commentators have argued that there is no empirical evidence that naked sovereign CDS had an impact on pricing in the sovereign bond market (see e.g. International Monetary Fund, 'Global Financial Stability Report' (April 2013).

140 Regulation (EU) No 236/2012 of the European Parliament and of the Council of 14 March 2012 on short selling and certain aspects of CDS.

141 Ibid., Recital 1.

This inhuman sport [insuring the life of (well-known) person] affected the minds of men depressed by long illness; for when such persons, casting an eye over a newspaper for amusement, saw their lives had been insured … they despaired of all hope, and thus their dissolution was hastened.[142]

Whilst this is not empirical evidence, arguably, there is something "mischievous"[143] and morally distasteful[144] in insuring someone else's life in which the policyholder has no interest. It widens the circle of persons that would benefit from the demise of the insured life. From the perspective of the owner of property that has been 'insured' by third parties without interest, the fact that such policies are in place may be worrying but it is suggested that the underlying concern goes back to 'moral hazard' (considered in Chapter 7) which increases as more policyholders without an insurable interest would stand to benefit from the loss or damage of the insured property.

Welfare-reduction and social cost: In addition to 'moral hazard', some commentators have expressed more general moral and societal concerns about CDS. Giving evidence to the House of Lords Select Committee on the Short Selling Regulations, the journalist and civil servant John Chapman denounced "the lack of morality in betting through short sales or CDS on the decline or even downfall of a company or country".[145] The argument that naked CDS transactions are immoral is not based upon moral objections to betting or gambling as such but on a perception that it is wrong to make a profit from speculating on the failure of a company or the financial ruin of a country. Professor Sinn has coined the term "casino capitalism" for financial institutions engaging in financial gambling, "privatizing profits" whilst "socializing [externalising] losses".[146] He argues that (pre-Financial Crisis) financial institutions took excessive risks whilst keeping minimal capital transacting in financial instruments such as CDS. In the short term, this allowed those institutions to maximize profits for distribution to shareholders. However, when losses materialized, the limited liability corporate status of those institutions, and the systemic importance of some of them, meant that losses were borne by unpaid creditors or, in the case of government bailouts, the taxpayer. According to Sinn, financial bets such as CDS attract moral opprobrium because they carry a cost to society.[147] Banks and other financial institutions can incur losses as result of their financial gambling that will exceed their capital reserves and may result in losses to depositors and other creditors,

---

142 T Mortimer, *'Every Man His Own Broker'* (London, WJ & J Richardson 1801) quoted in J Lowry and P Rawlings, *Insurance Law: Cases and Materials* (Hart Publishing 2004), 315 [701]; also see R Merkin, *'Gambling by Insurance – A Study of the Life Assurance Act 1774'* (1980) 9 Anglo-Am L R 331, 332.
143 LAA 1774, Preamble.
144 See n 37 and 38.
145 EU Economic and Financial Affairs and International Trade Sub-Committee, *Credit Default Swaps and Short Selling: Written Evidence* (HL 2010/2011 session).
146 H-W Sinn (n 139) ch 4.
147 See also EA Posner and EG Weyl (n 15) 1314.

and in the event of state guarantees or bail-outs, in additional costs to taxpayers. In contrast, insurance contracts are generally regarded as fulfilling a useful social function – namely to transfer or distribute risk, thereby mitigating the parties' aggregate exposure to risk resulting in an overall social gain.[148] Posner and Weyl argue that an insurable interest test can differentiate between socially beneficial insurance contracts and welfare-reducing (financial) gambling contracts[149] since an insurable interest in the insured subject-matter indicates that a risk transfer takes place, whereas the absence of an interest in the subject-matter is indicative of the wagering nature of the contract. They also propose that a quasi-insurable interest test could be applied to CDS to distinguish between covered CDS and naked CDS. In their opinion, naked CDS fall into the category of welfare-reducing gambling contracts, which increase the parties' aggregate risk exposure since one party will gain at the expense of the other. A naked CDS exposes each party to a greater risk than they were exposed to immediately prior to the conclusion of the contract and may produce negative externalities. A quasi-insurable interest test has been introduced by the Short Selling Regulations in relation to sovereign CDS, which restricts naked sovereign CDS (i.e. CDS that do not hedge against the risk of default of the underlying sovereign debt(or)).[150]

Multiple exposure: The US Financial Crisis Inquiry Commission found that CDS transactions in relation to US sub-prime mortgage collateralized debt obligations contributed to the Financial Crisis since they provided a mechanism for multiple bets to be placed on the performance of the same referenced pools of mortgage loans, regardless of whether or not the Protection Buyer had a credit exposure to any of the underlying mortgage loans.[151] Rather than spreading risk of default of the underlying mortgage loans, this led to a concentration of risk inflating the losses of Protection Sellers and thereby multiplied exponentially the effect of the collapse of the US sub-prime mortgage market. It is for that reason that George Soros has described CDS as "toxic".[152] In contrast, in contracts of insurance the multiple exposure risk is minimized by insisting upon an insurable interest in the insured subject-matter which ensures that the classes of persons eligible to insure a single risk remain limited, predictable and transparent and any pay-outs are limited to each insured's loss suffered in respect of his insurable interest.

The foregoing discussion illustrates that not only does the doctrine of insurable interest delineate insurance contracts from CDS for the purposes of contract classification but the doctrine's inapplicability to CDS also highlights the negative implication which the absence of an interest can have: the moral hazard

---

148 See above.
149 EA Posner and EG Weyl (n 15) 1307–1311, 1344–1350.
150 Articles 14 and 4.
151 The US Financial Crisis Inquiry Commission (n 125) ch 3, 7–8, in particular 142–146. The FCIC heard witness evidence that a significant portion of the total outstanding value of CDS of $58.2 trillion at the end of 2007 were speculative or naked CDS transactions.
152 G Soros (n 139).

associated with the empty creditor and manufactured credit event scenarios, the potential devaluing effect on the underlying asset, the potential social cost of gambling by financial institutions and the (inadvertent) creation of multiple exposure risk, catastrophe or correlated risk endangering the financial stability of financial institutions. Considering that a contract of insurance devoid of an insurable interest requirement would be very similar in form and effect to a CDS, it is at least arguable that insurance contracts without an insurable interest requirement would be susceptible to the same risks. Far from being an out-dated concept, an insurable interest requirement is a mechanism that "reinforces market discipline"[153] and restrains the insurance industry from overly specula-tive transactions. The LC expressly noted that restraining effect, so that "there would appear to be merit in retaining the requirement of insurable interest".[154] The recent history of CDS is a warning example of the potential consequences of abolishing the requirement for an insurable interest in insurance contracts.

The anti-wagering justification and the definition of insurable interest

Thus far it has been argued that the doctrine of insurable interest operates as a doctrinal dividing line between insurance contracts and other types of con-tracts. A separate question is whether, in relation to property insurance, the anti-wagering justification compels a narrow (legal interest test) definition of insurable interest or whether it would equally support a doctrine of insurable interest with a wide (factual expectation test) definition. A doctrine of insurable interest with a wide definition that allows economic interests should, prima facie, serve equally as well as a narrowly defined doctrine to differentiate contracts of insurance from wagers since wagers are characterized by neither of the contract-ing parties being required to have any interest in that contract other than the sum or stake. Similarly, the distinction between insurance contracts and CDS could be maintained as CDS are characterized by the Protection Buyer not being required to have an insurable interest or to have suffered any loss. According to Hartnett and Thompson, the dichotomy between (welfare-enhancing) contracts of insurance and (welfare-reducing) wagers is maintained, and the anti-wagering justification remains satisfied, if the insured has "some valuable relationship" to the property "which equals the pecuniary value of the insurance, regardless of the legal nature of that relationship".[155]

Nevertheless, it is tentatively suggested that an insurable interest based on an economic interest could blur the distinction between insurance contracts and other types of speculative contracts. Parties to financial contracts designed to speculate on, or hedge, financial risks (such as CDS) in their capacity as

---

153 LC, *Post Contract* (n 2) para 12.15.
154 Ibid.
155 (n 15) 433.

participants in the international financial markets may have some incidental or indirect market exposure to the reference entity or reference obligation that is the subject-matter of the contract. Consultees have expressed their concerns to the LC that the mere presence of such incidental interests might qualify as an insurable interest under the widened definition previously proposed by the LC and thus obscure the dividing line between contracts of insurance and derivative contracts.[156] Ince & Co note:

> Some members of the (re)insurance industry are already wary about the convergence of the (re)insurance industry and capital markets and the proposed reforms [to widen the definition of insurable interest to include economic interests] would facilitate the further erosion of boundaries between the two.[157]

Conversely, an insured with no more than an expectation of a bare economic loss has a minimal 'stake' in the insured property that is purely financial and merely anticipated. Rather than indemnifying the insured for something he has lost, such an insurance contract would position the insured so that, on the occurrence of the specified event, he would be able to claim for a future economic profit, that he might have or might not have made, thereby converting an expectation of a future profit into a present benefit and legally enforceable right. The more speculative the interest in the subject-matter of the contract is, the less risk transfer there will be and the more the contract will resemble a wager. Thomas notes that a "pecuniary [= economic] interest is not a stable and certain factual state ... This difficulty renders the test uncertain ... and does not result in a clearly drawn boundary".[158] American case law indicates that not all economic interests constitute an insurable interest.[159]

Considering the wide spectrum of economic interests, it is arguable that interests that are at the weak, incidental and speculative end of that spectrum would not necessarily be a convincing demarcator that differentiates contracts of insurance from wagers and CDS. Moreover, at that end of the spectrum, the multiple exposure risk and moral hazard risk noted in relation to wagers and CDS would start to materialize. It is accepted that the distinction between contracts of insurance and wagers can generally be maintained with a doctrine of insurable interest that includes economic interests based on a factual expectation test, but the policies behind the anti-wagering justification can be better served with a narrow meaning of insurable interest.

---

156 LC, '*Summary of Responses to Issues Paper 10: Insurable Interest*' (April 2016) para 2.53.
157 Ince & Co, '*Blurred Lines: The Impact of the LC's Proposals on Insurable Interest on Parametric Policies*' (July 2016).
158 D Rhidian Thomas, 'Insurable Interest – Accelerating the Liberal Spirit' in D Rhidian Thomas (ed), *Marine Insurance: The Law in Transition* (Informa 2006) para 2.69.
159 See Chapter 5.

A clear dividing line remains relevant since different governmental policies, regulatory and tax regimes apply to contracts of insurance and different kinds of wager contracts and financial contracts of speculation such as CDS. The FSMA regulatory framework limits the extent to which insurers can engage in 'gambling' in order to protect policyholders' and the insurers' financial stability by restricting insurers from carrying on non-insurance business, by requiring insurers to hold capital resources and from investing their assets imprudently. Wagering under the guise of insurance is contrary to fair and open dealings as between the parties to the contract as well as other market participants, courts and regulators. The case study of CDS has highlighted a number of negative implications to which insurance contracts without an insurable interest could become susceptible: the moral hazard associated with the empty creditor and the manufactured credit event scenarios, the potential devaluing effect on the underlying asset, the potential social cost of gambling by financial institutions and the (inadvertent) creation of multiple exposure risk endangering the financial stability of financial institutions. The anti-wagering justification for the doctrine of insurable interest is not obsolete, although its focus has shifted from moral concerns about gambling by individuals to the potential effect of gambling on the financial stability of insurers.

7   The moral hazard justification

The moral hazard justification for the doctrine of insurable interest derives from the idea that an insured without any interest would stand to benefit from the destruction of, or damage to, the insured subject-matter without any personal loss or detriment which, in turn, might tempt him to bring about its destruction in order to gain the benefit of insurance. This Chapter examines the criticisms of the moral hazard justification drawing on empirical data, doctrinal legal analysis and case studies. In relation to property insurance, it will be argued that the relationship between insurable interest and moral hazard can be better understood if insurable interest is seen as a mechanism for aligning the interests of the insured and the insurer in keeping the insured subject-matter safe. The example of the US STOLI schemes highlights that moral hazard is a real concern in life insurance.

Historical background and economic analysis

In *Sadlers' Company v Badcock* Lord Hardwicke summarized the moral hazard issue as follows: "...if any person may insure, whether he has property or not, it may be a temptation to burn houses, to receive the benefit of the policy", and "... the temptation to [destroy ships] has arisen from interest and no interest inserted in policies".[1] Similarly, it was thought that insuring the life of another person in whose life the insured had no interest could lead to the temptation to kill that person.[2] From the Preamble of the MIA 1746 it is clear that one of the main mischiefs the Act sought to address was the deliberate destruction of insured ships and cargo by insureds without any interest:

> ... the making of assurances, interest or no interest, or without further proof of interest than the policy, hath been productive of many pernicious practices, whereby a *great number of ships, with their cargoes, have either been fraudulently lost and destroyed* ...

> (Emphasis added)

---

1 (1743) 2 Atk 554 (Ch) 556.
2 R Merkin, '*Gambling by Insurance – A Study of the Life Assurance Act 1774*' (1980) 9 Anglo-Am L R 331, 331–333.

Conversely, by limiting the application of s.1 of the MIA 1746 to British vessels and cargo, Parliament pursued a strategy of encouraging moral hazard in relation to foreign vessels: permitting wager policies on foreign vessels would encourage fraud and aggression against enemy ships as it would make such ships, if insured against capture by British subjects, attractive targets for 'friendly' British privateers.[3]

Traditionally, the moral hazard justification has focussed on the deterrent effect of the doctrine of insurable interest – that is, that the existence of an insurable interest should discourage the insured from the deliberate destruction of insured property. The underlying explanation is that an insured without any interest in the insured property has no personal stake in the insured subject-matter and, accordingly, would not suffer any detriment, but gain, from its destruction. In contrast, an insured with an insurable interest in the insured subject-matter would suffer a disadvantage if the insured subject-matter is lost or destroyed. As under a contract of indemnity insurance, a claims payment is merely compensating the insured to the extent of his indemnifiable loss, he would not gain from the destruction of the insured subject-matter and, in practice, may even remain 'undercompensated'.[4] Excluding other incentives or motives, it is not to the rational insured's advantage to bring about the destruction of the insured property since the costs are at best equal the benefits from making a claim.

In life insurance, any moral hazard arising from the temptation to kill for the purpose of obtaining the policy proceeds is considered to be outweighed by an insurable interest:

1   in the insured's own life as he or she is unlikely to commit suicide "to gain a Pyrrhic victory by his own death"[5];
2   based on close familial ties between the insured and the life insured since the presumed "affection and mutual assistance"[6] between them make it likely that the insured would wish for the insured life to continue; and
3   based on a pecuniary interest in the insured life continuing.

Insurers rely on the doctrine of insurable interest to reduce the moral hazard element in their underwriting.[7]

The moral hazard justification can also be explained in microeconomic terms. The paradigm contract is assumed to be 'efficient': absent externalities,

3 AB Leonard, '*Underwriting Marine Warfare: Insurance and Conflict in the Eighteenth Century*' (2013) 15 Int JMH 173, 183.
4 See Chapter 8.
5 *Griffith v Fleming* [1909] 1 KB 805 (CA) 815, 821 (Vaughan Williams LJ). There are cases of suicide for the purposes of bestowing policy benefits on the estate of the insured. They are counter-acted by provisions which define a time period (typically two years) running from the inception of the policy in which, if a suicide is committed, a pay-out will not be made.
6 *Griffith v Fleming* (n 5) 823 (Kennedy LJ).
7 LC, '*Insurance Contract Law: Post Contract Duties and Other Issues*' (Law Com CP No 201, December 2011) para 12.13.

rational parties operating in a competitive market will enter into contracts to maximize their joint self-interest and will thereby also increase overall social welfare.[8] This efficiency can be impaired by a party's (hidden) strategic behaviour and informational asymmetries.[9] In the absence of any interest in the insured subject-matter, an insured might be incentivized to bring about a loss of the insured subject-matter to obtain a claims payment. A contract of insurance lacking insurable interest can give rise to negative externalities: first, assuming the insurer is unaware of the lack of interest, the additional moral hazard risk has not been priced into the premium. The cost of the moral hazard risk will be externalized onto the insurer's relevant pool of insureds. As a result, the pool cross-subsidizes the insured without interest.[10] Secondly, even if, following full disclosure of the lack of interest, an insurer would be prepared to underwrite the risk (for an increased premium), any third party who owns the insured property (or has another kind of insurable interest therein) – the 'TP' – and who is not a party to the insurance contract would be exposed to an increased risk of loss or damage to that property on account of the moral hazard risk.[11] Similarly, a TP whose life is insured faces an increased risk of being murdered. That risk represents a cost to the TP for which it is not compensated.[12] Absent any actual damage to the insured property, the TP is unlikely to have a cause of action in tort: the torts of trespass to goods and trespass to land require an unpermitted physical contact between the third party and the property; and the tort of nuisance only applies to land and if the tort victim can prove special damages arising from the unpermitted interference with his ownership rights. Making a threat to kill, contrary to s.16 of the Offences against the Person Act 1861, is a criminal offence but requires for the threat to be conveyed to the victim (i.e. the life insured). In economic theory, the doctrine of insurable interest can therefore be explained as a mandatory legal rule to counteract moral hazard and its consequences (impaired contract efficiency and negative externalities).[13]

Criticisms

The moral hazard justification for the doctrine of insurable interest is frequently dismissed as 'unsupported by evidence'.

---

8 R Avraham, '*The Economics of Insurance Law – A Primer*' (2012) 19 Conn Ins LJ 29, 42.
9 Ibid., Part II.
10 Ibid., 66.
11 T Baker and KD Logue, 'Mandatory Rules and Default Rules in Insurance Contracts' in D Schwarcz and P Siegelman (eds), *Research Handbook on the Economics of Insurance Law* (Edward Elgar Publishing 2015) 396.
12 J Loshin, '*Insurance Law's Hapless Busybody: A Case against the Insurable Interest Requirement*' (2007) 117 Yale LJ 474, at 481.
13 R Avraham (n 8) 76–78; T Baker and KD Logue (n 13) 396–397.

Doubtful deterrent effect

Several commentators query whether having an insurable interest in the insured subject-matter does in fact deter an insured from bringing about a loss in order to obtain the claims payments from his insurer.[14] What evidence is there to prove or disprove the deterrent effect of an insurable interest? In 2017, the annual cost of detected insurance claim frauds was estimated at £1.3 billion,[15] and undetected insurance fraud has been estimated to be at a similar level.[16] These numbers are totals for all types of insurance fraud. There appears to be no publicly available sub-set of data on the annual number, or monetary value, of fraudulent claims that involve the deliberate destruction of insured property, or the murder of insured lives, by the insured.[17] The doctrine of insurable interest makes no claim to be capable of deterring all kinds of insurance fraud, such as pre-contractual fraudulent misrepresentation, exaggerated or fictitious claims and 'cash for crash' scams by third parties.

Some empirical research on the deterrent effect of insurable interest in relation to life insurance has been carried out by Professor Davey.[18] He collated and analysed homicide statistics[19] that show that:

1   the largest category of those who committed murder for financial gain is spouses (37.5%);
2   of 69 cases that represented murder/murder-related offences in which obtaining life insurance monies was raised as evidence of a motive by the Prosecution, 41 (69.49%) were committed by a spouse and a further 3 cases (5.1%) included a spouse amongst a group of offenders; and
3   in the majority of cases, life insurance policies were purchased in good faith and without premeditation long before the intent to murder the insured life formed.

---

14 B Hartnett and JV Thornton, '*Insurable Interest in Property – A Socio-Economic Reevaluation of a Legal Concept*' (1949) Ins LJ 420; 433; Malcolm Clarke, *The Law of Insurance Contracts* (Service Issue 37, Informa 2016) para 4-2A; Robert Merkin, *Colinvaux's Law of Insurance* (12th edn, Sweet & Maxwell 2019) para 4-002; James Davey, '*The Reform of Gambling and the Future of Insurance Law*' (2004) 24 LS 507, 513–514. See also: *Kosmopoulos* (1987) 1 SCR 2 [37] (Wilson J).

15 ABI, '*One Scam Every Minute – ABI Reveals the True Extent of Insurance Fraud in the UK*' (22 August 2018).

16 ABI, '*Fraud Statistics*' (2016).

17 No such data is available from the Insurance Fraud Bureau's website <https://www.insurancefraudbureau.org>. The ABI confirmed that it does not hold such data.

18 J Davey, '*Dial M for Moral Hazard? Incentives to Murder and the Life Assurance Act 1774*' (2014) 25 ILJ 120.

19 Davey's statistics come from the Home Office's Homicide Index for the years 1997/98 to 2009/10 and "specific tables provided [to him] by the Government Statistics Inspectorate" – see J Davey (n 18) 132–133.

Given that a person has an insurable interest in the life of his or her spouse, Davey concluded that "[c]learly, the insurable interest rule does not prevent murder".[20] Whilst this is a compelling argument, a number of observations can be made on Davey's conclusion and its transferability, mutatis mutandis, to property insurance: first, the 1880s burial club murders by the 'Black Widows' of Liverpool is a historical example of homicides motivated by financial gain from the proceeds of life insurance unsupported by an insurable interest – an example that lives on in the collective memory of the insurance industry.[21] There are examples from both sides of the Atlantic illustrating the moral hazard inherent in life insurance where the insured does not have an insurable interest: *Wainwright v Bland*[22] (insured suspected of poisoning sister-in-law, on whose life he had purchased life insurance shortly before) and *Liberty Nat. Life Ins. Co. v Weldon*[23] (insured poisoned her two-year-old niece, on whose life she had purchased life insurance shortly before).

Secondly, the moral hazard justification does not claim that the existence of an insurable interest rules out completely the murder of an insured life (or the destruction of insured property). More modestly, it is said that the absence of an insurable interest can tempt an insured to bring about the loss in order to gain financially, whereas the presence of an insurable interest minimizes the incentive to do so. The unavailability of life insurance to persons without an insurable interest in the life insured means that such persons cannot be incentivized to murder the life insured for the insurance proceeds. A recent news report illustrates this point: a couple living in London are facing calls to be extradited to India over allegations that they arranged for the murder of their adopted son in India in order to claim the insurance proceeds under an Indian law-governed life insurance policy they had taken out on their adopted son's life for that purpose.[24] The insurer declined to pay out – presumably on the basis of an Indian law equivalent to the forfeiture rule[25] – but declining liability did not save the boy's life. In contrast, had English law applied, and the application for life insurance on an adopted son's life had been declined for lack of insurable interest, the couple would most likely not have proceeded with his murder.

The moral hazard justification cannot address any other reasons or motives of the insured. There may be a number of operative factors that might tempt, or deter, the insured from destroying the insured subject-matter that outweigh or overshadow the presence or absence of an insurable interest. Modern deterrence

---

20 J Davey (n 18) 135.
21 G Anderson and G Clark, '*Capturing Uncertainty: The Role of Insurance in the Construction of Modern Life*' (2007) 96 Zeitschrift für die gesamte Versicherungswissenschaft 129, 139.
22 (1835) 1 M & Rob 481.
23 267 Ala. 171,100 So.2d 696.
24 BBC, '*London Couple Accused over Adopted Son's Murder in India*' (16 October 2019).
25 The 'forfeiture rule' means the rule of public policy which in certain circumstances precludes a person who has unlawfully killed another from acquiring a benefit in consequence of the killing (Forfeiture Act 1982, s.1(1)).

theory in criminal law recognizes that, rather than just being deterred by the legal consequences of criminal conduct, decision-makers may base their decision to commit or refrain from committing an offence on a wide range of factors and their subjective perception of their relative importance.[26] Viewed in this light, the existence of an insurable interest is a factor but not a conclusive or all-overriding one in deterring the destruction of the insured subject-matter.

Thirdly, the statistics on spousal homicide are not directly translatable into proof that an *actual* insurable interest has no deterrent effect in relation to property insurance, since the law *presumes* that spouses possess an unlimited insurable interest in their respective lives "founded on affection and mutual assistance",[27] but no actual interest is required. Arguably, an insured who purchases a life insurance policy on the life of his or her spouse with the intent of murdering the spouse in order to obtain the policy proceeds may have a presumed insurable interest but could hardly be said to have an actual interest based on affection for his or her spouse. In contrast, there is no concept of a presumed insurable interest in property insurance – an actual interest, or an expectation of acquiring one, is required at the outset, and an actual insurable interest must exist at the time of the loss.

Davey and others argue that in life insurance, where an insurable interest in life is only required to exist at the time the contract is made,[28] any deterrent effect of an insurable interest may be lost during the term of the contract if the insured subsequently ceases to have an insurable interest. Thus, an insured who insures the life of her spouse might subsequently divorce yet still have a valid life policy.[29] Nor does the subsequent discharge of a debt render void a life policy purchased by a creditor upon the life of his debtor. This is a flaw in the insurable interest requirement in life insurance which is inconsistent with the moral hazard justification, although there is the practical consideration that insurers and courts cannot easily examine the true level of affection and the amortization of debts periodically after the inception of a life policy and therefore testing for insurable interest at the start is a "cost-effective solution".[30]

Fourthly, Davey acknowledges that the cases where a life insurance policy was bought by an insured with an insurable interest and with the intention of murdering the life insured to benefit from the insurance proceeds are very rare: only 19 cases over a period of 16 years (from 1985 to August 2011) in England and Wales.[31] To put this in context, there were 726 homicides recorded by the

---

26 PH Robinson and JM Darley, '*Does Criminal Law Deter? A Behavioural Science Investigation*' 24 (2004) OJLS 173, 184.
27 *Griffith v Fleming* (n 5) 823 (Kennedy LJ).
28 *Dalby v The India and London Life Assurance Company* (1854) 15 CB 365 (ExchCham).
29 In most US federal jurisdictions a divorce ordinarily terminates the insurable interest of the spouse (see RH Jerry II and DR Richmond, *Understanding Insurance Law* (5th edn, LexisNexis 2012) 277).
30 J Davey (n 18) 125. Davey criticizes that is as "cheap solution to a problem, that is imagined, but not understood".
31 Ibid., 137.

Table 7.1 Offences currently recorded as homicide in furtherance of theft or gain by relationship of victim to principal suspect, 2005/06–2017/18 in England and Wales[a]

	2005/ 06	2006/ 07	2007/ 08	2008/ 09	2009/ 10	2010/ 11	2011/ 12	2012/ 13	2013/ 14	2014/ 15	2015/ 16	2016/ 17	2017/ 18
Known	17	13	16	20	15	10	16	13	14	9	16	12	21
Not known	25	20	40	25	23	22	25	16	24	12	8	15	26

a   Office for National Statistics (n 32) Appendix Table 10a.

police in the year ending March 2019 in England and Wales.[32] Moreover, any empirical evidence of the deterrent effect of the doctrine of insurable interest is incomplete without any data on how many people would, if they could, take out life insurance on another person in whose life they have no insurable interest and would then be tempted to bring about the death of that person for the purpose of obtaining the policy proceeds. Although that data is unavailable, the statistics show that fewer homicides are committed for financial gain[33] where the suspect/perpetrator is known to the victim than where the suspect/perpetrator is unknown to the victim:

An inference to be drawn from these statistics is that people are more reluctant to kill for financial gain if they have some kind of pre-existing relationship with the victim. This in turn lends some tentative support to the contention that the presumed insurable interest said to exist in a spouse's life operates to reduce the insured's temptation to murder his or her spouse to obtain the life insurance policy proceeds. This hypothesis echoes Merkin's assessment that

> [i]t would, of course, be wrong to assume that requiring interest can prevent all murders ... Nevertheless, so long as some murders can be prevented by requiring interest, the law should so require.[34]

Fifthly, the homicide statistics do not prove or disprove that, in relation to property insurance, an insurable interest in the insured subject-matter is capable of deterring an insured from bringing about a loss in order to obtain the claims payments from his insurer. The absence of any data corroborating or disproving the doctrine of insurable interest's deterrent effect in relation to property insurance has already been noted. Basic probability theory would suggest that the greater the number of policyholders without an insurable interest insuring a specific property, the greater the circle of people who might benefit from its destruction without suffering any (significant) prejudice from its loss, and the greater the likelihood that one or more of them might be tempted to act to bring about the destruction of the insured property.

32 Office for National Statistics, '*Homicide in England and Wales: Year Ending March 2018*' (7 February 2019), Appendix Table 1.
33 'Financial gain' refers to any homicide that was primarily money-motivated.
34 R Merkin (n 2) 333.

Finally, the deterrent effect of laws has been challenged more broadly. Behavioural science studies have shown that the criminal law does not generally have a deterrent effect since potential offenders often do not know the legal rules and, even if they do, that knowledge may not influence their decision-making process.[35] The deterrent effect of tort law has been questioned on the same basis, as well as on the grounds that the chance of being held liable in tort is perceived to be low and often mitigated by liability insurance.[36] Applying the same reasoning to insurance law, it could be argued that any deterrent effect of the doctrine of insurable interest is undermined by that (1) most insureds do not have any knowledge of the doctrine, and (2) there are no sanctions for lack of insurable interest unless the point is raised by insurers and successfully litigated in court. Whilst it may be in the interest of the insurer to raise the lack of an insurable interest as a defence to a claim, neither the current law nor the IIB imposes any duty on the insurer to consider the insured's interest at the pre-contractual stage. This 'enforcement' defect will be considered further in Chapter 12.

In summary, a lack of an insurable interest can create the specific moral hazard that the insured would be positioned to benefit from the destruction of the insured property/life. Whilst the existence of an insurable interest should tend to reduce the moral hazard risk, there can be other factors at play in the "moral hazard calculus"[37] which override its deterrent effect.

Conducive effect

Some commentators argue that the presence of an insurable interest can in fact have the opposite effect for three reasons: first, an insured with an insurable interest "has intimate access to [the insured property] and is in a position to destroy it without detection"[38] (the 'opportunity argument'). Secondly, an insured with an insurable interest may have reason to destroy the insured property "to convert an asset, which is difficult to sell on a depressed market, into ready cash"[39] (the 'cash conversion argument'). Thirdly, an insured with an insurable interest may seek to profit by deliberately destroying the insured property "in situations in which insured property has been overvalued, and in the context of marine insurance where the value of the insured subject-matter is taken at the date of the policy and not at the time immediately prior to the loss"[40] (the 'profit argument').

The *opportunity argument* on its own is weak: without any other motive or incentive, it would be irrational behaviour for an insured to destroy the insured

---

35 PH Robinson and JM Darley (n 26) 173.
36 WJ Cardi, RD Penfield and AH Yoon, '*Does Tort Law Deter Individuals? A Behavioral Science Study*' (2012) 9 J Emp LS 567, 592–594.
37 J Loshin (n 12) 488–489.
38 *Kosmopoulos* (n 14) [37]. See also: B Hartnett and JV Thornton (n 14) 433.
39 Malcolm Clarke (n 14) para 4-2A.
40 Robert Merkin (n 14) para 4-002.

subject-matter just because he has access and/or control over it and might get away without his insurance fraud being detected. However, easy access to the insured property combined with a low risk of detection can be supporting factors if there are other motives or incentives to destroy the insured property. In relation to life insurance, it is noteworthy that in 96 out of 706 homicides in 2016/17, the victim was the principal suspect's (ex)partner. However, no granular information is available on motives other than that in the same period in 64% of 333 homicides where the principal suspect was known to the victim, the motive was classified as "quarrel, revenge or loss of temper", whilst only 4% were "in furtherance of theft or gain".[41]

The *cash conversion argument* and the *profit argument* wrongly assume that the existence of an insurable interest can provide an incentive to destroy the insured property. Ceteris paribus, an insured cannot hope to make a profit from the proceeds of an indemnity policy as he would only be compensated for his actual loss. In the situations described in the cash conversion argument and the profit argument, an incentive to destroy the insured property arises not because of an insurable interest but because the insured needs to liquidate assets or the insured value exceeds the actual (market) value of the insurable interest. Although the law allows some valuation flexibility in the form of valued policies,[42] it is well-established that over-insurance constitutes a moral hazard in its own right because the insured may be tempted to destroy the insured subject-matter to profit from a loss.[43] The moral hazard exists because the insurable interest does not extend into the over-insured portion.

In relation to life insurance, as an insurable interest in life is only required to exist at the time the contract is made, (1) the insured may cease to have an insurable interest subsequently, or (2) his pecuniary-style insurable interest may subsequently become less valuable than the policy proceeds payable upon death. In the first scenario, an incentive to bring about the death of the insured life arises upon the subsequent loss of the insurable interest, not its existence. In the second scenario, the insured would benefit financially from the death of the insured life because he or she has a pecuniary interest that has become overvalued (e.g. where the policy proceeds payable upon death exceed the insured's interest based upon an amortizing debt). This is another example of over-insurance. In both situations the underlying cause of moral hazard is that the insured is not required to have an insurable interest at the time of the insured event: it highlights the correlation between moral hazard and the absence of sufficient insurable interest, rather than that the presence of an insurable interest is conducive to creating moral hazard. It is therefore contended that neither the opportunity

---

41 Office for National Statistics (n 32) Appendix Tables 1, 7a, 10a and 10b.
42 MIA 1906, s.27(3).
43 In *Chapman v Pole* (1870) 22 LT 306 (ExchCham) 307, Cockburn CJ said: "…if a person were allowed to insure goods to a greater amount than the real value, it is obvious that a door would be open to fraud and wickedness of the most abominable description".

argument nor the cash conversion argument nor the profit argument convincingly undermines the moral hazard justification.

Reverse moral hazard

Loshin has argued that the doctrine of insurable interest does create reverse moral hazard – that is that, helped by the doctrinal uncertainty as to the meaning of insurable interest, insurers are incentivized to accept insureds with no, or ambiguous, interests in the knowledge that the contract is not enforceable in the absence of a valid insurable interest.[44] The reason for that, he argues, is that, as long as the probability of invalidating an insurance contract on the grounds of lack of insurable interest is greater than the probability of liability loss due to the moral hazard, the insurer can make a marginal gain.[45] It is suggested that, under English law, the doctrine is not generally abused in that way. Whilst "underwriting at claims stage" was one of the problems identified by the LC in relation to the old law on non-disclosure and misrepresentation,[46] no such allegation has been made against the doctrine of insurable interest.[47] Insurers rarely use the defence of lack of insurable interest because the courts have made it clear that their approach is "to lean in favour of an insurable interest". The small number of insurable interest cases in the courts and before the Financial Ombudsman indicates that insurers do not generally exploit the uncertainty as to what constitutes an insurable interest as a means of escaping liability for claims.[48] It is doubtful whether there is significant moral hazard in relation to life insurance in the United States given insurers' potential liability for wrongful death.[49]

It is also suggested that reverse moral hazard issues could be minimized by requiring insurers to decline to enter into contracts of insurance which they know would be void for lack of insurable. This will be explored further in Chapter 12.

Inappropriateness of contract law

It has also been questioned whether the doctrine of insurable interest, which is an insurance contract law doctrine rooted in common law and statute, is the appropriate medium to keep in check moral hazard. Clarke suggests that the destruction of insured property for fraudulent gain is "primarily a matter for the criminal law".[50]

---

44 J Loshin (n 12) 490–498.
45 Ibid., 492–493.
46 LC, '*Impact Assessment: Updating Insurance Contract Law: The Business Insured's Duty of Disclosure*' (June 2012) para 6.
47 LC, '*Post Contract*' (n 7) paras 12.22–12.24.
48 See Chapter 5.
49 *Liberty Nat. Life Ins. Co. v Weldon* (n 23); and see Chapter 5.
50 Malcolm Clarke (n 14) para 4-2A.

Criminal law and civil law often overlap or operate in parallel. For example, many criminal offences, such as murder, criminal damage, arson and fraud, have a tort equivalent. There is also frequent overlap where criminal conduct gives rise to an illegality defence to the enforcement of legal rights arising under trust, in contract, unjust enrichment or tort. There are other general contract law doctrines aimed at restraining one contract party from taking advantage of another.[51] In relation to the doctrine of insurable interest, the functional overlap is minimal: the criminal offences of murder and unlawfully destroying property belonging to another fulfil the broader functions of the criminal law and the criminal justice system, such as the protection of the public, the punishment of offenders and the deterrence of crime. The doctrine of insurable interest has a role to play in insurance contract law since, as will be argued below, it is a doctrinal tool to align the contractual interests of the insurer and the insured. Moreover, as will be shown in Chapters 9 and 10, the requirement for an insurable interest is an integral part of the insurance contract law and as well as being part of the fabric of standard property policy wordings.

'Skin in the game' in property insurance

Rather than exclusively focusing on the doctrine's ability to prevent the destruction of the insured property by the insured, the doctrine of insurable interest should be re-evaluated as a mechanism for aligning the interests of the insured and the insurer: namely the preservation of the insured subject-matter. Once the parties have entered into a contract of insurance, the insured may take less than optimal care in protecting the insured subject-matter against loss or damage, or fail to mitigate a loss, in the knowledge that the insurer will indemnify him for any insured loss.[52] As Heimer notes, policyholders' "motivation to control losses is greatly reduced by insurance coverage".[53] This behavioural pattern would be prejudicial to the insurer and may be contrary to the principle of good faith. There is a (potential) conflict of interests since the insurer wishes for the insured subject-matter to be protected against loss so that he is not called upon to pay claims. This apparent conflict of interests can be moderated if the insured has a personal stake in the insured subject-matter – what Kees van der Klugt refers to as "skin in the game".[54] A requirement for an insurable interest is a mechanism to ensure that the insured has skin in the game.

51 E.g. promissory estoppel, duress and undue influence.
52 This attitude is also referred to as 'moral*e* hazard' (as opposed to 'moral hazard') in insurance theory – see Emmett J Vaughan and Therese Vaughan, *Fundamentals of Risk and Insurance* (10th edn, John Wiley & Sons, Inc 2008) 5.
53 Carole Heimer, *Reactive Risk and Rational Action: Managing Moral Hazard in Insurance Contracts* (University of California Press 1985) Preface 8–9 and 35–36.
54 Interview with Kees van der Klugt, Director of Legal & Compliance at the Lloyd's Market Association (London, 29 September 2015).

How does an insurable interest constitute skin in the game?

To answer this question it is useful to imagine a spectrum of interests, ranging from the insured having outright ownership of the insured property to the insured having no relationship at all with the insured property.

Full ownership: An outright owner of the insured property is likely to have a significant 'investment' in the property because, in addition to the monetary value of the property, he would also stand to lose the 'use and enjoyment' of the property and suffer the inconvenience (or even trauma) of its loss. To the extent that the insured property was of sentimental value to the insured, such non-material value is usually not covered under a property policy[55] and, by definition, cannot be adequately compensated financially. The insurer will indemnify the insured merely up to the extent of his actual loss and, in practice, an insured can also remain 'undercompensated' if policy deductibles and limits apply.[56] Behavioural economists and psychologists have labelled the increased loss aversion and greater sentimental attachment that comes with ownership as the "endowment effect".[57] Therefore, it is both in the insurer's and the insured's interest that the insured property is kept safe from loss or damage. The insured is incentivized to take measures to safeguard the property and to mitigate any loss. Burrel speaking in the debates on the Marine Insurance Bill in 1741/42 thought this to be self-evident:

> It is, Sir, too well known to require Proof, that Interest is the Parent of Diligence, and that Men attend to the Performance of their Duty, in Proportion as they must suffer by the Neglect of it …[58]

Heimer, too, recognizes that an insured can be incentivized to prevent loss by creating a "community of fate".[59] Having a strong insurable interest in the insured property means that the insured and the insurer are jointly exposed to the risk of loss. The insured has substantial skin in the game. In addition, an insurable interest based on proprietary or contractual rights over the insured property serves as a legal platform from which the insurer can meaningfully impose contractual obligations on the insured to protect the insured property from loss since an effective performance of such obligations is likely to depend on the insured having access or control over the insured property either directly or through a third party.[60]

---

55 *Richard Aubrey Film Productions Ltd v Graham* [1960] 2 Lloyd's Rep 101 (QB) 103 (Winn J).
56 See Chapter 10.
57 CK Morewedge and CE Giblin, '*Explanations of the Endowment Effect: An Integrative Review*' (2015) 19(6) Tre Cogn Sci 339, 340–342.
58 As recorded in *The Gentleman's Magazine, and Historical Chronicle*, London 1742, vol. XII, 8.
59 Carole Heimer (n 54) 13 and 201. Heimer refers to a number of techniques aimed to achieve a community of fate but does not include the doctrine of insurable interest (which she only considers in the context of the indemnity principle).
60 See Chapters 9 and 10.

Economic interest: An insured with no more than an expectation of economic benefit if the insured property is preserved, or economic loss if the insured property is damaged or destroyed, has a purely financial 'stake' in the insured property. There is no endowment effect; he does not lose the use and enjoyment of the insured property, and there would generally be very little personal or sentimental 'investment' in the insured property. Rather than compensating for something actually lost, such an insurance contract would position the insured to claim for a future profit or expenses. An insured with a mere economic interest would have less incentive to take active steps to protect the insured property from harm as, by definition, his loss would be purely economic. Moreover, an economic interest is usually insufficient to give the insured the access and control rights to take loss prevention and mitigation measures.[61] Therefore, an economic interest equates to less 'skin in the game' and, consequently, a weaker community of interests of the insurer and the insured.

No interest: A contract under which the 'insured' has no interest in the subject-matter would not be a contract of insurance but a wager on the continuing safety of the property. The parties take diametrically opposite positions: the 'insured' would wish to see the property to be damaged or destroyed in order to benefit from a pay-out, whereas the 'insurer' wants the property to remain unharmed to avoid payment. Neither party is concerned with the property beyond the fact that any loss will trigger a payment.[62] The party betting on the subject-matter being damaged or destroyed may not go as far as actively bringing about its destruction but, nevertheless, the parties' respective interests are in direct conflict.

Relationship with other anti-moral hazard techniques

There are other techniques that insurers use to reduce moral hazard, and more specifically to counteract a misalignment of interests, by changing the incentive structure of the insured to align it to that of the insurer. Examples include contractual provisions for deductibles, retentions, limits of liability, reasonable precautions clauses and Risk Control Terms.[63] However, it is suggested, and argued more fully in Chapter 10, that the effectiveness of some of those anti-moral hazard techniques is dependent upon the existence, and the strength, of the insured's interest in the insured subject-matter. Moreover, these techniques are not in the nature of contractual default rules, so that their negotiation and inclusion in a specific contract of insurance requires express terms and may incur

---

61 Ibid.
62 *Carlill v Carbolic Smoke Ball Company* [1892] 2 QB 484 (QB) 490–491 (Hawkins J).
63 See Carole Heimer (n 54) 7–9. 'Risk Control Terms' are property policy terms such as exclusions, conditions precedent, warranties, notice provisions or termination events relating to the use of the insured property and changes in circumstances relating to the property, aimed at protecting the insurer from an increase in risk after inception. See Chapter 10.

additional transaction costs.[64] In contrast, the doctrine of insurable interest is a mandatory statutory or common law rule aligning the interests of the parties at no extra cost.

Relationship between insurable interest and moral hazard restated

Based on the foregoing discussion and the analysis in Chapter 10, the following propositions are put forward:

1   The strength of the relationship between the insured and the insured property directly affects the extent to which the insured has 'skin in the game'.
2   The extent to which the insured has skin in the game is correlated to the extent to which the insurer and the insured have a common interest in preserving the insured property.
3   The stronger the alignment of interests between the insurer and the insured, the more forcefully this alignment counteracts specific moral hazard risks, including the risk that the insured may take less than optimal care in protecting the insured property against loss or damage, the risk that the insured may fail to mitigate a loss and the risk that the insured may deliberately destroy the insured property in order to obtain a claims payment.
4   If the insured has no interest, or a bare economic interest, he is unlikely to have the access and control rights over the insured property necessary to protect the insured property against loss or damage, or, in the event of a loss, to take steps to mitigate.

If these propositions are correct, it should follow that there is an inverse correlation between the existence and relative strength of an insurable interest and the moral hazard risk. A substantial insurable interest should disincentivize behavioural patterns associated with moral hazard and furnish the insured with access and/or control rights over the insured property that allow him to take steps to protect it from loss or damage. It is acknowledged that there could be other factors that could misalign the insurer's and insured's interests and/or the insured may not act rationally and in accordance with what is in his self-interest. Nevertheless, the doctrine of insurable interest is a starting point for aligning the parties' interests, which, as discussed, can be reinforced by contractual means (such as deductible/retention clauses and reasonable precautions clauses) that build upon the 'skin in the game' provided by an insurable interest.

The idea of aligning the insurer's and the insured's interests during the currency of the insurance policy on the basis of an insurable interest cannot be coherently applied to life insurance: a person insuring his or her own life is presumed to prefer staying alive to his or her death with an insurance pay-out to his

---

64 T Baker and KD Logue (n 11) 380.

or her estate. When insuring the life of another person (A), an insurable interest in A's life might counter-balance any sentiments of desiring A's death in order to gain financially from the insurance proceeds, but A's individual autonomy would limit what steps the insured could take to protect A from death, or, in the event of a potentially fatal illness or injury, to take steps to mitigate.

Moral hazard in the capital markets

Whilst insurance law recognized the relationship between an insurable interest and moral hazard over 250 years ago, regulators and legislators only recently acknowledged the significance of the link between (the absence of) skin in the game and moral hazard in the banking and capital markets sector. In the years leading up to the Financial Crisis, a number of banks increasingly lowered their lending standards, issuing mortgage-backed loans irrespective of the borrowers' ability to repay. They were generating sub-prime loans for the purpose of selling them on as repackaged collateralized debt obligations into securitization pools. Under this so-called 'originate-to-distribute' business model, the originating banks had no incentive of ensuring that the loans would meet prudent lending standards since the credit risk would be sold on to investors further down in the securitization chain. When a significant proportion of the borrowers started defaulting, their defaults 'rippled' through the securitization and security structures. The US Financial Crisis Inquiry Commission found that the "collapsing mortgage-lending standards and the mortgage securitisation pipeline lit and spread the flame of contagion and crisis".[65]

To align the interests of the originating lenders (sponsors) and investors, US regulators have now adopted a 'skin in the game'-style credit risk retention rule under the Securities and Exchange Act of 1934, s.15G, as amended pursuant to s.941 of the Dodd-Frank Act. Broadly speaking, and with some exceptions, the credit risk retention rule requires sponsors of securitizations to retain at least 5% of the credit risk of the securitized exposure. Similarly, a new EU risk retention regime[66] prohibits specified investors from becoming exposed to the credit risk of a securitization unless any of the sponsor, the originator or the original lender in the transaction retains an interest of not less than 5% of the securitized exposures (and failure to comply will result in the imposition of an additional risk weighting charge and regulatory breaches). The US and EU risk retention

---

65 The US Financial Crisis Inquiry Commission, '*The Financial Crisis Inquiry Report – Final Report of the National Commission on the Causes of the Financial and Economic Crisis in the United States*' (February 2011) xxiii.

66 Regulation (EU) No 575/2013 Of the European Parliament and of the Council of 26 June 2013 on prudential requirements for credit institutions and investment firms and amending Regulation (EU) No 648/2012, Art.405; and Regulation (EU) 2017/2402 of the European Parliament and of the Council of 12 December 2017 laying down a general framework for securitization and creating a specific framework for simple, transparent and standardized securitization, and amending Directives 2009/65/EC, 2009/138/EC and 2011/61/EU and Regulations (EC) No 1060/2009 and (EU) No 648/2012, Art.6.

measures are intended to provide an economic incentive for sponsors and investors to monitor the quality of securitized assets. Other countries have adopted similar rules under the Basel III framework. In relation to CDS, the moral hazard risk arising from empty creditors, and the relevant legislative measures, has been discussed in Chapter 6. Posner and Weyl have advocated the adoption of a more sophisticated insurable interest rule across all financial instruments for regulatory purposes in order to assess ex ante whether they are socially valuable or socially costly and argue that all socially costly financial instruments should be banned.[67] To abolish the doctrine of insurable interest in contracts of insurance would be a development at odds with the introduction of 'skin in the game' concepts into banking regulation at supra-national and international level.

Moral hazard and STOLI

In a STOLI scheme, the investor (who takes an assignment of the life policy and pays the premium) has an economic incentive to hasten the death of the insured life (A). This moral hazard would be mitigated by an insurable interest in A's life, but, as US STOLI cases have highlighted, there is a tension between the insurable interest requirement and allowing the requirement to be circumvented in order to uphold the free assignability of life insurance policies.[68]

Whilst there are no reported cases of STOLI-related murders, the 'creepiness' of STOLI schemes is illustrated by a Florida case that involved a STOLI scheme in which members of a Colombian drug cartel had invested to launder money.[69] The original assignee of the policy may transfer the policy to another investor who could then on-sell it again, and so on. Bundles of life policies might be securitized, thus reaching numerous capital markets investors. Even if A consented to the assignment of the policy to the original assignee, he or she has no control over or knowledge of any subsequent investors who are anxious for A's early death and who may contact A to check if their investment has 'matured' yet.[70] A is at risk that his identity and personal data are disclosed to unauthorized individuals in the chain of investors and beyond. The idea that certain personal information should not be the subject of wagers because it is 'injurious' to the data subject was one of the grounds for not enforcing a wager on the sex of the Chevalier d'Eon in *Da Costa v Jones*.[71] Thus, there is moral hazard in the sense of causing injury to the privacy of A.

---

67 EA Posner and EG Weyl, '*An FDA for Financial Innovation: Applying the Insurable Interest Doctrine to the 21ˢᵗ Century Financial Markets*' (2013) 107 Nw U L Rev 1307, 1308, 1357.
68 See Chapter 5.
69 Mentioned in: M Fleisher, '*Stranger Originated Life Insurance: Finding a Modern Cure for an Age-Old Problem*' (2011) 41 Cum L Rev 569, 588.
70 Ibid. (Fleisher) 589.
71 (1778) 2 Cowper 729 (per Lord Mansfield).

There are other abuses and fraudulent practices associated with STOLI.[72] Often A is an elderly person who is talked into participating in a STOLI scheme by the scheme's promoters with promises of 'risk free' cash without fully understanding the financial obligations undertaken and the risks involved. A may be 'helped' with completing the life insurance application form in a manner that conceals or misrepresents that the life policy is acquired as part of a STOLI scheme. A material misrepresentation may negatively affect A's future insurability.

As for insurers, STOLI schemes can disrupt premium pricing, which relies on a significant proportion of life policies lapsing or being surrendered to the insurer for a comparatively low cash surrender value, rather than paying out policy proceeds. As fewer policies will lapse and more death benefits are paid out, insurers must raise premium rates for all insureds in order to stay profitable. Although some commentators have condemned 'lapse-supported pricing' and have argued that a secondary market in life policies (which also includes traditional life settlements and viaticals) is beneficial to consumers as it gives them more options when they wish to sell existing life policies,[73] Nurnberg and Lackey point out that only a small minority (namely wealthy elderly policyholders who are the STOLI target market) will benefit from STOLIs, whilst the large majority of consumer insureds will lose out by paying higher premiums for life insurance: "[STOLI] is an example of parasitic 'free-riding', made possible by the public good of existing insurance law, but in no way contributing to the public good".[74] As such, STOLI schemes are unfair and contrary to public welfare.

In addition, STOLI schemes create moral hazards to society at large: they infringe upon human dignity and condone attitudes that people's lives can be treated as an investment asset to speculate on,[75] and that it is acceptable to wish for the death of another human being. Nurnberg and Lackey contend that these attitudes are not shared by most civilized people and, accordingly, the "market right" of free assignability of life insurance policies in a STOLI context which is only relevant to few market participants must be balanced against the need "to preserve socially desired virtues" for the general public.[76] The insurable interest requirement plays a role in forestalling the creation of circumstances or an environment that entice homicide and can counteract any financial incentives to bring about A's death. The debate on STOLI schemes, and the subsequent anti-STOLI legislation enacted in many US States, highlights that moral hazard

---

72 For a detailed account of STOLI-associated risks to insureds, insurers and investors, see Fleisher (n 70) 587–596

73 DR Richmond, '*Investing with the Grim Reaper: Insurable Interest and Assignment in Life Insurance*' (2012) 50 Tort Trial Ins Prac LJ 657, 660.

74 H Nurnberg and DP Lackey, '*The Ethics of Life Insurance Settlements: Investing in Lives of Unrelated Individuals*' (2010) 96 J BE 513, 521 and 526.

75 SR Leimberg, '*Stranger-Owned Life Insurance: Killing the Goose that Lays Golden Eggs*' (May 2005) Ins Tax Rev 811.

76 H Nurnberg and DP Lackey (n 75).

and ethical concerns associated with the absence of an insurable interest are certainly not anachronistic and are taken seriously by the legislators.

Moral hazard and the definition of insurable interest

Does the moral hazard justification compel a narrow (legal interest test) definition of insurable interest or would it equally support a doctrine of insurable interest with a wide (factual expectation test) definition in property insurance? It has been suggested that, in property insurance, there is an inverse correlation between the presence of an insurable interest, and its relative strength, on the one hand, and the risk of moral hazard, on the other. A strong insurable interest in relation to the insured property aligns the interests of the insurer and the insured more closely and would tend to furnish the insured with the access and control rights over the property necessary to take loss prevention and mitigation measures. In contrast, an insured with a bare economic interest in the insured subject-matter is a comparatively inferior risk from a moral hazard perspective, since he has less 'skin in the game' incentives and is unlikely to have the access and control rights over the insured property necessary to actively safeguard the insured property.

In *Kosmopoulos* Wilson J expressed the opposite view: in relation to an insured with a bare economic interest, the moral hazard risk "may well decrease" because the insured with a bare economic interest is "not usually in the possession or control" of the insured property that would give him "intimate access to it", thereby putting him "in a position to destroy it without detection".[77] This is the opportunity argument which, as argued above, on its own is implausible since a rational insured would be unlikely to destroy the insured property just because he has access or control over it. The moral hazard justification does not compel, but favours, a narrow definition of insurable interest.

The focus of the traditional understanding of moral hazard justification has been on the deterrent effect of the doctrine of insurable interest. Although there is no reliable data available corroborating or disproving the doctrine's deterrent effect, it has played a key role in the STOLI discussion. By refocusing the moral hazard justification on the doctrine of insurable interest's ability to align the interests of the insured and the insurer in property insurance, it can be explained more convincingly and without the need for empirical evidence as to how many incidents of deliberate loss the existence of an insurable interest has prevented or failed to prevent. The proposition that having skin in the game is a means of creating a community of interest between contract parties whose interests would otherwise diverge is supported by legislative developments in the capital markets sector.

---

77 n 14 [37].

8   The indemnity justification

The indemnity justification for the doctrine of insurable interest rests upon the policy that claims payments should be limited to an indemnity for the insured's loss. As such, the doctrine of insurable interest is valued by the insurance industry as an additional barrier against invalid claims.[1] In this Chapter, the indemnity justification, and the criticisms raised against it, will be evaluated in the course of a doctrinal analysis of the relationship between the doctrine of insurable interest and the indemnity principle in property insurance.

The indemnity principle does not apply to contingency insurance contracts, such as life insurance, where the insurer undertakes to pay a certain sum of money upon a specified event for premium fixed upon the value of the insured's interest at the time the contract is made.[2] The indemnity justification has therefore no direct application to the doctrine of insurable interest in relation to contingency insurance.

The indemnity principle

Hold harmless: One party's obligation to indemnify the other is an essential characteristic of a contract of indemnity insurance. The primary obligation of an insurer under an indemnity insurance contract is to hold the insured harmless against loss by an insured peril. This has four doctrinal consequences: first, a failure by the insurer to hold the insured harmless constitutes a breach of contract.[3] Secondly, the insured will have a cause of action for breach of contract which arises if a loss caused by an insured peril is sustained. Thirdly, the insured's claim

---

1 LC, *'Insurance Contract Law: Post Contract Duties and Other Issues'* (Law Com CP No 201, December 2011) paras 12.16–12.19; LC, *'Issues Paper 10 – Insurable Interest: Updated Proposals'* (March 2015) para 2.3.
2 *Dalby v The India and London Life Assurance Company* (1854) 15 CB 365 (ExchCham). Note, however, that some types of life insurance have an indemnity element – see Chapter 5.
3 *Firma C-Trade S.A. Respondents v Newcastle Protection and Indemnity Association (The Fanti)* [1991] 2 AC 1 (HL) 35 (Lord Goff); *Ventouris v Mountain (The 'Italia Express' (No. 3))* [1992] 2 Lloyd's Rep 281 (Comm) 292 (Hirst J).

is a claim for damages,[4] and not a claim in debt. The insurer is responsible to compensate the insured so as to put him in the position he or she would have been in (financially) had the contract been performed.[5] Fourthly, at common law, if the insurer refused or failed to pay a valid claim, the insurer was not liable to the insured for any damages over and above the amount of the indemnity since no such remedy was available for late payment of damages.[6] The IA 2015, s.13A introduced a statutory implied duty on insurers to "pay any sums due in respect of claims within a reasonable time", upon breach of which remedies (including damages) will be available, but it did not re-characterize the nature of the insurer's primary 'hold harmless' obligation.

In the context of property insurance, the insurer must indemnify the insured for the loss caused to him by an insured peril to the insured property but no more than that – the insured is not entitled to make a profit at the expense of the insurer. In *Castellain v Preston* Brett LJ summarized the indemnity principle as follows:

> [T]he contract of insurance contained in a marine or fire policy is a contract of indemnity, and of indemnity only, and that this contract means that the assured, in case of a loss against which the policy has been made, shall be fully indemnified, but shall never be more than fully indemnified.[7]

The MIA 1906, s.67(1) fixes the measure of indemnity to the insurable value of the insured's interest. The indemnity payable is for the loss in relation to the insured's interest in the property[8] and does not extend to every loss suffered by the insured as a result of the insured event.[9] Thus, in *Castellain v Preston* Cotton LJ noted that in property insurance only losses that are an "incident of the property ... ought to be brought into account in estimating the loss".[10] Unless the contract provides otherwise, the insured is not entitled to damages for consequential loss since "loss which, although resulting from loss or damage to the property insured, is not itself loss in the value of that property".[11]

Imperfect indemnities: The indemnity principle applies to all contracts of indemnity insurance but the parties are, within certain limits, free to agree how the indemnity is to be calculated.[12] In relation to insurance of real property, the parties may agree that the measure of indemnity is determined by reference to the cost of reinstatement. Policies insuring personal property may offer 'new for

---

4 *Sprung v Royal Insurance (UK) Ltd* [1997] CLC 70 (CA); *Ventouris v Mountain* (n 2).
5 *Robinson v Harman* (1848) 1 Ex 850 (Exch).
6 *President of India v Lips Maritime Corp (The Lips)* [1988] AC 395 (HL).
7 (1883) 11 QBD 380 (CA) 386.
8 *Wasa International Insurance Co Ltd v Lexington Insurance Co* [2009] UKHL 40, [33].
9 Malcolm Clarke, *The Law of Insurance Contracts* (Service Issue 37, Informa 2016) para 28-8E.
10 (n 7) 395.
11 Malcolm Clarke (n 9) para 28-8E.
12 *North of England Iron Steamship Insurance Asc v Armstrong* (1869–70) LR 5 QB 244 (QB) 250 (Cockburn CJ).

old' coverage – for example, a lost or destroyed second-hand television set will be replaced with a new one. Unless a deduction is made for the 'betterment' of the property reinstated or replaced,[13] such policies extend the notion of an indemnity since, strictly speaking, they offer the insured more or something better than he or she has lost. Unless the valuation is fraudulent[14] or so excessive that the policy is in the nature of a wagering contract,[15] it is also open to the parties to agree the value of the subject-matter at the time of the contract in so-called valued policies, so that the insured need not prove the actual value of the subject-matter for the purposes of calculating the measure of indemnity (or for any other purpose specified in the policy).[16] An insured with a limited interest in the insured property, such as a bailee or trustee, may also recover an amount in excess of his own actual loss, but he must account for any recovery in excess of his interest to the true owner of the property.[17] The measure of indemnity can also be curtailed by agreement by providing for deductibles, retentions and limits of liability.

Criticisms

Lowry and Rawlings have suggested that the indemnity principle, which prevents claims by insureds who have not suffered a loss, is in itself sufficient to render the doctrine of insurable interest redundant.[18] Similarly, the LC initially took the view that "[i]n indemnity insurance it is difficult to see what a statutory requirement of insurable interest added to the common law indemnity principle", since the latter "will prevent wagering being disguised as insurance" and "minimize moral hazard".[19] For Hartnett and Thornton the indemnity justification represents "merely another head of the hydra that is the policy against wagering".[20] In *Kosmopoulos* Wilson J declared a narrow concept of insurable interest (which does not take into account economic benefits or detriment) to be inconsistent with the indemnity principle.[21] To evaluate these criticisms it is

13 *Reynolds v Phoenix Assurance Co Ltd* [1978] 2 Lloyd's Rep 440 (QB) 450 (Forbes J).
14 MIA 1906, s.27(3); *Thames and Mersey Marine Insurance Co Ltd v 'Gunford' Ship Co Ltd* [1911] AC 529 (HL).
15 *Lewis v Rucker* (1761) 2 Burr 1167 (KB).
16 MIA 1906, s.27(2) and (3).
17 *Hepburn v A Tomlinson (Hauliers) Ltd* [1966] AC 451 (HL); *Lonsdale & Thompson Ltd v Black Arrow Group plc* [1993] 2 WLR 815 (Ch); *Ramco (UK) Ltd v International Insurance Co of Hannover Ltd* [2004] EWCA Civ 675, [2004] 2 Lloyd's Rep 595.
18 J Lowry and P Rawlings, 'Rethinking Insurable Interest' in Sarah Worthington (ed), *Commercial Law and Commercial Practice* (Oxford, Hart Publishing 2003) 335, 361–363.
19 LC, '*Issues Paper 4 – Insurable Interest*' (January 2008) paras 7.44–46. The LC have since accepted that the indemnity principle does not render the doctrine of insurable interest redundant – see LC, '*Post Contract*' (n 1) para 12.4.
20 B Hartnett and J V Thornton, '*Insurable Interest in Property – A Socio-Economic Reevaluation of a Legal Concept*' (1949) Ins LJ 420, 434.
21 [1987] 1 SCR 2, [35].

necessary to examine the relationship between the doctrine of insurable interest and the indemnity principle.

The relationship between the doctrine of insurable interest and the indemnity principle

In the absence of any interest in the insured subject-matter the policyholder will not be able to prove a loss for which an indemnity is payable, since without such an interest, he cannot suffer any indemnifiable loss.[22] In *Lucena*, Lawrence J reasoned that one could only suffer such disadvantage (loss) by "having some relation to, or concern in the subject of the insurance ...".[23] Thus, an interest in the insured property is a precondition to the insured's exposure to risk and his capacity to suffer loss.

Where the insured has no interest, the application of the doctrine of insurable interest and the indemnity principle may have the same practical outcome that a claim is not payable. However, they are distinguishable: First, they are of different legal natures – the doctrine of insurable interest is a statutory and common law requirement, and the indemnity principle is of contractual nature. As a result, the indemnity principle can be varied by the agreement of the parties, whereas the requirement for an insurable interest cannot be waived by the parties.[24] Secondly, the legal consequences of non-compliance are different: a lack of insurable interest at the relevant time renders the whole insurance contract, depending on its type, void and/or illegal,[25] whereas the absence of an insured loss merely means that the insured has no enforceable claim (but does not impact on the validity of the contract). Thirdly, in contracts of contingency insurance the indemnity principle does not apply but the insured would still be required to have an insurable interest.

A separate question is whether the indemnity principle renders the doctrine of insurable interest redundant. It is suggested that the doctrine of insurable interest and the indemnity principle serve different purposes and operate at different levels and at different points in time and are therefore not interchangeable concepts. Insurable interest is concerned with who can insure a property: a current or prospective interest in the insured property establishes the exposure to the risk of loss or damage to the property which, in turn, is a pre-condition to the capacity to suffer an insured loss and the risk of transfer to the insurer under the contract of insurance.[26] The doctrine of insurable interest should operate at the underwriting stage to prevent any person without an interest from insuring

---

22 *Lucena v Crafurd* (1806) 2 Bos & Pul (NR) 269 (HL) 302 (Lawrence J).
23 Ibid.
24 See Chapter 3.
25 Ibid.
26 See Chapter 6 and *Lucena* (n 22) 302 (Lawrence J).

in the first place.[27] Moreover, the nature of the proposer's interest informs what type of insurance cover should be obtained. In contrast, the indemnity principle is relevant at claims stage, being concerned with the quantum of loss, and therefore only comes into play if and when a claim is made. The doctrine of insurable interest sets the parameters for the interest to which the quantification of loss is to be applied, but it does not prescribe how a claim is to be quantified. Thus, in *Wasa International Insurance Co Ltd v Lexington Insurance Co* Lod Mance said:

> The insurable interest which entitles the insurer to reinsure in respect of that subject matter is the insurer's exposure under the original insurance. The principle of indemnity limits any recovery from reinsurers to the amount paid in respect of that insurable interest.[28]

The insurer does not agree to hold the insured harmless against any loss, for the indemnity principle fixes the measure of indemnity to the insurable value of the insured's interest. If the insured has no insurable interest, the question how to value it does not arise – something that is not there cannot be valued. Conversely, the insured may have an insurable interest in the (whole) insured property, but if the property is only partially damaged, the insured can recover only to the extent of his loss. If the insured's interest is not affected by any damage to the insured property, he cannot claim an indemnity. The indemnity principle cannot stand on its own without the doctrine of insurable interest since the latter is the basis for the requirement of an interest that is relevant to the valuation of the loss. The nature and extent of the interest will inform its value. The doctrine of insurable interest gives meaning and effect to the indemnity principle, but it cannot quantify the loss.

There are further reasons why the indemnity principle cannot stand on its own: first, the indemnity principle is of contractual nature and, as has been noted above, can be varied or substituted with a different basis for the quantification of claims. The indemnity principle is therefore no guarantee that any other policy reasons said to be supported by the doctrine of insurable interest can be given effect. Secondly, if it is accepted, as will be argued in Chapter 11, that the requirement for an interest is a defining characteristic of contracts of insurance, an obligation to pay an indemnity, decoupled from an insurable interest, cannot be determinative of the characterization of the contract as a contract of insurance. Thirdly, the indemnity principle does not protect a prospective insured from entering into a contract that will be worthless to him since, on account of his lack of interest in the insured subject-matter, he will never suffer an insured loss for which he can claim. The doctrine of insurable interest, in contrast, by rendering a contract of insurance lacking an insurable interest void, seeks to ensure that

---

27 Graham Douds, '*Insurable Interest in English Marine Insurance Law: Do We Still Need It*' (2012) 25 USF Mar LJ 323, 338–340.
28 n 8 [33].

a person who has no prospect of suffering a loss is prevented from insuring ex ante.[29] At the time of loss when the indemnity principle becomes relevant, it is too late for the insured to make alternative arrangements, such as purchasing a more suitable policy that would have covered the interest he has or refraining from purchasing, and paying premium for, insurance cover he does not need. It has been argued that the suitability of a policy to the policyholder's circumstances is a matter that should be left to insurance regulation;[30] however, this argument ignores that a suitability assessment (whether by the insurer or the prospective insured) can only be made by reference to the relationship between the prospective insured and the subject-matter to be insured – that is, by considering his insurable interest. In Chapter 12 it will be argued that both parties should consider the insurable interest position at the outset and that regulatory oversight is needed not instead of but in conjunction with the doctrine of insurable interest.

The indemnity justification and the definition of insurable interest

Indemnity dependent on nature and extent interest

The LC has noted that a narrow definition of insurable interest based on the legal interest test limits the insured's "recoverable loss to that arising out of a legal or equitable relationship with the subject-matter of the insurance".[31] It is for this perceived limitation that Wilson J opined in *Kosmopoulos* that a narrow concept of insurable interest is inconsistent with the indemnity principle since it does not allow indemnification "for ... genuine pecuniary loss ...".[32]

Doctrinally, there is no inconsistency between a narrowly defined insurable interest and the indemnity principle as the quantum of the indemnifiable loss is circumscribed by the nature and extent of the insured's interest. The indemnity principle dictates neither a narrow nor a wide meaning of insurable interest; rather, the measure of indemnity principle is dictated by a number of factors, including the nature and extent of the insured's insurable interest. Other factors that can limit or expand the measure of indemnity include the policy terms (e.g. valued policies, deductibles, limits of liability, applicable exclusions) and the operation of the doctrine of causation.[33] However, a wider meaning of insurable interest that includes mere economic interests gives rise to two issues – multiple claims and valuation – that impact on the indemnity principle, and ultimately on the insurability of a risk.

---

29 See Chapter 12.
30 LC, '*Post Contract*' (n 1) para 12.33.
31 LC, '*Issues Paper 4*' (n 19) para 5.10.
32 n 21 [35].
33 See Chapters 7, 9 and 10.

Multiple claims

Whilst the indemnity principle is usually expressed as limiting the insured's recoveries,[34] the corollary is that the indemnity principle also limits an insurer's liability. As a contractual principle, the indemnity principle can only operate between the parties to a specific contract of insurance. Its capacity to protect insurers from multiple pay-outs in respect of the same loss is more problematic. Where a number of persons insure their respective interests in the same insured subject-matter, multiple insurance and loss scenarios can arise. The prudential and insurability implications of the multiple exposure risk have been explained in Chapter 6.

The multiple exposure risk can also create legal and practical issues. The 'loss' suffered by an insured with a mere economic interest in the insured subject-matter (such as a shareholder or unsecured creditor in relation to the corporate assets) may merely be reflective of the loss suffered by a third party with a proprietary interest in the subject-matter. In tort law, the reflective loss of a shareholder is not recoverable[35] as to do so would be contrary to the rule against double recovery of the same loss and would be prejudicial to the interests of creditors as the shareholder could recover ahead of the company, thereby reducing the assets available for distribution.[36] It is suggested that the same double recovery point and the detriment to creditors issue could arise if a shareholder insures and recovers under a policy of insurance in respect of the company's assets: if both the shareholder and the company insure company assets under separate policies, the same loss may be indemnified twice. If a shareholder would be allowed to insure corporate assets and claim for reflective loss, the insurance position would be at odds with tort law, and also with company law on account of piercing the corporate veil.[37] Conversely, if the shareholder is allowed to recover but the company is not (on the grounds that the shareholder has already been indemnified for the loss), the company's creditors would be prejudiced because they would have no recourse against the insurance proceeds in the hands of a shareholder.

Similarly, if an unsecured creditor can claim under a property policy for his economic loss in respect of loss or damage to an asset belonging to his debtor, there could be double recovery issues as the debtor may have already been compensated for the loss to the relevant asset by third parties or through its own insurance arrangements. Moreover, allowing an unsecured creditor to insure assets of the debtor company could also have the effect of him being treated equally, or even preferentially, in relation to secured creditors: if an insured event occurs in relation to the asset of the debtor which is subject to a fixed charge, the insured

---

34 *Castellain v Preston* (n 7).

35 *Prudential Assurance Co Ltd v Newman Industries Ltd (No.2)* [1982] Ch 204 (CA) and *Johnson v Gore Wood & Co* [2000] UKHL 65.

36 *Johnson v Gore Wood & Co* (n 35).

37 A company has a separate legal personality that is separate, and distinct, from its shareholders – see *Salomon v Salomon* [1897] AC 22 (HL).

unsecured creditor would be in a better position than an uninsured creditor with a fixed charge over the insured asset. Upon the company's insolvency, this might have the effect of circumventing the secured creditor's charge over the secured asset and contravene the anti-deprivation rule.[38] Unsecured creditors could also be affected detrimentally if a recovery by one unsecured creditor in respect of a debtor's asset means that the debtor itself cannot recover under its own insurance arrangements, thereby reducing the total value of assets available for distribution to all unsecured creditors.[39]

There is also a practical problem as to whether the shareholder's or unsecured creditor's proof of loss would reveal that his loss has already been (or will be) made good if the company itself has been (will be) compensated for the loss to the relevant asset, thus creating a risk of multiple pay-outs on the same loss. A legal interest-based concept of insurable interest affords insurers some protection from multiple claims in respect of the same loss and, as has been shown above, aligns insurance law recoveries with rules and principles from other areas of law.

Valuation

A pecuniary insurable interest must be capable of valuation.[40] If the expected loss is not determinable and measurable, the interest in question may not be suitable for insurance.[41] The problem of measuring an economic loss based on an expected profit or expense was noted by Lawrence J and Lord Eldon in *Lucena*.[42] In *Macaura*, Lord Buckmaster noted the difficulty of tracing the loss of a company's assets into the diminution of the company's share value:

> If he were at liberty to effect an insurance against loss by fire of any item of the company's property, the extent of his insurable interest could only be measured by determining the extent to which his share in the ultimate distribution would be diminished by the loss of the asset – a calculation almost impossible to make. There is no means by which such an interest can be definitely measured and no standard which can be fixed of the loss against which the contract of insurance could be regarded as an indemnity.[43]

38 Contracts purporting to exclude or vary the statutory order of distribution of the company's assets are void – see *British Eagle International Air Lines Ltd v Compagnie Nationale Air France* [1975] 1 WLR 758 (HL); *Mayhew v King* [2011] EWCA Civ 328.

39 This could contravene the pari passu principle that all (unsecured) creditors must be treated equally. See also Insolvency Act 1986, s.107.

40 Nicholas Legh-Jones, John Birds and David Owen, *MacGillivray on Insurance Law* (10th edn, Sweet & Maxwell 2003) para 1-069, cited with approval in *Feasey v Sun Life Assurance Co of Canada* [2003] EWCA Civ 885, [66] (Waller LJ).

41 Emmett J Vaughan and Therese Vaughan, *Fundamentals of Risk and Insurance* (10th edn, John Wiley & Sons, Inc 2008) 42–43.

42 n 22, 303 (Lawrence J) and 325–326 (Lord Eldon).

43 [1925] AC 619 (HL) 627.

In *Kosmopoulos* Wilson J rejected this line of reasoning:

> The difficulty of measuring the loss suffered by an individual shareholder should not, in my view, prevent a broadening of the definition of insurable interest. Modern company statutes ... require courts in certain circumstances to value shares. The task is obviously not considered impossible.[44]

It is suggested that difficulty lies not so much in ascertaining a share price or the amount of profit that could have been achieved but in valuing the loss that is attributable to the insured peril. Suppose a minority shareholder in a public listed company takes out insurance on corporate assets. If one out of numerous insured assets is lost or destroyed by an insured peril, it would be difficult to trace that loss into the corresponding reflective loss in the share value, in particular as share prices can be affected by numerous other factors. An unsecured creditor's loss might need to be valued by reference to a proportionate share in the insured asset equal to his share in the assets that would be available for distribution to unsecured creditors on (a hypothetical) insolvency. As noted above, the company itself may be compensated for the loss it suffered by third parties or through its own insurance arrangements, which, if a shareholder could insure the corporate asset independently, could give rise to a double recovery scenario. There is also timing issues: immediately after the loss of an insured corporate asset, the share price may be unaffected until the loss becomes known in the market. By the time a shareholder insured makes a claim, the share value is likely to have changed again due to numerous factors, and the proof of loss would be in relation to a historic share value as at the time of the loss.

The indemnity principle dictates neither a narrow nor a wide meaning of insurable interest. Merely expanding the meaning of insurable interest to include economic interests does not necessarily mean that the insured can recover for economic loss – the terms of the policy and the doctrine of causation also limit the insured's recoverable loss and, as will be discussed in Chapters 9 and 10, standard policy terms and the doctrine of causation are calibrated towards a doctrine of insurable interest with a narrow meaning based on the legal interest test.

44 n 21 [26].

9 The integral dimension of insurable interest – insurance contract law

Legal rules and doctrines do not operate in a vacuum but in a legal and social context. They interact with other legal doctrines and principles and, in the commercial sphere, they can have a dynamic relationship with market and industry practices. This Chapter and the next will explore this interconnectedness on a doctrinal level, and by reference to market practice and economic analysis: the interaction of the doctrine of insurable interest with other doctrines and principles of insurance law (this Chapter) and the extent to which the doctrine is an integral part of property insurance policy wordings (Chapter 10). In this Chapter it will be argued that the doctrine of insurable interest is integral to the operation of a number of doctrines and principles of insurance law.

Utmost good faith and pre-contractual risk presentation

Utmost good faith

Insurance contracts are contracts of utmost good faith,[1] imposing on both parties a general duty to act in good faith in their mutual dealings at the contract formation stage, and to a more limited extent during the term of the contract.[2] The IA 2015, s.14 has preserved the overarching principle of utmost good faith, although the remedy of avoidance for breach of good faith has been abolished.

In Chapter 7 it was argued that the doctrine of insurable interest serves as a doctrinal mechanism that counters the risk that the insured may take suboptimal care in protecting the insured property against loss or damage once cover is in place and that the insured may deliberately destroy the insured property. Both behavioural patterns are prejudicial to the insurer and may be incompatible with fair and open dealings on the part of the insured. By creating a community of interests, the doctrine of insurable interest supports the observance of utmost good faith. Viewed through a 'Law and Economics' lens, Avraham considers

---

1 MIA 1906, s.17 as amended by the IA 2015, s.14(3)(a).
2 See *Manifest Shipping Co Ltd v Uni-Polaris Insurance Co Ltd (The Star Sea)* [2001] UKHL 1; *Versloot Dredging BV v HDI Gerling Industrie Versicherung AG (The DC Merwestone)* [2016] UKSC 45.

that moral hazard is the post-contractual counterpart to the adverse selection problem at the pre-contractual stage. Both issues are rooted in what he calls "information impediments": the information advantage of the proposer at the pre-contractual stage, and the insurer's ignorance of an insured's post-inception behaviour that would tend to increase the probability of a loss.[3] The doctrine of insurable interest is a "doctrinal solution" to the moral hazard problem,[4] which the law imposes in relation to insurance contracts because they are contracts of utmost good faith. In Chapter 12 it will be argued that good faith also requires the insurer to consider the proposer's interest and to decline to enter into a contract of insurance which it knows would be void for lack of insurable interest.

Pre-contractual risk presentation under the IA 2015

The most significant aspect of the duty of utmost good faith in relation to *non-consumer insurance* is the insured's pre-contractual duty to make a fair presentation of the risk to the insurer.[5] The insured must disclose circumstances material to the risk or, failing that, give the insurer sufficient information to put a prudent insurer on notice that it needs to make further enquiries for the purpose of revealing those material circumstances.[6]

The rationale for the duty of fair presentation derives from the perception that the insured holds all the information about the risk, whereas the insurer is dependent upon the proposer providing full disclosure of all circumstances relevant to his underwriting assessment.[7] The duty of fair presentation, and its predecessor – the duty of disclosure, serve(d) to redress this informational asymmetry, preventing the insured from taking advantage of his "private knowledge" and allowing the parties to strike a fair agreement that is priced on the risk the insurer assumes.[8] The duty is also said to counter 'adverse selection' in the insurance market, whereby customers are more likely to seek insurance for risks they know to be high than for low risks. The pool of insureds would become smaller and more 'high risk', forcing the insurer to increase premiums. This cycle of adverse selection could repeat until the relevant insurance pool is no longer viable.[9]

The doctrine of insurable interest plays a role in discharging the duty of fair presentation. The scope of the duty of fair presentation is defined by reference to the insured's actual or deemed knowledge of material circumstances or information that would put the insurer on notice to make further enquiries[10] – "you

---

3 R Avraham, '*The Economics of Insurance Law – A Primer*' (2012) 19 Conn Ins LJ 29, 42–43.
4 Ibid., 45 and 76.
5 IA 2015, s.3(1).
6 IA 2015, s.3(4).
7 *Carter v Boehm* (1766) 3 Burr 1905 (KB) 1909–1911 (Lord Mansfield).
8 Ibid. See also *HIH Casualty and General Insurance Limited and Others v Chase Manhattan Bank* [2003] UKHL 6, [85] (Hobhouse LJ).
9 R Avraham (n 3) 44.
10 IA 2015, s.3(4).

cannot disclose what you do not know".[11] Material circumstances relating to property to be insured may include an accurate description of the property, its age, ownership, its previous, current and intended use, its location and proximity to physical hazards, the qualifications of the persons in whose charge or custody the property may be kept, the condition of the property, the arrangements that have been made for its safekeeping, its value, its insurance and claims history and other contracts and arrangements in place affecting the property.[12] A proposer without an insurable interest or a bare economic interest in the property is less likely to have any *actual knowledge* of that kind of information. Van der Klugt (Director of Legal and Compliance at the LMA) explains that, whilst insurable interest is not always an express topic of pre-contractual discussion in the Lloyd's Market, it would almost certainly become apparent on the information presented if the insured had no, or very little, connection with the property to be insured: there would be "something odd about the risk" and underwriters might decline cover for that reason.[13] In contrast, an insurable interest in the property based on a proprietary or contractual right would usually serve as a platform for knowledge of physical hazards and any special or unusual facts relating to the risk, or any particular concerns,[14] as such rights would usually allow for access to the property itself and to the property's records and other information about the property. In (non-consumer) life insurance, an employer's or a creditor's insurable interest in the life of the employee or debtor respectively means that the proposer is likely to be in a position to request the life to be insured (A) to provide the information on A's health, lifestyle and medical history that would be required for a fair presentation of the risk.

Deemed knowledge is assessed by reference to "what should reasonably have been revealed by a reasonable search of information *available to the insured*"[15] (emphasis added). O'Neill (Class Underwriter for Onshore Power and Energy at XL Catlin) notes that, even a proposer with a relatively weak insurable interest (e.g. a contractor) would still be expected to provide a full presentation of the risk, and, if that information is not held by him (or his organization), he would be asked to obtain the relevant information from elsewhere.[16] A reasonable search may reveal publicly available information, such as information from public records or publicly accessible Internet databases, and from enquiries of third parties, but such a search may not yield much that insurers (who themselves have access to publicly available information, statistical data and use sophisticated

11 *Joel v Law Union and Crown Insurance Company* [1908] 2 KB 863 (CA) 884–885 (Fletcher Moulton LJ).
12 Peter MacDonald Eggers and Simon Picken, *Good Faith and Insurance Contracts* (4th edn, Informa Law 2018) ch 15.
13 Interview with Kees van der Klugt, Director of Legal & Compliance at the Lloyd's Market Association (London, 29 September 2015).
14 IA 2015, s.7(4)(a) and (b).
15 IA 2015, s.4(6).
16 Interview with Peter O'Neill, Class Underwriter for Onshore Power and Energy at XL Catlin (now AXA XL Insurance; London, 9 September 2015).

risk models) do not already know. A disclosure based exclusively on public information is unlikely to satisfy an insurer. Non-public information about a property to be insured is less likely to be available to a proposer with no, or a bare economic, interest in that property. The kind of personal data required for an application for life insurance, even if it were held within the organization of the insured, is likely to be protected from onwards disclosure to a life insurer without the data subject's (i.e. A's) consent under data protection laws.[17]

A prudent insurer provided with insufficient information would want to make further enquiries,[18] and failing satisfactory responses, it would decline the risk or accept the risk subject to conditions and exclusions. O'Neill explains that brokers often assume a "screening role" by declining to present a risk to insurers on behalf of a client who does not have any, or an insufficient, interest in the subject-matter to be insured or who is unable to provide sufficient information on the risk.[19]

Actual and deemed knowledge of material circumstances relating to the property to be insured is more likely to be rooted in a relationship with the property based on ownership rights or proprietary or contractual rights to access, use or take possession. As such rights are also a basis for an insurable interest, it is suggested that there is a correlation between the requirement for, and nature of, an insurable interest and the scope of the duty of fair presentation: the presence of an insurable interest based on proprietary or contractual rights in relation to the insured property provides an optimal environment for the proposer to hold, and gain access to, the knowledge necessary for an efficient and effective risk presentation process. Without the relevant knowledge, the duty of fair presentation owed by a proposer with no, or a bare economic, interest in that property is much narrower in scope and affords less protection to insurers. Similarly, an insurable interest based on a pecuniary relationship between the insured and A is more likely to give leverage to the insured to ask A for the information, or A's consent to use information already held by the insured, for the purposes of making a presentation of the risk for life insurance. Without sufficient information on which an underwriting assessment can be based, insurers are likely to decline a risk.

In contrast, in relation to gambling contracts, neither party has a precontractual duty of disclosure since, without "any other interest in that contract than the sum or stake",[20] neither party has an inherent informational advantage. Adverse selection and information asymmetry is not an issue in gaming

---

17 Regulation (EU) 2016/679 of the European Parliament and of the Council of 27 April 2016 on the protection of natural persons with regard to the processing of personal data and on the free movement of such data, and repealing Directive 95/46/EC (General Data Protection Regulation).
18 IA 2015, s.3(4)(b).
19 Interview with Peter O'Neill (n 16).
20 *Carlill v Carbolic Smoke Ball Company* [1892] 2 QB 484 (QB) 490–491 (Hawkins J); see Chapter 6.

contracts of pure chance, such as roulette or games of dice. In all other types of gambling contracts, each party takes the risk that the other party is exploiting an informational advantage. The costs of adverse selection are reflected in the stake, the odds or the pay-out.[21]

Pre-contractual representations under CIDRA

Consumer insureds are under a pre-contractual duty to take reasonable care not to make a misrepresentation to the insurer.[22] Accordingly, insurers must ask questions about circumstances they consider relevant to their underwriting decision. Doctrinally, the absence of a requirement for an insurable interest, or a weak insurable interest, is not inconsistent with a duty not to make misrepresentations. However, the absence of an insurable interest – or a weak economic-interest-based interest in property insurance, or a weak familial link in life insurance – is likely to be a practical impediment to the proposer's ability to answer satisfactorily an insurer's questions as the following sample survey indicates:

1   Ten standard home and contents insurance proposal forms reviewed contained detailed questions about the property, including its physical characteristics, its value, its use, its claims history, hazard factors and risk mitigation measures, or made a series of assumptions about the property which the proposer must confirm as correct.
2   Six standard motor insurance proposal forms and the questionnaire of Go-Compare.com, an aggregator car insurance website (which has access to 120 car insurance brands), reviewed contained questions about the mileage, use (purpose and by whom), purchase date, overnight parking location, value and insurance/claims history of the car to be insured.
3   Preliminary questionnaires for initial quotes by three life insurance providers (Aviva, Legal & General and Post Office) and three aggregator websites (GoCompare.com, Confused.com and QuoteLifeCover.com) contained questions on A's date of birth, A's height and weight, whether A is/has been a smoker, whether A is a member of the Armed Forces or Army Reserve and A's address. The Legal & General proposal form for life insurance is a 36-page document which contains detailed questions on A's engagement in hazardous activities, residence in high-risk countries in the recent past, general health and lifestyle (present and past), medical family history and other life insurance products that A has in place or applied for. Moreover, it is standard practice for the insurer to request a medical report from A's doctor which would only be forthcoming if A has given its consent to the request and provided contact details for the doctor.

21 A Bruce and J Johnson, 'Market Ecology and Decision Behaviour in State-Contingent Claims Markets' in J Johnson and A Bruce (eds), *Decisions: Risk and Reward* (Routledge 2008) 313, 316–318 and chs 16 and 17.
22 CIDRA, s.2(2).

The structure and methodology of the proposal forms and questionnaires reviewed suggest that they were drafted with a proposer in mind who, in relation to:

1   home and contents insurance, is an owner or occupier of the property and, in relation to motor insurance, is the registered keeper, owner or regular authorized user of the car. A proposer with no, or a bare economic, interest would not ordinarily be in a position to complete these proposal forms unless he could draw upon the actual owner/occupier/registered keeper's knowledge; and
2   life insurance, is insuring its own life or is in a very close familial relationship with A, such as a spouse or partner.

A prudent insurer confronted with insufficient representations on which to base his underwriting assessment would decline to insure the property or life or, in the case of property insurance, insure it subject to exclusions and limitations of liability in relation to the risks affected by missing information.

In relation to the main property-related consumer insurance products (home/ content and motor insurance), many insurers' information-gathering processes are standardized and automated and do not allow for the acceptance of non-standard proposals. For example, incomplete online submissions are unlikely to be processed. The proposal forms for other types of consumer insurance may be more flexible and be dealt with on a case-by-case basis, but it is suggested that proposal forms aimed at the highly commoditized consumer insurance market cannot generally accommodate non-standard proposers who cannot make all the presentations required.

Causation

'Causation of loss' in insurance contract law is concerned with the degree of connectedness, temporal and spatial,[23] between the insured peril or event and the loss. As life-related insurance contracts are contingency contracts, and not contracts of indemnity, there is generally speaking no requirement that the contingent event causes a loss.[24] The following discussion is therefore limited to property insurance.

In the absence of special terms in the policy, the insurer is only liable for any loss proximately caused by a peril or event insured against and not proximately caused by an excepted or excluded peril or event.[25] A "proximate cause" does not

---

23   J Lowry and P Rawlings, '*Proximate Causation in Insurance Law*' (2005) 68 MLR 310, 311. For further discussion of causation see John Birds, Ben Lynch and Simon Paul, *MacGillivray on Insurance Law* (14th edn, Sweet & Maxwell 2018) paras 21-001–21-005.
24   *Dalby v The India and London Life Assurance Company* (1854) 15 CB 365 (ExchCham).
25   MIA 1906, s.55(1). This is also the general rule for non-marine insurance: John Birds, Ben Lynch and Simon Paul (n 23) para 21-001.

have to be the last one in time,[26] or the sole cause,[27] but it must be the dominant[28] or effective cause.[29]

No interest

In the absence of an (insurable) interest in the insured subject-matter the policyholder will not be able to prove a loss for which an indemnity is payable,[30] since any loss or damage to the insured subject-matter would not be a loss suffered by that policyholder.

Economic interests

In *Lucena*, Lawrence J highlighted the potential difficulty of proving a causational link between the peril insured against and the loss suffered by the insured if his insurable interest in the insured subject-matter is in the nature of an anticipated economic benefit:

> The objection to insuring that in which the assured has no property, seems to me to rest … on this, that if the interest intended to be protected by the assurance is liable to be affected by other matters than the perils insured against, of which matters some might happen in the interval between the time of the loss and the probable time when the risk would have ceased had no loss happened, it may be impossible to refer to those perils the prejudice or damage against which the insured meant to protect himself…[31]

Lawrence J's "objection" must be understood in the context of the then prevailing causation test: at that time, the courts' approach was to consider the last cause in time as the proximate cause.[32] Although the "proximate cause" doctrine is now focussed on the dominant or efficient cause, in property insurance, losses arising in relation to bare economic interests in property still present causational and coverage challenges in that the property loss or damage caused by the insured peril must result in economic loss to the insured that is in itself covered by the policy. The insured who has a bare economic interest in the insured property must be able to point to a chain of events in which the insured peril remains the proximate cause of his loss without the intervention of new and independent

---

26 *Leyland Shipping Co v Norwich Union Fire Insurance Society* [1918] AC 350 (HL) ('*Leyland*').
27 *Reischer v Borwick* [1894] 2 QB 458 (CA).
28 *Leyland* (n 26).
29 *Samuel & Co v Dumas* [1924] AC 431 (HL); *Global Process Systems Inc v Syarikat Takaful Malaysia Board (The Cendor Mopu)* [2011] UKSC 5.
30 See Chapters 6 and 8.
31 *Lucena* (1806) 2 Bos & Pul (NR) 269 (HL) 303. See also Chambre J's opinion on the same point and same grounds (at 299).
32 That is prior to the decision in *Leyland* (n 26).

causes. If the insured's relationship with the insured property is weak, causes other than the insured peril are likely to affect the insured's interest and it will be comparatively harder to isolate the insured peril as the proximate cause.

Taking Lord Eldon's example of the warehouse porter in *Lucena* transposed into present day, it could be argued that the warehouse porter has an economic interest in a ship: the loss of a ship and her cargo caused by 'perils of the sea' could result in financial difficulties of the ship owner, any charterer and the cargo owner which in turn could lead to their respective employees and contractors not being paid or their contracts being terminated. However, it is suggested that the warehouse porter's loss of wages is not proximately caused by 'perils of the sea' but would be the result of being made redundant (as an employee), or his contract being terminated (as a contractor).

Arguably, there would be a greater degree of proximity in a *Macaura*[33] situation where the destruction of the company's sole profit-generating asset by an insured peril causes a loss to the company's sole shareholder. Nevertheless, in *Macaura* (a post-*Leyland*-decision) Lord Sumner rejected that the insured peril (fire) was the proximate cause of Mr Macaura's loss: he had suffered loss as result of the decrease in share value, and not as result of the destruction of the timber by fire.[34] There are numerous performance-dependent and market-related factors that could concurrently and independently influence the price of a company's shares, in particular:

> ... if the asset be regarded as only one in an innumerable number of items in a company's assets and the shareholding interest be spread over a large number of individual shareholders.[35]

Conversely, the loss of a corporate asset may leave the share price unaffected, for example because the company itself may be compensated for the loss by third parties or through its own insurance arrangements.[36] In relation to an unsecured creditor, there is no loss until the debtor actually defaults and, with the passage of time and as other factors impact on the debtor's liquidity, the insured peril would become an increasingly remote cause of the loss. In situations where the insured's interest in the insured property is based exclusively on anticipated profits (i.e. the insured has no proprietary or contractual rights in relation to the insured property), it may be challenging to prove an unbroken chain of causation of insured peril → property damage → loss of anticipated profit, if such profits were contingent upon other (non-peril) events.

33 [1925] AC 619 (HL).
34 Ibid., 630.
35 Ibid., 627 (Lord Buckmaster).
36 For this reason shareholders cannot generally recover their 'reflective loss' – see Chapter 8.

Consequential loss

Economic loss that is consequential upon the loss of or damage to the insured property may not be covered under an unvalued property policy either because it is too remote under the proximate cause rule[37] or because on the true construction of the policy consequential loss is not covered.[38] The difficulty of valuing an economic loss based on an expected profit attributable to an insured peril was noted in Chapter 8.

Duty to mitigate loss

An insured with no, or a bare economic, interest in the insured property may be unable to mitigate effectively any loss of, or any damage to, that property for two reasons: first, he may not have (timely) notice of the loss that would allow him to take effective mitigation steps. Secondly, an insured with no or a bare economic interest who has no legal rights to control, deal with or access the insured property is unlikely to be in a position to take precautionary steps preventing the loss, or to avert or minimize a loss that has already occurred.[39] Conversely, an insured with a strong legal interest in the insured property would, generally speaking, be in a better position to protect the insured property against loss or damage, or, in the event of a loss, to take steps to mitigate and, in addition, it would be in his self-interest to do so.

Duty to prevent, avert and mitigate loss

Self-interest aside, is there a duty on the insured to prevent, avert or mitigate loss? Clarke maintains that, at common law, the insured has no duty to take care to avoid or *prevent an insured loss*: "… as a matter of contract interpretation, there is a strong presumption that insurance is intended to cover policyholder negligence. To cover human fallibility is one of the purposes of insurance".[40] However, as will be discussed in Chapter 10, property policy wordings often impose a general contractual obligation on the insured to take all reasonable precautions to prevent a loss and specific warranties or other terms that require specific safe-keeping and preventative measures to be in place. There is no equivalent term in life-related insurance policies, but critical illness and personal accident covers rely on medical certification which suggests that the insured life has sought medical advice and is likely to receive treatment.

---

37 *Shelbourne & Co v Law Investment & Ins Corp Ltd* [1898] 2 QB 626 (Comm Ct). See also Robert Merkin, *Colinvaux's Law of Insurance* (12th edn, Sweet & Maxwell 2019) paras 11-216 and 11-218.
38 John Birds, Ben Lynch and Simon Paul (n 23) para 21-014.
39 See Chapter 7.
40 Malcolm Clarke, *The Law of Insurance Contracts* (Service Issue 37, Informa 2016) para 28-8G1, citing *State of the Netherlands v Youell* [1998] 1 Lloyd's Rep 236 (CA).

Once an insured loss under a contract of marine insurance is imminent, or has occurred, the insured and his agents come under a statutory duty "to take such measures as may be reasonable for the purposes of *averting or minimising a loss*",[41] also known as the duty to sue and labour. In non-marine insurance, the existence of any duty to avert an imminent loss, in the absence of an express contractual term to that effect by operation of law, is less clear. In the absence of an express term, it is doubtful whether the courts would imply a duty to mitigate into a non-marine property insurance contract,[42] although MacDonald Eggers argues that the duty of mitigation applicable upon breach in general contract law should apply to insurance contracts.[43] It appears that the courts' approach would be to consider this as a matter of causation: if the insured fails to take reasonable measures to avert or minimize a loss, the chain of causation between the originally operative insured peril and the loss may be broken.[44] Unless the insured's negligence in failing to take mitigation measures is covered by a separate insured peril under the policy in question, the insured would then be unable to prove that the insured peril was the proximate cause of his loss and would thus fail to have an indemnifiable claim.

Reasonableness and insurable interest

Where a duty to take reasonable measures to avert or mitigate loss is imposed by statute or by contract, and to the extent that there is a corresponding common law duty, the question what is reasonable is assessed by reference to a hypothetical prudent uninsured,[45] who has the characteristics of the insured in question.[46] One of these characteristics should be the insured's relationship with the insured property – in other words, the nature and extent of his insurable interest – since it is his interest that will determine what precautionary or mitigation measures he is able and entitled to take.

If the insured has full ownership rights in the insured property, a wide range of precautionary and mitigation measures are, in theory, available to him. An insured with lesser legal rights in relation to the property may have contractual rights against a third party entitling him to require that third party to take mitigation measures. In contrast, an insured with no, or a bare economic, interest

---

41 MIA 1906, s.78(4).

42 In *Yorkshire Water v Sun Alliance & London Insurance plc* [1997] 2 Lloyd's LR 21 (CA) 30, Stuart-Smith LJ declined to imply a general duty to mitigate into a contract of liability insurance on the grounds that such a duty is usually incorporated as an express term.

43 Peter MacDonald Eggers, '*Sue and Labour and Beyond: The Assured's Duty of Mitigation*' [1998] LMCLQ 228.

44 *National Oilwell* [1993] 2 Lloyd's Rep 582 (Comm Ct) 618 (Colman J); *Yorkshire Water v Sun Alliance & London Insurance plc* (n 42) 33 (Otton LJ); *State of the Netherlands v Youell* (n 40) 53–54 (Philips LJ).

45 *Integrated Container Services Inc v British Traders Insurance Co Ltd* [1984] 1 Lloyd's Rep 154 (CA).

46 *Stephen v Scottish Boatowner Mutual Insurance Association* [1989] 1 Lloyd's Rep 535 (HL).

in the insured property who has no access to or control rights in the insured property is not in a position to take steps to prevent or mitigate loss of, or damage to, the insured property. Moreover, he may not have timely notice of the loss that would have allowed him to take effective steps to mitigate. Under a duty to take *reasonable* measures the insured would not be expected to take any steps (1) without notice of loss, or (2) contrary to his commercial interest[47] or (3) any steps that are unlawful (e.g. to trespass, or to commit any other tort), in order to avert or minimize loss. An insured who stands in no legal or equitable relation to a property cannot be expected to take any steps to protect such property from loss or damage or mitigate loss or damage to such property as there is no general legal duty to rescue property belonging to another, or any general liability for failing to act to prevent loss or damage to property of others.[48] A duty to take reasonable mitigation measures would be rendered meaningless. An insured with a bare economic interest can, at most, mitigate the economic consequences from the loss of the insured property that affect him. Any duty to take reasonable measures to avert or mitigate loss is likely to afford poor protection to the insurer if the insured is not in a position to take any such steps on account of his limited interest.

In contrast, as will be discussed in Chapter 10, if the contract of insurance requires specific precautionary or mitigation measures which are expressed as absolute obligations on the insured (i.e. not qualified by reasonableness), an insured with a bare economic interest may be incapable of performing such an obligation, or ensuring compliance with it, on account of having no legal rights in relation to the insured property that would allow him to take such measures.

Failure to mitigate as an intervening cause

Could a third party's failure to take mitigation measures break the chain of causation? Consider the following example: a supplier of components insures the buyer's factory premises and machinery. The supplier has an economic interest in the buyer's factory and the machinery as he would suffer economic loss if the factory and machinery were destroyed, production stopped and the factory owner ceased to buy the components. A fire (an insured peril) breaks out on the factory's premises. The (uninsured) owner of the factory decides not to call the fire brigade immediately, thereby allowing the fire to spread. The factory and machinery burn down completely. If the fire brigade had been called immediately, the fire could have been contained and production could have been

---

47 Case law on 'reasonable endeavour' obligations (as opposed to 'best endeavours' obligations) suggests that discharge of such obligations does not require the relevant contract party to sacrifice its own commercial interests – see *Yewbelle Ltd v London Green Developments Ltd* [2006] EWHC 3166 (Ch), discussed in *Jet2.com Ltd v Blackpool Airport Ltd* [2012] EWCA Civ 417, [20–32] (Moore-Bick LJ).

48 See Michael Jones, Anthony Dugdale and Mark Simpson, *Clerk & Lindsell on Torts* (22nd edn, Sweet & Maxwell 2017) paras 1–55 and 1–56.

resumed within hours. The insured does not learn about the fire until a few days later. A court may take the view that the proximate cause of the supplier's loss is the owner's inaction, not the fire itself. If the supplier's policy is a fire policy that does not cover perils other than fire, the insured has no claim. If the insured's policy is a property all risks policy, he would be covered unless there is a specific exclusion applying to the owner's failure to mitigate. In both scenarios, although the original peril (fire) is covered under the policy, the insurer's ultimate liability depends on the conduct of a third party over which neither the insured nor the insurer can exercise control. Thus, in some situations, the insurer may (unknowingly) take on the additional risk of a third party failing to mitigate loss in relation to the insured subject-matter, whereas in other cases, the insured's cover may be compromised on account of the (in)action of a third party. The third party does not owe any contractual mitigation duties under the insurance contract, the performance of which the insured can compel, or if breached, entitle, the insurer to decline liability. This 'third party failure to mitigate risk' does not arise (to the same extent) in contracts of property insurance where the insured has an insurable interest based on legal or contractual rights in relation to the property that are consistent with taking mitigation measures or contractually requiring a third party to do so.

Although insurers could seek to exclude expressly liability for loss resulting from a third party's failure to avert or minimize loss, the duty to mitigate is another example of a legal principle that operates more efficiently with a doctrine of insurable interest that is based on legal or contractual rights in the insured subject-matter and is rendered meaningless if the insured does not have any interest.

Abandonment

Abandonment is a legal principle that arises in indemnity insurance.[49] As life-related insurance contracts are contingency contracts, and not contracts of indemnity,[50] the principle of abandonment has no application.

Abandonment refers to the insured's election, and its acceptance by the insurer, to transfer the insured's proprietary rights in the insured subject-matter to the insurer if the insured is being indemnified for a total loss.[51] In the early history of insurable interest, the ability to transfer salvage rights appears to have been one of the rationales of the doctrine of insurable interest: "… and the reason the law [requiring an interest in the insured ship] goes upon, is that … where one would have the benefit of insurance, he must renounce all interest in the ship".[52] As the concept of abandonment entails the transfer of title in the

---

49 *Kaltenbach v McKenzie* (1887) 3 CPD 467 (CA) 471 (Brett LJ).

50 See n 24.

51 In relation to marine insurance, see MIA 1906, ss.61–63. An adapted concept of abandonment also applies to non-marine property indemnity insurance – see John Birds, Ben Lynch and Simon Paul (n 23) para 24-008.

52 *Goddart v Garrett* (1692) 23 ER 774.

insured subject-matter to the insurer,[53] an insurable interest based on proprietary rights in the insured subject-matter is essential to the insured's election to abandon. It is not argued that the insured must have an insurable interest based on proprietary rights; however, it is suggested that a lesser interest precludes the operation of abandonment. An insured without an insurable interest, or indeed even an insured who has mere contractual rights, or a bare economic interest, in relation to the insured property cannot make a valid abandonment of the insured property.[54]

Subrogation

An insurer is entitled to exercise rights of subrogation if the insurer has made an indemnity payment to the insured in respect of the insured loss[55] and his rights of subrogation are not otherwise excluded. In so far as the insured has been indemnified, the insurer becomes subrogated to all rights and remedies of the insured in and in respect of the insured subject-matter insured,[56] principally being rights of action against third parties and rights to recoveries (see below).

Relationship with the doctrine of insurable interest

The principle of subrogation only applies to indemnity insurance contracts,[57] but not to life-related insurance contracts that are contingency contracts.[58] In the absence of any interest in the insured subject-matter the policyholder will not be able to prove a loss for which an indemnity is payable, since without such an interest one cannot suffer any indemnifiable loss.[59] A contract under which payment is due to one party which is not in the nature of an indemnity for loss is not an indemnity contract. It follows that the principle of subrogation is not applicable if the insured has no interest in the insured subject-matter since the insured cannot suffer an indemnifiable loss, and any payment made to the insured would not be in the nature of an indemnity. In relation to property insurance, the doctrine of insurable interest, the indemnity principle and the principles of abandonment and subrogation operate in concentric circles: without an insurable interest, there can be no indemnifiable loss; without an indemnifiable and indemnified loss, abandonment or subrogation rights do not arise;

---

53 MIA 1906, s.63(1).
54 *Kulen Kemp v. Vigne* 1786) 1 TR 304 (KB) 308. Lord Mansfield said: "A necessary consequence of this being a wagering policy is, that the insured cannot abandon".
55 *John Edwards and Co v Motor Union Insurance Co Ltd* [1922] 2 KB 249 (KB) 254–255 (McCardie J).
56 MIA 1906, s.79(2). For further discussion see John Birds, Ben Lynch and Simon Paul (n 23) ch 24.
57 *Castellain v Preston* (1883) 11 QBD 380 (CA).
58 *The Solicitors' General Life Assurance Society v Lamb* (1864) 2 De GJ & S 251 (Ch).
59 See Chapters 6 and 8.

and, accordingly, without an insurable interest, abandonment and subrogation rights cannot be pursued.

Rights of action against third parties

Upon payment of an indemnity to the insured, the insurer is entitled to exercise, in the name of the insured, all rights and remedies of the insured against third parties who are legally responsible for the loss suffered by the insured.[60]

No interest: An insured without any interest in the insured property would not be able to establish any cause of action against a third party responsible for the loss of, or damage to, the insured property since he would not be able to show that the third party failed to perform an obligation or breached a duty owed to the insured in relation to the insured property, or violated one of the insured's rights in the insured property. If the insured had any rights or remedy in relation to the insured property, he would have an (insurable) interest.

Economic interest: An insurer would generally not be able to take advantage of subrogation rights in respect of actions against third parties if the insured has a bare economic insurable interest since the insured would not usually have any rights of action against third parties in those circumstances:

1   In the absence of proprietary rights in the insured property, there can be no claims in tort for physical damage to property: the torts of trespass to land, nuisance, trespass to goods and negligence causing property damage all protect property interests[61] and are not concerned with pure economic loss.
2   In the absence of rights in relation to the insured property deriving from a contract between the insured and the third party, there can be no action for breach of contract.
3   Within the boundaries of a proximate relationship between the claimant and the defendant giving rise to a duty of care, economic loss may be recoverable under the tort of negligence.[62] However, no such duty of care is generally owed by a defendant who negligently damages property belonging to a claimant who suffers economic (but no physical) loss as a result.[63] The reasons for this no-recovery rule are that there will generally be no proximate relationship between the wrongdoer and the party suffering pure economic loss as a result, and there could potentially be indeterminate claims.[64]

---

60 *Castellain v Preston* (n 57) 388 (Brett LJ).
61 Michael Jones, Anthony Dugdale and Mark Simpson (n 48) paras 1-39 to 1-41.
62 *Hedley Byrne v Heller* [1964] AC 465 (HL); *Caparo Industries Plc v Dickman* [1990] 2 AC 605 (HL); *Robinson v Chief Constable of West Yorkshire* [2018] UKSC 4.
63 *Cattle v Stockton Waterworks Co* (1875) LR 10 QB 453 (QB); *Candlewood Navigation Corp Ltd v Mitsui OSK Lines Ltd* [1986] AC 1 (PC); *Leigh & Sillivan Ltd v Aliakmon Shipping Co* [1986] AC 785 (HL). For further discussion see Michael Jones, Anthony Dugdale and Mark Simpson (n 48) paras 8-144 to 8-146.
64 *Cattle v Stockton Waterworks Co* (n 63) 457 (Blackburn J); *Spartan Steel & Alloys Ltd v Martin* [1973] QB 27 (CA) 38–39 (Lord Denning MR).

Therefore, unless the facts of the case support a duty of care owed to the (insured) claimant by the wrongdoer, an insured with a bare economic interest in the property insured will not have any cause of action in negligence against a wrongdoer responsible for the loss of, or damage to, the insured property.

4   The 'no reflective loss' principle prevents a shareholder from recovering damages in relation to contractual or tortious claims against a third party where the company also has a claim against the same third party arising out of the same set of facts.[65] Thus, in a *Macaura*[66] scenario, where an insurer indemnifies a shareholder for loss in respect of company assets, there would be no subrogated action in respect of reflective loss.

Rights to recoveries

Upon payment of an indemnity to the insured, the insurer is entitled to claim from the insured any benefits received by the insured in extinction or diminution of the loss for which he has been indemnified to the extent they exceed the insured's total loss and up to the amount paid by the insurer.[67] The insured holds the benefit subject to an equitable lien in favour of the insurer in respect of the insurer's share.[68]

No interest: An insured without any interest in the insured property cannot suffer an indemnifiable loss.[69] Any payment made by the insurer would not be in the nature of an indemnity, and any benefits received by the insured from third parties would not be 'in respect of the loss', and, accordingly, no subrogation rights would arise.

Economic interest: Could an insured with a bare economic interest receive benefits in respect of his loss? As discussed above, an insured with a bare economic interest in the property insured is unlikely to have any cause of action against any third party responsible for the loss of, or damage to, that property. Accordingly, such an insured is unlikely to receive any damages payments or other compensation from such a third party which, once received, would constitute benefits to which an insurer could be subrogated. An insured with a bare economic interest may receive an ex gratia payment or a gift from a third party. It is now accepted that if an ex gratia payment or gift was made to the insured with the intention of extinguishing or diminishing the loss indemnified by the insurer, the insurer is entitled to be subrogated to such a payment.[70] As ex gratia payments and gifts made in respect of an economic loss are rare, in the majority of cases, an insurer

---

65 See Chapter 8.

66 n 33.

67 *Castellain v Preston* (n 57) 388 (Brett LJ); *Darrell v Tibbits* (1880) 5 QBD 560 (CA).

68 *Lord Napier and Ettrick v Hunter* [1993] AC 73 (HL).

69 See Chapters 6 and 8.

70 See *Colonia Versicherung AG v Amoco Oil Co* [1997] 1 Lloyd's Rep 261 (CA); John Birds, Ben Lynch and Simon Paul (n 23) para 24-07.

could not expect to be able to take advantage of subrogation rights in respect of recoveries if the insured has no, or a bare economic, insurable interest.

Significance of abandonment and subrogation

It may be argued that the availability of abandonment/salvage rights and subrogation rights is not in itself a justification for the retention of the doctrine of insurable interest for a number of reasons: first, even if the doctrine of insurable interest is retained, abandonment and subrogation rights are not available in every type of insurance and for every type of loss: for example, neither principle applies in non-indemnity insurance and third party liability insurance, abandonment does not apply in instances of partial loss[71] and subrogation rights against third parties will not arise if the loss was caused by natural causes. Secondly, the operation of the principle of subrogation itself is not uncontroversial: some commentators have queried its rationales (preventing double recovery and fixing liability on the wrongdoer) and have argued that it can operate unfairly and lead to wasteful litigation.[72] Thirdly, it has been questioned whether the availability of subrogation rights is in fact material to insurers' underwriting decisions and is not reflected in premium rates.[73] Whilst these points are noted, whether or not subrogation rights are available in other types of insurance and whether the principle of subrogation itself is justified has no direct bearing on the argument put forward in this thesis that the doctrine of insurable interest, requiring the insured to have an insurable interest in the insured property, is apposite to the operation of the principles of subrogation and abandonment in property insurance.

In addition, it is suggested that permitting insureds with bare economic interests to insure property could compound subrogation issues arising from multiple insurance coverage on the same risk. It was argued in Chapter 6 that multiple exposure risk is likely to arise on a larger scale and would be more difficult to detect and to anticipate if persons with no interest or a bare economic interest in the insured subject-matter are entitled to insure. If there is a multiplicity of

---

71 MIA 1906, s.60(1).

72 For a discussion of whether subrogation is justified see R Hasson, '*Subrogation in Insurance Law: A Critical Evaluation*' (1985) 5 OJLS 416; SR Derham, *Subrogation in Insurance Law* (Sydney, The Law Book Company 1985) excerpted in J Lowry and P Rawlings, *Insurance Law: Cases and Materials* (Hart Publishing 2004) [1222]; R Merkin and J Steele, *Insurance and the Law of Obligations* (OUP 2013) ch 5.

73 There is no comprehensive and up-to-date data on how the availability of subrogation rights affects premium rates and the amount/percentage of subrogation recoveries actually made. See R Merkin and J Steele (n 72) fn 76 in ch 5; SR Derham (n 72). Matters relevant to subrogation rights and recoveries can be material to a prudent underwriter: see *Tate v Hyslop* (1883) 15 QBD 368 (CA); *Société Anonyme D'Intermediaries Luxembourgeois v. Farex Gie* [1995] LRLR 116 (CA); contra *Marc Rich & Co AG v Portman* [1996] 1 Lloyd's Rep 430 (Comm Ct). O'Neill (n 16) said that in energy downstream underwriting potential subrogation rights are not taken into account in pricing because subrogation rights are assumed to be available. Stahl (Head of Complex Claims at Allianz Group) indicated that policyholders without any subrogation rights would be a "less attractive" underwriting proposition.

insurance contracts in relation to the same subject-matter, there could be considerable uncertainty as to which policies should respond and to what extent a claims payment in relation to one insured would, directly or indirectly, compensate other insureds. Once claims have been paid, there could be very complex subrogation issues as a result of such overlapping coverage. Such issues would give rise to additional litigation risk.

Overlapping actions: A third party wrongdoer may be pursued in subrogated actions by several insurers who have insured different interests in the insured property. Hasson noted that this can result in wasteful litigation.[74] The risk of complex and potentially wasteful litigation increases the more interests in the same property are insured and could be compounded by an additional layer of insurance contracts in respect of economic interest in the property. Such litigation may entail difficult legal and factual questions as to the extent different insureds have definable individual interests from the aggregate interest[75] and whether or not loss in respect of an individual interest is merely 'reflective' of loss that has already been compensated in relation to a loss suffered by another party.[76] There is also a practical problem in that these subrogated actions may be brought independently and not on a consolidated basis.

Overlapping benefits: As regards an insurer's subrogation right to any benefits received in respect of the indemnified loss, the question arises whether, and in what circumstances, benefits received by other parties interested in the insured property that nevertheless indirectly benefit insureds with bare economic interests should be taken into account. For example, consider a *Macaura*[77] situation, where a company insures one of its major corporate assets: one of its shareholders insures that asset independently with another insurer. The asset is destroyed by a third party (which is an insured peril) and the shareholder successfully claims under his insurance policy. Subsequently, the company is paid a claim, or the asset is reinstated, under its insurance policy. Later, the company also receives compensation from the third party in respect of the loss. Clearly, the company's insurer has subrogation rights in respect of that recovery. But what rights by way of subrogation would the shareholder's insurer have? Would he have any direct entitlement to the compensation payment of the third party? This is unlikely as it would mean that the compensation payment in the hands of the company is subject to two equitable liens[78] – one in favour of the company's insurer and another lien in favour of the shareholder's insurer. Would the shareholder's insurer be entitled to the benefit of any increase in share price of the shares held by the insured shareholder that is attributable to receipt of the compensation payment? Would he be entitled to a return of the claims payment?

74 R Hasson (n 72) sec III.
75 Ibid.
76 See above and Chapter 8.
77 *Macaura* (n 33).
78 *Lord Napier and Ettrick v Hunter* (n 68).

Similar and additional issues could arise in debtor and creditor scenarios, where the debtor, secured and unsecured creditors each insure a major asset of the debtor independently, the asset is destroyed by a third party and all parties claim under their respective insurances. Subsequently, the debtor makes a recovery from the third party responsible for the loss. If a secured creditor applies his insurance proceeds towards the extinction of the debt, this would be a benefit in respect of the debtor's loss and may therefore be available to the debtor's insurer.[79] As the debtor is discharged from this debt, could this in turn be considered a benefit accruing to the debtor (i.e. the reduction of his total liabilities) to whom the unsecured creditor's insurer could be subrogated? A practical problem might be that the insurers of the shareholders, or the creditors (as the case may be), may be unaware of other insurance arrangements in respect of the insured property and any recoveries made.

The principles of indemnity, abandonment and subrogation all depend upon the existence of an insurable interest. As regards the duty of fair presentation, the principle of utmost good faith and the concept of causation and the duty to mitigate loss, it has been argued that their operation is underpinned by the doctrine of insurable interest. The presence of an insurable interest provides an optimal environment for the proposer to hold, and gain access to, the knowledge necessary for an effective risk presentation. The duty to mitigate is rendered meaningless if the insured does not have an insurable interest and operates more efficiently with a doctrine of insurable interest that is based on legal or contractual rights in the insured subject-matter. A strong insurable interest based on proprietary or contractual rights in property also helps to establish that the insured's loss was proximately caused by an insured peril. Further, the doctrine of insurable interest also supports the observance of utmost good faith since it operates as a doctrinal mechanism that counters specific types of moral hazard. These propositions indicate that the doctrine of insurable interest is interconnected with other legal doctrines and principles of insurance law. The doctrine of insurable interest could not be abolished without its removal having a fundamental impact on the remaining body of insurance law as the absence of an insurable interest requirement would render some of its doctrines and principles inapplicable, inoperable or meaningless. It is therefore suggested that the doctrine of insurable interest can be rationalized on a novel ground: its existence is integral to the operation of other doctrines and principles of insurance law. Moreover, in relation to property insurance, this Chapter has highlighted that the existing body of insurance contract law favours a narrow meaning of insurable interest based on proprietary or contractual rights in the insured property as some legal doctrines and principles (pre-contractual risk presentation, mitigation and subrogation) would operate less efficiently and more unpredictably if the insured had a bare economic interest in the insured property, as well as creating additional litigation risk.

---

79 John Birds, Ben Lynch and Simon Paul (n 23) para 24-092.

10 The integral dimension of insurable interest – policy terms

Building upon the argument that the doctrine of insurable interest is integral to the operation of other doctrines and principles of insurance law made in the previous Chapter, this Chapter will examine the extent to which the doctrine is part of the fabric of standard property insurance policy wordings. To that end, a sample of 50 property policy wordings was collected and reviewed. A full list is contained in Table 10.1, and for ease of reference, each wording has been given an identification number.

Methodology for survey

This survey includes 14 Institute Clauses,[1] one marine cargo policy incorporating the Institute Cargo Clauses (A) 1/9/2009,[2] 19 consumer policy wordings (mostly standard home/content and motor insurance)[3] and 16 non-consumer policy wordings relating to different types of property.[4] Forty-five out of the 50 policy wordings are standard wordings that were obtained from published wording collections and through Internet searches in 2016 and 2019.[5] The author also contacted 12 insurance companies and insurance brokers, which yielded property insurance wordings from two insurance companies provided on conditions of confidentiality and anonymity.[6] The author was unable to obtain sample wordings for parametric policies and ILW but, in any event, the focus of the survey is on standard, not bespoke, property policy wordings. Only policies governed by English law were included in the survey.

The purpose of this survey was to establish to what extent the doctrine of insurable interest is reflected in specific contractual terms commonly found in

---

1 Nos.1–14, all Institute Clauses except Freight. Institute Clauses are standard marine insurance policy terms devised for the incorporation into contracts of marine insurance.
2 No.15.
3 Nos.16–24.
4 Nos.25–48.
5 Nos.1–14; 16–23 and 25–45.
6 Nos.15, 24 and 46–48. The relevant entries in Table 10.1 have been anonymized.

Table 10.1 List of property policies included in the survey

ID No	Type	Insurer/ Organisation	Title
1.	Marine	Institute	Institute Time Clauses Hulls 1/10/83
2.	Marine	Institute	Institute Voyage Clauses Hulls 1/10/83
3.	Marine	Institute	Institute Time Clauses Hulls 1/11/95
4.	Marine	Institute	Institute Voyage Clauses Hulls 1/11/95
5.	Marine	Institute	International Hull Clauses 1/11/03
6.	Marine	Institute	Institute Cargo Clauses (A) 1/1/82
7.	Marine	Institute	Institute Cargo Clauses (B) 1/1/82
8.	Marine	Institute	Institute Cargo Clauses (C) 1/1/82
9.	Marine	Institute	Institute Cargo Clauses (A) 1/9/09
10.	Marine	Institute	Institute Cargo Clauses (B) 1/9/09
11.	Marine	Institute	Institute Cargo Clauses (C) 1/9/09
12.	Marine	Institute	Institute War Clauses (Cargo) 1/1/82
13.	Marine	Institute	Institute Strike Clauses (Cargo) 1/1/82
14.	Marine	Institute	Institute War Clauses (Cargo) 1/1/09
15.	Marine	[Anonymous]	Marine Cargo Policy
16.	Consumer Home & Content	More Than (RSA)	Home Choice Policy
17.	Consumer Home & Content	Aviva	Home Policy
18.	Consumer Home & Content	AIG	Home, Contents & Collections Policy Wording
19.	Consumer Home & Content	AXA	HomeSmart
20.	Consumer Home & Content	Direct Line	Home Insurance Plus
21.	Consumer Home & Content	Allianz	Home Policy
22.	Consumer Home & Content	Hiscox	Home Insurance
23.	Consumer Home & Content	Legal & General	Home Insurance
24.	Consumer Home & Content	[Anonymous]	[xxx] Home Insurance Policy Wording
25.	Consumer Motor	More Than (RSA)	Car Insurance
26.	Consumer Motor	Aviva	Car Policy
27.	Consumer Motor	AIG	Motor Policy
28.	Consumer Motor	AXA	Car Insurance
29.	Consumer Motor	Direct Line	Car Insurance
30.	Consumer Motor	Allianz	Car Insurance Policy
31.	Consumer Motor	Legal & General	Motor Policy
32.	Consumer Yacht	AIG	Yacht Policy
33.	Consumer Valuables	AIG	Collections Policy

ID No	Type	Insurer/ Organisation	Title
34.	Consumer Valuables	Hiscox	Fine Art Policy
35.	Business Motor	More Than (RSA)	Van Choice Policy
36.	Business Motor	More Than (RSA)	Business Car Insurance Policy
37.	Commercial Property	More Than (RSA)	Office Policy
38.	Commercial Property	Aviva	Business Insurance Policy
39.	Commercial Property	AIG	Commercial Combined Policy
40.	Commercial Property	AXA	Shops Policy
41.	Commercial Property	AXA	Offices Policy
42.	Engineering	Allianz	All Machinery Policy
43.	Engineering	Allianz	Construction Project All Risks Policy Wording
44.	Commercial Property	Hiscox	Office Buildings & Contents Policy
45.	Commercial Property	Hiscox	Charity Buildings & Contents Policy
46.	Commercial Property	[Anonymous]	[xxx] Global Commercial Property Policy
47.	Commercial Property	[Anonymous]	[xxx] Global Protection Policy
48.	Aircraft	[Anonymous]	[xxx] Aircraft Insurance Policy
49.	Aircraft	Kiln / Lloyd's of London	Unmanned Aircraft Systems ('UAS') Operators Insurance Policy Wording
50.	Commercial Property	Zurich	Shop – Retailers, Salons, Pubs and Restaurants Policy

standard property policy wordings. All 50 wordings were reviewed term-by-term to identify:

1   terms that require the insured to have an insurable interest;
2   terms that would be rendered inapplicable, or operate differently, or be incapable of being discharged, if the insured had no insurable interest, or a bare economic interest; and
3   terms that expressly or implicitly reject the existence of an insurable interest (no such terms were found).

Any policy terms that were neutral vis-à-vis the doctrine of insurable interest are not part of the discussion below. The survey excluded from review the liability cover sections in mixed/combined policies. Also excluded from the survey are life(-related) insurance policies as an insurable interest in the life insured is only required at the time of the contract, and the requirement is therefore less relevant to the terms and performance of a contract of life(-related) insurance.

Insurable interest and title requirements

Policies Nos.6–15 require the insured to have an insurable interest as a condition precedent to liability for a claim. Policies Nos.37 and 40–43 stipulate that the contract of insurance becomes void, voidable or cancellable if the insured ceases to have an insurable interest (and fails to give notice thereof). Some policies, whilst not expressly referencing the term 'insurable interest', require the insured to have a specific relationship with the insured property that is based on ownership, possession, use, control or legal responsibility.[7] Yet other policies leave the exact nature of the relationship between the insured and the insured subject-matter unspecified and refer more generically to "your property", "your home", "your car", "your building", "your yacht" or "your fine art".[8] The use of the possessive pronoun "your" in itself is unlikely to be interpreted as requiring the insured to have legal title to the insured subject-matter, but it is indicative of the parties' intention that the insured should have some relationship with the insured subject-matter. In particular its use in consumer insurance contracts can be seen as 'plain English' for a number of proprietary or contractual relationships as between the insured and the insured subject-matter.

There are also some policy terms that presuppose that the insured subject-matter is 'owned' by the insured: for example, it is a claims condition under Policy No.24 that the insured provides proof of ownership of the insured contents for which he claims. Policy No.49 requires the insured property to remain the property of the insured. Other wordings require notification of change in ownership of "your car/vehicle",[9] notice of a "change in ownership"[10] or consent to sale or transfer of "your yacht".[11] Some policies provide for cover being extended to property "acquired" by the insured after inception of the policy[12] – the inference being that such newly acquired property will be insured alongside specified property that is already in the insured's ownership or possession at the inception date.

The home and contents policy wordings reviewed tended to cover contents and personal effects which "belong" or are "owned" by the insured or family members and other (permanent) household members, or for which the insured is "legally responsible".[13] What is the basis for an insurable interest in items

---

7 Defining insured property by reference to the insured's relationship with it is prevalent in contents and personal belongings cover: see e.g. Nos.15, 17, 18, 23, 25, 35, 38, 40, 41, 42 and 46.
8 See e.g. Nos.18–20, 25, 26, 28–30, 32, 34, 35, 38, 44, 45 and 50.
9 See e.g. Nos.25 and 26.
10 See e.g. Nos.1 and 3.
11 No.32, General Condition 9.
12 No.33, Pt III, Condition C 4; No.38, Other Cover section.
13 No.17, Definition 'You'; No.18, Definition 'You'; No.19, Definition 'Content'; No.20, Definition 'You'; No.22, Definition 'You'.

belonging to family members and other household members? First, as may be the case with furniture and household goods, they may be owned jointly by the insured and another family member (e.g. as between husband and wife). Secondly, the insured may be insuring on behalf of himself and as agent for his family. It is for this reason that the schedule to a home and contents policy usually lists the insured's partner, any children, family members and any other household members who live with them permanently. Thirdly, the insured may have an insurable interest as a bailee of the goods.[14]

These contractual terms requiring a relationship between the insured and the insured property are consistent with the current law that requires an insured to have an insurable interest in the insured subject-matter which, in relation to property insurance, is based on a proprietary or contractual right in the property insured. They reflect the parties' intention that a contract of property insurance provides insurance cover for specified (categories of) property with which the insured has a relationship and are evidence that it is the parties' understanding that contracts of property insurance must be supported by an insurable interest.

Clauses requiring loss and exclusion of consequential loss

All policy wordings reviewed are indemnity policies, covering the insured for loss or damage to the insured property. The relationship between the indemnity principle and the doctrine of insurable interest has already been considered, and it was argued that the insured cannot suffer an indemnifiable loss without any interest in the insured property.[15]

Twenty-three wordings expressly restrict cover to direct physical loss of the insured property and/or expressly exclude from cover consequential or indirect loss or subsequent damage.[16] Typical forms of wordings are cover "… against all risks of direct physical loss or damage to [the property] …",[17] and exclusion from coverage of "…consequential loss or damage of any kind …".[18] Some of the business property policies exclude consequential loss generally but then provide for a specific type of consequential loss – such as business income loss, or emergency expenses, as a result of physical loss to the insured property – to be covered.[19] Any loss suffered by an insured with a bare economic interest is likely to be a financial loss consequential to actual physical loss or damage to the insured property and, accordingly, may fall into one of the categories of loss that are not covered by the policy. Such a policy would be worthless to the insured. Given that many property policy wordings require direct physical loss, and excluding consequential loss, is evidence that these policies operate on the assumption that

---

14 *Hepburn v A Tomlinson (Hauliers) Ltd* [1966] AC 451 (HL).
15 See Chapters 6 and 8.
16 Nos.16, 18, 22–24, 28–30, 32–38, 42, 50.
17 No.18, Pt IV Sec A.
18 No.38, Property Damage Cover, Exception 11.
19 See e.g. Nos.44–46, 49–50.

the insured has an insurable interest based on proprietary or contractual rights in the insured property, and the notion of such an insurable interest is embedded in the policy terms.

Retention, deductibles and limits of liability

Deductibles and retention provisions specify a fixed amount or a percentage of the loss for which the insured remains responsible. If a loss occurs, the insured will not be indemnified for the deductible or the retention. This ensures that the insured bears a portion of the cost of a loss and, thus, he is incentivized to protect the insured property against loss and, if a loss occurs, to take steps to minimize it. It also means that insurers do not have the administrative burden of dealing with a large number of small claims. Limit of liability provisions set out maximum amounts either for specific losses or the total amount that can be recovered under a policy even if the insured's actual loss exceeds such limit. Their purpose is to set a limit to the insurer's maximum potential exposure under any given policy and to encourage the insured to take loss mitigation measures. In property policies, the maximum limit of liability is often tied to the (aggregate) property value, which also is another means of excluding unforeseen consequential losses.

All of the wordings reviewed, except for the Institute Cargo Clauses,[20] either contain express provisions as to retentions, deductibles and limit(s) of liability or make reference to retentions, deductibles and limit(s) of liability being set out in the relevant policy schedule. As for the Institute Cargo Clauses, it should be borne in mind that they are not used as stand-alone contracts but that they are standard terms for incorporation into specific contracts of insurance. In the London marine insurance market, the prevalent form of contract now in use is the London Market Group's Market Reform Contract, which contains limits of liability and excess (deductible) provisions.

Limits of liability, retentions and deductible provisions in property policies would be rendered inapplicable without an underlying insurable interest in the insured subject-matter. Without any interest in the insured subject-matter, the policyholder cannot sustain an indemnifiable loss[21] to which limits of liability, retentions and deductibles could be applied. Moreover, it is the insured's interest in the insured subject-matter that is relevant to the valuation of the loss. A limit of liability provision which limits the insurer's liability for an insured loss suffered by the policyholder would be rendered redundant if there is no chance that the insurer incurs any liability for loss, and could not be applied if the amount of loss has not been given a value. Similarly, without any interest in the insured subject-matter, there would be no possibility of an insured loss and, accordingly, the insurer would not become liable to pay any indemnity to which a deductible or excess could be applied. Any deductible or excess provisions would

20 Nos.6–14.
21 See n 15.

be rendered redundant. Unless there is any interest that is at risk of being lost or damaged by an insured peril, any retention of risk provisions would remain inoperative since, mathematically, a percentage share of zero is zero. In other words, the presence of an insurable interest is essential to the operation of limits of liability, retentions and deductible provisions in property policies.

However, such provisions are not inherently inconsistent with an insurable interest based on the insured's economic interest in the insured subject-matter. It is conceivable to apply them to economic loss, always provided that the insured can furnish proof of loss, which may be difficult as a matter of coverage and causation.[22] If there are sub-limits of liability and/or deductibles applying to specific types of losses, it would be a matter of construction as to whether or not they would be applicable to economic loss consequential upon direct physical loss or damage to the insured property.

Loss prevention and loss mitigation

Forty-nine out of the 50 wordings reviewed contain express provisions relating to loss prevention and/or loss mitigation:

1   Seventeen wordings impose specific loss prevention obligations on the insured.[23]
2   Twenty-eight wordings impose general duty to take reasonable precautions to prevent loss.[24]
3   Fifteen wordings impose a duty to sue and labour.[25] and
4   Fourteen wordings impose loss mitigation duties on the insured once a loss has occurred.[26]

These contractual obligations supplement or modify any duties to prevent or minimize loss arising at law.[27] The prevalence of the contractual loss prevention and mitigation terms indicates that property policies assume that the insured is someone who has a relationship with the insured property that allows him to take precautionary loss prevention measures and, upon a loss, to take loss mitigation steps in relation to the insured property.

It is contended that such provisions would not operate as intended if the policyholder has no insurable interest or a bare economic interest in the insured property. By way of example, let us consider the *specific loss prevention measures* that More Than (RSA) requires its insureds to have in place under the Home Choice Policy:

22 See above and Chapter 9.
23 Nos.16, 18, 20, 23–25, 28, 29, 33, 35–37, 42–45, 47.
24 Nos.16, 17, 20–30, 32, 34–36, 40–50.
25 Nos.1–15.
26 Nos.16, 19, 24, 31–33, 37–43, 50.
27 See Chapter 9.

"Six Steps to a more secure home" Clause

1   The final exit door must be secured by either a deadlock conforming to British Standard 3621 or with a minimum of five levers, or by a multi-point locking system that includes a lever or cylinder deadlock.

2   Upper floor opening windows, including skylights which are accessible from adjoining roofs, walls, downpipes, balconies or external stairs, must be fitted with key-operated locks.

3   Any louvre windows must be fixed into their brackets with suitable adhesive.

4   Ground floor and basement opening windows, or any other ground floor openings measuring more than 23cm x 23 cm (9" x 9"), must be fitted with key-operated locks.

5   All other external doors must be secured with either a deadlock with a minimum of five levers or conforming to BS 3621, by a multi-point locking system that incorporates lever or cylinder deadlock, or by key-operated horizontal security bolts fitted internally top and bottom.

6   Patio or French doors or windows must be secured by a multi-point locking system with a lever or cylinder deadlock. As an alternative, hinged-type doors can be fitted with key-operated vertical security bolts fitted internally top and bottom. Sliding-type doors or windows can have key-operated bolts fitted internally top and bottom also.

... You must make sure all doors and windows are locked when you leave your home.[28]

To those policyholders to whom the security measures apply, compliance is expressed to be a condition precedent to the insurer's liability for loss or damage to the property through theft.[29] An owner/occupier insured is in a position to install the required locks and to ensure that they remain in place throughout the policy period. In contrast, a policyholder with no, or a bare economic, interest in the insured property is not in a position to know, or to find out, which of these security measures are in place. He or she does not have any rights of access to the insured property, to make any changes to comply with the security requirements, or to control and prevent changes being made that would be in breach of those requirements. He or she does not have the ability to manage the risk. Moreover, the policyholder cannot compel the owner of the insured property to comply in the absence of a contract with the owner to that effect. If he or she did have legally enforceable rights in relation to the insured property that would allow the insured to comply, or require the owner to comply, such rights might be the basis for a relationship giving rise to an insurable interest.[30] If the owner of the insured property does not have all the specified locks installed or leaves

28 No.16, p. 11.
29 Ibid.
30 See Chapter 4.

a window unlocked when leaving the house, the insured would be in breach of the security measures condition[31] regardless of whether or not the insured knew about it and despite the fact that the insured was not in a position to control compliance. This scenario shows that a contractual provision which was intended to manage the risk of theft is likely to fail in its purpose if the policyholder does not have any interest or has a bare economic interest: rather than preventing loss, the provision may operate to impair the policyholder's insurance coverage since he may be unable to comply with the required security measures.

General contractual *duties to take reasonable precautions, the duty to sue and labour and any contractual mitigation duties* in the wordings reviewed tended to be qualified by 'reasonableness' – that is, the insured must take reasonable precautions to prevent loss and must take reasonable steps or measures to minimize a loss. Reference is made to the discussion in Chapter 9 as to what is 'reasonable' by reference to the prudent uninsured: the standard of 'reasonableness' would differ considerably between a prudent uninsured with ownership or use and management rights in the insured property, on the one hand, and a prudent uninsured with no interest, or a bare economic interest, in property on the other. The former can take a wide range of precautions and mitigations steps because he has access and/or control over the insured property and he is likely to have early notice of a precaution failure, a threatened or impending loss and a loss that has actually occurred allowing him swift and effective action. The latter has no access to, or control rights in, the insured property that would allow him to take steps to prevent or mitigate loss of, or damage to, the insured property. Moreover, he may not have timely notice of the loss to take effective steps to mitigate. In those circumstances, any duty to take reasonable mitigation measures would be rendered meaningless and would fail to protect the insurer from liability for preventable loss.

The presence of an insurable interest based on proprietary or contractual rights permitting access to, and control over, the insured property, as well as being the basis for timely notice, is essential to the effective operation of all kinds of loss prevention and loss mitigation duties of the insured. In the absence of such an interest, such duties (1) if expressed as absolute obligations can be harmful to the insured's coverage, and (2) if expressed as obligations qualified by 'reasonableness', fail to protect the insurer.

O'Neill confirmed that the nature and extent of the insured's insurable interest can have an impact on the terms of the policy which, in his area of downstream energy underwriting, are usually bespoke. A relatively weak insurable interest might mean that additional risk management obligations are imposed on the insured,[32] indicating that risk prevention and mitigation may be of even greater concern to the insurer if the insured does not have full control over the property.

---

31 The consequences for a breach of terms and conditions in insurance contracts are now subject to the IA 2015, ss.9–11, which are subject to contracting-out restrictions (IA 2015, ss.15–18).
32 Interview with Peter O'Neill, Class Underwriter for Onshore Power and Energy at XL Catlin (now AXA XL Insurance; London, 9 September 2015).

Risk Control Terms

Most wordings in the survey contained exclusions, conditions precedent, warranties, notice provisions or termination events relating to the use of the insured property and changes in circumstances relating to the property, aimed at protecting the insurer from an increase in risk after the inception of the policy (collectively, 'Risk Control Terms'). Typical Risk Control Terms from the policy survey are detailed in Table 10.2.

Table 10.2 Policies containing Risk Control Terms

Type of Policy	Provision	Examples: Policy Nos.
Marine	Warranty that vessel not towed	1–5
	Automatic termination upon change of flag or transfer to new management	1, 3 and 5
	Change of voyage warranty	2, 4–5
	Maintenance of classification (termination event or warranty)	1, 3 and 5
	Navigating limits (warranty)	5
Home/content/ valuables	Property unoccupied for more than [30] consecutive days (exclusion for specified perils and/or prior consent requirement)	16–22
	(Prior) notice of changes affecting property	16–24, 32 and 33
	Use of home/items for unpermitted or illegal purposes exclusion	20, 24, 32 and 33
	Prior consent to works on home	18, 20, 22 and 33
	Prior consent to removal of jewellery from bank vault/safe	33
Motor	Use of car outside territorial limits (exclusion or notice requirement)	All motor (25–31, 35 and 36)
	Use of car (a) outside permitted uses by non-permitted users or (b) for illegal activities exclusion	All motor (25–31, 35 and 36)
	No cover whilst car not taxed/without MOT	30 and 31
	Notice of change of registered keeper and other circumstances relating to car	25–27, 29, 35 and 36
Business premises	Property unoccupied for more than [30] consecutive days (exclusion for specified perils and/or prior consent requirement)	39, 40, 44, 45, 47 and 50
	Change of use or other circumstances relating to premises (exclusion, termination or notice requirement)	37–41, 44–46, 50
Plant and machinery	Incorrect use exclusion	42
	Notice of alteration of risk	42 and 43
Aircraft	Non-permitted dealings with damaged aircraft exclusion	48
	Illegal and unauthorized uses exclusion	48
	Unauthorized pilot exclusion	48
	Excess passengers exclusion	48
	Notice of variation of risk	49

All Risk Control Terms have in common that they require the insured to deal with the property in a way which does not increase or change the risk assumed by the insurer at inception unless the insurer has been given notice and has consented to an increase or change in the risk.

An insured with an insurable interest based on proprietary or contractual rights allowing control of the insured property has the ability to ensure that the property is being used in compliance with all relevant Risk Control Terms. In contrast, a policyholder with no, or a bare economic, interest in the insured subject-matter is unlikely to be in a position to ensure compliance with these Risk Control Terms since he or she cannot control the use of, and dealings with, the insured property by third parties. Any third party who is in control of the insured property is not a party to the insurance contract, would not be bound by, and may be unaware of, its terms. Accordingly, such a policyholder's (continued) insurance cover would depend on third parties dealing with the insured property in a way that is consistent with any Risk Control Terms that are not binding upon them and of which they may not be aware. The policyholder's position could be accidentally (or even intentionally) prejudiced by the conduct of third parties. In the absence of any contract with such third parties, the policyholder cannot control their conduct in relation to their dealings with the insured property and he or she does not have any recourse against them if their dealings result in non-compliance with any of the Risk Control Terms. Similarly, the insurer has no contractual rights against such third parties under the contract of insurance and yet his position could be adversely affected. For example, he could mistakenly indemnify a loss in circumstances where, as a result of third party dealings with the insured property, unbeknownst to the insurer and the insured, a Risk Control Term was breached or not complied with. It is implausible that the parties to the insurance contract intended that compliance with the Risk Control Terms should be a matter for third parties over which neither of the parties can exercise any control. Risk Control Terms are another example of property policy terms that reflect the parties' implicit presumption that the insured has an insurable interest based on proprietary or contractual rights in relation to the insured property as without such an interest such terms do not operate as intended.

Notice of loss

All wordings reviewed, except for the Institute Cargo Clauses,[33] contain provisions that require the insured to notify a loss (and circumstances likely to give rise to a loss)[34] to the insurer. Being notified of a loss in a timely fashion is important to insurers to "test the genuineness of the claim"[35] by starting inves-

---

33 Nos.6–14. The Institute Cargo Clauses are not stand-alone policies but are incorporated into cargo insurance policies that are likely to contain notice and claims provisions.

34 Nos.15, 17, 18, 22, 27–30, 32–34, 39–43, 47 and 48.

35 John Birds, Ben Lynch and Simon Paul, *MacGillivray on Insurance Law* (14th edn, Sweet & Maxwell 2018) para 21-036.

tigations when the evidence is fresh, to become involved in, or give directions in relation to, loss mitigation measures and to set in motion any subrogation or reinsurance recovery actions.[36] It is a matter of construction of the wording in question whether the notice provision in question is a condition precedent to liability or an innominate term which, if breached, would give rise to a claim in damages for any loss flowing from the insured's failure to give notice within the prescribed time.[37] Some wordings also appear to adopt an intermediate position, which allows for claims to be rejected if failure to give timely notice prejudices the insurer's position.[38]

Most wordings impose a time limit for notification which may start running (1) from the (potential) event of loss, (2) from the insured's knowledge thereof or (3) by reference to what is practicable or reasonable. The significance of whether a notice requirement is triggered by a loss event, or by the insured's knowledge of a loss event, or by other criteria that take into account the individual characteristics of the insured is that an insured who has a close relationship with the insured property based on proprietary or contractual rights is likely to become aware of loss or damage to the insured property much sooner than an insured with a more remote interest or a policyholder with no interest in the insured property. For example, the owner/occupier of property insured under a home and contents policy is likely to realize that his house is on fire as it happens, and he is likely to become aware of a burglary of his home relatively soon after the event. In contrast, a shareholder who is not involved in the company's management may not learn of significant windstorm damage to one of the company's factories until he reads about it in the company's annual report and accounts several months later. It is acknowledged that these polar opposites have many shades in-between and that it is possible for shareholders, creditors, suppliers and other insureds with economic interests to have up-to-date information about key assets of a company, or neighbours knowing of a loss before the owners do, whereas an owner of many properties may not be in residence at the time one of his properties is damaged and may not learn of the loss until he is informed by a third party. However, it is suggested that the likelihood of an insured's prompt awareness of a loss is higher if the insured has a proprietary or contractual rights in relation to the property since that would ordinarily mean that he or his agents are frequently in close physical proximity to the property.

If the *notice requirement is triggered by the loss event* itself, whether or not the insured knew about the loss is irrelevant. Lack of knowledge of the loss would be prima facie no defence to a breach of the notice provision. Clearly, event-triggered notice provisions put an insured who has no close relationship with the

---

36 *Friends Provident Life & Pensions Ltd v Sirius International Insurance* [2005] EWCA Civ 601, [31] (Mance LJ).
37 Ibid.
38 No.18, Pt II; No.19, Claims Conditions.; No.20, Claims Conditions; No.22, Claims Conditions.; No.23, Claims Conditions; No.27, Pt VII cl 1(a); No.32, Claims Conditions.; No.33, Pt II.

property at a disadvantage as he may not become aware of the loss until after the notice period has expired.

In contrast, *knowledge-triggered notice provisions* start running from the time the insured became aware of the loss event. Whilst this favours insureds who may not themselves learn of a loss for some time, it could cause prejudice to an insurer who may find it more difficult to investigate a claim after the passage of time it took for the insured to become aware of the loss. For example, it may be more difficult to establish the exact cause and extent of loss from a site inspection, and to track down (reliable) witnesses,[39] or the insurer may "lose the opportunity to make or recover a reinsurance claim or a subrogation claim",[40] several months after the event. The insurer would have no remedy against the insured provided the insured gave notice within the time limit starting from the point in time when he became aware of the loss.

As for *notice provisions that rely on 'reasonableness' or 'practicality' qualifications*, "all existing circumstances" will be taken into account,[41] and it is suggested that this should include taking into account when the insured had become aware of the loss. By analogy, 'held covered' notice provisions requiring notice of a deviation from a vessel's contemplated voyage "within reasonable time" or "as soon as possible" have been held to require notice to be given "within reasonable time" or "as soon as possible" (as the case may be) from the time of the insured's discovery, or receiving advice, of the deviation.[42] It would neither be 'reasonable' nor be 'practicable' to give notice of a loss of which the insured is unaware. A potential difference to notice provisions that are triggered by knowledge is, perhaps, that 'reasonable' and 'practicable' notice provisions might also take into account if the insured would have had an opportunity to become aware of the loss sooner than he actually did. In any event, 'reasonable' and 'practicable' notice provisions can pose essentially the same problem for insurers as 'knowledge' triggered notice provisions.

If the proposition that the likelihood of an insured's timely awareness of a loss is higher if the insured has a proprietary or contractual rights in relation to the property (and vice versa: a policyholder without any interest in the insured property is far less likely to know about a loss immediately after the event) is correct, the same claims notice provision can produce very different practical outcomes depending on the nature of the insured's interest and produce unfair and unexpected results contrary to the parties' intention as to how notice provisions should operate. It is suggested that the notice provisions in the policy wordings

---

39 In *Bankers Insurance Co Ltd v South* [2003] EWHC 380 (QB), [2004] Lloyd's Rep IR 1, Buckley J at [37] said that the insurer had been prejudiced by a late notice of claim: "This is just the sort of case in which memories will fade, albeit most dramatically in the months immediately following the accident. Some witnesses may now be hard or practically impossible to trace".

40 This is one of Lord Mance's examples of serious prejudice as a result of late notice: *Friends Provident Life & Pensions Ltd v Sirius International Insurance* (n 36).

41 *Verelst's Administratrix v Motor Union Insurance Co* [1925] 2 KB 137 (KB).

42 See Hirst J's discussion of the case law held on covered notice provisions in *Black King Shipping Corp v Massie (The Litsion Pride)* [1985] 1 Lloyd's Rep 437, 463–471.

reviewed were drafted with an insured with a proprietary or contractual interest in the insured property in mind who would ordinarily be in a position to give timely notice of a loss.

Claims conditions

The majority of wordings reviewed contain additional claims conditions that become applicable once the insured has given notice of a claim and require the insured to take certain steps or provide documentation in relation to the insured property. Table 10.3 gives some examples of such provisions from the policy survey and explains why such a policyholder may not be able to comply with them unless he or she has an insurable interest based on proprietary or contractual rights in the property.

These provisions are drafted as absolute obligations – their performance is not qualified by reference to what is practicable, or reasonable, for the insured to do. Accordingly, if the insured cannot comply, he or she will be in breach of contract, regardless of whether the discharge of these obligations was practically impossible. It would be irrational to enter into a contract that creates obligations that one party is unable to perform where this inability to perform exists as from the inception of the contract. In the absence of ambiguity, it is not for the court to rewrite the parties' bargain[43] to make the claims conditions fit the circumstances of the policyholder and thus the courts would be required to give effect to those terms even if they produce unreasonable or unexpected results. It is suggested that the claims conditions in standard property policy wordings were drafted with an insured with a proprietary or contractual interest in the insured property in mind who is capable of complying with the claims conditions. They do not contemplate a policyholder with no, or a bare economic, interest.

Basis of settlement (reinstatement and repairs)

The insurer, upon accepting liability for a claim, will compensate the insured for his loss by paying the insured a sum of money representing his loss (based on the insurable value or the agreed value of the insured subject-matter). The insured can use the settlement proceeds as he pleases.[44] However, property policies frequently contain basis of settlement terms providing for the reinstatement or repair of insured buildings or personal property that have been damaged or the replacement of lost items (collectively, 'reinstatement'). Twenty-two wordings in the survey contained reinstatement provisions in respect to certain types of claims: some confer upon the insurer the right to elect reinstatement (i.e. an option as an alternative to cash settlement),[45] others are expressed as an absolute

---

43 *Arnold v Britton* [2015] UKSC 36 [19–20] (Neuberger PSC).
44 *Rayner v Preston* (1881) 18 Ch D 1 (Ch).
45 Nos.17, 20, 22, 23, 25, 27–31, 34, 35, 39, 42, 43 and 48.

Table 10.3 Policies containing claims conditions

Claims Conditions	Examples: Policy Nos.	Compliance Issues for an Insured without an Insurable Interest or with Only a Bare Economic Interest (the 'Policyholder')
The insurer is entitled to appoint a surveyor and to decide which port a damaged vessel is to be taken for repair.	1–5	The Policyholder and its insurer cannot give directions to the vessel's owner, its insurer or its management.
Insured is required to give the insurer and his agents access to/allow inspection of the damaged insured property.	16, 18–21, 24, 26, 30–33, 42, 43, 46, 50	The Policyholder is not in a position to grant access to the insurer.
Preservation of/provision of/ making available for inspection documentation to support the claim. In particular (all relating to the insured property): invoices, delivery receipts, transit documents, (original) purchase receipts, deeds/proof of ownership, instruction booklets, utility bills, driving licence of driver involved in car accident, vehicle documentation, financial information relating to the insured property.	5, 15, 16, 18–22, 26, 28, 32, 33, 37, 39, 40–43, 46, 49	The Policyholder is unlikely to be in possession of these documents or to be entitled to copies from third parties.
If the loss or damage to the insured property is the result of criminal action (malicious damage, theft, etc.), the insured must inform the police promptly and obtain a crime reference number (which is to be provided to the insurer).	16–20, 22–25, 27, 32, 33, 35, 37, 39, 40–43, 46, 47, 50	The Policyholder may not be able to report this kind of crime to the police, and obtain a crime reference number, because (1) he may be unaware that such a crime has been committed; (2) not being the owner (or otherwise legally entitled to the property) he would not be the primary victim of a crime against property.
The insured must obtain/provide to the insurer (in writing) details of the event of loss (date, time, what happened, witnesses).	19, 21, 23, 25, 30, 31, 33, 35, 40, 41, 48–50	The Policyholder is unlikely to have this information if he was not present at the scene and time of the loss or immediately thereafter.

obligation on the insurer to reinstate if a valid claim is made (i.e. reinstatement or repair is compulsory, subject to any applicable limits of liability)[46] and yet others give the insured the right to choose between a cash settlement (based on a reduction in market value) or reinstatement.[47] It should be noted that there is also a statutory right to require the reinstatement of buildings lost or damaged by fire where the insurer suspects arson or fraud, or where the insurer himself

46 Nos.16, 26.
47 Nos.21, 23, 24, 36 and 37.

is requested to do so by any person 'interested' in that property.[48] The purpose of reinstatement is to protect insurers from excessive multiple claims and to discourage arson, deliberate destruction and fraud.[49]

Reinstatement provisions are generally only triggered when an insured has a valid claim based on an indemnifiable loss and, accordingly, will not be applicable to a policyholder without any interest in the insured property. They could be triggered if the policyholder has a bare economic interest in the insured property, which is nevertheless sufficient to generate an indemnifiable loss. However, there a number of potential issues:

1   Reinstatement of the insured property does not compensate the policyholder with an economic interest as his loss is not the actual physical damage to the property but lost profits consequential upon such physical damage. Inevitably, there would be a time lag between the date of the event of the physical loss and the date by which the insured property has been reinstated. The policyholder's loss arises as a result of being unable to benefit economically from the insured property during that period.

2   The costs of reinstatement may significantly exceed any economic loss suffered by the policyholder. There is no concept of proportionate reinstatement – once the insurer is committed to reinstatement (whether as a matter of obligation or once an election by the party entitled to elect has been made), unless the policy provides otherwise, he must reinstate the property in full to a condition equal to immediately before the loss.[50] Clearly, an insurer who has the option to reinstate would choose a cash settlement in those circumstances, but, as has been noted above, some policies do not give the insurer the right to elect and in those circumstances an insurer could incur claims costs that are disproportionate to the actual loss suffered by the policyholder. This would defeat one of the main purposes of reinstatement clauses (keeping claims costs down) and is contrary to the indemnity principle.[51]

3   In the absence of other contractual arrangements,[52] neither the policyholder nor his insurer has any rights to compel the owner of the insured property to accept reinstatement. They cannot insist on reinstatement against the owner's wishes or proceed without the owner's or occupier's consent to enter the

---

48 Fires Prevention (Metropolis) Act 1774, s.83. Although s.83 is stated to apply to London, it has been held to apply to buildings and fixtures in England and Wales – see *Re Quicke's Trusts/ Poltimore v Quicke* [1908] 1 Ch 887 (Ch).

49 For further discussion of reinstatement see John Birds, Simon Milnes and Ben Lynch (n 35) ch 23; Robert Merkin, *Colinvaux's Law of Insurance* (12th edn, Sweet & Maxwell 2019) ch 11 sec 4.

50 Robert Merkin (n 49) paras 11-158 to 11-159, citing *Home Mutual Fire Insurance v Garfield* (1871) 4 Am Rep 74.

51 See Chapter 8.

52 For example, in *Western Trading* [2016] EWCA Civ 1003 the insured tenant was contractually obliged to reinstate.

land to carry out the work. In *Sadlers' Company v Badcock* Lord Hardwicke said that the insurer's option to reinstate:

> … shews most manifestly they meant to insure upon the property of the insured, because nobody else can give them leave to lay even a brick, for another person might fancy a house of a different kind.[53]

If reinstatement is physically or legally impossible before the insurer (or the insured, as the case may be) makes his election, any purported election is void and, subject to any other terms of the policy, the insurer's obligation reverts to making a cash settlement.[54] As for those policies that do not provide for an option to reinstate but make it an obligation of the insurer to do so in the event of a valid claim, the doctrine of frustration may operate to discharge the insurer from his obligation to reinstate.[55] It could be argued that in those cases, by analogy to the election cases, an obligation to make a cash settlement arises as an alternative performance by the insurer so that he does not become totally absolved from any performance under the contract of insurance. Alternatively, it could be said that the insurer's obligation to reinstate was accepted on the assumption that the policyholder would be in a position to allow the insurer to fulfil that obligation and, if he cannot do so, the insurer is entitled to regard himself discharged from his obligation to reinstate and, there being no contractual alternative for cash settlement, he is under no obligation to make an indemnity payment. In those circumstances, premium may be returnable on the grounds of total failure of consideration.

4   Even if the consent of all relevant third parties in relation to the reinstatement of the property were to be forthcoming, the owner of the Property, and other interested third parties, may have their own insurance arrangements covering the Property. If all parties involved and their insurers have full knowledge of each other's insurance arrangements and agree on the reinstatement of the Property, the insurers might bear the costs of reinstatement proportionately among themselves. However, if that is not the case, any rights to elect between reinstatement and cash settlement arising under different policies could be exercised inconsistently. For example, under a contract of property insurance covering the Property between the owner of the Property and his insurer, the latter, being entitled to elect, may decide on a cash settlement of the owner's claim. Another policyholder with

---

53   (1743) 2 Atk 554 (Ch), 557.
54   *Anderson v Commercial Union Assurance Corp* (1885) 55 LJQB 146 (CA), 150 (per Bowen LJ).
55   The doctrine of frustration is governed by common law and the Law Reform (Frustrated Contracts) Act 1943. The Act does not apply to contracts of insurance (see s.2(5)(b)), but Clarke notes that the Act could be said to apply in these circumstances since the contract of insurance has become one of reinstatement – see Malcolm Clarke, *The Law of Insurance Contracts* (Service Issue 37, Informa 2016) para 29-2C. Merkin (n 49) para 11-170 rejects the possibility of frustration.

a different interest in the Property insured under a separate policy may be entitled to reinstatement under his policy. In this scenario, the owner of the Property would, in effect, be compensated twice and, under the doctrine of subrogation, his insurer would be entitled to recover any amount by which the total benefits received by the owner exceed his loss up to the amount paid by the insurer.[56] This would produce the strange result that the net liability of the insurer who should primarily be responsible to indemnify for the loss or damage to the Property (i.e. the owner's insurer) is zero, whereas an insurer of a much more remote interest incurs significant costs for reinstatement.

Ergo the operation of reinstatement clauses in property policies with a policy-holder with a bare economic interest can produce unexpected or even absurd results that are (1) likely to be contrary to the parties' intention, (2) at odds with the usual purposes of reinstatement clauses, (3) in conflict with third party rights in relation to the insured property and (4) possibly inconsistent with, or creating uncertainty in relation to, other legal principles. Assuming that the parties to an insurance contract do not usually intend to achieve senseless or absurd results, the prevalence of reinstatement provisions in the property insurance wordings reviewed indicates that they were drafted with an insured with a proprietary or contractual interest in the insured property in mind and do not contemplate a policyholder with no, or a bare economic, interest.

Subrogation provisions

The relationship between the principle of subrogation and the doctrine of insurable interest has already been discussed in Chapter 9. It remains to be added that many of the property policies wordings reviewed include contractual subrogation rights of the insurer, often together with attendant duties imposed on the insured, that supplement, or vary, the rights and obligation arising as a matter of law.[57] O'Neill said that in his field (downstream energy underwriting) contractual subrogation clauses are included as a matter of course, and there is an expectation that subrogation rights are available in the event of a claim.[58]

Insurable interest as part of contractual fabric

The survey of 50 property-related policy wordings shows that the doctrine of insurable interest is embedded in specific contractual terms commonly found in standard property policy wordings. These wordings operate on the assumption that the insured has an insurable interest based on proprietary or contractual

56 See Chapter 9.
57 Nos.5, 15, 17–20, 22–39, 42–48.
58 Interview with Peter O'Neill (n 32).

rights in the insured property. They contain terms that would be rendered inapplicable, or are inconsistent with, the absence of an insurable interest or can create conflicts with the proprietary or contractual rights of third parties. Furthermore, standard property policy wordings contain a significant number of Risk Control Terms that impose obligations on the insured (either directly as duties or indirectly as exclusions from coverage) which cannot be discharged, or be complied with, by an insured who has no access to or control over the insured property. It has been argued that a policyholder without any interest in the insured property will not generally have, and a policyholder with a bare economic interest is unlikely to have, the kind and degree of control necessary to perform any absolute obligations that require access to, or control of, the insured property. From inception, a policyholder without any interest, or a bare economic interest, will be at risk of being in breach/non-compliance of such Risk Control Terms and, consequently, at risk of compromising his cover and/or entitlement to claim. On the other hand, where Risk Control Terms, mitigation obligations and notice requirements are qualified by 'reasonableness' or 'practicality', they offer no, or very little, protection to the insurer in relation to a policyholder for whom, on account of having no interest, or a bare economic interest, it would not be reasonable or practicable to take any steps which he cannot practically or legally take on account of having no rights in relation to the insured property. Standard property policy wordings applied to a policyholder with no interest, or a bare economic interest, can produce unreasonable and unexpected results which would be unlikely to accord to the intention of the parties.

The contractual framework of standard property policies presumes an insurable interest based on proprietary or contractual rights in order for their terms to operate efficiently and meaningfully. More specifically, in relation to home and contents insurance and commercial property insurance, these wordings envisage that the insured is the owner and/or authorized occupier/user of the property. In relation to motor insurance, the wordings envisage that the insured is the owner or registered keeper of the insured car or fleet. In every one of these cases, the insured would have an insurable interest firmly based on a proprietary or contractual right in the property. This indicates that insurers, as the draftsmen of these standard wordings, have an expectation that policyholder have such an insurable interest in the property to be insured. Whilst policyholders, especially consumers, may not in fact give any detailed consideration to what extent their interest allows them to perform and comply with the terms of their contract, no policyholder would knowingly wish to pay a premium for insurance cover that would be worthless to him or her: a policy insuring property in which the insured has no, or insufficient, interest would be worthless because without an indemnifiable loss the policyholder would not be able to claim, and because the insurance cover may become impaired for breach of terms with which the policyholder cannot comply on account of having no, or an insufficient, interest in insured property. The doctrine of insurable interest does not operate in a vacuum but in a legal and contractual framework and in the context of market practice which, in relation to standard property policy wordings, assumes that the policy-holder has an insurable interest based on proprietary or contractual rights.

It would, of course, be possible to adapt some of the terms discussed in this Chapter to make them more suitable to the specific circumstances of an insured with a bare economic interest, or remove them altogether, but such adjustments (1) would incur additional transaction costs in a commoditized market, (2) could not be made in respect of all relevant terms without also changing their purpose and (3), most importantly, would move the policy wording in question along the spectrum away from what is a contract of property insurance towards other types of insurance covering profits/receivables or liabilities, or contingency insurance, and, where there is no insurable interest at all, into the realm of non-insurance contracts. The policyholder with an insurable interest based on proprietary or contractual rights in the insured property is not just the paradigm case in property insurance; an insurable interest of that nature is integral to the operation of key standard terms in this type of insurance and, on a proper construction of the contract, should be regarded as what the parties intended consistent with the commercial purpose of such policies.

In this Chapter and the preceding one it has been argued that the doctrine of insurable interest can be rationalized on a novel ground in relation to property policies: the existence of an insurable interest is integral to the operation of other doctrines and principles of insurance law and the operation and performance of (standard terms-governed) contracts of property insurance in accordance with the parties' intention. Not only is there no industry demand for the abolition of the doctrine of insurable interest, there is no case for it either. To the contrary, the doctrine continues to be justified on the grounds of differentiating insurance contracts from wagers and other speculative contracts, counteracting moral hazard and aligning the insurer's and the insured's interests (as argued in Chapters 6 and 7), as well as being an integral part of insurance contract law and part of the fabric of property insurance contracts.

11 The definitional dimension of insurable interest

Contracts of all types of insurance are required to be supported by an insurable interest, either on the basis of legislation or as a matter of common law. This chapter will explore whether, independently of a requirement arising at law, an insurable interest is a definitional characteristic of contracts of insurance. Reference has already been made to the definitional role that an insurable interest plays in distinguishing contracts of insurance from wagers and other types of speculative contracts and the interconnectedness of the doctrine of insurable interest and other doctrines and principles of insurance law. The LC's description of the doctrine of insurable interest as a "hallmark of insurance"[1] suggests a definitional role and is indeed one of the LC's reasons for the retention of an insurable interest requirement in indemnity insurance.

Yet, if the requirement for an insurable interest is a definitional element of contracts of property insurance, how can this definitional role be reconciled with its role as validity requirement assigned to it by statute and at common law? There is a logical inconsistency between an insurable interest as a definitional element and an insurable interest as a validity requirement, as a contract that cannot be characterized as a contract of insurance would not be subject to the requirement for an insurable interest, and accordingly, such a non-insurance contract should not be rendered void for lack of insurable interest. This Chapter will therefore also examine whether the two roles can be reconciled. The extent to which the requirement for an insurable interest is part of the definition of a contract of insurance is not just a theoretical question but impacts on the characterization of contracts as contracts of insurance, which in turn has legal, regulatory and tax consequences.

Historical background to definition of 'contract of insurance'

Inherent in the concept of a contract of insurance under the lex mercatoria was that, in consideration for a specified sum of money, one party should 'become security to' (= indemnify) the other for loss in relation to a risk to which the second

---

1 LC, *'Insurance Contract Law: Post Contract Duties and Other Issues'* (Law Com CP No 201, December 2011) para 12.6–12.12; LC, *'Issues Paper 10 – Insurable Interest: Updated Proposals'* (March 2015) para 2.3.

party would be exposed. The advisory opinions in *Lucena* relied on works of continental jurists such as Grotius, Pothier and Scaccia for definitions of contracts of insurance.[2] It was from these continental definitions of (indemnity) insurance that Lawrence J extrapolated a requirement for an insurable interest based on the benefit from the preservation of the subject-matter or a prejudice upon its destruction: "If this be the general nature of the contract of insurance, it follows that it is applicable to protect men against uncertain events which may in any wise be of disadvantage to them...". He reasoned that one could only suffer such disadvantage (loss) by "having some relation to, or concern in the subject of the insurance ...".[3] On this line of reasoning, whilst not quite a definitional element itself, the existence of an insurable interest is a precondition to two definitional characteristics: the exposure to risk and the capacity to suffer loss. In contrast, Lord Eldon looked at insurable interest as a statutory validity requirement under the MIA 1746.[4]

The early cases are not consistent on whether the absence of an insurable interest meant that the policy would not be a contract of insurance at all, or would be void, or indeed whether any claims thereunder would simply be unenforceable. In *Goddart v Garrett*,[5] the court stated that a policy without an insurable interest would be void. In *Lynch v Dalzell*[6] and *Sadlers' Company v Badcock*,[7] in the absence of any interest the policyholders were simply not entitled to claim, although in *Sadlers' Company* Lord Hardwicke also struck a definitional tone, noting that an insurable interest was necessary "for it cannot properly be called insuring the thing" if the insured cannot sustain a loss requiring the insurer "to make satisfaction".[8] In the pre-LLA 1774 case of *Earl of March v Pigot*[9] a bet on whose father would live longer was documented in an insurance policy and was held to be an enforceable wager. In the twin cases of *Da Costa v Jones*[10] and *Roebuck v Hammerton*[11] (concerning wager policies on the gender of the Chevalier d'Eon) Lord Mansfield treated the pre-LAA 1774 policy in *Da Costa* as a wager (albeit unenforceable on public policy grounds), whereas in *Roebuck* he held the policy to be an insurance contract void under the LLA 1774.

The MIA 1746, the LAA 1774 and the MIA 1906 have in common that they treat(ed) contracts of insurance lacking an insurable interest as void – that is, the existence of an insurable interest is a precondition to the validity of the contract. However, the historical context of the legislation, as acknowledged

---

2 (1806) 2 Bos & Pul (NR) 269 (HL) 295 (Graham, Le Blanc, Rooke, Grose, Heath, Macdonald and Sir James Mansfield JJ), 300 (Lawrence J).
3 Ibid, 301–302.
4 Ibid, 321.
5 (1692) 23 ER 774.
6 (1729) 4 Bro PC 431.
7 (1743) 2 Atk 554.
8 Ibid, 556.
9 (1771) 5 Burr 2802.
10 (1778) 2 Cowper 729, 736.
11 (1778) 2 Cowper 737.

in the Preambles to the MIA 1746 and to the LAA 1774,[12] also had a definitional dimension: it was precisely to distinguish between (1) genuine contracts of insurance (with an insurable interest) and (2) gaming contracts and wager policies under the guise of insurance that did not require the insured to have an insurable interest, that the latter kind of contracts were to be rendered void for lack of insurable interest. Similarly, s.4(2) of the MIA 1906 deems a contract of marine insurance without interest (or the expectation of acquiring one) "to be a gaming or wagering contract ...", which suggests that a contract of insurance lacking an insurable interest would not just be void but may not be a contract of insurance at all.

Doctrinal analysis of definition of 'contract of insurance'

The existing statutes do not contain a definition of contracts of insurance. The courts too have been reluctant to define contracts of insurance, preferring to describe the defining features of insurance contracts as required for the purposes of the case under consideration.[13] In *Prudential Insurance Company v Commissioners of Inland Revenue* Channell J listed the existence of an 'interest' as one of the defining features of contracts of insurance (the other characteristics being the payment of money or the provision of a benefit, upon the occurrence of an uncertain event, in consideration for premium):

> The remaining essential is that ... the insurance must be against something. A contract which would otherwise be a mere wager may become an *insurance by reason of the assured having an interest in the subject-matter* – that is to say, the uncertain event which is necessary to make the contract amount to an insurance must be an event which is primâ facie adverse to the interest of the assured.[14]
>
> (Emphasis added)

Channell J's description was cited with approval in subsequent decisions,[15] including most recently by the Supreme Court in *Digital Satellite Warranty Cover Ltd v FSA*.[16] Similarly, in *Equitas Insurance Ltd v Municipal Mutual Insurance Ltd*, Leggatt LJ described the "basic nature of an insurance contract" in terms of a risk transfer to the insurer, whereby the risk insured is "a loss occurring

---

12 Both Preambles note that the respective statutes are intended to counteract a "mischievous kind of gaming" under the pretext of insurance.
13 *Medical Defence Union Ltd v Department of Trade* [1980] Ch 82 (Ch) 95 (Megarry V-C); *Department of Trade and Industry v St Christopher Motorist Association Ltd* [1974] 1 WLR 99 (Ch) 104 (Templeman J).
14 [1904] 2 KB 658 (KB) 663.
15 *Medical Defence Union Ltd v Department of Trade* (n 13); *Department of Trade and Industry v St Christopher Motorist Association Ltd* (n 13).
16 [2013] UKSC 7, [19] (Sumption JSC).

or a liability incurred or a claim made against the insured".[17] As noted above, Lawrence J derived the requirement for an insurable interest from a definition for indemnity insurance.[18] In *John Edwards and Co v Motor Union Insurance Co Ltd*, McCardie J said that a contract that does not require an insurable interest "is not a contract of indemnity at all".[19] In *Belmont Park Investments Pty Ltd v BNY Corporate Trustee Services Ltd*, the Supreme Court commented that a swap agreement without an insurable interest is not credit insurance.[20] Thus, the doctrinal evidence suggests that the existence of an interest in the insured subject-matter is a definitional characteristic of contracts of indemnity insurance.

In contrast, following *Prudential*, a number of decisions considering life endowment policies have stressed that contracts of life insurance are characterized by the payment of a sum of money (or other benefit) on an uncertain event contingent upon human life, regardless of whether the event is 'adverse' to the insured or whether the insurer is exposed to the risk of loss.[21] In *Fuji Finance Inc. v Aetna Life Insurance Co. Ltd*, the Court of Appeal considered that, to be within the scope of s.1 of the LAA 1774 (prohibition of contracts of life insurance without interest), it had to be established first that the contract is one of life insurance.[22] In *Feasey* too, the Court of Appeal distinguished between the characterization of a contract as contract of life insurance or wager and the question whether there was an insurable interest.[23] These analyses are consistent with treating insurable interest as a validity requirement, but not as a definitional element. Treating 'insurable interest' solely as a validity requirement for contracts of life insurance is also consistent with the requirement for an insurable interest at the time of the contract[24]: if it were a definitional element only applicable at the time of the contract and subsequently the insurable interest ceased to exist, the contract would be at risk of re-characterization during its currency.

The IIB defines a "contract of life-related insurance" as "a contract of insurance under which the insured event is the death, injury, ill-health or incapacity of an individual, or the life of an individual continuing".[25] Although the first four events ("death, injury, ill-health or incapacity") could all be broadly described as 'adverse', and therefore import into the definition of 'contract of life-related insurance' the concept of an 'interest' based on the capacity to be exposed to the relevant 'adversity' at the time of the contract, the "life … continuing" event is akin to the life endowment policy cases discussed above, where there is not

---

17 [2019] EWCA Civ 718 (CA), [132].
18 See n 3.
19 [1922] 2 K.B 249, at 255.
20 [2011] UKSC 38, [135] (Mance JSC).
21 *Flood v Irish Provident Assurance Co. Ltd* [1912] 2 Ch 597; *Joseph v Law Integrity Insurance Co. Ltd* [1912] 2 Ch 581 (CA); *Gould v Curtis* [1913] 3 KB 84 (CA); *Fuji Finance Inc. v Aetna Life Insurance Co. Ltd* [1997] Ch 173 (CA) ('*Fuji*') at 188 (Morritt LJ) and 198 (Hobhouse LJ).
22 *Fuji* (n 21), at 186 (Morritt LJ).
23 [2003] EWCA Civ 885 (CA), [54–58] and [150–151].
24 *Dalby v The India and London Life Assurance Company* (1854) 15 CB 365 (ExchCham).
25 IIB, cl.1.

necessarily any 'adversity' involved. Moreover, given that the IIB cl.2(1) requires an insurable interest only at the time of the contract, the IIB's treatment of insurable interest in contracts of life-related insurance is more consonant with insurable interest as a validity requirement rather than a definitional element.

Given that (1) life-related contracts of insurance tend to be contingency insurance contracts to which the indemnity principle does not apply,[26] (2) the contingent event does not necessarily result in loss or adversity and (3) the requirement for an insurable interest needs to be satisfied only at the time of the contract, it is arguable that in life-related insurance, the existence of an insurable interest is more in line with a validity requirement. On the other hand, an insurable interest may be the sole distinguishing factor between a contract of life-related insurance and other types of contract of speculation which supports the definitional character of (insurable) interest.

At European level, the Expert Group on European Insurance Contract Law noted that, although the law on the doctrine of insurable interest varies across Member States, the concept "relates to the definition of an insurance contract …".[27] The New York State Insurance Act, §1101(a) defines an 'insurance contract' by reference to the insured's "material interest" that would be adversely affected upon the happening of a fortuitous event.

Interest – v – insurable interest in property insurance

The LC note that Channell J's notion of 'interest' based on adversity and loss is not the same as the meaning of 'insurable interest' in property insurance as defined by statute and by the courts.[28] Similarly, Waller LJ's Principle 5 in *Feasey* suggests that not every interest qualifies as a valid insurable interest in property insurance.[29] The capacity to suffer 'adversity' or a 'loss' does not necessarily require an insurable interest based on proprietary or contractual rights in the insured subject-matter, although it does presuppose an interest based on the risk of economic loss. The focus on an 'adverse event' or a 'loss-causing event', rather than explicitly referring to the existence of an insurable interest, is also evident in some of the textbook definitions of contracts of indemnity insurance.[30] In Chapter 6 it was argued that the distinction between insurance contracts and wagers could be generally maintained by an economic interest since wagers are

---

26 *Dalby v The India and London Life Assurance Company* (n 24). Note, however, that some types of life-related insurance have an indemnity element – see Chapter 6.

27 Expert Group on European Insurance Contract Law, '*Final Report of the Commission Expert Group on European Insurance Law*' (27 February 2014) para 106.

28 LC, '*Issues Paper 4 – Insurable Interest*' (January 2008) para 7.20.

29 *Feasey* (n 23) [97].

30 John Birds, Ben Lynch and Simon Paul, *MacGillivray on Insurance Law* (14th edn, Sweet & Maxwell 2018) para 1-005; Robert Merkin, *Colinvaux's Law of Insurance* (12th edn, Sweet & Maxwell, 2019) para 1-040.

characterized by neither of the contracting parties being required to have **any** interest in that contract other than the sum or stake.

It is suggested that under the current law, there is a dichotomy between the notion of a wider (economic) interest, which is sufficient as a definitional characteristic of contracts of indemnity insurance, and a narrower 'insurable interest' within the meaning of the applicable statutes and as established by case law, which is required for a contract of property insurance to be valid. There is a "middle ground"[31] of contracts that are neither wager contracts nor valid contracts of insurance supported by an insurable interest. This middle ground is occupied by contracts that can be characterized as contracts of insurance as their form and terms are consistent with the definition/description of insurance contracts, and the insured has an 'interest', but which are void or unenforceable because the insured lacks an 'insurable interest' as defined by statute and by the courts. The middle ground was implicitly accepted in *Feasey* when Waller LJ rejected Counsel's argument that an insurance contract which is not a wager automatically demonstrates an insurable interest.[32] Whilst the requirement for a more general economic 'interest' based on 'adversity' and 'loss' may be a sine qua non definitional characteristic without which a contract cannot be classified as a contract of property insurance, the more narrowly defined 'insurable interest' is a validity requirement (although lack of an 'insurable interest' may not necessarily be fatal to the characterization of a contract as a contract of insurance).

Definition for regulatory and tax purposes

The RAO, art. 3 defines a "contract of insurance" in a circular fashion as "any contract of insurance which is a contract of long-term insurance or a contract of general insurance", which falls into the lists of specific contracts set out in Schedule 1 to the RAO. PERG 6.5.1G endorses Channell J's description of contracts of insurance as a starting point for the identification of contracts of insurance for regulatory purposes which, as noted above, regards an 'interest' as an essential characteristic. In addition, PERG, 6.6.2G notes the "assumption of risk" by the insurer as "an important descriptive feature of all contracts of insurance". In contracts of property insurance, the insurer assumes risk by agreeing to indemnify the insured for loss suffered in relation to the property insured as a result of a specified event. Without any interest in the property that pre-exists independently of the contract, there is no risk since the insured is not exposed to the possibility of loss or damage to the insured property – and, accordingly, there

---

31 Jonathan Gilman, Mark Templeman and others, *Arnould's Law of Marine Insurance and General Average* (19th edn, Sweet & Maxwell 2018) para 11-01. But query whether a 'middle ground' can exist in marine insurance as under the 'deeming' language in the MIA 1906, s.4(2)(a) a marine insurance contract without (expectation of acquiring) an insurable interest is automatically *deemed* to be a wager contract.

32 *Feasey* (n 23) [58].

can be no risk transfer to the insurer.[33] In life insurance, although the insurer's exposure to the risk of loss is not a requirement at common law,[34] the insurer usually assumes risk by agreeing to pay a specified sum upon the occurrence of an event contingent upon human life which may exceed the premium received if the event occurs too soon.

HM Revenue & Customs' Notice IPT1 mentions 'insurable interest' as a feature that characterizes contracts of insurance for the purposes of insurance premium tax,[35] and Notice 701/36 cross-refers to the identification of contracts of insurance under the FSMA regulatory regime.[36]

Conceptual analyses

A detailed discussion of the scholarly debate on what insurance is falls outside the scope of this work. This section examines two contributions to the concept of insurance by Abraham,[37] and Merkin and Steele,[38] as to whether they support or contradict the validity and/or definitional roles of insurable interest.

Abraham's four conceptions of insurance

Abraham identifies four conceptions of insurance – the contract conception, the public utility/regulated industry conception, the product conception and the governance conception – which, he argues, when examined in combination, give a "more rounded and complete picture" of insurance, which can serve to explain insurance law doctrines and highlights the normative choices to be made in insurance law.[39]

The *contract conception of insurance* perceives a contract of insurance as a voluntary agreement between an insurer and one or more insureds. This traditional model conforms to the description of contracts of insurance by Channell J and Lawrence J. If the parties have agreed to enter into a contract of indemnity insurance, the requirement for an insurable interest is not merely an independent validity requirement but the existence of an interest in the insured subject-matter is also a definitional characteristic of the type of contract they have chosen. However, according to Abraham, one issue with this analysis is that "most actual insurance transactions do not involve subjective assent" since many policyholders lack understanding of and real choice and bargaining power in relation to standard form contracts.[40] In relation to the doctrine of insurable interest, many

33 See Chapters 6 and 8; *Lucena* (n 3) 302 (Lawrence J).
34 See n 21.
35 HMRC, 'Notice IPT1: Insurance Premium Tax' (October 2014).
36 HMRC, 'VAT Notice 701/36: insurance' (February 2013).
37 KS Abraham, '*Four Conceptions of Insurance*' (2013) 161 U Penn LR 653.
38 R Merkin and J Steele, *Insurance and the Law of Obligations* (OUP 2013), ch 2 and 3.
39 KS Abraham (n 37) 698.
40 Ibid., 659–662.

policyholders do not have any real understanding that an insurable interest is required, whether as a matter of definition or as a separate validity requirement, and how this requirement is embedded in standard contract terms.[41] How this lack of awareness could be addressed will be considered in Chapter 12.

The *public utility/regulated industry conception* of insurance understands insurance as a cartelized industry providing a fundamental service used by a large proportion of people. This conception has gained currency in the United States as the US insurance industry operates under a grant of immunity from federal anti-trust law.[42] Given the perceived quasi-public nature of insurance and the anti-trust/competition privileges the insurance sector enjoys in the United States, the regulated industry conception of insurance considers it to be in the public interest to regulate contracts of insurance in relation to the general availability of the product/service, their contractual terms and conditions and pricing.[43] In the UK, the insurance industry is regulated under the FSMA 2000 regulatory framework, and, as noted above, for regulatory purposes, a 'contract of insurance' is identified by reference to Channell J's description of contracts of insurance, which includes 'insurable interest' as one of the elements. Other than that, the regulated industry conception of insurance neither supports nor contradicts a definitional role of insurable interest.

The *product conception* of insurance sees an insurance contract as a product bought by the insured to cover him against the financial consequences of specified risks. Like goods, insurance policies should be of "satisfactory quality" and "fit for the purposes" for which they are supplied.[44] This translates into requiring the policy to satisfy a degree of suitability to the policyholder's needs and the insurer to provide information about key features of the policy at the pre-contractual stage.[45] If a specific term of the policy renders the policy defective (i.e. unsuitable), proponents of the product conception suggest that such a term should be held invalid or be replaced with a more suitable term, so that the insurer is liable to pay the loss either by way of a claims payment or by way of product liability-style damages.[46]

The product conception of insurance cannot answer whether the existence of an insurable interest is a definitional element or a validity requirement as it does not seek to describe the features that an 'insurance product' should have. However, by highlighting the possibility of a remedy against the insurer if the

41 See Chapter 10.
42 KS Abraham (n 37) 668. See also: McCarran-Ferguson Act (15 U.S.C.) §§1011–1015.
43 Ibid., 668–669.
44 Ibid., 674–675. The relevant UK legislation is the Consumer Rights Act 2015, s.9 and the Sale of Goods Act 1979, s.14.
45 D. Schwarcz, '*A Products Liability Theory for the Judicial Regulation of Insurance Policies*' (2007) 48 Wm Mary L Rev 1389, 1436–1438.
46 ibid; JW Stempel, '*The Insurance Policy as Thing*' (2009) 44 Tort Trial Ins Prac LJ 813, 828–829.

policy is defective, the product conception of insurance puts into focus one of the criticisms levelled at the doctrine of insurable interest as a validity requirement, namely that insurers are not held accountable if the contract of insurance is rendered void for lack of insurable interest.[47] Any policy that contains an insuring clause or definition of the insured subject-matter that does not cover the policyholder's interest, but which could have been covered with more appropriate drafting or under a different kind of policy, is prima facie 'defective'. Under the product conception of insurance, the insurer should be held liable either on the basis of a 'defective warning' by the insurer as to the features of the policy or on the basis that the policy is 'defective in design'. Chapter 12 will argue the case for a remedy against the insurer in these circumstances.

The *governance conception* of insurance breaks down into two aspects: first, insurance can perform quasi-governmental function. Ericson, Doyle and Barry identify several ways in which the insurance industry acts as an "institution of governance" which, cumulatively, approach a function-oriented description of insurance.[48] Some of the 'functions' are indicative of an underlying assumption of the existence of an insurable interest as a definitional characteristic of indemnity insurance:

1   financial protection against risk through indemnification of loss by insurer;
2   the conversion of risk into costs and probabilities;
3   the pooling of risk by people wishing to minimize loss; and
4   risk management.[49]

Functions 1 to 3 assume a policyholder's exposure to risk, and Function 1 specifically refers to 'indemnification'. An interest in the insured subject-matter is a precondition to the insured's exposure to risk and his capacity to suffer an indemnifiable loss. Function 2 is concerned with attaching a monetary value to the risk. The value of the risk reflects the value of the interest insured and the probability that an insured loss will occur.[50] In property insurance, both components presuppose an interest of the policyholder in the insured property: there must be an interest to be valued and capable of resulting in a loss if the insured property were to be lost or damaged upon the occurrence of an insured peril. In life insurance, the LAA 1774 requires the insurable interest (other than presumed interests) to have a pecuniary value. Function 4 is concerned with how insurers seek to control or influence the behaviour of their policyholders to avoid

---

47 LC, *Issues Paper 4* (n 28) paras 4.19–4.23.
48 RV Ericson, A Doyle, D Barry, *Insurance as Governance* (University of Toronto Press 2003) 43–52.
49 Ibid., 47–49. The authors identify nine quasi-governmental functions but the functions not listed above have little bearing on the doctrine of insurable interest.
50 F Ewald (trs J-M Dautrey and CF Stifler), '*Risk in Contemporary Society*' (2000) 6 Conn Ins LJ 365, excerpted in J Lowry and P Rawlings, *Insurance Law: Cases and Materials* (Hart Publishing 2004) [101].

or minimize losses. In Chapters 7 and 10 it has been argued that the existence of an insurable interest contributes to an alignment of the insured's interests with those of the insurer in seeking to avoid or minimize loss and that it furnishes the insured with access and/or control rights over the insured property that allows him to take steps to protect it from loss or damage.

The second sub-category of the governance conception sees insurance as a set of relationships between all the policyholders of a particular insurer where the insurer acts as intermediary to prevent or deal with conflicts of interests between majority and minority policyholders.[51] However, as Abraham points out, this sub-category of the governance conception does not inform on the substance of any rights and obligations of policyholders inter se.[52] Without any detail as to the substance of the rights and obligations that govern the relationship between policyholders, no inference as to the role of the doctrine of insurable interest within this conception of insurance can be drawn.

Merkin and Steele's models of insurance

Merkin and Steele discuss two models of insurance: the "actuarial model" and the "relational model".[53]

The *actuarial model* is based on a vision of insurance that "involves premium paid in advance, guaranteed indemnity in the event of a covered loss, and a risk-based premium based on the best available information regarding the expected losses of the individual insureds".[54] The insurer pools the risks transferred, and premiums received, from a large group of policyholders. The risk of loss and the cost of actual losses are spread across the whole pool.[55] Compared to risk at an individual level, across a large pool of policyholders, the probability of loss becomes statistically more predictable so that the cost of risk becomes more calculable.[56]

The actuarial model does not describe insurance by expressly referencing the existence of an insurable interest. However, it implicitly assumes the existence of an interest as a component in contracts of insurance in so far as it relies on a policyholder's exposure to risk, the transfer of risk to the insurer and the policyholder's capacity to suffer an insured loss. Moreover, the pooling/collectivizing aspect of the actuarial model suggests some degree of solidarity and mutuality,[57] which could become diluted if the same pool included policyholders with and without interests in the insured subject-matters. This

51 KS Abraham (n 37) 693–694.
52 Ibid., 697.
53 R Merkin and J Steele (n 38) ch 2.
54 T Baker and J Simon, *Embracing Risk: The Changing Culture of Insurance and Responsibility* (Chicago University Press 2002), 10.
55 R Merkin and J Steele (n 38) 17–18.
56 Ibid.
57 R Merkin and J Steele (n 38) 18; F Ewald (n 50).

dilution could occur because there would no longer be (1) a shared exposure and expectation of loss across all policyholders in the pool, and (2) a cohesive community of interests in seeking, and being able, to avoid and minimize loss.[58] Conversely, the pooling/collectivizing aspect of the actuarial model does not make sense from the perspective of a policyholder without an insurable interest as such a policyholder would be subsidizing the pool with his premium contribution without obtaining any benefits. Finally, if policyholders were able to recover for losses in relation to insured property in which they do not have any interest, this would have a significant impact on the assessment of risk-based premium: first, the information on the risk provided by a policyholder without any interest may be of comparatively poor quality,[59] introducing a higher degree of uncertainty. Secondly, the likelihood and magnitude of loss may be different, and more difficult or impossible to value.[60] If policyholders are not required to have an insurable interest, there is a greater risk of multiple policies being taken out on the same risk,[61] which would distort or reverse the risk-spreading philosophy behind the actuarial model of insurance. Whilst there are actuarial methods of calculating stakes and pay-outs in betting pools, the actuarial model of insurance is based upon risk-spreading, not risk creation.[62]

The *relational model* of insurance does not seek to describe the characteristics of insurance contracts but "considers insurance in terms of the party relations of which it is an inherent part".[63] These relations are not just the contractual relationship between the insurer and the insured but also include relations to other (re)insurers, other parties providing indemnities, contract parties of the insured and third parties to whom the insured owes tortious duties. Merkin and Steele argue that any risk allocation and risk transfer arrangements should be considered in the context of these relationships. The relational model does not explain the parties' relationship with the insured subject-matter, except that, to the extent the relational model emphasizes risk transfer, there is an inherent assumption of the transferor's exposure to that risk based upon some interest in the subject-matter at risk. An examination of the relational context, and in particular the allocation of risk, may assist in identifying what interests each party has, which party should insure or has an obligation to insure and what kind of insurance would be the most suitable to cover the interest/s in question. Beyond that, the relation model does not support or contradict a definitional role of an insurable interest.

---

58 See Chapter 7.
59 See Chapter 9.
60 See Chapter 8.
61 See Chapter 6.
62 Ibid; EA Posner and EG Weyl, '*An FDA for Financial Innovation: Applying the Insurable Interest Doctrine to the 21st Century Financial Markets*' (2013) 107 Nw ULR 1307, 1314.
63 R Merkin and J Steele (n 38) 19.

Insurable interest and market perception

This section examines the insurance market's perception of insurable interest drawing on industry and stakeholder responses (collectively, the LC respondents) received, and other data collected, by the LC as part of their consultations on reforming the law on insurable interest,[64] and interviews conducted by the author with representatives from the insurance market: (1) Peter O'Neill (then Class Underwriter Onshore Power and Energy at XL Catlin), (2) Kees van der Klugt (Director of Legal & Compliance at the LMA) and (3) Andreas Stahl (Head of Complex Claims at Allianz Group).[65]

Definitional role

There has been continuing broad industry support for a requirement for an insurable interest in indemnity insurance[66] and life insurance.[67] Only three (all of them academics) out of 24 LC respondents to Issues Paper 10 advocated the abolition of the doctrine of insurable interest.[68]

Van der Klugt[69] commented that in the Lloyd's market "insurable interest is part of the DNA of the Market". In his opinion, the concept is a definitional element of a contract of insurance. Its purpose is to ensure an alignment of the insurer's and the insured's interests ('to have skin in the game') as it prevents or reduces moral hazard. For Stahl, the doctrine of insurable interest is one of two important principles which characterize contracts of insurance (the other one being fortuity).[70]

Several LC respondents noted the role of the doctrine of insurable interest as a "hallmark of insurance" or "distinguishing feature", delineating contracts of insurance from gambling and other types of speculative contracts.[71] The ABI acknowledged that the doctrine of insurable interest is embedded in market practice:

---

64 The author assisted the LC with reviewing and analysing the feedback received in response to Issues Paper 10 (n 1) and obtained their permission to cite from non-confidential responses to Issues Paper 10. In relation to all other responses, reliance is placed on the quotes and extracts published by the LC.

65 Interview with Peter O'Neill, Class Underwriter for Onshore Power and Energy at XL Catlin (now AXA XL Insurance; London, 9 September 2015); interview with Kees van der Klugt, Director of Legal & Compliance at the Lloyd's Market Association (London, 29 September 2015); interview with Andreas Stahl, Head of Complex Claims at Allianz Group (London, 14 October 2015).

66 LC, *Issues Paper 10* (n 1) para 2.3.

67 LC, '*Summary of Responses to Issues Paper 10: Insurable Interest*' (April 2016) para 3.60.

68 Ibid. paras 2.4 and 2.8–2.10.

69 Interview with Kees van der Klugt (n 65).

70 Interview with Andreas Stahl (n 65).

71 LC, *Post Contract* (n 1) paras 12.6, 12.9–12.10 (citing the ABI, the City of London Law Society, the International Swaps and Derivatives Association and the LMA); LC, '*Summary of Responses to Second Consultation Paper: Post Contract Duties and Other Issues*' (February 2013) para 2.2 (citing the LMA and NFU Mutual).

Insurers will not issue policies where there is no insurable interest. ... The requirement of an insurable interest for indemnity contracts maintains the distinction between insurance and gambling, and avoids undesirable social risks such as the potential for an increase in invalid or even fraudulent insurance claims.[72]

Similarly, the International Underwriting Association stressed the role of the doctrine of insurable interest as an essential, and differentiating, characteristic of contracts of insurance:

... we support retaining the requirement of insurable interest ... [which would] have value in clearly outlining the parameters and requirements of an insurance contract against other forms of contracts and wagers. Insurable interest is, we think, a useful indicator that a contract is one of insurance but is not the sole indicator.[73]

The Insurance Law Committee of the City of London Law Society ('ILC') responded:

... the insured should be required to have an insurable interest at the time of the loss ... this is a hallmark of insurance and distinguishes it from other contracts, such as derivative contracts ...[74]

Linklaters urged caution that under the LC's proposals, the requirement for an insurable interest would remain "part of the definition of insurance" and "to ensure that the boundary between insurance contracts and derivative contracts is not blurred ..."[75]. The concern is that by not clearly treating the requirement for an insurable interest as a definitional element of contracts of insurance, there is a risk that CDS could be re-characterized as contracts of insurance and be rendered void for lack of insurable interest. The LC have acknowledged the "demand for a dividing line" between insurance contracts and derivative products.[76] The majority of LC respondents agreed that investment-linked insurance contracts should fall within the definition of 'life-related contracts of insurance', accepting that their characterization as such would import a requirement for an insurable interest.[77]

The above sample of insurance market voices suggests that there is a deep-rooted understanding that the doctrine of insurable interest is a hallmark of

---

72 Note from the ABI to the LC dated 25 June 2015 in response to Issues Paper 10 (n 1).
73 Letter from the IUA to the LC dated 3 July 2015 in response to Issues Paper 10 (n 1).
74 Note from the ILC to the LC dated 29 June 2015 in response to Issues Paper 10 (n 1).
75 Email from Mark Brown/Linklaters to the LC dated 29 June 2015 in response to Issues Paper 10 (n 1).
76 LC, *Insurable Interest and Parametric Policies* (April 2016) para 1.20.
77 LC, *IIB Notes* paras 2.13 and 4.19.

insurance. The market's perception of the doctrine is consistent with the proposition that it is an integral part of the legal and contractual framework. Moreover, the language used by the insurance market points towards an understanding of insurable interest as a definitional element characterizing contracts of insurance and differentiating contracts of insurance from other types of contracts.

Economic interest

The ILAG on behalf of life insurers lobbied the LC to reconsider widening the existing restrictive categories of on insurable interest in life insurance which are "hindering the development of socially useful products".[78] In addition to widened categories of presumed interest based on natural affection, the IIB in cl.2(2) sets out a broader economic interest test – an insured would have an insurable interest in any circumstance where they have a "reasonable prospect" of suffering economic loss on the occurrence of the insured event – which has been welcomed by all LC respondents addressing that proposal in the 2016 version preceding the IIB.[79]

In relation to indemnity insurance, although van der Klugt,[80] O'Neill[81] and many LC respondents[82] said that the doctrine of insurable interest had not caused any problems as a matter of market practice, it has already been noted that there is some appetite for a wider non-exhaustive definition of insurable interest with a view to seeing potential selling and product development opportunities across all classes of insurance maximized.[83] As argued in Chapter 10, standard property policies are designed to apply to a policyholder who has proprietary or contractual rights in relation to the property in order for their terms to operate efficiently and meaningfully, and those insurers and brokers who responded in favour of a wider definition may not in fact wish to offer standard property insurance cover to policyholders with bare economic interests. If the policy survey in Chapter 10 reflects market sentiment, insurers are likely to hold more conservative views on the definition of insurable interest in property insurance if expanding the definition means that they would be exposed to expanded coverage and an erosion of their rights and protections under those policies.[84] As Stahl notes, the insurance industry is concerned about claims from policyholders with no, or with a weak, connection to the insured subject-matter and multiple exposure risk.[85] Respondents, such as Royal & Sun Alliance ('RSA')[86] and

---

78 Ibid. para 1.11.
79 LC, '*Summary of Responses to Issues Paper 10*' (n 67) para 3.16
80 Interview with Kees van der Klugt (n 65).
81 Interview with Peter O'Neill (n 65).
82 LC, '*Post Contract*' (n 1) para 12.26; LC, '*Summary of Responses to Issues Paper 10*' (n 67) para 2.7, citing Direct Line; ABI (n 72); IUA (n 73).
83 See Chapter 5.
84 See Chapter 10.
85 Interview with Andreas Stahl (n 65).
86 Note from RSA to the LC (undated) in response to Issues Paper 10 (n 1).

the ILC,[87] pointed out that widening the definition of insurable interest could extend coverage in (traditional) insurance contracts contrary to the intention of the parties. RSA also noted that the doctrine of insurable interest must work in tandem with the indemnity principle to protect against invalid, or unintended, claims.[88]

The LC accept that insurers rely on the doctrine of insurable interest as imposing a degree of market discipline and as a guard against moral hazard and claims by third parties that have no, or have a very tenuous, relationship with the insured property.[89] This 'barrier function' of the doctrine of insurable interest can be more easily fulfilled by an interest based on proprietary or contractual rights in the insured property, and some of the issues that may arise with economic interests have been highlighted in Chapters 9 and 10. To the extent that market practice is reflected in standard policy wordings, the survey of standard property policies has shown that these wordings assume the existence of an insurable interest based on proprietary or contractual rights in the insured property.[90] Policy wordings for policyholders with economic interests would require bespoke drafting or amendments that are not currently in place to ensure that their specific interests are covered and that the policy terms are suitable to be performed by such a policyholder whilst still offering the insurer sufficient protection against moral hazard, risk increases, expanded liability and invalid claims.[91]

Reconciliation between definitional and validity roles

If, on the basis of the historical, doctrinal and conceptual analyses and on the available evidence of market perception, it is accepted that the requirement for an (insurable) interest in the insured property is a definitional characteristic of contracts of property insurance, how can this definitional role be reconciled with a doctrine of insurable interest that operates as validity requirement? There is a logical contradiction in requiring an insurable interest for the purpose of classifying a contract as a contract of insurance and making it a validity requirement for that contract at the same time. If an insurable interest would only be a validity requirement, but not a definitional characteristic, there would be a risk that non-insurance contracts that have largely the same characteristics as insurance except for an insurable interest requirement (e.g. CDS) are rendered void for lack of insurable interest. This risk has been highlighted, and the need for an insurable interest-based boundary has been acknowledged, by the LC.[92]

---

87 ILC (n 74).
88 RSA (n 86): "... it must be made clear that there is a two tier test – insurable interest and loss (the indemnity principle). Where one of these is missing, a policy of indemnity does not respond ...".
89 LC, '*Post Contract Duties and Other Issues*' (n 1) paras 12.16–12.19.
90 See Chapter 10.
91 Ibid.; interview with Peter O'Neill (n 65).
92 See n 76.

Conversely, if an insurable interest is only a definitional element required to characterize a contract as a contract of insurance, a lack of insurable interest would merely result in a re-characterization of the contract. Whilst a re-characterization of the contract may have legal and regulatory consequences,[93] there would be no legal sanction to enforce the requirement for an 'insurable interest' and the policy reasons behind it. Moreover, without the invalidity consequence, policyholders without any interest would remain bound by contracts that are worthless to them, as without an insurable interest, there could not be any indemnifiable loss for which the insured would be entitled to claim.

The doctrine of insurable interest's role as a validity requirement and its definitional role can be reconciled if a wider meaning of 'interest' is adopted for definitional purposes than for 'insurable interest' as a validity requirement (Route A), and/or if a distinction is drawn between contracts of insurance, contracts under the guise of insurance and non-insurance contracts (Route B).

Route A: contracts with 'interest' but without 'insurable interest'

As argued above, it is the notion of an 'interest', but not an 'insurable interest', that is a sine qua non definitional element of contracts of property insurance, whereas the existence of an insurable interest (within the meaning of the applicable statutes and as established by case law) remains a condition precedent to the validity of such contracts. The definitional role of 'interest' and the validity role of 'insurable interest' are therefore distinct and compatible since it leaves room for a category of 'middle ground' (non-marine) contracts that can be characterized as contracts of insurance but are void because the insured lacks an (expectation of an) insurable interest. However, this distinction between 'interest' and 'insurable interest' has been eroded by the courts moving towards a factual expectation/moral certainty test for insurable interest as a validity requirement.[94] As a result, the validity role diminishes and could be absorbed in the definitional role, rendering the 'invalidity' consequence meaningless.

To the extent the current law recognizes certain economic interests as an 'insurable interest', the present dichotomy between an 'interest' for definitional purposes and an 'insurable interest' as a validity requirement could be maintained (albeit with shifted boundaries) as long as the former category remains wider in scope than the latter. In Chapters 6–10 it was argued that in relation to property insurance a narrow meaning of insurable interest based on proprietary and contractual rights gives better effect to the anti-wagering justification and the moral hazard justification, interacts more coherently with the existing body of insurance contract law and is reflected in standard policy wordings. One could add that a meaning of insurable interest that is narrower than the notion of a more general 'interest' based on 'adversity' and 'loss' is also essential to a

93 See below.
94 See Chapter 4.

conception of the doctrine of insurable interest that regards the existence of an insurable interest as a validity requirement.

Route B: non-insurance contracts under the guise of insurance

The second route to reconciling the doctrine of insurable interest's role as a validity requirement with its definitional role is to treat the requirement for an insurable interest as a definitional characteristic of contracts of property insurance and to regard the invalidity consequence merely as the sanction for non-insurance contracts lacking an insurable interest being documented and executed as contracts of insurance. This interpretation has historical foundations in the MIA 1746 and the LAA 1774, which were primarily directed at wager contracts under the guise of insurance.[95] It is also evident in the MIA 1906, s.4(2)(b). This interpretation has the advantage that it would not depend upon a distinction between a wider 'interest' for definitional purposes and a narrower 'insurable interest' as a validity requirement.

However, there is a risk that it could inadvertently render void other types of contracts such as CDS, which can look similar to, but are not intended to be, contracts of insurance.[96] The Potts Opinion concluded that CDS should not be treated as contracts of insurance since they were structured to pay out on the occurrence of a default irrespective of whether or not the protection buyer had an insurable interest or had suffered a loss.[97] In addition, it is suggested that a CDS executed and documented within the ISDA Master Agreement documentary framework – that is, not under any 'guise' – is unlikely to be regarded as a contract 'under the guise of insurance'.

How would this analysis apply to a contract that is documented as a contract of insurance, whose terms do not expressly exclude the requirement for an insurable interest but where the policyholder does not in fact have any interest in the insured property? If both parties are aware of the lack of interest at the time of the contract, the parties' agreement must be understood to be subject to a term that an insurable interest is not required even if that term is not reduced into writing. Accordingly, this would be an example, of a contract to be characterized as a non-insurance contract (on account of not requiring any interest) which is void for lack of insurable interest because it is written as a contract of insurance. In contrast, if at the time of the contract, both parties were under the common misapprehension that the policyholder had an insurable interest in the insured property, when he did not, the contract should be void for common mistake: being mistaken about a vital aspect of the contract – the absence of an insurable interest – that in itself would render the contract void should be sufficiently fundamental to vitiate that contract.[98] If the

95 MIA 1746, Preamble.
96 This risk has been highlighted by Linklaters (n 75).
97 See Chapter 6.
98 *Bell v Lever Brothers Ltd* [1932] AC 161 (HL).

policyholder misrepresents that he has an insurable interest at the time of the contract, the contract should be void for lack of insurable interest, regardless of the applicable remedies under the CIDRA, s.4 and Schedule 1 (consumers) or the IA 2015, s.8 and Schedule 1 (non-consumers), as it should not be open to an insurer to waive the requirement for an insurable interest.[99]

The two routes are not mutually exclusive and, taken together, can explain the definitional function of an (insurable) interest, whilst allowing the doctrine of insurable interest to target contracts that are written as contracts of insurance under the guise of insurance and insurance contracts where the insured lacks an insurable interest recognized at law.

Consequences of falling outside definition

If the requirement for an interest is a definitional characteristic of indemnity insurance contracts, any contract that does not have that characteristic should be (re-)characterized as a non-insurance contract. By way of high-level overview, the re-characterization of a contract as a non-insurance contract may have the following legal and regulatory consequences.

Consequences for policyholder

The classification of the contract as a contract of insurance may be important to policyholders who are subject to a mandatory statutory requirement to insure or who are under a *contractual obligation* to insure. Failure to have the required insurance may be a criminal offence in the case of mandatory insurance, or a breach of contract where it is a contractual obligation. In addition, policyholders under contracts of insurance enjoy special statutory,[100] counter-party insolvency[101] and regulatory protections[102] which may not be available if the contract in question is a non-insurance contract. Contracts of insurance attract special jurisdictional rules that are favourable to the insured and which do not apply to non-insurance contracts.[103]

Consequences for insurer

Legal consequences: Insurance contracts are contracts of utmost good faith imposing on both parties a general duty to act in good faith.[104] Specific breaches

---

99 See Chapter 3.
100 E.g. under the IA 2015, ss.9, 13A, 15–17.
101 Insurers (Reorganisation and Winding Up) Regulations, SI 2004/353, Part V.
102 FCA Handbook, ICOBS (consumer and non-consumer insureds); DISP and 'Compensation' (consumer insureds only).
103 Regulation (EU) No 1215/2012 of the European Parliament and of the Council of 12 December 2012 on jurisdiction and the recognition and enforcement of judgments in civil and commercial matters (recast), Section 3.
104 See Chapter 9.

of good faith, and of other terms, by the insured give rise to remedies for the insurer which may not be available under ordinary contract law applicable to non-insurance contracts.[105] If a contract of insurance is re-characterized as another type of contract, the insurer would not enjoy the protections of the specific rights and remedies that arise at law or are imposed by statute in relation to insurance contracts.

Regulatory consequences: Insurance companies operating in the UK are required to be authorized,[106] and, once authorized, they must stay within the specific permissions given, and comply with ongoing regulatory requirements imposed, by the regulators.[107] The re-characterization of a contract as a non-insurance contract could result in regulatory contraventions by the insurer who arranges, effects and carries out such contracts in relation to:

1   carrying on regulated activities outside their permissions granted under the FSMA 2000, Pt 4A (a 'Part 4A Permission');[108]
2   the Internal-Contagion-Restriction;[109]
3   compliance with the Solvency II regime, including reporting obligations;[110] and
4   mis-selling unsuitable insurance products in breach of the conduct of business regulations applicable to insurers.[111]

Fiscal consequences: A re-characterization of a contract as a non-insurance contract may also have tax and accountancy implications.[112] In addition, an insurer may find it difficult to obtain reinsurance in respect of non-insurance liabilities, and any claims or liability incurred under an underlying non-insurance contract may not be covered under existing reinsurance contracts.[113]

This snapshot shows that the characterization of a contract as a contract of insurance or a non-insurance contract may have significant legal, regulatory and fiscal consequences for both parties. Whether or not the requirement for an insurable interest is a definitional characteristic of contracts of indemnity insurance is relevant to the identification of the type of contract in question. On the evidence available, a requirement for an insurable interest in indemnity insurance is seen by the insurance market not just as a legal requirement but also as part

---

105 E.g. see CIDRA, s.4(1); IA 2015, ss.8, 10–12. See also: *Nextia Properties Limited v RBS* [2013] EWHC 3167 (QB) [77] (Behrens J).
106 FSMA 2000, s.19.
107 Ibid., s.20 and Part 4A.
108 FSMA 2000, s.20(1).
109 PRA Rulebook, 'SII Firms: Conditions Governing Business' 9.1. See also Section 5.2.3.
110 See PRA Rulebook, 'SS Firms: Solvency Capital Requirement – Internal Models' 6.1 and 'Reporting' 5.1–5.5.
111 See also Chapter 12.
112 See Chapter 6.
113 This may be so because non-insurance claims and liabilities may not be within the scope of the reinsurance contract.

of market practice and an essential characteristic of contracts of insurance. Description of the doctrine of insurable interest as the "DNA of the Market" and as "hallmark of insurance" exemplify the market perception that the doctrine has a definitional dimension. Historically and doctrinally, the existence of an interest in the insured subject-matter appears to be an inherent, and occasionally explicit, definitional characteristic of contracts of indemnity insurance, although an economic interest (which may not necessarily qualify as an insurable interest) appears to be sufficient for definitional purposes. It has been argued that the doctrine of insurable interest's role as a validity requirement and its definitional role can be reconciled. However, a wider definition of insurable interest extending to economic interests could result in the confluence of the doctrine's definitional role and validity role. This may lead to interpretational issues as to which contracts would be rendered void for lack of insurable interest. The role of insurable interest in life-related insurance is more ambiguous, and arguably more in the nature of a validity requirement, given the timing of the requirement at the time of the contract and that the contingent event triggering payment does not need to be adverse to the interest of the insured.

12 Remedies, enforcement and reform

The preceding discussion centred on the requirement for an insurable interest. The focus of this Chapter is on the law's responses to a lack of insurable interest. First, the remedies and enforcement regime under the current law and the IIB will be evaluated on the basis of doctrinal legal analysis and by reference to general contract law theory. It will then be examined to what extent the FSMA regulatory framework can assist a policyholder in the 'Unsuitable Policy Scenario'[1] to fill a remedial gap left by the insurance contract law. Finally, it will be proposed that the IIB and the FSMA regulatory framework should be supplemented by (1) a new statutory duty of insurers to decline to enter into contracts of insurance which they know would be void for lack of insurable interest, and (2) a regulatory obligation on insurers to provide information to the proposer on the insurable interest requirement specific to the type of policy in question before the contract is entered into.

As a matter of taxonomy, the terms 'consequence' and 'remedy' are used loosely: the doctrine of insurable interest does not confer any rights upon one party A which, if infringed by another party B, entitles A to a remedy from B. Rather, the requirement for an insurable interest is extra-contractual and, depending on the type of insurance, has different legal bases that determine the legal consequences that flow from a lack of insurable interest.[2] Moreover, the definitional dimension of the doctrine that overlays its role as a validity requirement introduces an additional layer of legal and regulatory consequences.[3]

Evaluation of remedies regime

The law's main response to a lack of insurable interest is to render the contract of insurance void and/or to hold claims made thereunder unenforceable. The LC criticized the current law for affording insurers the opportunity to write risks, collect premium and then decline the payment, whereas policyholders are "exposed to having neither their claims paid, nor their premiums returned if a policy

---

1 See below.
2 See Chapter 3.
3 See Chapter 11 and below.

is found to be illegal".[4] The perception that insureds are harshly penalized by the invalidity consequence but that insurers do not suffer any adverse consequences if the contract of insurance lacks an insurable interest, and may use the lack of an insurable interest as an opportunistic defence in order to escape liability for a claim,[5] is reflected in the courts' approach "to lean in favour of an insurable interest".[6] Davey criticized that the remedial regime for lack of insurable interest is rendered ineffective since its enforcement depends upon the insurer raising the matter as a defence.[7] Moreover, it has been suggested that the invalidity consequence is a disproportionate response that conflicts with what the parties have agreed and the performance of their respective promises.[8]

Fairness

Invalidity and unenforceability: Where the insured has no interest in the insured property, the invalidity consequence in combination with a return of premium to the policyholder (and ignoring any administrative costs) should leave the parties in a neutral position: without an insurable interest the policyholder is not exposed to any risk of loss, and the insurer does not assume any risk, in the insured subject-matter. The insurer returns the premium for which he has not given any consideration, and the policyholder can extricate himself from a contract that is worthless to him (since without an insurable interest, he cannot suffer an indemnifiable loss) without incurring any liability or costs. Neither party gains an unfair advantage over the other.

The current law is potentially unfair to the extent that premium is not returnable upon a contract of insurance being rendered illegal or void for lack of insurable interest. However, the insurer is not always entitled to retain the premium and there are a number of circumstances when the insurer must return the premium.[9] There is no unfairness in the premium not being returnable where the insurer has been 'on risk' but a claim is not payable because the insured does not have an insurable interest at the time of the insured event.

Unsuitable Policy Scenario: Nevertheless, there are circumstances where the invalidity consequence on its own could operate unfairly: a policyholder may suffer a genuine loss or contingency (the 'Uninsured Loss') in relation to which he or she had thought to have insurance protection but for which he is not in fact covered as that loss or contingency does not relate to an interest protected by the policy

---

4 LC, '*Issues Paper 4 – Insurable Interest*' (January 2008) para 4.19–4.23.
5 Ibid. See also *Feasey* [2003] EWCA Civ 885, [6] and [144].
6 See Chapter 3.
7 James Davey, '*Insurable Interest – A Rule in Search of a Rationale*', presentation at a BILA seminar at Lloyd's on 18 September 2015. The slides are available from BILA.
8 *Kosmopoulos* [1987] 1 SCR 2, [23] (Wilson J); J Lowry and P Rawlings, 'Rethinking Insurable Interest' in Sarah Worthington (ed.), *Commercial Law and Commercial Practice* (Oxford, Hart Publishing 2003) 335 at 361–363; James Davey (n 7); LC, *Insurance Contract Law: Post Contract Duties and Other Issues* (Law Com CP No 201, December 2011) para 4.4.
9 See Chapter 3.

in question. Unknowingly, the policyholder lacks an insurable interest in the subject-matter of the contract of insurance entered into (the 'Invalid Policy') but:

1   he or she would have had an insurable interest and, accordingly, an enforceable claim in relation to his or her Uninsured Loss under a different kind of policy, or
2   he or she has rights or control over a (legal) person (a 'controlled person') who would have had an insurable interest in the subject-matter insured under the Invalid Policy if it had been entered into by that person and he or she could have caused the controlled person to do so and, accordingly, the controlled person would have had an enforceable claim in relation to the Uninsured Loss (both are an 'Alternative Policy').

If the policyholder had known that the Invalid Policy would be void for lack of insurable interest, he or she would not have entered into it. Relying on the Invalid Policy for cover for the Uninsured Loss, at the time of entering into the Invalid Policy or indeed at any time before the Uninsured Loss, the policyholder did not consider and did not enter (or cause a controlled person to enter) into an Alternative Policy. In those circumstances, the invalidity of the Invalid Policy may be inadequate relief for the policyholder as it does not compensate for the loss of opportunity to enter (or cause a controlled person to enter) into an Alternative Policy (the 'Loss of Chance'). By way of shorthand, this situation is referred to as the 'Unsuitable Policy Scenario'.

The unfairness in the Unsuitable Policy Scenario is that both contract parties failed to consider the policyholder's interest and proceeded to enter into the Invalid Policy. Yet, the invalidity consequence has a disproportionately greater adverse effect on the policyholder who has suffered an Uninsured Loss and Loss of Chance, whereas the insurer would at most be liable to return the premium. The current law and the IIB do not require the insurer to take any responsibility for considering at the time of the contract whether or not the policyholder has an insurable interest. The courts have sought to alleviate the unfairness by "lean[ing] in favour of an insurable interest", but the courts' approach can be no more than a retrospective attempt to make an unsuitable (or unsuitably drafted) policy suitable to the interest that the policyholder does in fact have and cannot assist with cases where an Invalid Policy cannot be (re)construed as an Alternative Policy.

Remedial gap: A policyholder has no contractual redress against an insurer who fails to inform the policyholder at the time of the contract that the policyholder is or might be lacking an insurable interest and/or who fails to decline to enter into a contract of insurance he knows or suspects to be invalid for lack of insurable interest:

1   The invalidity consequence does not address those failures, and a return of premium does not compensate the policyholder for his Uninsured Loss and Loss of Chance.

2   If it is accepted that the requirement for an insurable interest cannot be waived,[10] an insurer cannot be liable for the Uninsured Loss based on (implied) waiver.

3   The IA 2015 does not impose any duty on the insurer to make precontractual disclosures of circumstances it knows or ought to know (but not known to the insured) and which are material to the risk or the enforceability of claims. Although such a duty was recognized in *Banque Financiere de la Cite SA v Westgate Insurance Co*,[11] even post-amendment of s.17 of MIA 1906, it is at best unclear whether such a breach affords the policyholder any remedy for the reasons discussed in Chapter 3.

4   An action for misrepresentation against the insurer could only be established if the insured has been induced to enter into the Invalid Policy by a false statement of fact (or some kind of misleading conduct) by the insurer. Although an insurer may know or suspect that the proposer does not have an insurable interest, he is unlikely to make a statement to that effect. In addition, traditionally, statements of law did not amount to statements of fact, but more recently the courts have accepted that a misrepresentation of law can be actionable.[12]

Under the current law and the IIB there is a 'remedial gap' in relation to the Unsuitable Policy Scenario, which creates an imbalance to the disadvantage of the policyholder. The LC suggested that it is a matter of insurance regulation, not primary legislation, whether insurers should take responsibility for ascertaining the insured's interest at the outset,[13] but as will be shown below, the current FSMA regulatory framework does not necessarily allow a policyholder recourse against the insurer in the circumstances of the Unsuitable Policy Scenario. Regulatory oversight is needed not instead but in conjunction with the doctrine of insurable interest.

Effectiveness and enforcement

The invalidity consequence is a relatively ineffective means of ensuring compliance with the insurable interest requirement and can remain undetected or unenforced:

1   In practice, the threat of a contract of insurance being void for lack of insurable interest cannot operate as an effective deterrent if, at the time of entering into the contract, the policyholder's (lack of) insurable interest is not actively considered by the parties and the insured is wholly unaware of the requirement of an insurable interest and the consequences of lacking an insurable interest.

10 Ibid.
11 [1990] 1 Q.B. 665 (CA), affirmed by House of Lords [1991] AC 249.
12 *Pankhania v Hackney LBC* [2002] EWHC 2441 (Ch).
13 LC, *Post Contract* (n 8) para 12.33.

2   Although a court must take notice of the lack of insurable interest if the issue arises in litigation even if neither party relies on it,[14] if the relevant contract is not litigated, the parties can deliberately choose to ignore the invalidity of their contract and perform their respective promises as if they were enforceable.

3   There is usually no practical or tactical advantage for policyholders to ask the courts to hold a contract of insurance void for lack of insurable interest.[15] In a claims scenario, the invalidity of the contract of insurance for lack of insurable interest would defeat the policyholder's claim and the premium may not be repayable.

4   Insurers do not often pursue the point as the courts have made it clear that they do not look favourably upon the lack of insurable interest being raised as a technical defence to a claim.[16]

5   The courts' approach "to lean in favour of an insurable interest" has introduced a significant degree of unpredictability as it relies upon the Three Strategies influenced by the courts' perception of whether the defence of lack of insurable interest is raised on technical grounds.[17] Professor Birks disapproved of what he called "discretionary remedialism" – the exercise of discretion by the court to give or withhold a remedy as it sees fit – for being contrary to legal certainty and transparency, and undermining the legitimacy of the judiciary within a democratic society.[18]

It is suggested that, if the IIB were to become law, the courts might display less discretionary remedialism in relation to life-related contracts of insurance: (1) the widened categories of 'insurable interest' in cl.2 would absorb some cases such as *Feasey*[19] where the courts have stretched the life insurance categories of insurable interest. (2) Constitutionally, the exercise of judicial discretion would be less acceptable once the doctrine of insurable interest has been freshly endorsed by Parliament. Nevertheless, the IIB fails to address the problem that the invalidity consequence cannot operate as an effective deterrent to entering into a contract of insurance lacking an insurable interest if this matter is not considered by the parties at the time of entering the contract. The IIB does not require insurers to take greater responsibility in that respect.

Interference with the parties' contract

Contractual freedom competes with social interests and public policies. In Chapters 6–10 it was argued that there are policy, doctrinal and market practice reasons for the retention of an insurable interest requirement. However, is the

14 See Chapter 3.
15 Ibid.
16 Ibid.
17 Ibid.
18 P Birks, '*Rights, Wrongs, and Remedies*' 20 OJLS (2000) 1, 23.
19 n 5.

invalidity or unenforceability of a contract of insurance a proportionate response to the insured lacking an insurable interest in the insured subject-matter? There is a general consensus that to render a contract of insurance unsupported by an insurable interest illegal, as well as void, is disproportionate and superfluous.[20] The courts, the LC and some commentators have reproached the doctrine of insurable interest, if used as a technical defence by insurers, for thwarting the performance of the contracting parties' respective promises when a contract of insurance is rendered void for lack of insurable interest.[21] These criticisms hark back to classical contract law theory, which places contracts, as obligations voluntarily assumed by agreement, in the private law sphere in which the state, unless called upon by one of the contracting parties to enforce any obligations, has no authority to interfere. The concept of 'freedom of contract' refers to the freedom of private parties to form a contract with whom they want and on whatever terms they choose without (government) intervention and interference.[22] Once a contract has been entered into, the parties should be held to their bargain – *pacta sunt servanda*. A number of observations are offered in response:

General contract law exceptions: The traditional 'contract conception' of insurance as a voluntary agreement has itself been criticized for being a theoretical ideal: in many insurance transactions, in particular in the commoditized consumer market, policies are offered by insurers on (non-negotiable) standardized terms and policyholders may have no real understanding of the terms and their meaning.[23] Abrahams suggests that the absence of a true understanding of the terms and the lack of opportunity to bargain undermines the contract conception and the assumption of freedom of contract in relation to insurance.[24]

Moreover, the principles of freedom of contract and *pacta sunt servanda* are not absolute. The *pacta sunt servanda* principle, as understood by English law, is permeable: leaving aside legislative intervention,[25] English contract law doctrine recognizes that not all promises are enforceable, that contracts can be rescinded or avoided and that contractual obligations can (instead of performance) be discharged by breach and by operation of the doctrine of frustration.

Agreement and failure of consideration: Arguably, the principles of freedom of contract and *pacta sunt servanda* are not necessarily undermined if, as has been argued,[26] the requirement for an insurable interest is regarded not merely as a validity requirement but also as an inherent part of the parties' agreement and a definitional element of contracts of indemnity insurance. If the parties have

---

20 LC, *Post Contract* (n 8) para 13.50. Under the IIB, cl.4 and 6, contracts of life-related insurance without an insurable interest would no longer be illegal.
21 See n 8.
22 J Adams and R Brownswood, '*The Ideologies of Contract Law*' (1987) 7 LS 205, 208.
23 KS Abraham, '*Four Conceptions of Insurance*' (2013) 161 U Penn LR 653, 660.
24 Ibid., 661.
25 E.g. Unfair Contract Terms Act 1977; Equality Act 2010; Consumer Rights Act 2015; Unfair Terms in Consumer Contracts Regulations 1999, SI 1999/2083.
26 See Chapters 10 and 11.

agreed to enter into a contract of indemnity insurance pursuant to which the insurer undertakes to hold the insured harmless against loss or damage to the insured property caused by an insured peril, it is in accordance with that agreement that a policyholder cannot claim if he has not suffered an indemnifiable loss.

Moreover, if the insured has no insurable interest in the insured subject-matter, and no prospect of acquiring one during the term of the contract, there would be a total failure of consideration on the part of the insurer since he would not be running the risk of being liable to indemnify the insured in the event of a loss. The contract would be worthless to the insured, since without any insurable interest, he cannot suffer an indemnifiable loss. Promises made without consideration are unenforceable. Therefore, any rule of law that any contract of indemnity insurance made without an insurable interest is void and unenforceable (i.e. the invalidity consequence) is largely consistent with the general contract law doctrine of consideration. However, it is suggested that the invalidity consequence is more than a specific example of the doctrine of consideration, as in the instance of contracts of insurance unsupported by an insurable interest, the absence of consideration can be neither remedied by the insurer nor waived nor circumvented by executing the contract by deed.

Softer remedies? If it is accepted that there are policy reasons for an insurable interest requirement, could these policy goals be pursued with less severe sanctions? The invalidity consequence appears harsh and inflexible in comparison to the proportionate remedies regimes that are now applicable in respect of 'qualifying misrepresentations' (consumers) or 'qualifying breaches' (non-consumers) in relation to the insured's pre-contractual information duties under the CIDRA, s.4 and Schedule 1, and the IA 2015, s.3(1) and Schedule 1, respectively. By analogy, it might be said that, instead of automatically rendering the contract of insurance void, the legal consequences flowing from a lack of insurable interest could be more sensitive to what the parties would have done, had they considered the insured's interest (or lack of interest) at the outset. However, a CIDRA/IA 2015 Schedule 1-style proportionate remedies regime would not necessarily be appropriate in relation to the doctrine of insurable interest. A mere premium increase or reduction in claims payments would not cure the absence of an insurable interest. Nor could amended terms rescue a policy insuring a subject-matter in which the policyholder has no interest whatsoever, although this could be a useful remedy if a different type of policy covering the insured's interest would have been available from the same insurer. The invalidity consequence is what Baker and Logue call a "mandatory rule"[27] since insurance contracts unsupported by an insurable interest can produce negative externalities, such as the costs of gambling on society,[28] the costs of financial speculation on

---

27 T Baker and KD Logue, '*Mandatory Rules and Default Rules in Insurance Contracts*' in D Schwarcz and P Siegelman (eds), *Research Handbook on the Economics of Insurance Law* (Edward Elgar Publishing 2015) 396 397.

28 See Chapter 6.

investors and taxpayers[29] and the moral(e) hazard risk that a policyholder without interest would destroy property belonging to a third party[30] and that such a policyholder would take less-than-reasonable care of the insured property.[31]

Davey argues that contracts of insurance should not be rendered void for lack of insurable interest but that the proper role of the doctrine of insurable interest should be as an "interpretative principle" that defines the extent of the cover, so that in the absence of an insurable interest, any loss would simply be irrecoverable.[32] Davey's proposal would keep the contract alive but would be of no benefit to a policyholder lacking an insurable interest in the insured subject-matter as he would not be able to claim under the policy whilst continuing to be liable for premium and other policy obligations.

In the Unsuitable Policy Scenario, could the parties' contract that is void for lack of insurable interest be replaced with an Alternative Policy which covers the policyholder's interest? In practice, the courts have already moved in this direction by seeking to construe a policy so that it embraces the interest that the insured has in the subject-matter.[33] It is suggested that, outside the bounds of contractual construction and rectification, a rewriting of the terms of the contract by the courts for the parties would be equally discordant with the principles of freedom of contract and *pacta sunt servanda*. Faced with a void contract, the parties would be free to enter into a fresh contract of insurance that covers a subject-matter in which the insured does have an insurable interest. However, this is unlikely to assist an insured who has already suffered a loss to his interest as a fresh contract of insurance could not cover any losses already known to the parties to have occurred.[34]

Sham transactions: Historically the doctrine of insurable interest was deployed to counteract wager policies – agreements in the nature of a bet but with the appearance of contracts of insurance that had been used as instruments of fraud.[35] Sham transactions remain unacceptable.[36] If the policyholder and the insurer collude in entering into a wager (or financial transaction in the nature of a bet or wager) under the guise of a contract of insurance with a common intention to give to third parties and to the courts the appearance that their contract is a contract of insurance, their transaction may be characterized as a 'sham'.[37] In this scenario, it is suggested that the invalidity of a contract aimed at the deception of third parties and the courts is not a disproportionate consequence.

---

29 Ibid.
30 See Chapter 7.
31 Ibid.
32 James Davey (n 7).
33 *Feasey* (n 5), [97]. See also Chapter 3.
34 An insurance contract requires an uncertain or fortuitous event – see *Prudential Insurance Company v Inland Revenue Commissioners* [1904] 2 KB 658 (KB) 663.
35 MIA 1746, Preamble.
36 See Chapter 6.
37 Ibid.

Support for the invalidity consequence: It is suggested that the invalidity consequence is not disproportionally harsh but incomplete. If the invalidity consequence were to be supplemented with a pre-contractual duty on insurers to decline to enter into a contract of insurance if the insurer knows or ought to know that the contract would be void for lack of insurable interest, there should be fewer occasions on which purported contracts of insurance are rendered void for lack of insurable interest.

In summary, if the policyholder has no (prospect of an) interest in the insured subject-matter, the invalidity of the contract of insurance paired with a return of premium is generally a fair and proportionate response (albeit ineffective in prospective deterrence) since it releases the parties from a contractual bargain that is worthless to the policyholder and for which the insurer cannot provide any consideration. However, in the Unsuitable Policy Scenario the policyholder is more severely affected by the invalidity consequence than the insurer, and there is a remedial gap in respect of the policyholder's Loss of Chance to cover the Uninsured Loss.

Remedial gap between legal consequences and regulatory sanctions

This section examines whether the FSMA regulatory framework can assist a policyholder in the Unsuitable Policy Scenario by filling the remedial gap left by insurance contract law by allowing a policyholder to recover for his Loss of Chance in a private action against the insurer. This section is not concerned with regulatory sanctions.

Authorization and permissions

A lack of insurable interest may mean that the contract in question is liable to be re-characterized as a non-insurance contract.[38] Arranging, effecting and carrying out a non-insurance contract may be in contravention of the insurer's Part 4A Permission.[39] Under the FSMA 2000, s.20(3), in prescribed cases[40] such a contravention would be actionable at the suit of a person who suffers loss as a result of that contravention (a 's.20(3) action'). However, it is unlikely that a s.20(3) action would assist a policyholder in the Unsuitable Policy Scenario:

1   The loss suffered by the policyholder is his Uninsured Loss and Loss of Chance. The Uninsured Loss is caused by a peril operating on the property, and the Loss of Chance is the result of the parties entering into the Invalid Policy. Neither loss is the result of a contravention by the insurer of his Part

---

38 See Chapter 11.
39 FSMA 2000, s.20(1).
40 Financial Services and Markets Act 2000 (Rights of Action) Regulations 2001, SI 2001/2256 (amended by SI 2013/472) ('Rights of Actions Regulations'), reg.4(1).

4A Permission. The causal connection between the loss and the unauthorized activity is an essential pre-condition to a s.20(3) action.[41]

2   If the re-characterized contract does not constitute another specified investment under Pt III of the RAO, arranging or entering into such a contract will not constitute a regulated activity for which the insurer would require any Part 4A Permission, and accordingly a s.20(3) action may not be available.

3   A s.20(3) action can only be brought by a private person, or a person acting in a fiduciary or representative capacity on behalf of a private person,[42] and it is "subject to the defences and other incidents applying to actions for breach of statutory duty".[43] Accordingly, a s.20(3) action would not be available to business insureds. It may also be unavailable, if, independently of the policyholder's lack of insurable interest, the insurer would have been entitled to decline liability under the Invalid Policy.

Prudential regulation

Prudential contraventions resulting from a contract of insurance lacking an insurable interest may include breaches of the Internal-Contagion Restriction[44] and non-compliance with the Solvency II regime.[45] However, these specific contraventions would not give rise to an action for damages by the policyholder as the relevant rules are not stated to be actionable.[46]

Conduct of business regulation

Contraventions: The FCA Handbook contains a number of provisions relevant to the Unsuitable Policy Scenario:

1   Principles of Business ('PRIN'), 2.1.1R, Principles 1 (Integrity), 2 (Skill, care and diligence), 3 (Management and control), 6 (Customers' interests), 7 (Communications with clients) and 9 (Customers: relationships of trust); and
2   ICOBS rules and guidance in 5.1–5.3, 6.1 and 6.3.

These provisions seek to regulate, inter alia, how insurance products are advertised, what information needs to be provided and to what extent an insurer must take steps to ensure that the insurance product meets the policyholder's needs. Failing to comply with these provisions can result in mis-selling, that is, the sale of an insurance policy that is unsuitable to a specific policyholder.

41 *City Index Limited (t/a FinSpreads) v Romeo Balducci* [2011] EWHC 2562 (Ch), [36] and [51] (Proudman J).
42 Rights of Actions Regulations (n 40) reg 4(2)(a)(i) and (ii).
43 FSMA 2000, s.20(3).
44 PRA Rulebook, 'SII Firms: Conditions Governing Business' 9.1. See also Chapters 6 and 11.
45 Ibid.
46 FSMA 2000, s.138D(1); PRA Rulebook (n 44).

Pursuant to ICOBS 5.1.1(1)G insurers should take reasonable steps to ensure that a policyholder only buys a policy under which he is eligible to claim. In the absence of an insurable interest, a policyholder would be ineligible to claim. In addition, ICOBS 5.1.4(4)G suggests that insurers should ask clear and specific questions about information relevant to the policy to be entered into at the pre-contractual disclosure stage. It is at least arguable that the insurer's responsibility "to take reasonable steps" to ensure eligibility to claim extends to (1) making enquiries as to the existence and nature of the proposer's interest at the time of entering into the policy, and (2) declining to issue/sell a policy which the insurer knows would be void for lack of insurable interest. In the context of the mis-selling of payment protection insurance, the FSA noted that it would expect insurers to ask specific questions aimed at eligibility either when speaking to customers directly or by using proposal/application forms fulfilling the same purpose, and to give customers "clear and balanced information that they can use to make an informed decision".[47]

ICOBS 5.2.2R (as amended by the Insurance Distribution Directive ('IDD'))[48] requires that, prior to the conclusion of a contract of insurance, the insurer, or an insurance intermediary if one is involved in the placement (either an "insurance distributor" as defined in art.2(1)(8) of the IDD), must specify, on the basis of information obtained from the prospective policyholder, that policyholder's demands and the needs. The proposed insurance must be consistent with the prospective policyholder's demands and needs (ICOBS 5.2.2BR). In non-advised sales, the insurer distributor should provide a "demands and needs statement" to that effect (ICOBS 5.2.4G), which must be clear, accurate and comprehensible.[49] In advised sales, the insurance distributor has more stringent obligations to take reasonable care to ensure the suitability of its advice to a policyholder (ICOBS 5.3.1R) and to explain why a particular insurance product would best meet that policyholder's demands and needs (ICOBS 5.3.4R). In direct sales by insurers, these provisions could assist in preventing the Unsuitable Policy Scenario from arising if the insurer assesses whether the policy under consideration is suitable to cover the prospective policyholder's interest. If he or she has no (prospective) insurable interest in the subject-matter to be insured he or she has no insurance 'need' even if he or she 'demands' such insurance. In sales through an intermediary, the same assessment made by the intermediary should flag up any issues with the prospective policyholder's interest.

Further to ICOBS 6.1.5R (as amended by the IDD), a prospective policyholder must be given by the insurer (or an insurance intermediary if one is involved in the placement) appropriate information about a policy before the contract is concluded so that he or she can make an informed decision about the

---

47 FSA, '*The Sale of Payment Protection Insurance – Results of Thematic Work*' (November 2005) para 4.5.
48 Directive (EU) 2016/97 of the European Parliament and of the Council of 20 January 2016 on insurance distribution (recast).
49 ICOBS 4.1A.2(2)(a)R.

arrangements proposed. In relation to each policy (other than 'pure protection contracts'), ICOBS 6.1.10AR and Annex 3 require that in advance of the contract, a prospective consumer policyholder is to be provided with an insurance product information document ('IPID') that provides, inter alia, a summary of the insurance cover and the main exclusions where claims cannot be made. Further to ICOBS 6.1.7A(2)G, such IPID information should also be provided to non-consumer policyholders. There is an equivalent information requirement for pure protection contracts (long-term life and sickness insurance) in ICOBS 6.3.1(2)R. The requirement to provide information on the scope of cover and the exclusions that have an adverse effect on claims being payable could be capable of being construed to include information on what types of interests in the insured subject-matter the policy covers but is more likely to be directed at providing details of express contractual exclusions and coverage limitations.[50] The insurable interest requirement, being a general restriction on insurability based on statute and/or common law, is unlikely to be captured by "objective information" on "key features of the insurance products".[51]

Based on the above FCA Handbook Principles, rules and guidance, it could be argued that insurance distributors should (1) be making enquiries as to the existence and nature of the proposer's interest to assess whether the policy under consideration is suitable to cover the proposer's interest, and (2) provide the proposer with clear and balanced information as to the insurable interest requirement under the proposed policy so that the proposer can make an informed decision.

Nevertheless, it is far from certain whether the FCA would regard an enquiry into the prospective policyholder's insurable interest to be part of an insurer's eligibility check under ICOBS 5.1.1G. FCA guidance is non-binding.[52] The 'demands and needs' assessment under ICOBS 5.2.2R and 5.2.2BR is based on 'information obtained', but there is no express obligation on an insurance distributor to enquire into the prospective policyholder's insurable interest in the insured subject-matter or to prompt the disclosure of information relating to the prospective policyholder's interest by making the insurable interest requirement a part of the product information provided. Consequently, the lack of interest may not be flagged up and taken into account when assessing the prospective policyholder's demands and needs. As noted above, ICOBS 6.1.5R, 6.1.7AR, 6.1.10AR and 6.3.1(2)R are unlikely to be concerned with extra-contractual policy features. There are no published FSA/FCA Decision Notices for breaches of ICOBS 5.1, 5.2, 6.1 and 6.3 in relation to the sale of insurance policies in which policyholders did not have an insurable interest. Neither the FCA nor the LC have pinpointed those regulatory provisions as an existing basis for mis-selling claims against insurers who failed to consider the existence and nature of the

---

50 See e.g. ICOBS 6 Annex 2, 2.1 6th bullet point; Annex 3 2.1, 3.9(e) and (f).
51 IDD, art.20(1) and (8); Recital (48).
52 FCA Handbook, 'The Enforcement Guide' 2.9.2.

proposer's interest. In *Figurasin v Central Capital Limited, Paragon Personal Finance*, the court noted that the ICOBS rules "are not required to accommodate any level of irresponsibility on the part of the consumer",[53] indicating that policyholders too must exercise some degree of judgement, although the Financial Ombudsman has decided some complaints on insurable interest by generalized references to mis-selling.[54]

Redress: Under the FSMA 2000, s.138D(2), a contravention by an authorized insurer of a FCA Handbook rule would generally be actionable by a policyholder who is a private person and who has suffered a loss as a result of the contravention, subject to defences and certain exceptions (a 's.138D(2) action'). However, there would be a number of potential obstacles to a successful s.138D(2) action in the Unsuitable Policy Scenario even if a contravention of the relevant FCA rules can be established:

1   The s.138D(2) action would not be available to business insureds.[55] Even certain categories of individuals may not fall within the categories of 'private person'.[56]

2   A s.138D(2) action does not arise upon contraventions of FCA guidance[57] and the provisions in PRIN.[58] Accordingly, a policyholder would not be able to establish a right of action in reliance on contraventions of ICOBS 5.1.1G/5.1.2G or the Principles in PRIN 2.1.1.

3   The policyholder must show that he has suffered a loss as a result of the contravention. The Uninsured Loss is not caused by a contravention of any rule but an insured peril. A contravention of ICOBS 5.3.1R may cause the Loss of Chance in an advised sale but the fact pattern might be such that other causative factors were at play when the policyholder entered into the Invalid Policy: for example, if the policyholder relied on his own judgement,[59] or the advice of a third party,[60] in entering into the Invalid Policy, there may be no causational link between the insurer's contraventions of FCA rules and the Loss of Chance. A contravention of ICOBS 6.1.5R cannot result in a Loss of Chance if no information on insurable interest is required to be provided. Moreover, no Loss of Chance arises if no Alternative Policy would have been available.

---

53 [2014] EWCA Civ 504, [23] (Patten LJ).
54 FOS Final Decisions DRN2653519; DRN5256949; DRN6435124.
55 Rights of Actions Regulations (n 40), reg.3(1).
56 *Sivagnanam v Barclays Bank Plc* [2015] EWHC 3985 (Comm).
57 FSMA 2000, s.138D(2). See also *R (British Bankers Association) v FSA* [2011] EWHC 999 (Admin), [71–94] (Ouseley J).
58 FSMA 2000, s.138D(3); PRIN 3.4.4R.
59 *Zaki v Credit Suisse (UK) Ltd* [2011] EWHC 2422 (Comm), [131–134] (Teare J); *Basma Al Sulaiman v Credit Suisse Securities (Europe) Limited, Plurimi Capital LLP* [2013] EWHC 400 (Comm), [160–165] (Cooke J).
60 *Basma Al Sulaiman v Credit Suisse Securities (Europe) Limited, Plurimi Capital LLP* (n 59).

4   The s.138D(2) action for damages is subject to defences. In the Unsuitable
Policy Scenario this limitation could apply if independently of the policyholder's lack of insurable interest, the insurer would have been entitled to
decline liability under the Invalid Policy. For example, in *Bate v Aviva Insurance UK Ltd*,[61] the court found that the insurer had not been in contravention of ICOBS rules and dismissed a claim for damages pursuant to the
predecessor of s.138D[62] as the insurer had been entitled to deny liability for
a claim on the grounds of misrepresentation, non-disclosure, breaches of
condition and forfeiture for use of fraudulent devices.

FOS

For consumer policyholders[63] the Financial Ombudsman Scheme could provide
an alternative route to redress.[64] The Ombudsman can determine a complaint
"by reference to what is, in his opinion, fair and reasonable in all the circumstances of the case"[65] taking into account, inter alia, law, regulatory rules, guidance and standards and good industry practice at the relevant time,[66] and can
make compensatory awards of up to £150,000.[67] Significantly, in the Unsuitable
Policy Scenario this would allow a consumer policyholder to make a complaint
in respect of contraventions of the Principles of Business and ICOBS guidance
not actionable under the FSMA 2000, s.138D(2) and (3).[68] A review of the reported FOS decisions between 2012 and 2017 showed that there were only 35
complaints with an insurable interest element, and only 3 decisions considered
complaints on insurable interest by reference to mis-selling.[69]

There are no consumer redress schemes in place, and the FCA has not exercised
any product intervention powers, relevant to insurable interest. In summary, although PRIN and ICOBS create a regulatory environment that is conducive to
the insurer taking steps to consider insurable interest issues at the time of the
contract, the current FSMA 2000 regulatory framework cannot fill the remedial
gap in the Unsuitable Policy Scenario as insurance distributors are not required
to provide information on the insurable interest requirement in their product

---

61   [2014] EWCA Civ 334.
62   FSMA 2000, s.150 (prior to amendment by the Financial Services Act 2012).
63   The definition of 'eligible complainant' includes consumers, micro-enterprises, charities which
     have an annual income of less than £1 million and trustees of trusts which have a net asset value
     of less than £1 million – see DISP 2.7.3R.
64   FSMA 2000, Part XVI.
65   FCA Handbook, 'Dispute Resolution: Complaints' ('DISP') DISP 3.6.1R.
66   DISP 3.6.4R.
67   FSMA 2000, s.404B(5); DISP 3.7.4R.
68   In *R (British Bankers Association) v FSA* (n 57) the court held that the restrictions on actionabil-
     ity under s.138D(3) and PRIN R.3.4.4 do not preclude redress through the Financial Ombuds-
     man Scheme.
69   See n 54.

information, and the scope for private actions for damages under the FSMA 2000 ss.20(3) and 138D(2) is limited.

Insurers' duties in relation to insurable interest

This section will argue the case for closing the remedial gap and re-balancing the parties' responsibilities in relation to ensuring that the insured has an insurable interest by introducing a statutory duty on the insurer to decline to enter into a contract of insurance that would be void for lack of insurable interest, supplemented by a product information requirement relating to insurable interest in the FCA Handbook ICOBS.

Suggested wordings

Suggested wordings for the duty to decline (for inclusion in the IIB) and a regulatory requirement (for inclusion in the FCA Handbook ICOBS, Table 12.1) on which the following discussion is based are set out below:

Duty to decline

IIB
[4A]   **Insurer's duty to decline**

1   If, at the time of entering into the contract, the insurer knows, or ought to know, or is presumed to know, that the contract of insurance would be void for lack of insurable interest in the insured subject-matter, the insurer must decline to enter into the contract.
2   The duty imposed by subsection (1) is referred to in this Act as 'the duty to decline'.
3   The insured has a remedy against the insurer for a breach of the duty to decline only if the insured shows that, but for the breach, the insured –

   a   would not have entered into the contract of insurance,
   b   would have entered into the contract of insurance only on different terms, or would have arranged for a person controlled by the insured to enter into it, so that the contract would not have been void for lack of insurable interest, and
   c   the insured suffered a loss as a result of the breach of the duty to decline.

4   For the purposes of section [4A], the knowledge of the parties is determined by reference to the Insurance Act 2015, sections 4 and 6 in relation to a non-consumer insureds and an insurer, and the Consumer Insurance (Disclosure and Representation) Act 2012, section 5(5)(a) in relation to a consumer insured.

[the 'duty to decline']

Table 12.1 Regulatory product information requirement

FCA Handbook ICOBS Insurance: Conduct of Business sourcebook
ICOBS 6.3.1R *– pure protection contracts*
[Table] Information to be communicated before conclusion
(8a)   Information on the insurable interest requirement as applicable to the contract.
ICOBS 6 Annex 3R *Providing product information by way of standardized insurance information document*
2   What information needs to be contained in the IPID? 2.1 R   The *IPID* must contain the following information: ...   (2a)   Information on the insurable interest requirement as applicable to the contract.

[together, the 'regulatory product information requirement']

The duty to decline

The duty to decline operates in two parts: first, the insurer owes a pre-contractual duty to prospective insureds to decline to enter into a contract of insurance which he knows, or ought to know, would be void for lack of insurable interest (cl.[4A](1)). The second part is a remedy of an insured for breach of the duty to decline if he can show an element of inducement (cl.[4A](3)(a) or (b)), and a loss as a result of the breach (cl.[4A](3)(c)). As the duty to decline should apply in respect of all types of contracts of insurance, it should be included into the IIB alongside with the generally applicable provisions and after the provisions that specifically relate to life-related contracts of insurance.

One of the key elements of the duty to decline is the knowledge of the parties as regards the absence of an insurable interest in the subject-matter to be insured at the time of the contract. The duty to decline only arises if the insurer has the pre-requisite knowledge. Indirectly, the insured's (absence of) knowledge of the lack of insurable interest is relevant to the availability of a remedy for breach of the duty. As the parties' pre-contractual knowledge is already the subject of provisions in the CIDRA, s.5(5)(a) and the IA 2015, ss.4–6, for consistency, they are adopted for the purposes of cl.[4A] in sub-cl.(4).

The *knowledge of the insurer* which determines whether the duty to decline arises would in many cases derive from the pre-contractual presentation of the risk by the insured in accordance with CIDRA (consumer insureds) or the IA 2015, Pt.2 (non-consumer insureds).

Non-consumer insureds must make pre-contractual disclosures of circumstances material to the risk or, failing that, give the insurer sufficient information to put a prudent insurer on notice that it needs to make further enquiries for the purpose of revealing those material circumstances.[70] Is the nature and extent of

70 IA 2015, ss.3(3) and (4).

the insured's interest material? In the absence of a specific enquiry, the editors of MacGillivray and the authors of 'Good Faith and Insurance Contracts' consider that it is not, the latter on the ground that an insured is not required to have an interest at the time of the contract.[71] However, under the IIB, cl.2(1) the insured would be required to have an insurable interest in a contract of life-related insurance at the time of the contract, and under the MIA 1906, s.4(2), the insured is required to have an insurable interest, or a reasonable prospect of acquiring one, at the time of the contract. The IA 2015 s.7(4)(a) states that "special or unusual facts relating to the risk" are material. Moreover, given the importance the insurance market accords to the requirement as a "hallmark of insurance", and its role in aligning the interests of the insurer, loss prevention, risk mitigation and subrogation,[72] it is arguable that the absence of any interest (or prospect thereof), or an unusually weak interest, in the subject-matter would affect the risk and, accordingly, should be material and disclosable. If information on the insured's interest becomes part of the insured's pre-contractual risk presentation, the insurer would have the relevant knowledge for the purposes of the duty to decline.

If, however, the nature and extent of the insured's interest is not considered to be material, there would be no duty to disclose those matters. In addition, consumer insureds are not required to volunteer information.[73] Some of the Financial Ombudsman decisions reviewed show that some insurers already operate under underwriting guidelines that require prescribed types of insurable interest and that it is already their standard procedure to enquire about a proposer's interest and to decline insurance for proposers without the required interest, at the outset.[74] This is also reflected in the proposal forms and questionnaires reviewed.[75] Nevertheless, not all proposal forms ask questions aimed at identifying the nature of the relationship between the proposer and the property to be insured (e.g.: 'Do you own or rent your home?' in a home insurance proposal form; 'Are you the legal owner and/or registered keeper of the car?' in motor insurance). It is therefore important to prompt prospective policyholders to consider and discuss their interest with the insurer or an insurance intermediary before the contract is entered into – this process could be triggered by the regulatory product information requirement (discussed below).

An insurer is also taken to have knowledge of any matters set out in ss.5 and 6(1) of the IA 2015 (including common knowledge and constructive knowledge). Thus, if the insurer suspects that the insured has no insurable interest in the subject-matter of the contract, or if it is common knowledge or industry

71 John Birds, Ben Lynch and Simon Paul, *MacGillivray on Insurance Law* (14th edn, Sweet & Maxwell 2018), para 17-076; Peter MacDonald Eggers and Sir Simon Picken, *Good Faith and Insurance Contracts* (4th edn, Informa Law 2018) para 15.21.
72 See Chapters 9–11.
73 CIDRA, s.2(2). See Section 8.1.
74 See e.g. FOS Final Decisions DR1190601, DRN2129054, DRN2557385, DRN4121567 and DRN5793832.
75 See Chapter 9.

knowledge that a particular insured has no relation to a specific subject-matter that could be the basis for an insurable interest, the insurer would be deemed to know so. Such deemed knowledge would be sufficient for the duty to decline to arise.

If the insured makes a misrepresentation as to his lack of insurable interest, the insurer is unlikely to have the pre-requisite knowledge for the purposes of the duty to decline to arise, and accordingly, the insured would have no remedy under cl.[4A](1).

The *knowledge of the insured* is relevant to whether or not a remedy for breach of the duty to decline is available. If, at the time of the contract, the insured knew that the contract (i.e. the Invalid Policy) would be void for lack of insurable interest, he will not be able to establish that he would not have entered the Invalid Policy but for the breach of the duty to decline. An insured with knowledge of the lack of insurable interest could not be said to have relied on the Invalid Policy for cover for his Uninsured Loss and he could have looked for, and entered into, an Alternative Policy at the time of entering into the Invalid Policy. Accordingly, such an insured would not have suffered any Loss of Chance as a result of the breach of the duty to decline.

Different standards of knowledge can calibrate the availability of a remedy for a breach of the duty to decline to consumer and non-consumer insureds. The knowledge accorded to a *non-consumer insured* under ss.4 and 6 of the IA 2015 is comprehensive and should impose a relatively high threshold to a damages claim for breach of the duty to decline as the circumstances where the insurer knows, but the insured does not know, that the insured lacks an insurable interest should be rare. In comparison, the meaning of 'knowledge' of a *consumer insured* is narrower: according to the CIDRA, s.5(5)(a) there is a (rebuttable) presumption that a consumer insurer has the "knowledge of a reasonable consumer". This presumption can be displaced by showing that the consumer insured in question had no actual knowledge. Given the lower standard of knowledge of consumer insureds, combined with any knowledge the insurer might acquire through the insured's answers in the proposal form and in compliance with the regulatory product information requirement, it should be easier for consumer insureds to obtain a remedy under cl.[4A](3).

Regardless of knowledge, a remedy for breach of the duty to decline would also be barred if no Alternative Policy would have been available at the time of the contract and in the absence of a loss as a result of the breach (cl.[4A](3)(b) and (c)). This should provide insurers with additional protection against unmeritorious claims under cl.[4A].

A regulatory product information requirement

The regulatory product information requirement proposed to be included in the FCA Handbook ICOBS would require an insurer to produce IPID information, and an insurance distributor to give the prospective policyholder information on the insurable interest requirement as applicable to the contract. This requirement would then tie in with the general rule in ICOBS 6.1.5(1)R, requiring information about the policy to be provided "in good time and in a comprehensible form" so that the policyholder can make an informed decision. By making the provisions part of ICOBS 6, the regulatory product information requirement would apply to insurance distributors, including insurers and insurance intermediaries, but the obligation to produce the IPID (or equivalent) is on the insurer.[76]

The regulatory product information requirement does not demand that insurance distributors must ask the prospective policyholder to confirm that he or she has an insurable interest or to determine the existence of an insurable interest with absolute certainty. However, by including information on insurable interest as applicable to the policy in question in the relevant pre-contractual product information, the prospective policyholder would be prompted to consider his or her insurable interest under the policy proposed, and if he or she had concerns, those concerns could be raised with the insurance distributor, who would then have additional information for the purposes of (re)assessing that policyholder's demands and the needs.[77] In the case of direct sales, such information would also be relevant to the insurer's knowledge for the purposes of the duty to decline.

The regulatory product information requirement ensures that insurers do not side-step the duty to decline by deliberately refraining from raising insurable interest as a matter for pre-contractual consideration. In non-consumer insurance, insurance intermediaries (such as brokers) will frequently act as insurance distributors. If so, the regulatory requirements in ICOBS 5.1.1G and 6.1.5R would apply to them and, if complied with, proposals for insurance unsupported by an insurable interest should not even proceed to the insurer. If an insurer is involved as an insurance distributor – which will be the case in direct sales – the regulatory product information requirement should prompt (supplemental) information flow in relation to the proposer's pre-contractual risk presentation. It is in line with the IA s.3(4)(b), which puts the onus on the insurer to make further enquiries if put on notice of the possible existence of further material circumstances.

Legal bases for the duty to decline and the regulatory product information requirement

Duty to decline: It is suggested that the duty to decline is a specific manifestation of the duty of good faith as applicable to insurance contracts.[78] In *Carter v Boehm*, Lord Mansfield explained 'good faith' as follows: "Good faith forbids either party by concealing what he privately knows, to draw the other into a bargain, from his ignorance of that fact, and his believing to the contrary".[79] An insurer who misleads the insured into believing that he has an enforceable contract

76 ICOBS 6.-1.1R and 6.-1.5R.
77 ICOBS 5.2.2R.
78 IA 2015, s.14.
79 (1766) 3 Burr 1905 (KB) 1910.

222 Remedies, enforcement and reform

knowing that the insured has no insurable interest in the subject-matter of the contract, and no reasonable prospect of acquiring one, does not act in good faith. Although in *Feasey* an insurable interest was established on the facts, the Court of Appeal indicated that the insurer's defence of lack of insurable interest was not raised in good faith given that the insurer had devised the contractual structure in full knowledge of the nature and extent of the insured's interest.[80] By analogy to pre-contractual non-disclosure/misrepresentation by the insured, there are some tentative (pre-IA 2015) dicta that the remedy of avoidance is subject to a requirement of good faith.[81] In a recent Financial Ombudsman decision,[82] a complaint that an insurer had been in breach of the duty of utmost good faith for failing to let the insured know that the policy should not be taken out for lack of insurable interest was considered, but no breach of good faith was found on the facts. Some US jurisdictions recognize that an insurer who knowingly issues a policy that clearly lacks an insurable interest may be liable to the insured for breach of the duty of fair dealings.[83]

In Chapter 3 it was noted that there are a number of issues with denying the defence of lack of insurable interest on the grounds of bad faith, but the duty to decline is no such defence – it recognizes that the lack of insurable interest renders the Invalid Policy void but seeks to give an alternative remedy in the circumstances set out in cl.[4A]. The approach to good faith under the IA 2015, s.14 is that the principle of good faith has been preserved, although the remedy of avoidance for breach of good faith has been abolished. It has been noted above that the LC consider the principle of good faith to be an "interpretative principle" that supports separate remedies regimes for breaches of more specific duties. It would be in keeping with this approach to create an independent duty to decline with accompanying remedies provisions. The IIB would be a suitable instrument for the duty to decline since it relates to insurable interest and could be easily amended prior to its enactment. If the IIB does not proceed, the provisions for the duty of decline could also be included independently in Part 5 of the IA 2015.

Regulatory product information requirement: The regulatory product information requirement – as part of the FCA Handbook – would be in part a particularization, and in part an extension, of the ICOBS provisions but re-cast as a separate and specific rules. The LC consider that it should be a matter for insurance regulation whether insurers should take some responsibility for ascertaining the insured's interest at the pre-contractual stage.[84]

---

80 n 5, [6] (Waller LJ), [121–122] (Dyson LJ); [144] (Ward LJ).
81 See *Drake Insurance Plc (In Provisional Liquidation) v Provident Insurance Plc* [2003] EWCA Civ 1834, [177] (Pill LJ), more cautiously [87] (Rix LJ) and [144] (Clarke LJ). Contra: *Brotherton v Aseguradora Colseguros SA (No.2)* [2003] EWCA Civ 705, [34] (Mance LJ).
82 FOS Final Decision DRN5335876.
83 For an overview see J Loshin, '*Insurance Law's Hapless Busybody: A Case against the Insurable Interest Requirement*' (2007) 117 Yale LJ 474, at 501–502.
84 LC, *Post Contract* (n 8) para 12.33.

The regulatory product information requirement would support the statutory duty to decline. There is precedent for primary legislation and insurance regulation dealing with issues in tandem, such as:

1   CIDRA, ss.2–3/IA 2015, s.3 and ICOBS 5.1.4G (pre-contractual presentation of the risk);
2   CIDRA, s.4 / IA, ss.8 and 10–11 and ICOBS 8.1.2R (rejection of claims);
3   IA, s.13A and ICOBS 8.1.1R (handling and payment of claims); and
4   MIA 1906, s.17 and IA s.14 and post-IDD ICOBS 2.5.1R (good faith and insurer acting honestly and fairly, etc.).

When making new rules, the FCA must, so far as reasonably possible, advance one or more of its operational objectives having regard to the regulatory principles.[85] One of its operational objectives is securing an appropriate degree of protection for consumers.[86] The FCA confirmed that the IDD amendments to ICOBS 5 and 6 are intended to further the consumer protection objective.[87] Given that in the consumer insurance market most policies are in the nature of contracts of adhesion and contain terms and conditions of which policyholders may have no real understanding,[88] consumers may not necessarily be focussed on, or capable of, assessing whether their interest is covered by a particular policy. It does not seem to strike a fair balance between the parties that the insurer is entitled to assume that a standard term policy suits a proposer's interest without making available information on the insurable interest requirement as it applies to the contract in question. It would be consistent with the FCA's consumer protection objective to make specific rules as expressed in the regulatory product information requirement to protect consumer policyholders from entering into contracts under which they would not be eligible to claim. The regulatory product information requirement should reduce the number of insurance contracts that are void for lack of interest by highlighting the insurable interest requirement to prospective policyholders before they enter into a contract of insurance. To advance the consumer protection objective in that way would not conflict with, and possibly be supportive of, the FCA's other objectives, being its strategic objective to maintain well-functioning markets, and its integrity and competition objective.[89] In particular, greater transparency on the insurable interest requirement in the IPID (or equivalent document), enabling prospective policyholders to make informed choices, should advance the FCA's competition objective.[90]

85 FSMA 2000, s.1B.
86 FSMA 2000, s.1C.
87 FCA, '*Insurance Distribution Directive Implementation: Consultation Paper I*' (CP 17/7, March 2017) 55.
88 See Chapter 11.
89 FSMA 2000, s.1B(2), 1C and 1D.
90 FSMA 2000, s.1D(2)(a).

The FCA must also have regard to the general principle of proportionality of a regulatory burden or restriction and the efficient use of its resources.[91] The regulatory product information requirement should not add any disproportionate burden:

1   As insurers are already required to produce IPIDs (or equivalent) for their policies, it should not be a significant burden to include information on the insurable interest requirement as applicable to a particular type of policy.
2   Any information obtained from the prospective policyholder regarding his or her interest would become part of the information relevant to that policyholder's insurance demands and needs. In direct sales, insurers are already under an existing regulatory duty to ensure that a proposed contract of insurance is consistent with those demands and needs. In mediated sales, this duty is placed on the intermediary.
3   The FCA carried out a cost-benefit analysis on the relevant ICOBS amendments pursuant to the IDD and noted that most firms that took part in the consultation had reported that "they would incur no additional costs resulting from the requirement that all contracts proposed are consistent with the customer's demands and needs, as they already had mechanisms in place to ensure this".[92]
4   As for the FCA's efficient and economic use of its resources, the FCA Handbook ICOBS could be amended by a short update, whereas the FCA's existing processes and procedures for supervision and enforcement would not need to be changed.

Benefits and detriments

The main arguments against introducing a duty to decline and a regulatory product information requirement are that these obligation would (1) add to the legal and regulatory burden of insurers, (2) complicate the law and (3) address a narrow issue that has not given rise to many cases or practical problems. These are valid objections but they are outweighed by the benefits, including (4) promoting compliance with the insurable interest requirement and good faith, (5) addressing the remedial gap in the Unsuitable Policy and (6) reducing the opportunistic use of the insurable interest defence and giving greater legitimacy to its proper use. These points are addressed in turn:

Legal and regulatory burden: Prima facie, the duty to decline and the regulatory product information requirement would add to the legal and regulatory burden of insurers but, it is suggested, they do not add significantly to existing obligations and insurers' procedures and practices. It has been argued above that insurers already owe a reciprocal duty of good faith to the insured and that the FSMA 2000 regulatory framework already contains product information

---

91 FSMA 2000, s.3B(1)(a) and (b).
92 n 87, 44.

requirements that point towards greater transparency as to what a specific contract of insurance does and does not cover to prevent specific instances of mis-selling. Some insurers already have in place procedures complying with the duty to decline and the regulatory product information requirement as a matter of good practice. The innovation of the duty to decline and a regulatory product information requirement would be to provide remedies for an insured who suffers loss as a result of their breach. From the above discussion it should be clear that an effort has been made to strike a fair balance between the interests of the insurer and that of the insured. Thus, the conditions attached to the availability of a remedy for a breach of the duty to decline ensure that, in the first instance, it should be the responsibility of the policyholder and his insurance advisers to ensure that the policy to be purchased is suitable to cover the policyholder's interest. A remedy for a contravention of the regulatory product information requirement following a s.138D(2) action would only be available to consumer policyholders and be subject to other limitations.

It could also be argued that a greater responsibility on insurers in relation to making available information on the insurable interest requirement as applicable to their products is a quid pro quo for the retention of the requirement that is valued by the insurance market as a 'hallmark of insurance' and as additional protection against invalid claims.[93] Clearly, insurers consider that the doctrine protects and benefits them, so that compliance with the duty to decline and the regulatory product information requirement would be in their own best interest. Having successfully lobbied the LC for the retention of the insurable interest requirement,[94] it would seem only fair that the insurance industry accept some responsibility for ensuring compliance with it.

Complexity of law: The complexity of the existing law on insurable interest has been one of the drivers for reform. The duty to decline would add a provision to the IIB but would not change the operation of its core provisions. For consistency, the 'knowledge provisions' from the CIDRA and the IA 2015 have been adopted.

Narrow legal issue: It is conceded that the Unsuitable Policy Scenario concerns a narrow issue. However, the alternative seems to be that the courts would continue to use the Three Strategies in cases involving an Unsuitable Policy Scenario, an approach which itself is open to criticism.[95] In addition, the duty to decline and a regulatory product information requirement could prevent or reduce the mis-selling of insurance products in the future.

Promoting compliance: It is suggested that the most important benefit of the duty to decline and a regulatory product information requirement would be that compliance with these duties would promote compliance with the requirement for an insurable interest and should forestall the situation where the parties enter into a contract of insurance in ignorance of the insured's lack of insurable

---

93 LC, '*Issues Paper 10 – Insurable Interest: Updated Proposals*' (March 2015) para 2.3.
94 LC, '*Post Contract*' (n 8) para 10.12.
95 See n 18.

interest in the insured subject-matter. The duties should encourage both parties to consider insurable interest issues at the outset and consequently should prevent those issues from being raised at claims stage. The availability of remedies against the insurer should incentivize those insurers who still adhere to a modus operandi of pleading the insured's lack of insurable interest at claims stage, rather than considering it at the pre-contractual stage, to change their procedures. In addition, the duty to decline should promote good faith and fair dealings as between the parties. The policy reasons behind the justifications of the requirement for an insurable interest would be given better effect if the requirement were to be supported by duties on the insurer that curtail non-compliance.

Closure of remedial gap: The remedies available against insurers for breach of the duty to decline and any contravention of the regulatory product information requirement would close the remedial gap in the Unsuitable Policy Scenario: a policyholder could claim damages for his Loss of Chance. This remedy would counter-balance the invalidity consequence which disproportionately penalizes the insured. One of the main objectives of recent insurance contract law reforms was to ensure "a better balance of interests between policyholders and insurers".[96] Closing this remedial gap would be in line with that aim.

Fewer opportunities for technical insurable interest defence: If insurers were to be under a duty to decline, there should be fewer occasions on which insurers could use the lack of an insurable interest as an opportunistic and technical defence in order to escape liability for a claim. Compliance with the duty to decline and the regulatory product information requirement by insurers should rule out situations like *Feasey* where (re)insurers appeared to have turned a blind eye to the (lack of) insurable interest position.[97] Conversely, insurers who have discharged their duty to decline and complied with the regulatory product information requirement should be able to raise insurable interest issues at claims stage as a genuine defence. The duty to decline and the regulatory product information requirement would give greater legitimacy to genuine insurable interest defences raised by insurers and should reduce the scope for the courts' "discretionary remedialism" by "lean[ing] in favour of an insurable interest". This, in turn, should make insurable interest litigation more predictable.

The combination of the duty to decline and the regulatory product information requirement would also affirm the growing partnership between insurance contract law and insurance regulation, of which there are already a number of examples. The regulatory product information requirement does not make the doctrine of insurable interest a regulatory requirement, but it is a regulatory tool that should assist in preventing parties from entering into contracts of insurance that are void for lack of insurable interest and consequently of no value to either party.

---

96 LC, *'Insurance Contract Law: Business Disclosure; Warranties; Insurers' Remedies for Fraudulent Claims; and Late Payment'* (Law Com No 353, July 2014) para 1.6.
97 n 5.

13 Conclusion

This book set out to examine the English law on insurable interest and to contribute to the debate whether the doctrine remains relevant to modern English insurance law and market practice and whether and how the doctrine of insurable interest should be reformed. The research outcome is a 'qualified defence' of the doctrine of insurable interest with recommendations as to how the doctrine could be reformed. There is a strong case for retaining the doctrine of insurable interest. The policies behind the Traditional Justifications for the doctrine of insurable interest remain relevant and, in the case of the anti-wagering justification and the moral hazard justification, have indeed acquired fresh significance following the Financial Crisis, the expansion of derivative contracts and the liberalization of gambling. The requirement for an insurable interest delineates insurance contracts from other types of speculative contracts, as well as setting a boundary for insurers' realm of operation and supporting their financial stability. It is a mechanism for aligning the interests of the insured and the insurer in the preservation of the insured subject-matter and supports post-contractual fair dealings between the parties.

The doctrine of insurable interest can also be rationalized on novel grounds: its existence is integral to the operation of other doctrines and principles of insurance law and, in relation to property insurance, to the operation and performance of standard contract terms. In addition, the insurance market perceives the requirement for an insurable interest to be part of market practice and as an essential characteristic of contracts of insurance. Doctrinally, the existence of an economic interest in the insured subject-matter appears to be a definitional or descriptive characteristic of contracts of indemnity insurance. There is a tension between the doctrine of insurable interest's definitional role and its role as a validity requirement, but it has been shown that these two roles can be reconciled. The LC's proposals as encapsulated in the IIB – although largely limited to contracts of life-related insurance – are an endorsement of the continuing applicability of the doctrine of insurable interest acknowledging its relevance as matter of policy and market practice.

Under the current law (and the IIB) the main legal consequences flowing from non-compliance with the insurable interest requirement – the invalidity of the contract of insurance and the unenforceability of claim – are predominantly weapons in the arsenal of the insurer. They are ineffective means of promoting compliance with the insurable interest requirement as they do not oblige or incentivize insurers to take greater responsibility to consider the policyholder's interest at the time of the contract. In the Unsuitable Policy Scenario, policyholders can face a remedial gap with no recourse against insurer in respect of their Uninsured Loss and their Loss of Chance. Founded upon good faith and by reference to existing rules and guidance in the FCA Handbook, the case was argued for the introduction of (1) a new statutory duty of insurers to decline to enter into contract of insurance which they know, or ought to know, would be void for lack of insurable interest, and (2) a regulatory obligation on insurers to provide information to the insured on the insurable interest requirement specific to the type of policy in question before the contract is concluded. The addition of these duties and their attendant remedies should support the observance of the doctrine of insurable interest by the parties, help to prevent contracts of insurance that are invalid for lack of insurable interest being entered into and strike a fairer balance between the interests of the insurer and the insured.

Over the last decade, English insurance contract law has been reformed to make it fairer, more predictable and more effective. The IIB is the final outstanding part of this reform project, but it remains to be seen whether, and how, the IIB is passed into law. As the IIB's main substantive provisions only apply to contracts of life-related insurance, it does not consolidate the fragmented legal bases of the doctrine of insurable interest. The IIB would alleviate the restrictiveness of the law on insurable interest in relation to life-related insurance: the economic interest test for insurable interest and the recast and new categories of automatic insurable interest would expand the scope of insurable interest, creating a more permissive regime. It is regrettable that the IIB excludes insurable interest in non-life-related insurance from the reforms. This is a missed opportunity to clarify the ambit of insurable interest in property/indemnity insurance with a view to making the definition of insurable interest clear enough to provide legal certainty, flexible enough to embrace market innovations but also sufficiently significant to maintain a doctrinal dividing line between contracts of insurance and other kinds of contracts of speculation. It has been suggested in this book that an extension of the meaning of insurable interest to include economic interests may not be needed in relation to property insurance and that, by reference to the Traditional Justifications and the novel rationales put forward, there is a good arguable case that the meaning of insurable interest should remain confined to legal or contractual rights in relation to property or that the notion of economic interest should be interpreted narrowly. In the commoditized consumer and business property insurance market the notion of a legal interest is strongly embedded in standard policy terms and interlinks with the (efficient) operation of other principles of insurance law. The acceptance of weaker interests would require the re-drafting of, and inclusion of special terms in, property policy wording to address the insured's weaker links to the insured property in the context of risk management and risk mitigation. A widened definition of insurable interest may be most appreciated at the fringes of insurance, such as parametric policies and innovative contingency insurance transactions. However, given the 'hallmark of insurance' role of the requirement for an insurable interest, a widened definition may blur the boundaries between insurance and non-insurance products, and this may in turn require the boundaries to be re-drawn by reference to other criteria. As the 'DNA of the Market', the doctrine of insurable interest cannot be excised without appropriate 'gene therapy' changes to the insurance market.

Bibliography

Books

Baker T and Simon J, Embracing Risk: The Changing Culture of Insurance and Responsibility (Chicago University Press 2002)

Birds J, *Birds' Modern Insurance Law* (10th edn, Sweet & Maxwell 2016)

Birds J, Lynch B and Paul S, *MacGillivray on Insurance Law* (14th edn, Sweet & Maxwell 2018)

Bruck (ed), *Kommentar zum Versicherungsvertragsrecht - Vol.5/2 – Lebensversicherung* (8th ed., De Gruyter Recht, Berlin 2013)

Bruck-Möller, *Kommentar zum Versicherungsvertragsrecht - Vol.3 – Feuerversicherung* (8th ed., De Gruyter Recht, Berlin 2002)

Bruck-Möller *Grosskommentar zum Versicherungsvertragsrecht - Vol.3* (9th ed., De Gruyter Recht, Berlin 2010)

Burling J and Lazarus K (eds.), *Research Handbook on International Insurance Law and Regulation* (Edward Elgar, Cheltenham 2011)

Chalmers M, *The Marine Insurance Act 1906* (1st edn, William Clowes & Sons 1907)

Clark G, *Betting on Lives: The Culture of Life Insurance in England, 1695–1775* (Manchester University Press 1999)

Clarke M, *Law of Liability Insurance* (Informa 2013)

———, *The Law of Insurance Contracts* (Service Issue 37, Informa 2016)

Couch on Insurance 3D (Thomson Reuters 2011)

Ehrenberg V, *Versicherungsrecht* (Verlag von Duncker & Humblot 1893)

Ericson RV, Doyle A and Barry D, *Insurance as Governance* (University of Toronto Press 2003)

Firth S, *Derivatives Law and Practice* (Sweet & Maxwell, Release 49 2019)

Gilman J, Templeman M, Blanchard C, Hopkins P and Hart N, *Arnould's Law of Marine Insurance and General Average* (19th edn, Sweet & Maxwell 2018)

Georgosouli A and Goldby M (eds), *Systemic Risk and the Future of Insurance Regulation* (Informa 2016)

Halsbury's Laws of Australia: Insurance (LexisNexis Loose-leaf, 6 May 2013)

Heimer C, *Reactive Risk and Rational Action: Managing Moral Hazard in Insurance Contracts* (University of California Press 1985)

Holmes EM (ed), *Appleman on Insurance* (St. Paul, Minn., West Pub. Co. 1996–2014)

Honsell H (ed), *Berliner Kommentar zum Versicherungsvertragsgesetz* (Springer Verlag 1999)

Jerry II RH and Richmond DR, *Understanding Insurance Law* (5th ed, LexisNexis 2012)

Jing Z, *Chinese Insurance Contracts* (Routledge 2017)

Johnson J and Bruce A (eds), *Decisions: Risk and Reward* (Routledge 2008)

Jones M, Dugdale A and others, *Clerk & Lindsell on Torts* (22nd edn, Sweet & Maxwell 2017)

Legh-Jones N, Birds J and Owen D, *MacGillivray on Insurance Law* (10th edn, Sweet & Maxwell 2003)

Lewis RP and Insua NM, *Business Income Insurance Disputes* (2nd ed., Wolters Kluwer 2012)

Lowry J and Rawlings P, *Insurance Law: Cases and Materials* (Hart Publishing 2004)

Lowry J, Rawlings P and Merkin R, *Insurance Law: Doctrines and Principles* (3rd edn, Hart Publishing 2011)

MacDonald Eggers P and Picken S, *Good Faith and Insurance Contracts* (4th edn, Informa Law 2018)

Marshall S, *A Treatise on the Law of Insurance: In Four Books*, vol 1 (Butterworth 1802)

Merkin R, *Colinvaux's Law of Insurance* (12th edn, Sweet & Maxwell 2019)

Merkin R and Steele J, *Insurance and the Law of Obligations* (OUP 2013)

Miers D, *Regulating Commercial Gambling: Past, Present and Future* (OUP 2004)

Mores ER, *A Short Account of the Society for Equitable Assurances on Lives and Survivorship; Established by Deed* (London 1762)

O'Neill PT and Woloniecki JW, *The Law of Reinsurance* (5th edn, Sweet & Maxwell 2019)

Park J, *A System of the Law of Marine Insurance* (6th edn, Butterworth 1809)

Postlethwayt M, *The Universal Dictionary of Trade and Commerce*, vol 1 (London 1751)

Reinecke FMB, Nienaber PM and van Niekerk JP, *South African Insurance Law* (Juta 2013)

Schwarcz D and Siegelman P (eds), *Research Handbook on the Economics of Insurance Law* (Edward Elgar Publishing 2015)

Sinn H-W, *Casino Capitalism* (OUP 2010)

Soyer B (ed), *Reforming Marine & Commercial Insurance Law* (Informa 2008)

Sutton K, *Insurance Law in Australia* (3rd ed., LBC Information Service 1999)

Thomas DR (ed), *Marine Insurance: The Law in Transition* (Informa 2006)

Vaughan EJ and Vaughan T, *Fundamentals of Risk and Insurance* (10th edn, John Wiley & Sons, Inc 2008)

Weskett J, *A Compleat Digest of the Theory, Laws, and Practice of Insurance* (London 1781)

Worthington S (ed.), *Commercial Law and Commercial Practice* (Oxford, Hart Publishing 2003)

Articles

Abraham KS, '*Four Conceptions of Insurance*' (2013) 161 U Penn LRev 653

Adams, J and Brownswood R, '*The Ideologies of Contract Law*' (1987) 7 LS 205

Anderson G and Clark G, '*Capturing Uncertainty: The Role of Insurance in the Construction of Modern Life*' (2007) 96 Zeitschrift für die gesamte Versicherungswissenschaft 129

Arnold-Dwyer F, '*Insurance Law Reform by Degrees: Late Payment and Insurable Interest*' (2017) 80 MLR 489

Avraham R, '*The Economics of Insurance Law –A Primer*' (2012) 19 Conn Ins LJ 29

Azeez YA and Ishola AS, '*Insurable Interest in Takaful: A Theoretical Contrivance for Islamic Insurers*' (2015) 6(S3) IJEFI 109

Bennett HN, '*Mapping the Doctrine of Utmost Good Faith in Insurance Contract Law*' [1999] LMCLQ 165

Birks P, '*Rights, Wrongs, and Remedies*' (2000) 20 OJLS 1

Bloink RS, '*Catalysts for Clarification: Modern Twists on the Insurable Interest Requirement for Life Insurance*' (2010) 17 Conn Ins LJ 56

Botes E and Kloppers H, '*Insurable Interest as a Requirement for Insurance Contracts: A Comparative Analysis*' (2018) 26 AJ Intl CL 130

Cardi WJ, Penfield RD and Yoon AH, '*Does Tort Law Deter Individuals? A Behavioral Science Study*' (2012) 9 J Emp LS 567

Davey J, '*The Reform of Gambling and the Future of Insurance Law*' (2004) 24 LS 507
——— '*Dial M for Moral Hazard? Incentives to Murder and the Life Assurance Act 1774*' (2014) 25 ILJ 120

Douds G, '*Insurable Interest in English Marine Insurance Law: Do We Still Need It*' (2012) 25 USF Mar LJ 323

Ewald F (trs J-M Dautrey and CF Stifler), '*Risk in Contemporary Society*' (2000) 6 Conn Ins LJ 365

Fleisher M, '*Stranger Originated Life Insurance: Finding a Modern Cure for an Age-Old Problem*' (2011) 41 Cum L Rev 569

Fulton LV, Mendez FA et al, '*Confusion between Odds and Probability, a Pandemic?*' (2012) 20 J Stat Edu 1

Harrington S, '*The Financial Crisis, Systemic Risk, and the Future of Insurance Regulation*' (2009) 76 J Risk Ins 785

Hartnett B and Thornton JV, '*Insurable Interest in Property – A Socio-Economic Reevaluation of a Legal Concept*' (1949) Ins LJ 420

Hasson RA, '*The Special Nature of the Insurance Contract: A Comparison of the American and English Law of Insurance*' (1984) 47 MLR 505
——— '*Subrogation in Insurance Law: A Critical Evaluation*' (1985) 5 OJLS 416

Hu HTC and Black B, '*Debt, Equity and Hybrid Decoupling: Governance and Systemic Risk Implications*' (2008) 14 Eur F Man 663
——— '*Debt, Equity and Hybrid Decoupling: Governance and Empty Voting II: Importance and Extension*' (2008) 156 U Penn L Rev 625

Kimball-Stanley A, '*Insurance and Credit Default Swaps: Should Like Things Be Treated Alike?*' (2008) 15 Conn Ins LJ 242

Koch P, '*100 Jahre Versicherungsvertagsgesetz*' (June 2008) 11 Versicherungswirtschaft Nr. 54

Kramer A, Harris A and Ansehl R, '*The New York State Insurance Department and Credit Default Swaps: Good Intentions, Bad Idea*' (2009) 22 JT Reg F Inst 29

Leimberg SR, '*Stranger-Owned Life Insurance: Killing the Goose that lays Golden Eggs*' (May 2005) Ins Tax Rev 811

Leonard AB, '*Underwriting Marine Warfare: Insurance and Conflict in the Eighteenth Century*' (2013) 15 Int JMH 173

Loshin J, '*Insurance Law's Hapless Busybody: A Case against the Insurable Interest Requirement*' (2007) 117 Yale LJ 474

Lowry J and Rawlings P, '*Proximate Causation in Insurance Law*' (2005) 68 MLR 310

MacDonald Eggers P, '*Sue and Labour and Beyond: The Assured's Duty of Mitigation*' [1998] LMCLQ 228

McDonald R and Paulson A, '*AIG- In Hindsight*' (2015) 29 J Econ Pers 81

Merkin R, '*Gambling by Insurance – A Study of the Life Assurance Act 1774*' (1980) 9 Anglo-Am L R 331

——— '*Australia, still a Nation of Chalmers?*' (2011) 30 UQLJ 189

Morewedge CK and Giblin CE, '*Explanations of the Endowment Effect: An Integrative Review*' (2015) 19(6) Tre Cogn Sci 339

Nurnberg H and Lackey DP, '*The Ethics of Life Insurance Settlements: Investing in Lives of Unrelated Individuals*' (2010) 96 JBE 513

Posner EA and Weyl EG, '*An FDA for Financial Innovation: Applying the Insurable Interest Doctrine to the 21ˢᵗ Century Financial Markets*' (2013) 107 Nw U L Rev 1307

Raskin M, '*The Law and Legality of Smart Contracts*' (2017) 1 Geo L Tech Rev 305

Richmond DR, '*Investing with the Grim Reaper: Insurable Interest and Assignment in Life Insurance*' (2012) 50 Tort Trial Ins Prac L J 657

Robinson PH and Darley JM, '*Does Criminal Law Deter? A Behavioural Science Investigation*' 24 (2004) OJLS 173

Schwarcz D, '*A Products Liability Theory for the Judicial Regulation of Insurance Policies*' (2007) 48 Wm Mary L Rev 1389

Schwarcz D and Schwarcz S, '*Regulating Systemic Risk in Insurance*' (2014) 1 U Chi L Rev 1569

Sjostrom Jr W, '*The AIG Bailout*' (2009) 66 Wash Lee L Rev 943

Swisher PN, '*Wagering on the Lives of Strangers: The Insurable Interest Requirement in the Life Insurance Secondary Market*' (2015) 50 Tort Trial Ins Prac LJ 703

Stempel JW, '*The Insurance Policy as Thing*' (2009) 44 Tort Trial Ins Prac LJ 813

Turk MC, '*The Convergence of Insurance with Banking and Securities Industries, and the Limits of Regulatory Arbitrage in Finance*' (2015) 2015:3 Col Bus L Rev 968

Walker-Bright P and Law TP, '*AIG's Financial Distress: How Credit Default Swaps and the Lack of Regulation Brought Down an Insurance Giant and Implications for the Insurance Industry*' (2009) Spring 2009 C Crit Issu Ins Law 1

Yeo HY, Jiao Y and Chen J, '*Insurable Interest Rule for Property Insurance in the People's Republic of China*' (2009) 8 JBL 787

Law Commission Reports and Papers

Law Commission and Scottish Law Commission, '*Issue Paper 4 – Insurable Interest*' (January 2008)

Law Commission and Scottish Law Commission, '*Insurance Contract Law: Post Contract Duties and Other Issues*' (Law Com CP No 201, December 2011)

Law Commission and Scottish Law Commission, '*Impact Assessment: Updating Insurance Contract Law: The Business Insured's Duty of Disclosure*' (June 2012)

Law Commission and Scottish Law Commission, '*Summary of Responses to Second Consultation Paper: Post Contract Duties and Other Issues*' (February 2013)

Law Commission and Scottish Law Commission, '*Insurance Contract Law: Business Disclosure; Warranties; Insurers' Remedies for Fraudulent Claims; and Late Payment*' (Law Com No 353, July 2014)

Law Commission and Scottish Law Commission, '*Issues Paper 10 – Insurable Interest: Updated Proposals*' (March 2015)

Law Commission and Scottish Law Commission, '*Summary of Responses to Issues Paper 10: Insurable Interest*' (April 2016)

Law Commission and Scottish Law Commission, '*Insurable Interest and Parametric Policies*' (April 2016)

The Law Commission and The Scottish Law Commission, '*Insurable Interest Bill*' (June 2018)

Law Commission and Scottish Law Commission, '*Updated draft Insurable Interest Bill for Review - Accompanying Notes*' (June 2018)

The Australian Law Reform Commission, '*Report No.20 – Insurance Contract's* (1984)

Other

Association of British Insurers, '*Fraud Statistics*' (2016) <https://www.abi.org.uk/products-and-issues/topics-and-issues/fraud/> accessed on 3 December 2019

———— '*One Scam Every Minute – ABI Reveals the True Extent of Insurance Fraud in the UK*' (22 August 2018) <https://www.abi.org.uk/news/news-articles/2018/08/one-scam-every-minute/> accessed on 3 December 2019

———— '*UK Insurance & Long-Term Savings – The State of the Market 2019*' (February 2019), 2 <https://www.abi.org.uk/globalassets/files/publications/public/data/abi_bro6778_state_of_market_2019_web.pdf> accessed on 3 December 2019

Bank for International Settlements, '*OTC Derivatives Outstanding*' (4 June 2019) <https://www.bis.org/statistics/derstats.htm> accessed 3 December 2019

BBC, '*London Couple Accused Over Adopted Son's Murder in India*' (14 October 2019) <https://www.bbc.co.uk/news/uk-england-london-49592362> accessed on 3 December 2019

British Horseracing Authority, '*The Rules of Racing*' (September 2019) <http://rules.britishhorseracing.com> accessed on 3 December 2019

Cleary Gottlieb Steen & Hamilton LLP, Letter to the Clerk of the US States Court of Appeals for the Second Circuit (29 March 2013) < https://argentine.shearman.com/> accessed 3 December 2019

Department for Culture, Media and Sport: Gambling Review Body, '*The Gambling Review Report*' (July 2001) <http://www.homepages.ucl.ac.uk/~uctyjow/Gambling/gamblingreviewcontents.pdf> accessed on 3 December 2019

EU Economic and Financial Affairs and International Trade Sub-Committee, '*Credit Default Swaps and Short Selling: Written Evidence*' (HL 2010/2011 session) <http://www.parliament.uk/documents/lords-committees/eu-sub-com-a/CDSandshortselling/WrittenevidenceCDS.pdf> accessed 3 December 2019

Expert Group on European Insurance Contract Law, '*Final Report of the Commission Expert Group on European Insurance Law*' (27 February 2014) <https://ec.europa.eu/info/business-economy-euro/doing-business-eu/contract-rules/insurance-contracts/expert-group-european-insurance-contract-law_en> accessed 3 December 2019

Financial Conduct Authority, '*Insurance Distribution Directive implementation: Consultation Paper I* (CP 17/7, March 2017) 55 <https://www.fca.org.uk/publication/consultation/cp17-07.pdf> accessed on 3 December 2019.

Financial Ombudsman Service Annual Review 2018/19, '*Data in More Depth 2018/2019*' <https://annualreview.financial-ombudsman.org.uk/files/2242/annual-review-2018-2019-data.pdf> accessed on 3 December 2019)

Financial Services Authority, '*The Sale of Payment Protection Insurance – Results of Thematic Work*' (November 2005) (hard copy held by author)

———— '*The Turner Review – A Regulatory Response to the Global Banking Crisis*' (March 2009) <http://news.bbc.co.uk/1/shared/bsp/hi/pdfs/18_03_09_turner_review.pdf> accessed 3 December 2019

Financial Stability Board, '*Guidance to Assess the Systemic Importance of Financial Institutions, Markets and Instruments: Initial Considerations*' (Report to G20 Finance Ministers and Governors, October 2009) <http://www.financialstabilityboard.org/wp-content/uploads/r_091107c.pdf> accessed 3 December 2019

Gambling Commission, '*Annual Report and Accounts 2018–19*' <https://www.gamblingcommission.gov.uk/PDF/Annual-Report1819.pdf > accessed on 3 December 2019

HM Treasury, '*The UK Insurance Growth Action Plan*' (December 2013) <https://www.gov.uk/government/publications/the-uk-insurance-growth-action-plan> accessed on 3 December 2019

Ince & Co, '*Blurred Lines: The Impact of the LC's Proposals on Insurable Interest on Parametric Policies*' (July 2016) < https://www.incegd.com/en/knowledge-bank/blurred-lines-the-impact-of-the-law-commissions-proposals-on-insurable-interest-on-parametric-policies> accessed 3 December 2019

International Monetary Fund, '*Global Financial Stability Report*' (April 2013) < https://www.imf.org/en/Publications/GFSR/Issues/2016/12/31/Transition-Challenges-to-Stability > accessed 3 December 2019

Journal of the House of Commons, From November the 26th, 1772, in the Thirteenth Year of the Reign of King George the Third, to September 15th, 1774, in the Fourteenth Year of the Reign of King George the Third, vol. 34 (26 November 1772 to 15 September 1774), <https://books.google.co.uk/books?id=tBlDAAAAcAAJ&printsec=frontcover&source=gbs_ge_summary_r&cad=0#v=onepage&q&f=false > accessed on 3 December 2019

Klugt, K van der, Interview with Kees van der Klugt, Director of Legal & Compliance at the Lloyd's Market Association (London, 29 September 2015)

Life Insurance Settlement Association, '*Life Settlement Regulation*' (September 2018) <https://www.lisa.org/industry-resources/life-settlement-regulation> accessed on 3 December 2019

Merkin R, '*Reforming Insurance Law: Is There a Case for Reverse Transportation? A Report for The English and Scottish Law Commissions on The Australian Experience of Insurance Law Reform*' (undated) <https://s3-eu-west-2.amazonaws.com/lawcom-prod-storage-11jsxou24uy7q/uploads/2015/03/ICL_Merkin_report.pdf> accessed on 3 December 2019

More Than (RSA), '*Home Choice Policy*' <https://www.morethan.com/media/filer_public/08/d6/08d63bc3-0ceb-4ec1-a1b2-8f7d629e55b5/more-than-home-choice-policy-wording-from-18-october-2015.pdf> accessed on 3 December 2019

Moses A, Russo C and Porzecanski K, '*Argentine Bonds Decline as Default Triggers $1 Billion of Swaps*' Bloomberg (2 August 2014) <http://www.bloomberg.com/news/articles/2014-08-01/argentina-default-triggers-1-billion-of-swaps-after-isda-ruling> accessed 3 December 2019

Neate R, '*Argentina Appeals against US Hedge Fund Ruling*' The Guardian (27 November 2012) <http://www.theguardian.com/business/2012/nov/27/argentina-appeals-hedge-fund-ruling> accessed 3 December 2019

Office for National Statistics, '*Homicide in England and Wales: Year Ending March 2018*' (7 February 2019) <https://www.ons.gov.uk/peoplepopulationandcommunity/crimeandjustice/datasets/appendixtableshomicideinenglandandwales > accessed 3 December 2019

Office of the Ombudsman for Long Term Insurance (MFB Reinecke – Assistant Ombudsman), '*Insurable Interest in the Context of Long-Term Insurance*' (undated)

<https://www.ombud.co.za/papers-and-presentations/insurable-interest> accessed on 3 December 2019

O'Neill P, Interview with Peter O'Neill, Class Underwriter for Onshore Power and Energy at XL Catlin (now AXA XL Insurance; London, 9 September 2015)

Report from the Select Committee Report on Gaming together with the Minutes of Evidence, dated 20 May 1844, vi (House of Commons Papers, Paper No. 297, vol 6, from the 19h Century House of Commons Sessional Papers Collection

Russo C, '*Singer Denial Failing to Quell Win-Win Charge: Argentina Credit*' Bloomberg (11 April 2013) <http://www.bloomberg.com/news/articles/2013-04-11/singer-denial-failing-to-quell-win-win-charge-argentina-credit> accessed 3 December 2019

Salmon F, '*Elliott vs Argentina: Enter the crazy*' Reuters (US edition, 27 August 2013) <http://blogs.reuters.com/felix-salmon/2013/08/27/elliott-vs-argentina-enter-the-crazy/> accessed 3 December 2019

Soros G, '*One Way to Stop Bear Raids*' Wall Street Journal (24 March 2009) <http://www.wsj.com/articles/SB123785310594719693> accessed 3 July 2019

Stahl A, Interview with Andreas Stahl, Head of Complex Claims at Allianz Group (London, 14 October 2015)

The Geneva Association (The International Association for the Study of Insurance Economics), '*Systemic Risk in Insurance – An Analysis of Insurance and Financial Stability*' (March 2010) <https://www.genevaassociation.org/media/99228/ga2010-systemic_risk_in_insurance.pdf> accessed 3 December 2019

The Gentleman's Magazine, and Historical Chronicle, vol XII (London 1742) <http://onlinebooks.library.upenn.edu/webbin/serial?id=gentlemans> accessed 29 November 2019

The National Lottery, '*Rules for Draw-Based Games*' (Edition 18a) < https://www.national-lottery.co.uk/games/in-store/rules accessed on 3 December 2019

The US Financial Crisis Inquiry Commission, '*The Financial Crisis Inquiry Report – Final Report of the National Commission on the Causes of the Financial and Economic Crisis in the United States*' (February 2011) <http://www.gpo.gov/fdsys/pkg/GPO-FCIC/pdf/GPO-FCIC.pdf> accessed 3 December 2019

US CFTC Chairman J. Christopher Giancarlo, US SEC Chairman Jay Clayton, and (UK) FCA Chief Executive Andrew Bailey, '*Joint Statement on Opportunistic Strategies in the Credit Derivative Markets*' (24 June 2019) < https://www.fca.org.uk/news/statements/joint-statement-opportunistic-strategies-credit-derivatives-markets> accessed 3 December 2019

Index

Printed in Great Britain
by Amazon

10387988R00154